THE LIST OF
BOOKS

Frederic Raphael
Kenneth McLeish

Harmony Books
New York

How to use this book

Titles are given in English throughout; foreign-language titles are given (in addition) where the usual English translation is markedly different, or (alone) where the book is better known by its original title or where there is no known translation. Authors' names are given in their most usual form (e.g. Auden, W.H., not Auden, Wystan Hugh), and pseudonyms are kept where regularly used (e.g. Mark Twain, not Samuel Clemens). The date given for each book is, wherever possible, the date of first publication; where there are important later editions, these are mentioned in the review. Author, title and publication date are generally sufficient to identify a book in a bookseller's or librarian's catalogue (such as *Books in Print*, a not infallible but usually helpful first resource); with older authors, foreign authors and especially classics, we recommend browsing through available editions to find the best. For many authors, we have listed a number of additional titles: these have been chosen for merit or for interest, and are not intended to be a comprehensive list ("etc" denotes that all the author's work seems to us well worth pursuing).

Since *The List of Books* is *an* imaginary library, one of the many possible, we have made selection rather than completeness the rule throughout; we have made *our* choice, not *the* choice. The Michelin-like symbols offer similarly partial, even biased, opinions on a book's particular merits and we have used them only where we feel they add usefully to our other remarks.

Cross-references are by subject and author's name. If, under the review of a particular book (say, in the Mythology list, Bloggs' *Myths*) there is a reference to another list (e.g. "see POETRY"), we mean that Bloggs also features in the Poetry list; if the reference is to another author's name (e.g. "see Jones"), we mean that Jones' book in the Mythology list is relevant to Bloggs'; if the reference is both to another list and to another author (e.g. "see POETRY (Jones)"), we mean that Jones' book in the Poetry list is relevant to Bloggs' here. Thus, following up (under Bloggs in Mythology) the following cross-references "See Jones; OCCULT: POETRY: TRAVEL (Jones)" will involve looking up Jones in the Mythology list, Bloggs in the Occult and Poetry lists, and Jones in the Travel list.

Symbols

🏛 A particular pleasure to read

! Seminal book that changed our thinking

📕 Standard work on the subject

𝒫 Difficult; worth persevering

✳ Infuriating; possibly illuminating

a Recommended for beginners in the subject

★ Not to be missed

✓ Contains good bibliography

_ℐℐ Exceptional illustrations

📗 Major masterpiece

📘 Minor masterpiece

📰 Of particular interest to readers in the USA

📰 Of particular interest to readers in the UK

Edited and designed by
Mitchell Beazley Publishers
87–89 Shaftesbury Avenue,
London W1V 7AD
© Mitchell Beazley Publishers 1981
© Text: Volatic Limited and Kenneth McLeish 1981
All rights reserved, including the right of reproduction in whole or in part in any form.

First published in the United States by Harmony Books
A Division of Crown Publishers, Inc.,
One Park Avenue, New York,
New York 10016.

Published in Canada by General Publishing Company Limited.

Library of Congress Cataloging in Publication Data
Raphael, Frederic, 1931–
The list of books.
Includes index.
1. Bibliography—Best books.
I. McLeish, Kenneth, 1940–, joint author.
II. Title
Z1035.R24 011 80-21151
ISBN 0-517-540177 (cloth)
ISBN 0-517-541521 (paper)

Contents

Introduction   4
Books of the decade, 1970–80   6
Editors' choice   7
Getting to grips with the twentieth century   8
Home reference books   9

Anthropology   10
Archaeology   13
Architecture   15
Art and Design   18
Autobiography and Memoirs   22
Biography   25
Children's Books   31
Diaries and Letters   36
Drama   41
Economics   47
Feminism   49
Fiction   51
   Crime Fiction and Thrillers   51
   Novels   54
   Science Fiction   66
   Short Stories   67
Film   71
Food and Drink   74
Geography and the Environment   77
History   79
   American History   79
   Ancient History   82
   Asian, African and Middle Eastern History   84
   British History   87
   European History   90
   Latin American History   92
   World History   93
Home and Garden   94
Humour   96
Literary Criticism   99
Mathematics, Science and Technology   102
Media   107
Medicine and Psychiatry   109
Music   111
Mythology   114
Natural History   117
Occult and Paranormal   121
Philosophy   123
Poetry   127
Politics   133
Psychology   136
Reference   138
Religion   142
Sex and Love   145
Sociology   147
Travel and Exploration   150

Index   155

Introduction

The intention of this book is to furnish an "imaginary library" of some three thousand volumes in which a reasonably literate person can hope to find both instruction and inspiration, art and amusement. It was André Malraux who first coined the term "*musée imaginaire*" to describe the choice of the world's art which a man might make to furnish his own private museum. Modern printing, Malraux proceeded to argue, has actually made such a collection a practical possibility. Masterpieces which men of the eighteenth century and before had to travel to see are now within the reach of all who can afford a postcard or a newspaper supplement. Mechanical reproduction has removed art from the hands of the few and made it accessible to all. Printing has done the same for books: the paperback is scarcely more expensive than the fine art print.

Our problem is no longer one of access; it is more likely to be one of choice. How are we to choose among the thousands of available titles? To enter a library is immediately to be seized by a kind of panic; one risks starving among such plenty. The confession that one does not know what to read next, or where to begin in an unfamiliar subject, is shameful in a society in which nobody wishes to be a beginner and where naïveté is likely to earn the scorn accorded to all newcomers. This book seeks to be a kind of reader's ticket to that immense library which man (dedicated or venal, brilliant or dogged, wise or witty) has put together ever since he first began to leave a written record of his experiences and his opinions.

Our first notion was to supply lists of unadorned titles in each of the standard library categories. But to give no information about the books proposed would be to leave the reader in the bemused condition of a guest at a crowded party to whom the host has nothing more to say than "You know everybody here, of course". So we decided that it was essential to give a brief account of each recommended book, however laughable or superficial an authority might find it. We have tried to be as specific as possible in the information conveyed, in order to avoid the kind of Shorter Notice which once said of Ezra Pound's *Cantos* that some were good and some were bad.

The method we adopted, in order to make our cull, was to ask our collaborators (for whose generosity and learning we cannot say enough) to make lists in the categories in which they were expert. (The categories began as standard Dewey headings, but gradually shifted and changed to accommodate a wider range both of interests and of books. They are now perhaps arbitrary, but, we hope, comfortably commodious.) We limited our collaborators to a given number of books, though we recognized that this limitation, like giving only so many visas to a huge concourse of worthy people, was bound to lead to unhappy exclusions. Many good things found no place in our narrow lifeboat. In particular, we have excluded technical books accessible only to specialists: a necessary restriction, reflecting the inevitable distinction between a menu and a list of all available forms of nutriment. We then circulated the lists among friends and those who were willing to lend us their time, so that no single person was, in the end, exclusively responsible in any given department. (The editorial decision was, however, final. Acknowledgements our collaborators deserve; the blame is ours.) Mavericks and texts of perhaps marginal value thus scrambled their way aboard, sometimes at the expense of worthy work which more blandly covered similar ground. It is, therefore, no scandal not to find your favourite (or your own) book in these pages; we are not judging, though we have been obliged to choose.

This is in short, *an* imaginary library, not *the* imaginary library.

It can, and should, be supplemented by further reading and broader research. (We have indicated, wherever possible, books with informative bibliographies: often these will provide an ancillary or alternative list, the part thus standing for the whole.) If first publication leads to a sort of informed common pursuit whereby new volumes are proposed for future editions, something more interesting, more exciting, may well be on the way. As for how *The List of Books* can best be read, we propose no prescription. One may browse; one may plough. We have made the index a straightforward author index, trying to imagine who a frustrated reader might be looking for, rather than merely supplying a dutiful rehash of earlier material, in alphabetical and inverted order, *Purists, For the satisfaction of.* (For those who relish indexes, the wittiest we know is in C. D. Broad's *Five Types of Ethical Theory.*)

"They said it couldn't be done—and it couldn't" is a joke at least as old as George Jean Nathan. The last man who knew everything died at the end of the eighteenth century: he will never be replaced. The Tower of Babel is an example that should be enough to deter anyone who seeks to make a self-importantly impertinent edifice of human intelligence—but there is no evidence that the suburbs of Babel, with their rows of modest bungalows whose occupants are too timid to attempt a second floor, are man's happiest environment. In fact, the collation of these lists has been enough to pull down most people's vanity, and certainly ours; for the more one looks at what is available in an unfamiliar field, the more urgent the desire one feels to abandon the affectations of the editor and assume the modesty of the student. We hope to revise *The List of Books* every second year, and we shall be vigilant for new titles to add to it. The next edition will carry a section devoted to important additions, in each category, and we welcome (though we cannot promise always to acknowledge) suggestions—perhaps in the form of short reviews—for additions to these imaginary shelves.

F.R.; K.M.; London, 1980

Acknowledgements

The Editors and the Publishers would like to thank the following people without whose witty, wise and erudite contributions (ranging from suggestions and advice to complete reviews) this book would never have reached its present form.

Valerie Alderson; Brian Aldiss; John Alexander; Roger Baker; Georgina Battiscombe; Robert Benewick; Ruth Binney; Nikolaus Boulting; William Boyd; Michael Broadbent; Henry Brougham; R. Allen Brown; Sandy Carr; Jeremy Catto; John Clark; W. Owen Cole; Leo Cooper; Jane Cousins; Nona Coxhead; Sarah Culshaw; Marcus Cunliffe; D. C. Earl; G. R. Elton; Barry Fantoni; Antony Flew; Anthony Fothergill; Christopher Hale; Ragnhild Hatton; Tim Heald; Roger Hearn; Christopher Hill; Christopher Hird; Richard Hollis; Richard Holmes; Antony Hopkins; Philip Howard; Joel Hurstfield; Tom Hutchinson; Angela Jeffs; Emrys Jones; H. R. F. Keating; Brian Klug; Alan Knight; Eric Laithwaite; Peter Levi; Sir Bernard Lovell; John Lynch; Rosemary McLeish; Valerie McLeish; Sir Philip Magnus; Stephen Mennell; Peggy Miller; Patrick Moore; Michael Morris; Raymond Mortimer; John Nicholson; Robert Nye; John Paterson; Stewart Perowne; David Robinson; John Robinson; Sheila Rowbotham; Martin Sherwood; Maurice Shock; Paul Sidey; Tony Smith; Vernon Sproxton; John Stevenson; Brian Street; Jonathan Sumption; John Russell Taylor; Ion Trewin; J. C. Trewin; Lord Vaizey; Gwynne Vevers; Jonathan Walters; Colin Wilson

Books of the decade, 1970–80

These lists cream the crop: one was compiled by the editors, the other by our American colleagues. By and large they represent some of the best, the most influential or most significant books published in each of our categories since 1970. Where books appear in both lists, we have left them there: duplication is an indication of one kind of specialness, at least.

British choice

Attenborough, D.: *Life on Earth* (1979)
Berger, J.: *Ways of Seeing* (1972)
Berryman, J.: *Selected Poems* (1972)
Boston Women's Collective: *Our Bodies, Ourselves* (1972)
Brown, D.: *Bury My Heart at Wounded Knee* (1972)
Clarke, R. and Hindley, G.: *The Challenge of the Primitives* (1975)
Davidson, A.: *Mediterranean Seafood* (1972)
Gerbi, A.: *The Dispute of the New World* (1973)
Greer, G.: *The Female Eunuch* (1970)
Halberstam, D.: *The Best and the Brightest* (1972)
Harvey, J.: *The Master Builders* (1971)
Hill, C.: *The World Turned Upside Down* (1972)
Hindley, G. (ed): *The Larousse Encyclopaedia of Music* (1971)
Johnson, H.: *The World Atlas of Wine* (1971)
Koestler, A.: *The Case of the Midwife Toad* (1971)
Ladurie, E. le Roy: *Montaillou* (1975)
Lovell, B.: *In the Centre of Immensities* (1979)
Mendelssohn, K.: *Science and Western Domination* (1976)
Morison, S.: *The Great Explorers* (1978)
Papanek, V.: *Design for the Real World* (1971)
Schumacher, E.: *Small Is Beautiful* (1973)
Sendak, M.: *Where the Wild Things Are* (1970)
Skinner, B. F.: *Beyond Freedom and Dignity* (1971)
Solzhenitsyn, A.: *The Gulag Archipelago* (1974)
Steadman, R.: *America* (1974)
Thorne, C.: *Allies of a Kind* (1978)
Ward, B.: *The Home of Man* (1976)
Wilson, C.: *The Occult* (1971)
Woodward, B. and Bernstein, C.: *All the President's Men* (1974)

American choice

Bellow, S.: *Mr. Sammler's Planet* (1970)
Bettelheim, B.: *The Uses of Enchantment* (1977)
Boorstin, D. J.: *The Americans: The Democratic Experience* (1973)
Boston Women's Collective: *Our Bodies, Ourselves* (1972)
Brand, S.: *The Last Whole Earth Catalog* (1975)
Brown, D.: *Bury My Heart at Wounded Knee* (1971)
Clavell, J.: *Shogun* (1975)
Collier, P. and Horowitz, D.: *The Rockefellers: An American Dynasty* (1976)
Comfort, A.: *The Joy of Sex* (1972)
Cooke, A.: *Alistair Cooke's America* (1973)
FitzGerald, F.: *Fire in the Lake* (1972)
Halberstam, D.: *The Best and the Brightest* (1972)
Haley, A.: *Roots* (1976)
Hardwick, E.: *Seduction and Betrayal: Women and Literature* (1974)
Hellman, L.: *Pentimento* (1973)
Herr, M.: *Dispatches* (1977)
Howe, I.: *World of Our Fathers* (1976)
Jong, E.: *Fear of Flying* (1973)
Kluger, R.: *Simple Justice: The History of Brown v. Board of Education* (1976)
Lash, J. P.: *Eleanor and Franklin* (1972)
McCullough, D.: *The Path between the Seas: The Creation of the Panama Canal, 1870–1914* (1977)
Márquez, G. G.: *One Hundred Years of Solitude* (1970)
Milford, N.: *Zelda: A Biography* (1970)
Morgan, M.: *The Total Woman* (1973)
Pirsig, R. M.: *Zen and the Art of Motorcycle Maintenance* (1974)
Singer, I. B.: *Enemies: A Love Story* (1972)
Skinner, B. F.: *Beyond Freedom and Dignity* (1971)

Terkel, S.: *Working* (1974)
Thomas, L.: *The Lives of a Cell* (1974)
Toffler, A.: *Future Shock* (1971)
Updike, J.: *Rabbit Redux* (1971)
Vidal, G.: *Burr: A Novel* (1973)
Vonnegut, K.: *Slaughterhouse Five* (1973)
Ward, B.: *The Home of Man* (1976)
Wolfe, T.: *Radical Chic and Mau-Mauing the Flak Catchers* (1970)
Woodward, B. and Bernstein, C.: *All the President's Men* (1974); *The Final Days* (1976)
Wouk, H.: *The Winds of War* (1971)

Editors' choice

Each editor was asked, independently, which twenty-five books he would pack for a desert island holiday. This list is the combined result. Several books were common choices; apart from them, each editor was surprised by several of the books on the other's list.
Aeschylus: *The Oresteia*
Albee, Edward: *Who's Afraid of Virginia Woolf?*
Attenborough, David: *Life on Earth*
Aristophanes: *Thesmophoriazusae*
Austen, Jane: *Emma*
Berlioz, Hector: *Memoirs*
Burke, Kenneth: *A Grammar of Motives*
Byron: *Letters and Journals*
Cavafy, Constantine: *Collected Poems*
Dante: *The Divine Comedy*
Donne, John: *Poems*
Dostoyevsky, Fyodor: *The Brothers Karamazov*
Durrell, Gerald: *My Family and Other Animals*
Durrell, Lawrence: *Reflections on a Marine Venus*
Eliot, George: *Middlemarch*
Eliot, T. S.: *Four Quartets*
Flaubert, Gustave: *Madame Bovary*
Ford, Ford Madox: *Parade's End*
Frazer, Sir James: *The Golden Bough*
Gibbon, Edward: *The Decline and Fall of the Roman Empire*
Heller, Joseph: *Catch 22*
Hockney, David: *Hockney*
Homer: *The Odyssey*
Innes, Michael: *Operation Pax*
Jarrell, Randall: *Pictures from an Institution*
Jonson, Ben: *The Alchemist*
Kafka, Franz: *The Trial*
McCabe, J. and Kilgore, A.: *Laurel and Hardy*
McCarthy, Mary: *The Groves of Academe*
Montaigne, Michel de: *Essays*
Nabokov, Vladimir: *Pale Fire*
Nietzsche, Friedrich: *Thus Spake Zarathustra*
Orwell, George: *Collected Essays*
Pascal, Blaise: *Pensées*
Proust, Marcel: *Remembrance of Things Past*
Rabelais, François: *Gargantua and Pantagruel*
Renoir, Jean: *Renoir, My Father*
Runciman, Steven: *A History of the Crusades*
Shakespeare, William: *Collected Works*
Singer, Isaac Bashevis: *A Crown of Feathers*
Stendhal: *The Charterhouse of Parma*
Thesiger, W.: *The Marsh Arabs*
Thucydides: *The Peloponnesian War*
Tolstoy, Leo: *War and Peace*
Villon, François: *Poems*
White, E. W.: *Stravinsky*
Wittgenstein, Ludwig: *Philosophical Investigations*

Getting to grips with the twentieth century

If books reflect historical, sociological and cultural growth, the ones recommended here may, we hope, help to account for or explain some of the directions human existence has taken in our century. Some of these books are dated, many are infuriating or partial; all are landmarks.

Acheson, D.: *Present at the Creation* (1967)
Anderson, P.: *Considerations on Western Marxism* (1976)
Austin, W.: *Music in the 20th Century* (1966)
Banham, R.: *Theory and Design in the First Machine Age* (1960)
Beauvoir, S. de: *The Second Sex* (1949)
Beckett, S.: *Waiting for Godot* (1952)
Berry, B. J. L.: *The Human Consequences of Urbanization* (1973)
Brittain, V.: *Testament of Youth* (1933)
Brownlow, K.: *The Parade's Gone By* (1968)
Bruce, L.: *The Essential Lenny Bruce* (1975)
Capote, T.: *In Cold Blood* (1966)
Carr, E. H.: *The Russian Revolution* (1979)
Carson, R.: *Silent Spring* (1962)
Cherry-Garrard, A.: *The Worst Journey in the World* (1912)
Clark, R. M.: *The Scientific Breakthrough* (1974)
Clarke, R. and Hindley, G.: *The Challenge of the Primitives* (1975)
Eliot, T. S.: *The Waste Land* (1923)
Esslin, M.: *The Theatre of the Absurd* (1961)
Fanon, F.: *The Wretched of the Earth* (1961)
Friedan, B.: *The Feminine Mystique* (1962)
Friedman, M.: *Capitalism and Freedom* (1962)
Frith, S.: *The Sociology of Rock* (1978)
Graves, R.: *Goodbye to All That* (1929)
Halberstam, D.: *The Best and the Brightest* (1972)
Harrison, J.: *Marxist Economics for Socialists* (1978)
Hebblethwaite, P.: *The Christian-Marxist Dialogue and Beyond* (1976)
Ionesco, E.: *The Bald Prima Donna* (1948)
Jones, E.: *The Life and Work of Sigmund Freud* (1953)
Joyce, J.: *Ulysses* (1921)
Kafka, F.: *The Diaries of Franz Kafka* (1948)
Kafka, F.: *The Trial* (1937)
Keynes, J.M.: *The General Theory of Employment, Interest and Money* (1936)
Klee, P.: *On Modern Art* (1943)
Kolko, G.: *Main Currents in Modern American History* (1976)
Le Corbusier: *Towards an Architecture* (1923)
Lichtheim, G.: *Europe in the 20th Century* (1972)
Lorenz, K.: *On Aggression* (1963)
McAleavy, H.: *The Modern History of China* (1967)
Macartney, C. A. and Palmer, A. W.: *Independent Eastern Europe* (1962)
McGlashan, A.: *Gravity and Levity* (1976)
Mailer, N.: *Marilyn* (1973)
Mailer, N.: *The Naked and the Dead* (1948)
Malaparte, C.: *Kaput* (1964)
Niebuhr, R.: *Moral and Immoral Society* (1932)
Orwell, G.: *Animal Farm* (1946)
Orwell, G.: *The Road to Wigan Pier* (1937)
Papanek, V.: *Design for the Real World* (1971)
Pirandello, L.: *Six Characters in Search of an Author* (1929)
Piven, F. F. and Cloward, R. A.: *Poor People's Movements* (1977)
Reich, W.: *The Sexual Revolution* (1930)
Rosen, S.: *Future Facts* (1976)
Rosenberg, H.: *The Anxious Object* (1964)
Schumacher, E.: *Small Is Beautiful* (1973)
Sinclair, A.: *Prohibition: The Era of Excess* (1962)
Solzhenitsyn, A. I.: *The Gulag Archipelago* (1974)
Stern, J. P.: *The Führer and the People* (1975)
Taylor, A. J. P.: *English History, 1914–1945* (1965)
Terkel, S.: *Work* (1974)
Wing, J. K.: *Reasoning about Madness* (1978)

Home reference books

There is a place in most home libraries for a small collection of general reference books. We provide two basic lists, by no means mutually exclusive; one British and one American.

British

Every collection should contain a dictionary, such as *The Concise Oxford English Dictionary* or *Chambers Twentieth Century Dictionary*, plus/or *Longman Dictionary of Contemporary English* (P. Proctor) and *The Complete Plain Words* (Ernest Gowers). Many people will also find a constant use for *The Concise Dictionary of 26 Languages* (compiled by Peter M. Bergman). Still concerned with words, the collection should contain *The Concise Oxford Dictionary of Quotations* or *The Penguin Dictionary of Quotations*.

There should be an atlas, such as *The Times Atlas of the World: Concise Edition* or *New Concise Atlas of the Earth*, the indexes of which can be used as a world gazetteer. For annually updated information on world affairs get *The Statesman's Year Book, Europa Year Book* or *Whitaker's Almanack*.

For biographical information consult *Who Did What* (historical and international) and *Who's Who* (contemporary and British); much international coverage is provided by a good one-volume encyclopaedia such as *Columbia Encyclopaedia* or *Hutchinson's New 20th Century Encyclopaedia*. The historical aspect of recent developments is summarized in *Chronology of the Modern World*.

Finally, two useful books on general medical and legal matters: *Reader's Digest Family Health Guide* and *Know Your Rights* (neither, of course, is meant to supplement professional advice). In any case, every home should have a book on first aid, such as *The Pocket Medical and First Aid Guide* (Dr James Bevan).

American

Every collection should contain a dictionary, such as *Webster's New Collegiate Dictionary* (the second edition is the recommended unabridged version; the seventh is the desk edition) or *The Random House College Dictionary*.

The collection might also contain *Roget's Thesaurus of Synonyms and Antonyms* and *Bartlett's Familiar Quotations*.

There should be an atlas. Two good ones are *The New York Times Atlas of the World* and the *Rand McNally New International Atlas*, the indexes of which can be used as a world gazetteer. Annually updated information on world affairs is contained in *The World Almanac and Book of Facts*.

For biographical information consult *Who's Who in America* and *Who's Who in the World*. There is also a *Who's Who* for each state.

Two reliable encyclopaedias for home use are *Encyclopaedia Britannica* and *The World Book Encyclopedia*. An excellent one-volume encyclopaedia is *The New Columbia Encyclopaedia*.

Every home should have a book on first aid, such as *Basic First Aid* or *Standard First and Personal Safety*, both published by the American National Red Cross.

Also useful: *Know Your Rights: A Guide to Everyday Law*, by Ronald Irving and Charles Anthony.

Anthropology

Anthropology was born as a formal discipline in the 19th century, when a previously haphazard interest in the cultural and social behaviour of remote peoples was supplied with a theoretical basis and scientific procedures. At first it was very closely linked with its sister-subject sociology; both were concerned with man the organizer, with the forces and movements which mould human society. Gradually, however, the disciplines began to grow apart: sociology became ever more political (and analytically "scientific"), anthropology more historical (and descriptively "artistic"). The books in this list follow the bias towards study of the cultures of "primitive" peoples; but there are also representatives of a more modern trend towards treating man as a single phenomenon (with local and historical variants) and extrapolating from the techniques and discoveries of "primitive" anthropology a series of proposed solutions to the self-destructive energy of technological man. Once again the wheel has come full circle: sociology and anthropology go hand in hand, and their concern is social change, their scenario nothing less than the future of the human race itself.

See AUTOBIOGRAPHY (Mead); GEOGRAPHY (Forde, Sauer); HISTORY/AMERICAN (Josephy); HISTORY/BRITISH (Thomas); MATHEMATICS (Bronowski); MYTHOLOGY (Frazer, Kirk, Huxley, Lévi-Strauss); RELIGION (Castaneda)

Agee, J. and **Evans, W.** *Let Us Now Praise Famous Men* (1941)
Study in words and photographs of three poor tenant families in the southern USA in 1936. Overpraised in its time, and the prose now seems self-consciously "poetic"; but the pictures especially are haunting, moving, devastating.

Asad, Talal (ed) *Anthropology and the Colonial Encounter* (1973)   ♀
A new generation of anthropologists turned on their teachers and accused them of compliance with colonialism. This collection of essays lays out their case.

Bailey, F. G. *Stratagems and Spoils* (1969)   🏛*
Descriptions of the devious and clever ploys that men get up to in different societies in order to get the (differently defined) spoils. Also: *Gifts and Poisons*

Boas, Franz *The Mind of Primitive Man* (1911)   ♀
One of the great revolutionary works (revised 1937); hard but essential. Boas was the first to proclaim that mankind is indissolubly one, and that all races have the potential to produce and create equally. The Nazis burned this book and civil rights activists everywhere bear it like a banner.

Bowen, E. S. *Return to Laughter* (1954)
Warm, amusing account of the everyday problems that an anthropologist encounters "in the field".

Chagnon, A. A. *Yanomamo: The Fierce People* (1977)
Aggression as a way of life. Text is as lively as the title; the sociological implications are wide and sharp. See Thrasher NATURAL HISTORY (Lorenz); SOCIOLOGY (Whyte)

Clarke, R. and **Hindley, G.** *The Challenge of the Primitives* (1975)   ★ ✓
As the future of technological society grows ever more doubtful, some anthropologists are suggesting that a return to "primitive" concepts of kinship with nature may provide viable alternatives. This book readably and succinctly distils the essence of this hopeful philosophy.

Cohen, Abner *Two Dimensional Man* (1974)
Accessible introduction to the thinking of anthropologists on symbolism, politics and their interrelationship.

Coon, C. S. and **Hunt, E. E.** *The Living Races of Man* (1965)   ▮★ ✓ ◢
Authoritative study of the racial composition of all peoples of the world. Also: *The Origin of Races*; *Seven Caves*

Dalton, George *Tribal and Peasant Economies* (1976)   ▮♀
Accessible textbook on all aspects of social economics.

Dodds, E. R. *The Greeks and the Irrational* (1951)   ▮★▮
Seminal case-study of a society moving from "mythology" to "religion". Different approaches to the irrational world lead to different kinds of social behaviour; by studying these (and literature, philosophy, their embodiment) we discover the governing systems and beliefs of an ancient society. Sounds narrow; is stimulating, wide-ranging. See MYTHOLOGY (Harrison, Kirk, Slater)

Douglas, Mary *Purity and Danger* (1966)
Classic example of anthropologists' attempts to see meanings in the apparently

trivial detail of everyday life—you'll never look at "dirt" in the same way again. Also: *Rules and Meanings*; *Natural Symbols*

Dumont, Louis *Homo Hierarchichus* (1966) 🏛🗋
Class, caste, hierarchies in general—the enabling structures of society, or its main inhibitors? Clear, readable introduction.

Eisley, Loren *The Immense Journey* (1957) 🏛
Intense, poetic, unforgettable essays by a distinguished anthropologist who later published several volumes of poems. The title refers to the long journey of man, from the beginnings in the primordial ocean to today—and beyond?

Epstein, A. L. *Politics in an Urban African Community* (1958) 🗋♀
Readable account of the changes brought to the 1950s Zambian copper belt by urbanization. Also: *Ethos and Identity*

Evans-Pritchard, E. E. *The Nuer* (1940) 🗋♀
The classic text on fieldwork, studied by every student of anthropology. Also: *Witchcraft, Oracles and Magic among the Azande*, etc

Frankenberg, R. *Communities in Britain* (1966) 📖
Anthropologists' studies in Britain, of rural communities and of urban groups, neatly and usefully summarized.

Fürer-Haimendorff, Christoph von *The Sherpas of Nepal* (1964) 🏛🗋 ⁄⁄
Readable field-study, a model of how such books can be made both authoritative and accessible to the general reader. Also: *The Naked Nagas*, etc

Geipel, John *The Europeans* (1969)
Ethno-historical survey of the various peoples of Europe: anthropology dominates, but archaeology, social history, linguistics and genetics are also brought into play. For modern Europeans—and immigrants to Newer Worlds—a fascinating study of how we came to be the way we are.

Gennep, Arnold van *Rites of Passage* (1977) 🗋
Points of transition in the development of an individual or a society are often traumatic, often accompanied by therapeutic or apotropaic ritual. A systematic study of such rituals in various primitive societies. See Mead.

Greenway, John *Down among the Wild Men* (1972) 🏛 ⁄⁄
Popular anthropology at its readable best: partly a witty autobiographical account of fifteen years' study of Old Stone Age aborigines in Australia, partly a scientific account of his findings and conclusions. Also: *Literature among the Primitives*; *The Inevitable Americans*; *Ethnomusicology*, etc

Gulliver, P. H. *Social Control in an African Society* (1963) 🗋♀
Fascinating field-study, with important general implications. See Dumont.

Hall, E. T. *The Silent Language* (1959) a
Hall was one of the first to write about what has become a cliché—we communicate not by ordinary language alone, but also by "body language" and by other signals that are not expressed in words. A fascinating, essential book. See PSYCHOLOGY (Argyle).

Kitzinger, S. *Women as Mothers* (1978)
Wide-ranging, well-written study of motherhood in different societies. Author's premise is that the "maternal instinct" does not exist as such; the role of mother varies as a direct response to the needs of society. Also: *The Good Birth Guide*. See PSYCHOLOGY (Rutter)

Kroeber, A. L. *Configurations of Culture Growth* (1945) *
An attempt by one of the most influential of 20th-century anthropologists to trace the growth and decline of human thought and art. Also: *Anthropology* (one of the first general texts in the field)

Kuper, Adam *Anthropology and Anthropologists* (1973) a
Easy introduction to the history, personalities, events and ideas of 20th-century British anthropology.

Leach, Edmund *Lévi-Strauss* (1970) a
Useful introduction to the work of leading French anthropologist. Also: *Political Systems of Highland Burma*; *Culture and Communication*. See Lévi-Strauss; MYTHOLOGY (Lévi-Strauss)

Lévi-Strauss, Claude *The Elementary Structures of Kinship* (1949) ⁄🗋♀★
One of the great 20th-century gurus in full flood: a study of kinship groups and their binding rituals throughout the world. Thorny style, but accessible with perseverance: he's a name to read as well as drop. Also: *The Savage Mind*, etc. See Leach; MYTHOLOGY

Lewis, I. M. *Ecstatic Religion* (1971) *
Attempts to make sense of "strange" religious practices by looking at the problems of the social groups which carry them out. For a Christian view of the same area, see RELIGION (Davies). Also: *An Introduction to Social Anthropology*

Lienhardt, Godfrey *Divinity and Experience: The Religion of the Dinka* (1961) 🗋
Fascinating attempt to explain another society's religion, with all the respect and complexity usually reserved for one's own. Also: *Social Anthropology*

Lisitzky, Gene *Four Ways of Being Human* (1956)
Elegant survey of four "Stone Age" groups surviving, more or less unchanged,
into the 20th-century: Eskimos, Hopi Indians, Maoris and Sepang of Malaya.
Mixture of anthropology and social psychology (behaviour as identity) is
successful and fascinating. See Mead.

Lloyd, P. *Classes, Crises and Coups* (1971)   **a**
Readable introduction to the study of modernizing societies and the political,
economic and social problems they face. Also: *Slums of Hope?: Shanty Towns of
the Third World*

Malinowski, B. *Argonauts of the Western Pacific* (1922)   **❗▌**
Account of the lives, trading, canoe-building and sailing of the inhabitants of the
Trobriand Islands in the Western Pacific. One of the first and best examples of
anthropological fieldwork. Also: *The Sexual Life of Savages in North-Western
Melanesia*; *Crime and Custom in Savage Society*, etc

Mead, Margaret *New Lives for Old* (1956)   **▌★**
The Manu Tribe of Papua New Guinea collapsed cultural evolution: between
1928 and 1953 they moved from the Stone Age to the Air Age. Mead's
book—typical of her wide-ranging generous scholarship—discusses the
interweaving of old and new, the psychological effects of change; draws parallels
with the general evolution of the rest of the human race. Also: *Coming of Age in
Samoa*; *Growing Up in New Guinea*; *Sex and Temperament in Three Primitive
Societies*, etc. See Lisitzky; AUTOBIOGRAPHY; SOCIOLOGY

Pocock, D. F. *Understanding Social Anthropology* (1976)   **a ✓**
Excellent layman's introduction (with set essays for the eager). Also: *Social
Anthropology*

Radin, Paul *Primitive Religion: Its Nature and Origin* (1937)   **▌**
Radin was a synthesizer of various strands in anthropology: economic and social
structure, religion, philosophy, psychology. His books vary in importance; this is
one of the best.

Sapir, Edward *Culture, Language and Personality* (1961)   **▌**
Collection of thoughtful essays by one of the great American cultural
anthropologists and linguists.

Schapera, Isaac *Married Life in an African Tribe* (1966)
Readable field-work study: specific tribal details lead to general conclusions
about marriage as a binding agent in society. See Evans-Pritchard.

Street, B. V. *The Savage in Literature* (1975)   **🏛**
Amusing, relevant account of the image of other societies purveyed by popular
19th-century adventure novels.

Sutherland, A. (ed) *Face Values* (1978)   **a ∥**
Glossy "pop" anthropology book based on a TV series set up by professional
anthropologists. Later articles, however, are quite difficult. Also: *Gypsies: The
Hidden Americans*

Thrasher, Frederic M. *The Gang* (1936)   **▌ρ**
Exhaustive, anthropological-sociological study of no less than 1,313 Chicago
gangs. Stiff read; absorbing and disturbing. See SOCIOLOGY (Suttles)

Tiger, L. S. and **Fox, R.** *The Imperial Animal* (1971)   **ρ**
Challenging study of man's socially divisive and cohesive instincts: historical,
anthropological and sociological disciplines luminously applied not to one small
tribe, but to the whole human race.

Turner, V. W. *The Forest of Symbols* (1967)   **ρ★**
Excellent example of anthropologists' attempts to understand the complex
symbols of even the "simplest" peoples: reads, at times, like literary criticism.
Also: *The Ritual Process*

Tylor, Edward B. *Researches into the Early History of Mankind*
(1865)   **▌ρ★**
Anthropology was once known, disparagingly, as "Mr Tylor's science". He was,
to the history of what he first called "culture" (ie, the linguistic, psychic,
emotional and material fabric of a society), what Darwin was to evolution. This
book is a synthesis of his work—of absorbing interest, and still of unique value.
Excellent abridged edition (1964) by Bohannan (himself a noted, and
recommended, anthropologist).

Archaeology

Modern archaeology was born in 1708, with the first excavations at Pompeii. At first it was informal and irresponsible, little more than an aristocratic upgrading of the treasure-hunting and tomb-robbing characteristic of any historical period. In the 19th century it became badged with more serious, systematic study, the archaeologists seeking for information about ancient cultures as eagerly as for their glittering artefacts. The great names of 19th-century archaeology—Schliemann, Evans, Petrie—made their subject a true sibling of anthropology and cultural history, the passion of the polymath, and it is mainly their enthusiastic work which led to our century's obsession with the minutiae of ancient life. Archaeology continued as a genial, gentlemanly pursuit for inspired individualists until World War II. Since then, it has evolved (or declined) from an art to a science. The exactitudes of statistics, aerial photography (itself a legacy of 20th-century warfare), chemical analysis and other scientific disciplines are applied, and the results are, first, that archaeology now has areas as arcane and specialized as nuclear physics or X-ray crystallography, and second, that as our view of the distant past comes into ever sharper focus, we find it extraordinarily like our own: the notion of what "civilization" is travels further backwards in time, and wider in geography, with every newly published paper. Art or science? Amateur or specialist? The list covers books in both areas—and shades (like archaeology itself, one of the most humane of disciplines) into history and cultural anthropology too.

See ANTHROPOLOGY (Geipel); ART (Frankfort); CHILDREN'S BOOKS (Brothwell); GEOGRAPHY (Sauer); HISTORY/ANCIENT (Grant, Lehmann)

Bellwood, Peter *The Polynesians: Prehistory of an Island People* (1978)   a✓ ⫽
Until AD 1500 the Polynesians were one of the most widely spread ethnic groups on earth. Their origins, history, languages and way of life are examined in this pioneering survey. Also: *Man's Conquest of the Pacific*

Bishop, W. and **Clark, J. D. (eds)** *The Background to Evolution in Africa* (1967)   ℗✓
The origins of the human race. Outline of essential work, includes contributions from most of the leading workers in the field.

Bray, W. and **Trump, D. H.** *A Dictionary of Archaeology* (1970)
Convenient one-volume reference work. Covers the whole field of archaeology from human evolution and the prehistoric period to the civilizations of Egypt, the Near East and the Americas.

Brothwell, D. R. and **Higgs, E.** *Science in Archaeology* (1969)   ▋✓⫽
"What the archaeologist is able to learn about the past depends to a great extent on the completeness and discrimination with which he avails himself of the resources being made available on an ever more generous scale by his colleagues in a growing range of scientific disciplines." The important contributions of science to archaeology are discussed: professionals' version of Wilson (qv). See CHILDREN'S BOOKS

Ceram, C. W. *Gods, Graves and Scholars* (1951)   a
Popular approach is over–breathless for specialists, and the book (despite new editions) is dating fast. But it remains an outstanding enthusiasm-builder for would-be archaeologists. Also: *The March of Archaeology*, etc

Chadwick, John *The Mycenaean World* (1976)   ▋a⫽
Terse, stimulating challenge to the orthodox view of Cretan prehistory by one of the pioneer code-breakers of Linear B.

Chang, Kwang-Chih *The Archaeology of Ancient China* (1963)   ℗✓⫽
Chinese civilization from its primitive farming beginnings (3rd millennium BC) to the early historic periods (2nd millennium AD). See FOOD; HISTORY/ASIAN (Eberhard, for later history)

Clark, Grahame *World Prehistory* (1969)   ▋a✓⫽
Comprehensive introduction (regularly updated) to the intellectual, material and social progress of mankind. A suitcase of a book: everything you need is here.
Also: *Archaeology and Society*

Coles, John *Archaeology by Experiment* (1973)
Vivid insights into the past can be gained by reconstructing and testing models of

ancient equipment. Revaluation of methods of food production, and of heavy and light industry. Unusual subject, expertly treated.

Cottrell, Leonard *The Land of Shinar* (1965)　　　　　　🏠 a ✓
Sniffed at by narrower academics for his easy style, Cottrell is one of the great popularizers of archaeology. This book deals with Sumeria, the possible site of the Garden of Eden, a "lost" culture as full of vitality as Egypt or Persia. Also: *Lost Cities; The Bull of Minos,* etc

Cunliffe, Barry *Fishbourne* (1971)　　　　　　　🗖🖼
Cunliffe's account of the dig at the Roman villa, Fishbourne, England, is a fine case-study of the modern archaeologist at work, balancing trowel and brush against sophisticated laboratory techniques.

Daniel, Glyn *150 Years of Archaeology* (1950)
Standard introductory textbook; should be followed by Wilson (qv) or by Brothwell and Higgs (qv) for accounts of up-to-date methodology.

Deuel, Leo *Conquistadors without Swords* (1967)　　　　　a ★ ✓
Narration of archaeological discovery in the Americas, interleaved with extensive, lively quotations from the archaeologists' own accounts. Also: *The Treasures of Time* (ancient Near East revealed in the same enthralling way)

Frere, Sheppard *Britannia* (1967)　　　　　　　🗖 ♀
History of Roman Britain, from archaeological evidence. Ponderous style never entirely engulfs the author's enthusiasm or the fascination of the subject.

Hawkes, Jacquetta *The World of the Past* (1963)
Excellent anthology of Hawkes' lively, expert articles and other smaller writings. Also: *Dawn of the Gods,* etc

Hume, Ivor *Historical Archaeology* (1969)　　　　　　🏠 ⁄⁄
Application of archaeological disciplines to a known historical period: colonial America. Good specialist book, of interest to the layman attracted by the period or by the unusual conjunction of disciplines.

Keating, Rex *Nubian Rescue* (1975)
The building of the Aswan Dam in the 1950s and 1960s led to unprecedented archaeological activity in Nubia, "Middle Egypt", in ancient times the corridor between Mediterranean and African civilizations. This book is a clear, if rather plainly written, summary of spectacular "rescue archaeology" (dig before the water comes).

Leone, Mark (ed) *Contemporary Archaeology* (1972)　　　　♀ ✳
Discusses the controversy surrounding the theories and aims of the "new archaeology", with particular reference to North America. Polemical; hard; engrossing.

Libby, W. F. *Radiocarbon Dating* (1955)　　　　　　　♀
MacKendrick, Paul *The Greek Stones Speak* (1962)　　　　🏠 a ⁄⁄
Elegant, stylish: ancient culture revealed by trowel. In its time, unrivalled for enthusiastic clarity; still an excellent general introduction. Updated edition badly needed—it's too good to lose. Also: *The Mute Stones Speak* (a less dated, but also less exciting, account of Italian archaeology)

Mulvaney, D. J. *The Prehistory of Australia* (1969)　　　　🗖
Aborigines. Neglected topic, expertly outlined.

Negev, Avraham (ed) *Archaeological Encyclopaedia of the Holy Land* (1972)　　　　　　　　　　　a ★ ⁄⁄

Oates, D. and **J.** *The Rise of Civilization* (1976)　　　　　a
Early agriculture; the first domestication of animals during the Neolithic period; the rise of urbanization in Mesopotamia and Egypt. Characteristic volume in recommendable *Making of the Past* series.

Phillipson, D. W. *The Later Prehistory of Eastern and Southern Africa* (1977)　　　　　　　　　　🗖 ⁄⁄

Piggott, Stuart *Ancient Europe: A Survey* (1965)　　　　　🏠 a
European prehistory from the beginnings of agriculture to Classical antiquity. The parallel development of barbarian cultures with the civilizations of antiquity, clearly explained and ably illustrated.

Raistrick, Arthur *Industrial Archaeology* (1972)　　　　🏠 a ⁄⁄
Sandars, Nancy K. *Prehistoric Art in Europe* (1968)　　　🏠 ★ ⁄⁄
Superb volume from recommended *Pelican History of Art* series. See
MYTHOLOGY

Ucko, P. J. and **Dimbleby, G. W. (eds)** *The Domestication and Exploitation of Plants and Animals* (1969)　　　　　　🗖 ♀
Analysis of innovatory collaboration between archaeologists and natural scientists, to their mutual benefit and enlightenment. Also: *Man, Settlement and Urbanism*

Willey, Gordon *An Introduction to American Archaeology* (2 vols, 1966–71)　　　　　　　　　　🗖 ✓ ⁄⁄
Wilson, David *Atoms of Time Past* (1975)　　　　　　🗖 a ✓
Up-to-date history, for the general reader, of the use of scientific techniques in archaeology: bones and shards treated with laboratory procedures as well as inspired individual guesswork. Notably clear, informative style.

Architecture

Architecture is, in a real sense, the measure of man's unnatural-ness. Ever since he adapted the cave for his convenience, he has rebelled against the kind of shelter which unshaped nature provides. Thus the history of architecture is that of man against nature, however naturally he has sought to harmonize his antagonism with the materials and environment he finds on earth. The story of architecture is told (and lived) principally by urban man, for whom buildings become the reflection of society, its organization and its myths. This means that the debate on architectural aesthetics is also about morals, politics, religion: hence its intense importance, its furious partialities. ("You say," said Nietzsche, "that there can be no argument about matters of taste? All life is an argument about matters of taste.") The architect makes his artistic and concrete statement—in obstinately durable form—and then moves on, sometimes with giant strides, sometimes on feet of clay, rarely leaving satisfactory explanation or justification. Vitruvius and Le Corbusier, in the following list, are distinguished exceptions (and prove, perhaps, the dangers of universalizing assertions, however impressive the credentials of the dogmatists). The majority of books cited here are by critics and scholars, though the true critic of the building is often and decisively the man who uses it. In the present century, however, the architectural critic has become an influential and creative force. Architecture is three-dimensional thought; hence the significance of the "philosophers" who are its critics and proponents.

See ART (Frankfort, Giedion, Pevsner, Stedman); CHILDREN'S BOOKS (Macaulay); GEOGRAPHY (Hall, Jacobs, Morgan, Pahl, *Scientific American*, Tunnard); HISTORY/BRITISH (Brown)

Banham, Reyner *Theory and Design in the First Machine Age* (1960) ★
Theories which complemented architecture and design, 1900–40, when architects and designers really tried to come to terms with the potential of industry and science. Banham's tone here, as always, is clear, fervent, readable. Leads usefully to Jencks (qv) and Newman(qv): the seeds are planted here. Also: *The Architecture of the Well-Tempered Environment; Los Angeles: The Architecture of Four Ecologies; A Guide to Modern Architecture*, etc

Boethius, A. and **Ward-Perkins, J.** *Etruscan and Roman Architecture* (1970)
Like most others in the *Pelican History of Art* series, competent and authoritative. No light read; but text, illustrations, exhaustive footnotes and detailed bibliography cover ground from 1400 BC to the decline of Rome.

Burnham, D. H. and **Bennett, E. H.** *Plan of Chicago* (1909)
By 1900 the Chicago School, led by Louis Sullivan and Frank Lloyd Wright, had established the city as the home of modern urban architecture. Burnham and Bennett's famous plan for the further development of the city was adopted in 1909; its lineaments may still be seen in the magnificent lakefront and other glories. Chapter 8 summarizes the plan.

Clark, Kenneth *The Gothic Revival* (1928)
The impetuous pioneer piece on the survival and revival of Gothic architecture, from the Dissolution of the Monasteries to full-blooded Victorian Revivalist styles. Depicts beautifully the interaction between literature, painting, architecture and landscape gardening, as Clark contrasts 18th- and 19-century concepts of "taste". See ART; AUTOBIOGRAPHY

Clifton-Taylor, Alec *The Pattern of English Building* (1960)
Lateral approach to architectural history; deals less with the development of "great styles" than with the close relationship between geology and traditional building materials, topography and the building types which characterize England's architecture.

Collins, Peter *Architectural Judgement* (1971)
Collins asks not about our response to buildings but why, in "their professional judgement", architects, planners and developers choose one building rather than another. For believers in absolute aesthetic standards, an essential antidote. Also: *Changing Ideals in Modern Architecture, 1750–1950*

Colvin, Howard *A Biographical Dictionary of British Architects, 1660–1840* (1954)

Conant, Kenneth *Carolingian and Romanesque Architecture, 800–1200* (1959)
Downing, A. J. *Rural Essays* (1853)
Downing designed many fine homes and gardens, but was especially intrigued by American "cottage architecture"—the homely constructions, often home-made, of the lower middle class; country churches, county courthouses and the like. His book makes for nostalgic imaginings. See Kouwenhoven.
Fleming, J., Honour, H. and **Pevsner, N.** *Penguin Dictionary of Architecture* (1966)
Basic guide to architects, architectural terms, building materials, ornamentation, styles and movements. See Pevsner; ART (Honour, Pevsner)
Frankl, Paul *Gothic Architecture* (1962)
Detailed analysis of style and structure; a good introduction, despite Frankl's insistence on divorcing architecture from sculpture, stained glass, etc, at a time when unity of the arts was of the essence.
Giedion, Sigfried *Space, Time and Architecture: The Growth of a New Tradition* (1941)
Polemical, path-finding book succeeds admirably in placing architecture, construction and city planning of the industrial era (mid 18th century onwards) in the wider context of art and science. See ART
Gropius, Walter *The Scope of Total Architecture* (1955)
Testament and manifesto of Bauhaus founder: "the approach to any kind of design, a chair, a building, a whole town or a regional plan, should be essentially identical."
Harvey, John *The Master Builders: Architecture in the Middle Ages* (1971).
Also: *The Gothic World, 1100–1600, The Medieval Architect*; *Cathedrals of England and Wales*
Heydenreich, L. and **Lotz, W.** *The Architecture of Italy, 1400–1600* (1970)
Hitchcock, Henry-Russell *Architecture: Nineteenth and Twentieth Centuries* (1958)
Despite limited illustrations, an excellent summary of 19th- and 20th-century European, British and American architecture. Also: *Modern Architecture in England*; *Rococo Architecture in Southern Germany*
Jencks, Charles *The Language of Post-Modern Architecture* (1977)
Stimulating analysis of recent trends. Useful adjunct to the more theoretical writings of such men as Venturi (qv); a literate, often witty guide. Also: *Modern Movements in Architecture*
Kouwenhoven, John *Made in America* (1948)
Readable examination, by a literary critic, of what he calls American "vernacular art"—the unselfconscious art of the "carpenter builders" who shaped the country's aesthetic sense. See Downing.
Lancaster, Osbert *A Cartoon History of Architecture* (1975)
Lancaster a true caricaturist: drawings pinpoint subject; waspish comments make equally vivid impact. "Wimbledon Transitional", "Stockbroker Tudor", "Bypass Variegated"—all begin here.
Lawrence, Arnold *Greek Architecture* (1957)
Authoritative, scholarly text; detailed footnotes and bibliography; essential.
Le Corbusier *Towards an Architecture* (1923)
Designer-in-chief of 20th-century city-scape, with its straight lines, cubes, glass, concrete and steel, Le Corbusier has had incalculable, perhaps undue, influence; his writings remain crucial to an understanding of modern urban life. Also: *Five Points of a New Architecture*, etc
Mumford, Lewis (ed) *Roots of Contemporary American Architecture* (1956)
Using original documents, Mumford analyses the intellectual germination of architecture in pre-Chicago America and the evolution of indigenous 20th-century styles. Contrast of quotations from architects—like Frank Lloyd Wright and Louis Sullivan—and critics (Mumford and others) is particularly stimulating. Also: *The City in History*, etc. See ART
Murray, Peter *The Architecture of the Italian Renaissance* (1963)
Readable, scholarly; useful luggage for travellers. Also: *A History of English Architecture*; *Piranesi and the Grandeur of Ancient Rome*; *A History of World Art*
Newman, Oscar *Defensible Space: People and Design in the Violent City* (1972)
Influential in promoting the view that architecture should be based on the study of people's psychological needs (eg for privacy, contact, security). Essential sociological balance for the theories of (for example) Le Corbusier (qv).
Norberg-Schulz, Christian *Meaning in Western Architecture* (1976)
Respected history of architecture, with strong theoretical bias; demanding, but usefully comprehensive.

Palladio, Andrea *Four Books on Architecture* (1570) ★ ∬
Treatise on Classical architecture; possibly the most influential pattern-book ever published. Need not be read, but should be perused, the pages turned, designs and drawings studied; they appear, repeated endlessly, on every "Classical" building in the Western world. For analysis, see Wittkower's *Architectural Principles in the Age of Humanism*

Pevsner, Nikolaus *An Outline of European Architecture* (1942) ⚑◧a★∬
In this and numerous other books, Pevsner revolutionized British attitudes towards architecture. The latest edition performs the same service in an American "Postscript". Also: *The Buildings of England* (series); *Essays on Art, Architecture and Design*; *A History of Building Types*, etc. See Fleming; ART

Rapoport, Amos *House Form and Culture* (1969) 🏛a
This fascinating volume associates the forms of domestic architecture with the cultures that surround and influence them.

Richards, James *An Introduction to Modern Architecture* (1940) ♀a∬
Recent history is often less digestible than the study of dead civilizations. Modern architecture is no exception; even so this book persuasively argues that architecture is a social art related to 20th-century life rather than (in the author's own words) an "academic exercise in applied ornament". Usefully read in conjunction with Giedion (qv), Mumford (qv), and Newman (qv). Also: *The Anti-Rationalists*; *The Castles on the Ground*; *The Functional Tradition in Industrial Building*

Richards, James (ed) *Who's Who in Architecture: From 1400 to the Present Day* (1977) ◧
Biographical and critical studies of professional architects from Alberti and Brunelleschi onwards. Comprehensive coverage of architects of the Western world, including the USA and Latin America; new edition adds names from Israel, Africa and the Far East.

Ruskin, John *The Seven Lamps of Architecture* (1849) 🏛!★∬
Though Ruskin himself later called it "a wretched rant", this book, together with Pugin's and Morris's writings, really paved the way for modern architectural history and criticism, laying down criteria by which to judge buildings which were not simply those of Vitruvius or Alberti dressed up in 18th-century tasteful finery. A founding father, Ruskin writes with grace as well as passion, and puts forward an eloquent case, among other things for the preservation of historic buildings. Also: *The Stones of Venice*. See LITERARY CRITICISM

Scott, Geoffrey *The Architecture of Humanism* (1914) 🏛✱
A furious attack on 19th- and early-20th-century "practicality" and a compelling psychological defence of the ornate forms of the baroque. Looking back, 60 years on, how right Scott was!

Smith, E. Baldwin *The Dome* (1950)
Smith has written several books, each treating a specific architectural feature which appears over large areas of the earth. This book is one of the best of them.

Soper, A. and **Sickman, L.** *The Art and Architecture of China* (1956) 🏛◧✓∬
From earliest times, traditionalism and resistance to change characterize Chinese architecture; an interesting contrast with the fashionable, ever-changing styles of the West. Also: *The Art and Architecture of Japan*

Summerson, John *The Classical Language of Architecture* (1964) ◧a★∬
Despite pockets of Gothic resistance, Classical architecture has dominated the "civilized" world from the Renaissance to the present century. Summerson explains its grammatical disciplines for expert and layman alike. His purpose is to make us think critically about, instead of just gazing at, architecture. Useful glossary of architectural terms. Also: *Georgian London*; *Victorian Architecture: Four Studies in Evaluation*; *Inigo Jones*; *Architecture in Britain, 1530–1830*, etc

Venturi, Robert *Complexity and Contradiction in Architecture* (1977)
In the late 20th century, architecture is evolving from "modernism", the human dimension reasserting itself. Seminal text by a leading US practitioner. Usefully read in conjunction with Jencks (qv).

Vitruvius *On Architecture* (43 BC)
Fascinating contemporary analysis of Classical architecture, including discussion of materials for building and decorating, and even of the design of catapults and "tortoises" (early tanks). Particularly influential in the Renaissance. Good translation: Loeb Library.

Wright, Frank Lloyd *Modern Architecture* (1931) ◧
As important for America as Le Corbusier (qv) was for France and Gropius (qv) for Germany, Wright in this famous book states with the passion that imbued all his work the principles of his very personal architecture. Also: *When Democracy Builds*, etc. See Mumford.

Art and Design

At first sight, it might seem that there are too many art books: too much reading goes on, and not enough looking. But for most people, art books are a personal gallery to the majority of the world's great pictures, the only possible ticket to the contents of far-flung galleries. For this reason, art books are recommended here for quality of pictures, standard of reproduction, first; second comes authority or accessibility of text. We have, however, chosen not so much picture books about individual artists, as books about trends, about art itself. Where art becomes a practical as well as an aesthetic matter, and particularly in the new, prescriptive discipline of design, things are a little different. Here theory and philosophy are crucial matters, and elegance of text bulks large. The best books of all—and it is interesting to see how many of them are by artists themselves—are those which combine experience, vision and articulacy of style. They are the cream of a rich and nourishing list.

See ANTHROPOLOGY (Agee, Kroeber, Turner); ARCHAEOLOGY (Sandars); ARCHITECTURE (Banham, Clark, Kouwenhoven, Lancaster, Lawrence, Newman, Soper); AUTOBIOGRAPHY (Cellini, Clark); BIOGRAPHY (Freud, Grigson, Hudson, Lindsay, Renoir, Thompson); DIARIES (Dali, Van Gogh); GEOGRAPHY (Tunnard); HISTORY/AMERICAN (Josephy, Jones); HISTORY/ASIAN (Basham); HISTORY/BRITISH (Burn, Burton, Dillon, George, Strong); HOME (Conran, Jeffs, Johnson, Kron); HUMOUR (Hollowood, Larry, *New Yorker*, Searle, Schulz, Steadman, Steinberg); LITERARY CRITICISM (Benjamin); MATHEMATICS (Hofstadter); MEDIA (Evans, Maclean); MEDICINE (Trevor-Roper); MUSIC (Hoffnung); NATURAL HISTORY (Audubon, Bewick, Holden)

Adburgham, Alison (ed) *A Punch History of Manners and Modes,*
1841–1940(1961)   ★ ⫽
Since few of us can house, let alone afford, the 7000 back numbers of *Punch*, this
volume suffices to show how valuable this magazine is, to social historians and the
inquisitive alike, as a marvellous source of information on changes in attitudes.
The cartoons offer an accurate guide to fashion from bloomers to the zip fastener.
Battock, Gregory (ed) *The New Art: A Critical Anthology* (1973) ℘ a ⫽
For those worried about deciphering the art of the post-machine age and
understanding the preoccupations of painters, sculptors, space enclosers, volume
envelopers, earth movers and esoteric talkers, this collection of essays provides
some useful insights. Also: *Idea Art*; *New Ideas in Art Education*. See Rosenberg.
Baudelaire, Charles *The Painter of Modern Life* (1863)
The poet on the visual arts of his time is wiser and more perceptive than many
full-time professional critics. Ostensibly about Constantin Guys, this book is
crammed with general judgements on artistic society at large. Also: *Art in Paris,*
1845–1862. See Delacroix; BIOGRAPHY (Starkie); DIARIES; POETRY
Behrman, S. N. *Duveen*(1952)
Witty, scathing account of the extraordinary career of one of the most successful
20th-century art dealers, who provided many newly rich Americans with
ancestors-to-order culled from the stately homes of England, and single-handed
made the unremarkable Romney into one of the world's most sought-after
painters.
Bell, Clive *Art*(1914)
Cornerstone of Bloomsbury Group aesthetics, with its emphasis on "significant
form" and the presentation of humane values in an increasingly inhuman world.
Also: *Civilization*. See Fry.
Berger, John *Ways of Seeing* (1972)   ℘ a ★ ⫽
Influential essays on the gap between what we *see* and the knowledge and beliefs
that we articulate in words. In particular Berger examines our assumptions that
there is such a thing as "art" and that the perception of art objects—aesthetic
experience?—is somehow set apart from other perceptions. Hard; rewarding.
Also: *Permanent Red*; *Art and Revolution*, etc.
Black, J. A. and Garland, M. *A History of Fashion* (1975)   🏛 ⫽
Audacious successful attempt to trace the history of fashion practically from
Adam and Eve, certainly from the age of skins and paint, to the kaleidoscopic
seventies. See Adburgham.

Clark, Kenneth *Looking at Pictures* (1960)　　　　　　　　　　🏛
The title expresses exactly what this book is about, and what Clark does as well as any living man. He makes a personal anthology of paintings—good reproductions accompany the text—and reading the book is like walking through a gallery with Clark at one's side. Also: *The Nude*, etc. See ARCHITECTURE; AUTOBIOGRAPHY

Conrad, Peter *The Victorian Treasure-House* (1973)
Switch-back progression through the labyrinth of the Victorian British mind, as manifested primarily in the visual arts, though there are constant vitalizing cross-references to poetry, fiction, technology and history. Also: *Shandyism*

Delacroix, Eugène *Journal* (1893)
Vivid, fetching picture of the French art world in the mid 19th century, seen through the eyes of one of its leading figures. Compare with Baudelaire (qv).

Frankfort, H. *The Art and Architecture of the Ancient Orient* (1954)　　　　　　　　　　　　　　　　　　a★✓ ⫽

Fry, Roger *Vision and Design* (1920)　　　　　　　　🏛
Essays on a variety of subjects which roused the passions of this most dynamic member of the Bloomsbury Group, exploring and explaining his sensations in front of a Claude, a Cézanne or a masterwork of the Renaissance in terms still illuminating to the layman. Also: *Transformations*; *Cézanne Letters*. See Bell.

Gaunt, William *The Pre-Raphaelite Tragedy* (1942)
Excellent introduction to the Pre-Raphaelites, their lives, their sometimes scandalous loves, and their deadly serious work. Also: *Victorian Olympus*; *The Aesthetic Adventure*

Giedion, Sigfried *Mechanization Takes Command* (1948)　　▯a★
The potter's wheel, the weaver's loom, iron casting and printing with movable type were early instances of the mechanization of design processes. From gradual beginnings, with the commercial exploitation of the innovations of the Industrial Revolution in the 18th and 19th centuries, mechanization does indeed take command. Giedion's account puts up all the hares—even, in 1948, feminism—in the race for comfort, convenience, cleanliness and, above all, not godliness, but commercial success. See ARCHITECTURE

Gilson, Étienne *The Arts of the Beautiful* (1965)
Gilson (a noted and dependable critic) writes with grace and style not of pictures only, but of art in general. An important and highly enjoyable book: aesthetics at their unpretentious best. Also: *Form and Substance in the Arts*; *The Choir of Muses*, etc. See PHILOSOPHY

Gombrich, Ernst *Art and Illusion* (1960)　　　　　　▯♀ ⫽
Exploration of the psychology of pictorial representation, covering the whole history of what artists actually did and what they thought they were doing (often two very different matters). Profound scholarship, lightly worn. Also: *The Story of Art*; *The Sense of Order*; *Meditations on a Hobby Horse*, etc.

Haydon, Benjamin Robert *Autobiography and Journals* (1853)　　★
Life and reflections of a painter with genius but no talent. Haydon knew everybody, and always has something interesting to say, not least about his own contradictory nature.

Hogarth, William *The Analysis of Beauty* (1753)　　　　　★
Hogarth's paintings and engravings attacked the conventions and hypocrisies of society in general and the art world in particular. In print too he kept up the good work, with broadsides against connoisseurship and especially against classicism as the current artistic credo, in an attempt to make the language of art understandable to more than a small dilettante élite. Stimulating, invigorating essays–with points still valid today. Facsimile edition (1969) recommended.

Honour, Hugh *Neoclassicism* (1968)　　　　　　　　▯a ⫽
Far-ranging, compact introduction to a whole climate of thought and feeling in the late 18th and early 19th centuries, as cool and graceful in style as the art it celebrates. Also: *Romanticism*; *Chinoiserie*. See ARCHITECTURE (Fleming)

Ivins, William M. *Prints and Visual Communication* (1953)　　🏛 ⫽
Apparently dry subject (how various graphic processes evolved conventions of representation in order to put over their meaning) transformed into a breathless historical detective story which illuminates far more than its immediate subject.

Jones, Owen *The Grammar of Ornament* (1856)　　　　　★ ⫽
Though it was not regarded as art, decoration was a subject of consuming interest to the Victorians. Industry, newly mechanized, had a voracious appetite for new patterns. What better, Jones and many others thought, than the study of nature and history? Theories still relevant; colour lithographs a joy for all.

Klee, Paul *On Modern Art* (1948)　　　　　　　　　　♀a ⫽
In this self-analytical sketchbook—collected thoughts and illustrations—Klee worries about the isolation (self-inflicted, he thinks) of the modern artist. Also: *Notebooks*

Laver, James *Taste and Fashion: From the French Revolution to the Present Day* (1937)　　　　　　　　　　　　　　🏛 ⫽
Elegant text; delightful plates. Revised edition (1945) recommended.

McGraw-Hill (publisher) *Encyclopaedia of World Art* (15 vols, 1963–68) ▲ a ★ ⁂

Mondrian, Piet *Plastic Art and Pure Plastic Art* (1937) ♀ ⁂
Mondrian, with the minimum of words and faded but adequate images, outlines the conversion of a realist landscape painter to abstract painting, his individual brand of Cubism being known as Neo-Plasticism. A great help in understanding what sort of activity painting has become in the 20th century.

Morison, Stanley *Politics and Script* (1972) ▲ ⁂
No mere catalogue of scripts and types this: Morison relates the history of lettering to political, social, religious, aesthetic, and commercial factors. Unusual subject; absorbing book.

Mumford, Lewis *Technics and Civilization* (1934) ★
Mumford removes our historical blinkers by relating advances in design since the Industrial Revolution to their wider historical context. His inventory of inventions is endlessly fascinating. See ARCHITECTURE

Murray, P. and **L.** *A Dictionary of Art and Artists* (1959) a

Newton, Stella M. *Health, Art and Reason* (1974) ▲ ⁂
Fascinating study of conflicting attitudes to female fashions in the wildly ambiguous Victorian era when reforms in dress were argued for, initiated and sometimes abandoned, on grounds of health and hygiene, art, and reason. Also: *Renaissance Theatrical Costume and the Sense of the Historical Past*. See Adburgham; Black.

Nochlin, Linda *Realism* (1971)
Forceful study of 19th-century relations between art and life, particularly in the work of those artists whose work contains specific social or political commitment.

Osborne, Harold *The Oxford Companion to Art* (1970) ▮ a ⁂
Alphabetical reference book, more chunky and full than Murray (qv). If you can afford just one art-reference book, this should be it.

Panovsky, Erwin *Meaning in the Visual Arts* (1955) ♀ ⁂
Provocative collection of essays by the inventor of "iconology"—the study of the artist's visual language and how artists have conveyed meaning to spectators in various historical periods. Also: *Studies in Iconology*; *The Life and Art of Albrecht Dürer*

Panek, Victor *Design for the Real World* (1971) ▲ ✳
Pied Piper Papanek cannot, even in the face of the worsening energy crisis and the polarization of wealth, persuade lemming-like designers to accept responsibility for solving *real* problems. Their ideals are submerged by the marketing idea of the "ideal consumer", and the poor—individuals and nations—the sick and the needy are neglected. See Schaeffer.

Pevsner, Nikolaus *Pioneers of Modern Design* (1936) ❗ ▮ ★ ⁂
The irresistible force of the Industrial Revolution meets the immovable object—the nostalgia of Victorian Revivalism—yet somehow "modern" architecture and design emerge. Revised edition (1960) recommended. Also: *The Englishness of English Art*; *Studies in Art, Architecture and Design* (especially volume II), etc. See ARCHITECTURE (Fleming, Pevsner)

Pissarro, Camille *Letters to His Son Lucien* (1943)
The great Impressionist writes regularly to his artist son in London over twenty years, mixing professional advice, art gossip and domestic details in a charming, revealing way.

Read, Herbert *Art and Industry* (1934) ❗ ⁂
Practical yet impassioned statement of faith on the principles of industrial design, by one of the major pioneers in its study. Catches the feeling of the earnest thirties; but the arguments are still relevant. Also: *The Philosophy of Modern Art*; *Icon and Idea*; *The Meaning of Art*, etc

Reitlinger, Gerald *The Economics of Taste* (3 vols, 1961–70) ▲ ⁂
Intimidating title disguises a riveting account of the rise and fall of prices and reputations in pictures (vol I) and *objets d'art* (vol II) since the mid 18th century. Vol III carries the tale through the swinging sixties.

Reynolds, Joshua *Discourses on Art* (1769–91) ♀
Classic statement of classical 18th-century academic attitudes, by the then President of the British Royal Academy and one of their most successful exponents. Who should know better? Who could put it more elegantly?

Richter, Jean Paul (ed) *The Literary Works of Leonardo da Vinci* (1939)
Richter's sleuth work in collating innumerable intriguing notes from the artist's notebooks and manuscripts, aided by his cultivated ability to read Leonardo's reversed writings without the use of a mirror, makes Leonardo's contributions to art and science seem all the more remarkable. 1970 reprint recommended. See BIOGRAPHY (Freud)

Rosenberg, Harold *The Anxious Object* (1964) ▲ a ⁂
Art critic of the *New Yorker* genuinely enjoys many of the more bizarre manifestations of "modern art". Enthusiasm is the best advocate, especially

when matched (as here) by style, common sense, and a very necessary sense of humour. Also: *The Tradition of the New*; *The De-Definition of Art*; *Artworks and Packages*. See Battock.

Rothenstein, John *Modern English Painters, 1952–1974* (1976) 🔖 a
Lively accounts of fifty 20th-century artists, most of whom the former director of the Tate Gallery, London, knew personally and describes with a fund of anecdote as well as crisp critical perception. Compare with his autobiography, *Brave Day Hideous Night*.

Sandler, Irving *The Triumph of American Painting* (1970) a ∥
Blow-by-blow account of the rise of Abstract Expressionism in America, by one who saw it all happen, knew and knows most of the principal characters, and is able, before even the dust of the battle has completely stilled, to step back and judge with unnerving sense and precision. Also: *The New York School*

Schaeffer, H. *19th-century Modern* (1970) ♀ a
The essential antidote to Pevsner's (qv) classic *Pioneers*, with its artist-craftsman bias. Victorian consumer products, like bicycles, spoons and even gynaecological forceps are examined and the roots of modernism are traced in this functional tradition. Schaeffer raises a moral question too: when the perfect solution to a design problem has been reached, why should "stylists" deceive consumers with seductive new models? See Papanek.

Scharf, Aaron *Art and Photography* (1968) 📖 ∥
Standard work on the tricky relations between the traditional arts and photography. Breezy; full of oddities as well as serious information; cheerily opinionated.

Sickert, Walter Richard *A Free House* (1947)
Fine (and eccentric) artist lays about him on subjects connected with painting, friends, enemies, the art establishment (which he abhorred) and the advantages and disadvantages of the English, both of which he was well placed to appreciate. Selection by Osbert Sitwell recommended.

Smith, John Thomas *Nollekens and His Times* (1828) ★
Sublimely bitchy anecdotal biography by his former pupil and assistant of one of the 18th century's great eccentrics, who happened also to be a sculptor of note.

Stedman, John *The Rule of Taste from George I to George IV* (1936)
Postulates general agreement upon what was considered "correct taste" in the period of the British Georges; traces the influence of Vanbrugh, Burlington, Kent, Walpole, and Adam in architecture and interior decoration and also that of Kneller, Gainsborough, Romney and other painters.

Sypher, Wylie *Four Stages of Renaissance Style* (1955)
A noted literary critic discusses the styles of the Renaissance as manifested not only in painting and sculpture, but also in literature, music and the other arts. A *tour de force* of enthusiasm and knowledge.

Vasari, Giorgio *Lives of the Artists* (1550–68) 📖 ★
Anecdotal and a pleasure to read, but also an interesting historical document which covers every aspect of art and artists in Renaissance Italy when, as Gombrich (qv) puts it, "artists became conscious and over-conscious of the great achievements of the past that weighed on them".

Autobiography and Memoirs

The opportunity to make a recension of one's own life is clearly difficult to resist—and results, more often than not, in mayfly publishing, a few hours' dance in the sun followed by oblivion. Our choice (a selective one) is based first on excellence (of perception or style), and second on relevance (a person of lasting interest or an age defined). Particularly interesting are memoirs which can be checked for bias, and those of writers whose main work is in other fields. The selection of material from one's own life is a critical act, sometimes as revealing as the incidents of that life themselves. If Beethoven had written an autobiography, would it have been about earache or symphonies?

See ART (Haydon); BIOGRAPHY (Trelawny); CHILDREN'S BOOKS (Durrell); DRAMA (Cibber); FILM (Brown, Fields, Griffith, Love, Montagu, Niven, Parrish); HISTORY/BRITISH (Burnet); HUMOUR (Milligan); MATHEMATICS (Heisenberg, Watson); MEDIA (Higham, Knopf); MEDICINE (Copeland); MUSIC (Berlioz, Kirkpatrick, Stravinsky, Varèse); NATURAL HISTORY (Bewick, Burton, Durrell, Maxwell, Waterton); OCCULT (Bennett, J. B., Lethbridge); RELIGION (Newman, Phillips); TRAVEL (Genet, Lawrence, Schultz, Twain)

Adams, Henry *The Education of Henry Adams* (1907)
Grandson and great-grandson of American presidents, Adams pretended that his own life as a scholar and novelist had been a failure. Ironic, third-person autobiography treats its subject as a victim of historic, indeed cosmic circumstance. See HISTORY/AMERICAN; RELIGION

Augustine *Confessions* (5th century)
Augustine felt that, until his conversion to Christianity at the age of 32, he had lived a life of sin. This is a moving personal account of one man's coming to terms with God; Augustine writes with particular sensitivity of his human relationships, too—with his mother, his friends, his mistress and his loved son Adeodatus ("Godgiven"), who died young.

Bamford, Francis (ed) *A Royalist's Notebook: The Commonplace Book of Sir John Oglander, Knight, of Nunwell, 1622–1652* (1936)
Oglander lived on the Isle of Wight during the English Civil War. The book transcends temporal detail as a picture of the horror evoked by such uprisings; particularly good on *social* horror, the bewilderment of the ruling class when the lower orders suddenly, inexplicably, get out of hand.

Betjeman, John *Summoned by Bells* (1960)
Verse autobiography; sensitive evocation of childhood in Edwardian London, Cornwall and Oxford, with Archibald the teddy bear and apparently total recall of everything he ever saw or heard.

Brittain, Vera *Testament of Youth* (1933)
Well-brought-up middle-class girl in Edwardian Britain finds her life and views changed by World War I, in which her fiancé, brother and many friends were killed. Fine portrait of the changing status and ideas of women at the time of the suffragettes. Also: *Testament of Friendship*; *Testament of Experience*

Caesar, Julius *The Civil Wars* (47–44 BC)
The very archetype of a general's memoirs. Ostensibly detached and objective, in fact Caesar's own justification for treason and the usurpation of autocratic powers. (He did it all in defence of his prestige and dignity.) Also: *The Gallic Wars*. See DIARIES (Cicero); HISTORY/ANCIENT (Selzer)

Cardigan, Countess of *My Recollections* (1909)
Shocking Scandal, Victorian style. Society women are said to have gone down on their knees to stop her publishing. Don't leave it in the spare room, however honest your guests.

Cellini, Benvenuto *Autobiography* (1728)
The artist as bohemian, free to disregard the laws and customs of ordinary men. Sculptor, goldsmith of genius, Cellini worked for popes, dukes and kings, led a colourful life full of amorous encounters and brushes with the law. Great fun, if you can stand the pace.

Chaplin, Charles *My Autobiography* (1964)
First part best: recollections of his Dickensian childhood in the slums of Victorian London. See FILM (McCabe)

Clark, Kenneth *Another Part of the Wood* (1974)
Clark was director of the National Gallery, London, and a skilled popularizer of art. The book is amusing, occasionally feline; good stories; memorable account of his own happiest of marriages. See ARCHITECTURE; ART

Fox, George *Journal* (1694)   ♀
Written by the founder of Quakerism, with hindsight, in sedater, pacifist old age;
a vivid picture of the social and religious crisis from which the Quakers emerged.
Franklin, Benjamin *Autobiography* (1771–88)
The quintessential American success story, from rags not only to riches, but also
to great political influence and power and an eternal warm spot in the hearts of all
his countrymen. Franklin the adventurer, the printer and businessman, the
scientist, the politician are here; Franklin the lover and friend must be assumed
from other sources. See BIOGRAPHY (Van Doren)
Gandhi, Mahatma *Autobiography: The Story of My Experiences with
Truth* (1924)
Written in and out of prison during the early 1920s, this simple, direct, revealing
document inspired millions, and led others to assume that Gandhi, however
great, was after all only a man.
Gosse, Edmund *Father and Son* (1907)   ▌♀
Study of a relationship: classic of the genre. Gosse senior was an eminent marine
biologist (he crossed swords with Darwin), and a fanatical member of the
Plymouth Brethren. A widower, he brought up his son (author of this book) "in
the nurture and admonition of the Lord", until the boy finally went to boarding
school and discovered his own soul.
Grant, Ulysses S. *Personal Memoirs* (2 vols, 1885–86)   ▣
Grant could not escape scandal by leaving the White House; he lent his name to
his son's brokerage firm, which failed, bringing the entire family into disrepute.
Grant, old and sick, determined to make up everyone's loss. Signing a contract
with his old friend Mark Twain, he set to work on the volumes that he just barely
completed before his death. Surprisingly they are full of pleasant humour and
insights about his colleagues and the president he had so greatly admired, Old
Abe; they endure as among the very best of military and political memoirs.
Graves, Robert *Goodbye to All That* (1929)   ▣▌∥▣
Argument about which is the finest set of British memoirs of World War I stops
here. Post-war pages tell of T. E. Lawrence, friends in Oxford and Bloomsbury,
marriage, children—and divorce in 1929, when he went to live abroad. If there
are standard works of autobiography, this is one. See FICTION/NOVELS;
MYTHOLOGY; POETRY
Hahn, Otto *A Scientific Autobiography* (1966)   ▣∥
"Father of nuclear chemistry" reviews his scientific work from the discovery of
radio thorium in 1904, via the splitting of the atom in 1938, to the Nobel Prize in
1944. The science is lucidly explained but may test the layman. See
MATHEMATICS (Irving)
Hart, Basil Liddell (ed) *The Rommel Papers* (1950)   ▣ ★
One of the best diaries from World War II. Charts Rommel's gradual
disillusionment with Hitler, from the time of his own early victories to his forced
suicide. Bitter, eloquent evidence for the grandeur and waste of war. See Speer;
BIOGRAPHY (Bullock); HISTORY/EUROPEAN; POLITICS (Stern)
Hellman, Lillian *An Unfinished Woman* (1969)   ▣∥
From raffish Jewish family in the American South came this distinguished,
successful dramatist: talented, nervous and difficult, friend of Dorothy Parker
and lover of Dashiell Hammett, whose left-wing views led her to politics. Sad and
moving. Also: *Pentimento*; *Scoundrel Time*, etc
Hervey, Lord *Memoirs of the Reign of George II* (1848)   ★
Nearest English equivalent to Saint Simon (qv). Lively account of George II, his
Queen and their court. Little-known; a rare delight.
Hudson, W. H. *Far Away and Long Ago* (1918)   ★
Poet's recollections of early childhood on the Argentinian pampas. Prose-poetic,
limpid, fine. Also: *Idle Days in Patagonia*, etc. See NATURAL HISTORY
Keller, Helen *The Story of My Life* (1903)
Perhaps we shall never cease to be fascinated and astounded by the story of this
extraordinary woman who triumphed over nearly complete sensory
deprivation—deaf, dumb and blind from early childhood—to become one of the
great figures of our time.
Kropotkin, Peter *Memoirs of a Revolutionist* (1899)   ♀∥
Kropotkin, born a prince, became an anarchist and leading thinker behind the
Russian Revolution. Geographer, explorer, political philosopher, he writes well
of early socialism in Russia, France and Britain. A fascinating world, as remote
now as the moon.
Lee, Laurie *Cider with Rosie* (1959)   ▣ ★∥
Superb evocation of childhood and 1920s British countryside, a book as good as
that of Hudson (qv). Also: *As I Walked Out One Midsummer Morning*, etc
Macmillan, Harold *The Winds of Change, 1914–1939* (1966)   ∥▩
World War I, Depression and the rise of Fascist dictators form the background to
the autobiography of this urbane British publisher-politician. Political memoirs
come and go: this one will endure. Also (sequels): *The Blast of War*; *Tides of
Fortune*. See MEDIA (Nowell-Smith)

Malcolm X *The Autobiography of Malcolm X* (1965)
Having been involved in drugs, crime, pimping, conversion to and dismissal from the Black Muslim movement, Malcolm X was murdered in 1965. If he had survived he might have been a major political force. His book will live.

Maugham, W. Somerset *The Summing Up* (1938)
Judicious look back at what life had taught a professional writer who chose never to wear his heart on his sleeve; dry, touching portrait of the artist as an old man. Also: *A Writer's Notebook.* See DRAMA; FICTION/CRIME; FICTION/NOVELS; FICTION/SHORT STORIES

Mead, Margaret *Blackberry Winter* (1973)   ★ //
Generation of ambitiously intellectual American women produced Margaret Mead, anthropologist, writer, traveller, whose life is here chronicled as far as 1939. See ANTHROPOLOGY; SOCIOLOGY

Miller, Merle *Plain Speaking: An Oral Biography of Harry Truman* (1974)   ▧
Miller captured the words of the ex-President on tape, had them transcribed and produced from them this marvellous, moving, quixotic book.

Morris, Jan *Conundrum* (1974)
James Morris was a successful British journalist, writer and traveller, happily married and with children—but this was a painful façade: since childhood he had felt that he was a woman trapped in a man's body. How body and spirit became one (through hormones and surgery) is told with charm, delicacy and humour. See TRAVEL (Morris, James)

Muggeridge, Malcolm *Chronicles of Wasted Time* (2 vols, 1972–73)   ▨
Like many British intellectuals of his late-Edwardian generation, Muggeridge always lived his life *à clef.* Turn the key deftly, and tiptoe into the wide-eyed, artfully candid world of a wastrel intellect, penitently impenitent, discreetly blabbering: enjoyable traipse through Kippsian Croydon and the Fabian world of the repellent Webbs, on to British India and a lifetime of journalism. Never did apprentice Christian more rabidly bite the hands that fed him.

Nabokov, Vladimir *Speak, Memory* (1966)   ▥ ★ //
Russian novelist writes of his childhood in a wealthy, pre-Revolutionary family—a never-forgotten dream of happiness irretrievably snatched away. See BIOGRAPHY; CHILDREN'S BOOKS (Carroll); FICTION/NOVELS; POETRY (Pushkin)

Rousseau, Jean-Jacques *The Confessions* (1782)   ★
Writer, thinker, composer, Rousseau fought with all his friends, was always in a disastrous amorous state, lived a humdrum life with a mistress whose five children went to the foundling hospital. Unrivalled self-portrait of a difficult, distracted genius at loggerheads with the everyday. See POLITICS

Saint Simon, Louis de Rouvroy, Duc de *Memoirs* (18th century)   ℘ ★
Discursive, ironic, waspish: among the best memoirs ever published. Vivid, caustic picture by a survivor of Louis XIV's court. Style at first indigestible, then compulsive.

Shostakovich, Dmitri *Testimony* (1979)   ✱
Distracted, dictated memoirs from Shostakovich's last years. Chillingly describes his 50-year persecution by bureaucratic tyrants, his continuous self-haunting misery. Not, perhaps, for lovers of his music, or of the Soviet state; for students of political repression or artistic neurosis, vital.

Simenon, Georges *When I Was Old* (1970)
Frightening book, by a man haunted by his own creativity. Frank comments on drinking, never-ceasing need for women, methods of writing, memories of children when young; musings on contemporaries and on other writers. Revealing; especially relevant to the debate about how much an artist's life inhabits his work. See FICTION/CRIME

Sitwell, Osbert *Left Hand, Right Hand* (1944–46)   ▨
The Sitwells were to 1920s and 1930s Britain what the Algonquin set was to the USA: inessential but definitive. Eccentrics all, they were often extremely funny, and never lost an iron grasp of their own self-importance and their putative place in English letters. (See John Pearson's *Façades* for efficient outside account.) See OCCULT (Sitwell, S.); POETRY (Sitwell, E.)

Speer, Albert *Inside the Third Reich* (1970)
Chilling, invaluable account of life as Hitler's pet courtier and political architect. Speer's intellectual quality illuminates but never explains his master's fatal power; he is the epitome of a man whose "honour rooted in dishonour stood" and whom faith unfaithful has kept falsely true. See Hart; BIOGRAPHY (Bullock); POLITICS (Stern)

Woolman, John *Journal* (1774)
For thirty years the elderly Woolman travelled about the American colonies trying to persuade his fellow Quakers that to own people was wrong. As a direct result the Quakers were the first important group to ban slavery, a fuse that led to the Civil War and beyond.

Biography

Modern biography combines the skills of historian, essayist, psycho-analyst, critic and (biographers like to think) novelist. The books in this list are chosen, like those in Autobiography and Memoirs, for the importance or interest of the subject and for evocation of period or character. They fall into two categories: objective, where historian and critic predominate, and subjective, where memoirist and analyst tend to take over (and where what a writer says about his subject is often deeply revealing of himself). One or two cases (for example Sartre on Genet and Troyat on Tolstoy) stray delightfully (or scandalously) into fiction. Whether biography is an art or not—and despite the documentary fetish which has led to renewed prolixity in recent times (for example in Michael Holroyd, after all the slimming work of Lytton Strachey)—it is nearly always metaphorical or allegorical; for a life can never be written: it must be lived.

See ART (Smith, Vasari); DRAMA (Fitzsimons); HISTORY/ AMERICAN (Aaron, Morgan, Woodward); HISTORY/ANCIENT (Selzer); HISTORY/ASIAN (Suyin); HISTORY/BRITISH (Hibbert, Longford, Magnus, Neale, Plumb, Scarisbrick, Willson); HISTORY/EUROPEAN (Geyl, Grey, Massie, Origo, Tyler); FILM (McCabe, Septon, Taylor); LITERARY CRITICISM (Hazlitt); MATHEMATICS (Davis, Moszkowski, Reid); MEDIA (Berg); MUSIC (Einstein, Nichols, Nolan, White); NATURAL HISTORY (Adams, Blunt); PSYCHOLOGY (Watson); RELIGION (Wat, Wendel); TRAVEL (Ronay)

Aldington, Richard *Lawrence of Arabia* (1955) ✳
Definitive example of the "irresponsible" hatchet-job. Priceless malice, eg over T. E. Lawrence's claim to have read every book in the Bodleian Library while at Oxford. To be taken with the pinch of the salt it so liberally supplies. Also: *Portrait of a Genius, but...* (about D. H. Lawrence). See TRAVEL (Lawrence)
Bainton, Roland H. *Here I Stand* (1950) ☿
Excellent short book on Luther and the Lutheran Reformation; religious aspects preponderant and thoughtfully discussed. Also: *Erasmus of Christendom*
Baker, Carlos *Ernest Hemingway: A Life Story* (1969)
Fast-talking, fast-moving mixture of punditry and pungency; "in-depth" journalism at its upmarket best. See FICTION/NOVELS (Hemingway); FICTION/SHORT STORIES (Hemingway)
Bate, W. J. *John Keats* (1963)
On the West side of the Atlantic, at least, now the standard biography. And Bate's *Life of Dr Johnson* is even better. Both are extraordinary: they carry their learning gracefully; they are also as dramatic as life itself. See Gittings; LITERARY CRITICISM (Keats); POETRY (Keats)
Bell, Quentin *Virginia Woolf: A Biography* (1972)
Two civilized volumes by Virginia Woolf's nephew, making extensive use of her intimate journals. Notable for fine analysis of Woolf's relationships with her friends; dubious jibes at Leonard. See Woolf; DIARIES (Woolf); FEMINISM (Woolf); FICTION/NOVELS (Woolf)
Boswell, James *The Life of Samuel Johnson Ll.D.* (1791) ☿★▤
Perhaps the one assured world classic in English biography. Remarkable for its almost proverbial re-creation of Johnson's talk; for acute observation of English foible and eccentricity; for power to set a scene and adjudge an encounter; for gathering sense of the moral greatness of its subject, and above all for deep underlying affection. Also: *A Journal of a Tour to the Hebrides.* See Bate; Johnson; Krutch; DIARIES; LITERARY CRITICISM (Johnson); REFERENCE (Johnson); TRAVEL (Johnson)
Bullock, Alan *Hitler: A Study in Tyranny* (1952) ▮☿ ∥
Measured, convincing, composedly British account of Hitler's extraordinary character and destructive genius. The narrative of the years up to 1940 is unsurpassed; more recent research, and re-assessment of evidence from the Nuremberg Trials, have challenged Bullock's picture of the final years. See AUTOBIOGRAPHY (Hart, Speer); POLITICS (Arendt, Stern)
Capote, Truman *In Cold Blood* (1966)
Biography as murder investigation: in this case a multiple murder executed by two footloose psychopaths in a small country township in Kansas. Interweaving factual reportage and fictive reconstruction, Capote builds up a detailed portrait of mid-West America.

Cecil, Lord David *Melbourne* (2 vols, 1939–54)
As a young man, Melbourne (Sir William Lamb) married Lady Caroline;
thus the first part of this life concerns the ensuing Byron scandal. Later,
Melbourne was twice Prime Minister, and became the fatherly confidant of the
young Queen Victoria. Common to sovereign and adviser is an abiding
melancholy, admirably treated by Cecil. Also: *Max: Sir Max Beerbohm*;
Visionary and Dreamer: Two Poetic Painters

Charters, Ann *Kerouac: A Biography* (1973)
Sad, panoramic re-creation of Kerouac's life and the "beat" circle of the 1950s:
Ginsberg, Burroughs, Cassady, Snyder *et al*. There was vision there, and hope;
but the elegiac tone was already strong. See DIARIES (Ginsberg);
FICTION/NOVELS (Kerouac)

Coleridge, Samuel Taylor *Biographia Literaria* (1817)
Subtitled *Biographical Sketches of My Literary Life and Opinions*, probably the
best criticism of a friend and collaborator by his friend: Coleridge on
Wordsworth. Ambitious philosophical criticism shows characteristic depth and
range of Coleridge's mind. Also: *Notebooks*; *Shakespearian Criticism*, etc. See De
Quincey; Lefebure; DIARIES (Wordsworth); POETRY (Coleridge, Wordsworth)

De Quincey, Thomas *Recollections of the Lake Poets* (1834–40)   ℗
Rambling perceptive reminiscences: the Opium Eater is a master of digression
and sly innuendo. See Coleridge; Lefebure; POETRY (Coleridge, Wordsworth)

Donaldson, Frances *Edward VIII* (1974)
Astringent (but never slick or malicious) antidote to modern royal "lives", with
their tendency to be impartial on the side of the famous. Edward had a hellish
childhood (oh those sewn-up trouser pockets, with all they say of the fear of sex
and small change), but he was a spoiled man of small brain and less judgement,
whose "romance" was perhaps a necessary escape from responsibilities he could
not face.

Edel, Leon *Henry James* (5 vols, 1953–72)   ▮ ℗
Ambitious, enthralling but uneven, fluctuating between Freudian psycho-
biography, detailed literary criticism, and urbane anecdote. The first three
volumes are the best. Also: *Literary Biography* (influential theoretical work). See
James; DIARIES (James); FICTION/NOVELS (James); FICTION/SHORT
STORIES(James); LITERARY CRITICISM (James)

Ellmann, Richard *James Joyce* (1959)   ℗ ⫽
Lovingly re-creates not only Joyce's Dublin, but his European cities too, and
establishes the autobiographical figure behind the fiction. Ellmann writes with a
unique combination of scholarship and pixie charm, ideally suited to his subject.
Also: *Golden Codgers: Biographical Speculations*; *Yeats: The Man and the
Masks*. See DIARIES (Joyce); FICTION/NOVELS (Joyce); FICTION/SHORT
STORIES (Joyce)

Flexner, James *Washington: The Indispensable Man* (1974)   ★
One-volume recension of Flexner's superb four-volume biography of
Washington, which appeared over a period of nearly twenty years. Now probably
the best short biography of *the* founding father—*pater patriae*. See Freeman.

Freeman, D. S. *Robert E. Lee* (4 vols, 1934–35); *Washington*
(6 vols, 1948–54)   ★
Seldom does a single biographer produce two standard and definitive
biographies, certainly not of two such august and eminent—and different—men
as Lee and Washington. Both were Virginians (as was Freeman); both were
soldiers; and both had a deep love of their country, differently expressed as this
obviously was. At any rate both these massive biographies are masterpieces.
Almost equally good is *Lee's Lieutenants*, on which Freeman worked in between
Lee and Washington. See Flexner.

Freud, Sigmund *Leonardo da Vinci* (1910)   ℗
This brief monograph of the links between Leonardo's art and his childhood
upbringing succinctly demonstrates what "Freudian biography" actually
means—and also contains some shrewd warnings from the sage himself on its
inherent risks. See Jones; ART (Richter); MEDICINE (Freud)

Froude, James *Thomas Carlyle* (4 vols, 1882–84)   ℗
One of the great Victorian classics of biography. Central to Carlyle's life was his
unhappy and unfulfilled marriage, which Froude depicted with a sympathy (for
the wife) and a frankness that outraged his contemporaries; yet Carlyle the writer
and prophet emerges with a bitter grandeur. Excellent one-volume abridgement
by John Clubbe (1979). Also: *My Relations with Carlyle*. See DIARIES (Carlyle);
LITERARY CRITICISM (Carlyle)

Gaskell, Elizabeth *The Life of Charlotte Brontë* (1857)   ℗
Mrs Gaskell knew Charlotte well; the biography, though sentimental and
reticent, gives an authentic picture of Brontë Yorkshire and is unique as a
contemporary account by another woman writer. Should be read in conjunction
with Gérin (qv). See FICTION/NOVELS (Brontë, Gaskell)

Gérin, Winifred *Branwell Brontë* (1961)   ℗ ★ ⫽
The most haunting of an impressive series of biographies which together

reconstruct the entire Brontë world. Also: *The Brontës* (2 vols). See Gaskell; FICTION/NOVELS (Brontë)

Gittings, Robert *John Keats* (1968) 🏛★*▯*
This moving biography has established itself as a classic of what might be called the "mainstream" school of modern biography. Also: *Young Thomas Hardy*; *The Older Hardy*; *The Nature of Biography*. See Bate; LITERARY CRITICISM (Keats); POETRY (Keats)

Green, Peter *Kenneth Grahame, 1859–1932* (1959) 🏛✳*▯*▭
Classical scholar subjects the author of much-loved *The Wind in the Willows* to a sensitive post-Freudian interpretation, emphasizing the passing of an Edwardian bachelor golden age. Provoking, and thought-provoking too. See CHILDREN'S BOOKS (Grahame)

Grigson, Geoffrey *Samuel Palmer: The Visionary Years* (1947) ♀*▯*▭
Grigson has written on folklore, herbalism, wild flowers, topography, poetry and painting; probably none of his books have combined these elements so magically as this early biographical study. The book put Palmer (the most English of rural painters) on the map after years of neglect. Also: *Samuel Palmer's Valley of Vision*

Holmes, Richard *Shelley* (1974) ♀
Almost in that class of biography typified by André Maurois' delectable *Byron* (and perhaps by his *Ariel*, also a study of Shelley) in which a poet's life is treated with narrative zest but with little serious attention to the poetry. Holmes, if prosaic, carried out his investigations with thoroughness and readability. The flame is missing, but the fuel is excellently assembled. See Trelawny; POETRY (Shelley); LITERARY CRITICISM (Shelley)

Holroyd, Michael *Lytton Strachey: A Critical Biography*
(2 vols, 1967–68) ♀★*▯*
This unbrief life, combining polished literary style with scandalous Bloomsbury material, discovered a huge new readership for modern British biography. Holroyd gives the fraught emotional life of Strachey and his circle the unexpected quality of comic epic. Also: *Augustus John*; *Hugh Kingsmill*. See Strachey.

Howarth, David *The Desert King: Ibn Saud, Founder of Saudi Arabia* (1964)
Wonderful swashbuckling biography of the father of his country—and also of more than 125 sons and an uncounted number of daughters (not uncountable, just uncounted).

Hudson, Derek *Munby: Man of Two Worlds* (1972)
Extraordinary story of a respectable Victorian gentleman with a passion for buxom working-class girls, who spent his life secretly drawing, photographing and interviewing them, and finally married the prize specimen, his housekeeper, Hannah. Bizarre; touching; great fun. Also: *Thomas Barnes of "The Times"*; *Lewis Carroll*; *Arthur Rackham*. See FEMINISM (Hiley)

Huizinga, Johan *Erasmus of Rotterdam* (1924) ♀*▯*
Elegant, moving biography of one of Europe's greatest humanists, freely illustrated with drawings by Dürer, Holbein, Cranach and others. See HISTORY/EUROPEAN; RELIGION (Phillips)

Hyde, H. Montgomery *Oscar Wilde* (1976)
Hyde conducts his biographies like court-hearings (they often centre on celebrated trials); his dramatic but detached approach is peculiarly effective in dealing with Wilde's mesmeric, histrionic personality. Also: *The Strange Death of Lord Castlereagh*; *The Trial of Sir Roger Casement*; *Carson*. See DIARIES (Wilde); DRAMA (Wilde); FICTION/NOVELS (Wilde)

James, Henry *Partial Portraits* (1913) ★
Supreme examples of the essayist as biographer. A great novelist looks with affectionate, sometimes sly acumen at eminent contemporaries. George Eliot, Trollope, Maupassant, Stevenson and Turgenev definitively abbreviated. See Edel; DIARIES; FICTION/NOVELS; FICTION/SHORT STORIES; LITERARY CRITICISM

Johnson, Dr Samuel *The Lives of the Most Eminent English Poets*
(1783) ♀★▯
Celebrated studies of 52 poets (including Donne, Milton, Dryden, Pope, Gray) from the early 17th century to the late 18th. 18th-century prose at its magisterial, grandiloquent best. See Bate: Boswell; Krutch; LITERARY CRITICISM; REFERENCE; TRAVEL

Jones, Ernest *The Life and Work of Sigmund Freud*
(3 vols, 1953–57) ♀*▯*
A Freudian on Freud (who emerges as a heroic and surprisingly attractive figure, set against a dark period of European history). Jones is a hagiographer: expect no objective analysis here, no dirt. See Freud; Pickering; MEDICINE (Freud); OCCULT (Vyvyan, for anti-Jones polemic)

Krutch, Joseph Wood *The Life of Samuel Johnson Ll.D.* (1945)
Krutch was a redoubtable scholar and one of the great raconteurs of his time (as well as a distinguished naturalist). All these strains came together in a fine but

little-known life of Dr Johnson, with whom Krutch had much in common. See Bate; Boswell; Johnson; LITERARY CRITICISM (Johnson); NATURAL HISTORY; REFERENCE (Johnson); TRAVEL (Johnson)

Lachouque, H. *The Anatomy of Glory: Napoleon and His Guard* (1978) 🔊 *∥*
It's said that there are over 300,000 books about Napoleon and at least one (a novel) by him. This is one of the best—we think. Napoleon was a startling combination of genius and monster; this author shirks not a single wart. See HISTORY/EUROPEAN (Chandler, Geyl)

Lefebure, Molly *Samuel Taylor Coleridge: A Bondage of Opium* (1974) ♀ *∥*
Coleridge's entire life seen in terms of his drug addiction, rather than (say) through his visionary poetry, his politics and journalism, or his position as a major English Romantic critic and philosopher. Readable, grim interpretation of a notably unhappy life. See Coleridge; De Quincey; POETRY (Coleridge)

Lindsay, Jack *J. M. W. Turner: His Life and Work* (1966) ♀ *∥*
Turner's difficult, withdrawn personality has often proved intractable to biographers. But by making use of his verse-jottings and sketchbooks, Lindsay produces a convincing psychological interpretation, set against a detailed evocation of the art-world of the period. See MATHEMATICS

Longford, Elizabeth *Wellington* (2 vols, 1969–72)
Readable and detailed, but never dull. This Wellington entertains all the contradictions of an English grandee, at once sensitive to the horrors of war and a great captain, a reactionary splendidly contemptuous of received ideas. Philip Guedalla's *The Iron Duke* is written with more style, but less authority. See HISTORY/BRITISH

Madariaga, Salvador de *Bolívar* (1951) ♀
Compendious literary account of the creator of South American independence (of a kind) from Spanish domination.

Mailer, Norman *Marilyn* (1973)
Ravishing photo-portraits of Marilyn Monroe; the text is written as a pastiche of American advertising copy—"a very Stradivarius of sex," etc—and a polemic against earnest show-biz biographies. The ironic form of the book is a rare delight. See FICTION/NOVELS

Marchand, Leslie *Lord Byron: A Biography* (3 vols, 1957) ♀ *∥*
Definitive example of the modern three-decker "definitive" life. Exhaustingly informative; a fascinating, if oddly unbalanced monument. Also: *Byron: A Portrait*; *Byron's Letters and Journals*. See Trelawny; DIARIES (Byron); POETRY (Byron)

Masters, John *Casanova* (1969) *∥*
Tragi-comic life of one of the world's most charming rogues. Admirably balances author's deflating research against the tumescence of Casanova's own memoirs. It's less like life than a Rossini comic opera—but Casanova's pervasive melancholy gives the book dark overtones. How sad to be the cynosure of half Europe, and the court jester of the other half!

Milford, Nancy *Zelda Fitzgerald: A Biography* (1970) 🔊 *∥*
Scott Fitzgerald's life seen from Zelda's standpoint. Written *con amore*, with a feminist edge. See DIARIES (Fitzgerald); FICTION/NOVELS (Fitzgerald); FICTION/SHORT STORIES (Fitzgerald)

Mitford, Nancy *Voltaire in Love* (1957)
Stylish account of 18th-century country life at the Chateau de Circy in Champagne, and also the pleasures of elegant Parisian intercourse at the Hotel Lambert on the Île Saint-Louis. Also: *Madame de Pompadour*; *Frederick the Great*. See FICTION/NOVELS (Voltaire)

Morison, S.E. *Admiral of the Ocean Sea: The Life of Christopher Columbus* (1942)
Standard English-language biography of the "discoverer" of America (who never touched the American continent). See HISTORY/AMERICAN; TRAVEL

Nabokov, Vladimir *Nicolai Gogol* (1944)
Brilliant, eccentric study, beginning with Gogol's "death and youth", and ending with a comic interview between Nabokov and his unsatisfied publisher. Captures the strangeness of Gogol's personality, and the peculiar Russian humour of *Dead Souls*. See AUTOBIOGRAPHY; CHILDREN'S BOOKS (Carroll); FICTION/NOVELS (Gogol, Nabokov); POETRY (Pushkin)

Nicolson, Harold *King George V: His Life and Reign* (1952) ♀ *∥*
Dignified, engaging portrait of a monarch at the centre of a declining empire. Also: *Curzon: The Last Phase; The Development of English Biography; Some People*. See DIARIES

Painter, George *Marcel Proust: A Biography* (1959–65) ♀ *∥*
This authoritative English biography produced a revolution in Proustian studies, largely by its reconstruction of *Remembrance of Things Past* in terms of Proust's own relationships and youthful experiences. Massive, but delicate as Proust himself in its perception of people and places; an exceptional piece of prose.

Also: *André Gide; Chateaubriand.* See Pickering; DRAMA (Johnson); FICTION/NOVELS (Proust); LITERARY CRITICISM (Beckett)

Parkman, Francis *La Salle and the Discovery of the Great West* (1879) 🔒📖
Biographical history, at times using La Salle's own words. La Salle was the indomitable but unlovely explorer who claimed Louisiana for France and was murdered for his pains by his own men. A Coriolanus in the American wilderness. See HISTORY/AMERICAN

Pickering, George W. *Creative Malady* (1974) ✱
Highly original study of how psychological illness contributed to the productivity of six well-known individuals. Fascinating biographical sketches of Darwin, Florence Nightingale, Mary Baker Eddy, Freud, Proust and Elizabeth Barrett Browning.

Plutarch *Parallel Lives* (105–115) 🔒📖
Regarded in the Middle Ages and Renaissance as one of the most important of classical books to survive, this had an enormous influence perhaps hard to understand today, when moralizing biography is not the height of fashion: without it, for example, Shakespeare's history plays would have been heavier on bland pageantry, lighter on the analysis of political motivation and influence.
Parallel Lives: famous Greeks compared with famous Romans. Sounds forbidding: in fact is light and a joy to read.

Renan, Ernest *The Life of Jesus* (1863) ✱
Renan was the first writer to apply modern biographical methods to Jesus. The result created an uproar similar to that following Darwin's *The Origin of Species*. Short, elegant and sceptical, in the best Voltairean tradition, it is still eminently readable. Also: *Marcus Aurelius*

Renoir, Jean *Renoir My Father* (1962) 🔒∥
Intimate, uninhibited picture of a great painter. From life—or studio portrait? The father-figure *is* very like a Michel Simon performance from one of Jean Renoir's early films. Still, a stylish evocation of French country life, and of the quirks and dedication of the creative mind.

Ricks, Christopher *Tennyson* (1972) 🔒✓∥
Short on day-to-day events, though never shirking psychological issues; sympathetic, uncensorious critique of a genius of verbal niceties, who perhaps became a little too nice for his own poetic good. See POETRY (Tennyson)

Rolt, L. T. C. *Isambard Kingdom Brunel: A Biography* (1957) 🔒∥▨
Rolt successfully presents the great bridge-builder and boat constructor as a heroic representative of Victorian energy and enterprise, a Michelangelo of engineering. The biography is given tension and excitement by accounts of the various disasters, collapses, and sinkings which accompanied Brunel's triumphant progress. Also: *George and Robert Stephenson: The Railway Revolution*; *James Watt*

Sandburg, Carl *Abraham Lincoln: The Prairie Years* (2 vols, 1926–29); *The War Years* (4 vols, 1939) ★
There are many biographies of Lincoln—he is an irresistible subject—and many are good, but Sandburg's *magnum opus* is probably the most monumental and endearing. See DIARIES (Lincoln)

Sartre, Jean-Paul *Saint Genet: Actor and Martyr* (1952) ♀
Existentialist biography of the criminal and playwright Jean Genet. Though long and analytico-rhetorical, it presents an interesting alternative to the Anglo-Saxon tradition of empirical biography. Also: *Baudelaire*; *Flaubert*. See DRAMA; FICTION/NOVELS; PHILOSOPHY; SEX (Genet); TRAVEL (Genet)

Starkie, Enid *Baudelaire* (1957) ♀
Meticulous with a warmth and sympathy rare in academic biography. Excellent on both Baudelaire's love affairs and his poetry. Usefully read in conjunction with Sartre's *Baudelaire*. Also: *Arthur Rimbaud*; *Flaubert*. See ART (Baudelaire); DIARIES (Baudelaire); POETRY (Baudelaire)

Steegmuller, Francis *Cocteau: A Biography* (1970)
Cocteau's chameleon personality (novelist, poet, painter, film-maker, impresario) provides a glittering, amusing guide through the avant-garde Paris of Diaghilev, Nijinsky, Picasso, Stravinsky, Radiguet and Isadora Duncan. Also: *Apollinaire: Poet among the Painters*; *Flaubert and Madame Bovary: A Double Portrait*; *Maupassant: A Lion in the Path*. See DIARIES

Strachey, Lytton *Eminent Victorians* (1918) ★
Elegant, mocking studies of Cardinal Manning, Florence Nightingale, Dr Arnold of Rugby School, and General Gordon of Khartoum. The book marks the beginning of the immense influence of Bloomsbury on modern British biography, destroying forever what Strachey called "the tedious panegyric" of Victorian biography. Also: *Queen Victoria*; *Portraits in Miniature*. See Holroyd.

Taylor, A. J. P. *Bismarck* (1955) ♀
Terse, critical but teasingly just appraisal of the Iron Chancellor by the emery paper of British historians. Also: *War Lords*; *Beaverbrook*, etc. See HISTORY/BRITISH

Thompson, E. P. *William Morris: From Romantic to Revolutionary* (1955) ℗

Brilliant, dogmatic biography by leading left-wing historian. "The transformation of the eccentric artist and romantic literary man into the socialist agitator may be counted among the great conversions of the world." See HISTORY/BRITISH

Tomalin, Claire *The Life and Death of Mary Wollstonecraft* (1974)

Short, admirably balanced life of the first British feminist (1759–97), author of *Vindication of the Rights of Women.* See FEMINISM (Wollstonecraft)

Trelawny, Edward John *Records of Shelley, Byron, and the Author* (1858) ★

Trelawny was a natural raconteur, and his bubbling, opinionated and often mendacious biography, packed with dramatic incident and reconstructed dialogue, reads with all the life and outrageousness of a Ken Russell film. See Holmes; Marchand; DIARIES (Byron); POETRY (Byron)

Trevor-Roper, Hugh *A Hidden Life: The Enigma of Sir Edmund Backhouse* (1976) 📖

Full of fantastic sexual adventures at the turn of the 19th century, this remarkable biography patiently reconstructs the life of a forger, swindler and conman who, among other things, sold the British Government 200,000 non-existent rifles in 1915. Also: *Archbishop Laud; The Last Days of Hitler*

Troyat, Henri *Tolstoy* (1965) ★ ⫽

Rich, imaginative presentation of Tolstoy as a man of enormous inner contradictions and appetites, vividly re-created through the eyes of his long-suffering wife, children, and literary contemporaries. The style is self-consciously Tolstoyan, but retains a very French ironic detachment. Should be a novel—and very nearly is. Also: *Pushkin; Gogol.* See FICTION/NOVELS (Tolstoy); LITERARY CRITICISM (Tolstoy)

Van Doren, Carl *Benjamin Franklin* (1938)

Franklin is an immense subject for a biographer—scientist, politician, philosopher, lover, he was all things to all men. Van Doren captures the many-sidedness of the man in this popular, well-written book. See AUTOBIOGRAPHY (Franklin); REFERENCE (Adler)

Wall, Joseph F. *Andrew Carnegie* (1970)

Gigantic biography of the giant industrialist and philanthropist; particularly good on his Scottish background, and on the operation of his early corporations in the late-19th-century heyday of American industrial enterprise. (Carnegie had interests in oil, railways, bridges, telegraphy, iron and steel—among other things.) Interesting comments on how the Civil War affected businessmen in the next two generations, and on Carnegie's attitude to business rivals and to labour relations. Sober; thorough; absorbing. Also: *Henry Watterson, Reconstructed Rebel*

Woodham-Smith, Cecil *Florence Nightingale, 1820–1910* (1950) 📖 ★ ⫽ 🖼

One of the most outstanding and readable narrative historians of her generation, Woodham-Smith concentrated all her knowledge of the ways of the Victorian establishment in this splendid vindication of Miss Nightingale's rumbustious career. See Pickering; Strachey; HISTORY/BRITISH

Woolf, Virginia *Flush* (1933)

Whimsical biography of Elizabeth Barrett Browning's red cocker-spaniel, complete with line-drawings by sister Vanessa. Woolf carries it off by prose style alone, and gives a splendidly confused vision of the elopement to Italy, with striking effects of light, shade, scent, and lapsing time. Also: *Roger Fry; Orlando: A Biography* (a spoof). See Bell; DIARIES; FEMINISM; FICTION/NOVELS

Zweig, Stefan *Three Masters* (1920) ★

These studies of Balzac, Dickens and Dostoyevsky show the early influence of Freudian psychology, and Zweig's own special brand of imaginative-biographical criticism. Also: *Master Builders* (Hölderlin, von Kleist, Nietzsche). See FICTION/NOVELS (Balzac, Dickens, Dostoyevsky)

Children's Books

Any list of children's books should make nostalgic browsing for adults; but it should also include the sort of books children actually still read. This list is a choice of classics (all recommendably readable, and read) and good contemporary books, potentially of classic status too.

See DIARIES (Frank); FICTION/NOVELS (Swift, Twain); FICTION/SHORT STORIES (Grimm); HUMOUR (Schulz); REFERENCE (Merit, New Arthur Mee, Opie); RELIGION (Bible)

Adams, Richard *Watership Down* (1972)
Long, allegorical novel about rabbits; occasional turgidities offset by strong story-line. Adam's later books are full of detailed violence, could be a test for the squeamish. (10+)

Aiken, Joan *Tales of Arabel's Raven* (1974)   ♪
Slapstick adventures of ordinary little girl and pet raven in contemporary London. Expert comedy for the 7+ set; older children (11+) may prefer her densely-plotted historical novels (*Go Saddle the Sea*; *The Wolves of Willoughby Chase*) or her collections of short stories (*A Harp of Fishbones*; *The Kingdom under the Sea*, etc).

Alcott, Louisa May *Little Women* (1868)
One of the great progenitors of the family story. Alcott writes from her own life with a sincerity and warmth which transcend the often pious particularity. (10+)

Almedingen, E. M. *Ellen* (1971)
Ellen Polotratzky, the author's grandmother, is the central character; five other biographical novels complete the sequence, and build a fascinating picture of pre-Revolutionary Russia. (12+) Also: *A Candle at Dusk*; *The Knights of the Golden Table*, etc

Andersen, Hans Christian *Fairy Tales* (1835–72)   ▣
Among the plethora of available translations, two may be singled out: Corrin's in *Ardizzone's Hans Andersen* (1978, illustrated by Edward Ardizzone); and Haugaard's *Hans Andersen: His Classic Fairy Tales* (1976, illustrated by Michael Foreman). (6+)

Atwater, F. and **R.** *Mr Popper's Penguins* (1938)
Where do you keep a flock of penguins in a city apartment? Naturally, in the bath. So how do you take a bath? Splendid, deadpan humour, like children's Thurber. (8+)

Baum, Frank L. *The Wonderful World of Oz* (1900)
This famous century-inaugurating story was followed by several others by Baum and dozens of others by inferior copiers. Sentimental and foolish at times, but the characters of Dorothy and her loyal friends are warm and—with Judy Garland's help—unforgettable. (10+)

Bawden, Nina *Carrie's War* (1973)
World War II evacuee children in Welsh mining community. Strong on period detail—and that includes period attitudes, adult emotions seen through a child's eyes. (10+) Also: *A Handful of Thieves*; *The Runaway Summer*, etc

Boston, Lucy M. *The Children of Green Knowe* (1954)
Boston's own historic house is central to all her Green Knowe stories. In this one, Tolly from the present and the ghost-children from the house's past share adventures and troubles in a time-free world. (8+) Also: *Castle of Yew*, etc

Brothwell, D.R. (ed) *The Rise of Man* (1976)   a ★ ♪
Superb account for children of man's evolution from fossil evidence to remains of great civilizations. Demanding text is offset by the clarity and simplicity of the illustrations (drawings and diagrams are especially good, and well-captioned). In the same series, and of the same quality: *The Universe* (Kerrod); *The Prehistoric World* (Sheehan); *The Living World* (Chinery). (12+) See ARCHAEOLOGY

Brunhoff, Jean de *The Story of Babar* (1934)   ♪ ▣
Exploits of young elephant acquiring and passing on the trappings of bourgeois society, told with a gentle satire not lost on today's readers. Delightful illustrations. Original, large-format edition best; continuations of saga by author's son Laurent are markedly less good. (6+) Also: *Babar's Travels*; *Babar the King*; *Babar at Home*

Buchan, John *The Thirty-nine Steps* (1915)
First class thriller. The stuff of every schoolboy's dreams: stiff upper lips, gripping adventures, good Scottish scenery. (10+) Also: *The Three Hostages*, etc

Burnett, Frances Hodgson *The Secret Garden* (1911)   ★ ▣
A story in true Romantic tradition: two lonely, spoilt children (one an invalid who is miraculously cured) discover a secret, forbidden and neglected garden in which, through working to restore its former glory, they discover their own better natures. Sharp, sympathetic characterization; her best book. (10+)

Carroll, Lewis *Alice's Adventures in Wonderland* (1865) ★ 〃 ▯
Among the editions in print, those with Tenniel's original illustrations are the
best. For the adventurous or curious, a translation into Russian by Nabokov is
available. (8+) Also: *Through the Looking Glass*

Christopher, John *The White Mountains* (1967)
Together with *The City of Gold and Lead* and *The Pool of Fire*, this makes up a
science-fiction triology in which man, dominated by an alien race, painfully
throws off his servitude. Racy style; good introduction to major SF children's
author. (9+) Also: *The Lotus Caves; The Guardians; The Prince in Waiting*

Cole, William (ed) *Oh, What Nonsense!* (1968)
Collection of nonsense rhymes, illustrated by Tomi Ungerer—sure winner with
younger children. Sample: "The time to tickle a lizard is before, or right after, a
blizzard . . ." (6+)

Cooper, Susan *Over Sea, Under Stone* (1965)
First of a series of five novels. Light battles with Dark for control of the world,
with children for warriors. (11+)

Dahl, Roald *Charlie and the Chocolate Factory* (1964) ★
Charlie's passion for chocolates was made worse by living within sight of Willie
Wonka's chocolate factory. How he got into the factory and came to run it is told
with an off-beat humour and a lateral view of reality that goes down especially
well with young children. (6+) Also: *James and the Giant Peach*, etc

De La Mare, Walter *Come Hither* (1923) ★
Wide-ranging poetry anthology by one of the best-loved 20th-century poets. If
you buy no other poetry anthologies, buy this one. (8+) Also: *Collected Stories for
Children; Three Royal Monkeys*, etc

Dickinson, Peter *The Changes* (1975)
Combined edition of three books (*The Weathermonger, Heartsease* and *The
Devil's Children*) that make up a dystopian fantasy in which present-day Britain
has reverted to a medieval way of life and all machines are regarded as
intrinsically evil. (12+) Also: *The Blue Hawk*, etc. See FICTION/CRIME

Dixon, E. (ed) *Fairy Tales from the Arabian Nights* (1958) ★ 〃
Arabia, China and India all contributed to these folk tales of the East, which have
been used as bedtime stories since Scheherazade first captured her audience. This
well-illustrated edition (pictures by Kiddell-Monro) recommended. (7+)

Durrell, Gerald *My Family and Other Animals* (1956) ★
Winning combination of animals, insects, and the author's slapstick family (he is
the brother of Lawrence Durrell), all set in Corfu between the wars. Amusing,
affectionate, observant: a modern classic. (9+) Also: *Birds, Beasts and Relatives;
Fillets of Plaice*, etc. See NATURAL HISTORY

Fleischman, Sid *Jingo Django* (1971) ★
Orphan chimney-sweep in 19th-century Boston begins a treasure-hunt which
takes him by stagecoach, river-scow and gipsy caravan to Mexico. Fast and funny;
poetic style juicy with period slang and atmosphere. (10+)

Forbes, Esther *Johnny Tremain* (1943)
Moving, enduring novel about a young hero in Boston during the American
Revolution. (10+)

Gág, Wanda *Millions of Cats* (1928)
"Hundreds of cats, thousands of cats, millions and billions and trillions of
cats"—so goes the silly refrain of this lovely book in which the author-artist
draws, or seems to draw, every one of those remarkably proliferating cats. (3+)

Garfield, Leon *The Strange Affair of Adelaide Harris* (1971)
Garfield is a leading exponent of the historical novel with an 18th- or 19th-
century setting; this book introduces an element of farce, which allows full play
for his ironic wit. Alarums and excursions at Dr Bunnion's Academy after Harris
attempts to expose his infant sister according to the customs of ancient Sparta. (10+)

Garner, Alan *Elidor* (1965) 🏚
Elidor marks the peak of Garner's fantasy writing for children (*The Weirdstone of
Brisingamen; The Moon of Gomrath; The Owl Service*). Here, the battle between
good and evil in mythological Elidor breaks through into this world, involving
four children in a strange power-struggle before balance is restored. (10+)
Garner has also written four books of a different kind (*The Stone Book; Tom
Fobble's Day; Granny Reardun; The Aimer Gate*): prose-poetic in style, they
build up a portrait of a family of British village craftsmen (stonemasons and
blacksmiths) spanning five generations from the mid 19th century to the
outbreak of World War II.

Grahame, Kenneth *The Wind in the Willows* (1908) ★ 〃 ▯
Rat, Mole, Badger and Toad are part of the mythology of childhood; life on the
river bank is an experience not to be forgotten, especially when assisted by E. H.
Shepard's illustrations. (7+) See BIOGRAPHY (Green)

Haggard, H. Rider *King Solomon's Mines* (1885)
Masterly adventure story of speculators in southern Africa. With Conan Doyle's
The Lost World (hereby recommended), a fine tale from a splendid era of
adventure fiction. The jargon has dated; the pace hasn't. (10+)

Hoban, Russell *The Mouse and His Child* (1969)
Carefully plotted, engaging story—a modern classic of children's fantasy. (8+)
Hughes, Ted *The Iron Man* (1968)   ★ 🖻
Superb mixture of science fiction and fable. The Iron Man appears from nowhere, disastrously gobbling up anything metal, until he is sent to the scrap yard where he grows sleek and "gleaming blue like a new gun barrel". In gratitude he helps earth against an invading space-creature. As with most classics, bald account tells nothing of style, imagination, quality. (8+) See POETRY
Hunter, Norman *The Incredible Adventures of Professor Branestawm* (1933)   🏛 ∥
Excruciating schoolboy humour, mad professor and friends in style of 1930s *Punch*. Stories more than match the zany genius of their illustrator, Heath Robinson. (7+) Also: *The Peculiar Triumph of Professor Branestawm*, etc
Jansson, Tove *Finn Family Moomintroll* (1950)
The Moomintrolls, looking like small, amiable hippos, live in the forests of Finland. During the long, dark winters they sleep, but in spring they come to full-blooded life and have wonderful, magical summer adventures. (7+)
Kingsley, Charles *The Heroes* (1856)   🏛 ∥
Retelling of Greek myths in simple, direct style. Perseus, Jason, Theseus—Kingsley's first, most likeable children's book. (9+) Also: *The Water Babies*; *Hereward the Wake*; *Westward Ho!*
Kipling, Rudyard *Just So Stories* (1902)
Adults may find these whimsical stories of how the animals got their characteristics the most dated and arch of all Kipling's work; but young children (4+) always come back for more. *The Jungle Book* is darker, more disciplined, on a level nearer that of his adult writing. (8+) Also: *Puck of Pook's Hill*, etc. See FICTION/SHORT STORIES; POETRY
Konigsburg, E. L. *From the Mixed-up Files of Mrs Basil E. Frankweiler* (1968)   ★
Witty, sensitive story of two adolescents who run away, take up residence in a museum, discover a beautiful statue and set out to find its maker. Particularly good on brother-sister relationships, everyday detail of museum life, dialogue between adults and children. (10+) Also: *Jennifer, Hecate, Macbeth, William, McKinley, and Me, Elizabeth*, etc
Lang, Andrew *The Blue Fairy Book* (1889)   🏛 ∥ 🖻
First of twelve "colour" fairy books. Stories from all over the world; available either as a straight reprint of 19th-century editions, or in a newly edited version by Brian Alderson, with fresh illustrations and (in part) new translations. (7+)
Le Guin, Ursula *A Wizard of Earthsea* (1968)
Dark-versus-Light trilogy, set in fantasy world with echoes of Tolkien (qv) and Lewis (qv). This is the first of the books, in which Sparrowhawk attains full magical powers and begins his journey towards his destiny. (11+) Also: *The Tombs of Atuan*; *The Farthest Shore*. See FICTION/SF
Lewis, C. S. *The Lion, the Witch, and the Wardrobe* (1950)
Pevensie children enter the world of Narnia through a wardrobe and become agents of change, subject to the Christ-like figure of Aslan the lion. Religious symbolism troubles some adults, but is rarely explicit and seems to pass most children by as they are carried forward by the adventures. (8+) Also: *Prince Caspian*; *The Voyage of the "Dawn Treader"*, etc. See FICTION/SF
Lindsay, Norman *The Magic Pudding* (1918)
Australian classic with unique brand of humour. Bunyip Bluegum, Bill Barnacle and Sam Sawnoff, keepers of the irascible Magic Pudding, enjoy riotous adventures, defending it from thieves and feeding well from it, as they travel the country. Antipodean odyssey, Mark Twain crossed with Roald Dahl. (5+)
Lines, Kathleen *Lavender's Blue* (1954)
Harold Jones's delicately coloured illustrations help to make an appealing collection of nursery-rhymes for very young children. Nicola Bayley's picture book of *Nursery Rhymes* sits neatly on the fence between the frankly popular and self-consciously artistic, while Helen Oxenbury's *Cakes and Custard* will appeal to an older age group.
Lively, Penelope *The House in Norham Gardens* (1974)
The seedy atmosphere (deteriorating house, aged academic lady owners) is cleverly established, as is the character of the young niece who uncovers a tambour in the attic and thereby releases a dream-fantasy from ancient New Guinea. (12+) Also: *The Wild Hunt of Hagworthy*; *The Ghost of Thomas Kempe*
Lobel, Arnold *Frog and Toad Are Friends* (1970)   🏛 ∥
Designed for children taking their first steps in independent reading; delightful story of Frog's and Toad's summer frolics, full of good natured humour and wit. (6+) Also: *Small Pig*; *The Great Blueness*
Lofting, Hugh *The Story of Dr Dolittle* (1920)   ★ ∥ 🖻
Dr Dolittle talks every animal's language, keeps a collection of weird animal friends (eg the Pushmi-pullyu), with whom he has adventures of a Heath Robinsonesque imagination. Gentle, delightful, warm. (8+)

Macauley, David *Cathedral* (1973) ★ ✄
Superb account of why and how a cathedral (imaginary, but typical) was planned and built. Author an architect; drawings pin-sharp and accurate as well as evocative. Especially good on detailed working-methods of masons, carpenters, glass-blowers, etc, and on how the building grew on its site (dizzy perspectives of medieval scaffolding). (8+) Also: *City; Castle; Pyramid*, etc

MacDonald, George *The Princess and the Goblin* (1872)
Published in a rich period for children's classics, this unusual fairy tale retains freshness, originality, draws its readers into the magical world of Celtic folktale and legend. (8+) Also: *The Princess and Curdie; At the Back of the North Wind*

Marshall, James Vance *Walkabout* (1959)
Two American children stranded in the Australian desert after an aircrash are led to food and water by an Aborigine boy. The young American boy soon learns from their guide; but the older girl, full of adolescent fears, shies away and inadvertently destroys the Aborigine, for he believes she has seen the Spirit of Death in his eyes. (12+) Original title: *The Children*

Masefield, John *The Midnight Folk* (1927)
Led by Nibbins the cat through secret passages in the old house, Kay escapes from dreary governesses and guardians to the magic world of the Midnight Folk; meets witches, smugglers and talking animals in his search for Great Grandfather's lost treasure. (9+) Also: *The Box of Delights; Jim Davis*. See DRAMA

Mayne, William *Earthfasts* (1966)
Nellie Jack John, the drummer boy, comes marching out of the castle mound into the 20th century after 200 years of searching for Arthur and his sleeping knights. (10+) A varied and prolific writer, for almost each age-group, his work has consistent quality. Also: *A Game of Dark; The Jersey Shore*, etc

Milligan, Spike *Silly Verse for Kids* (1963) ✄ ▣
Title tells all. "There are holes in the sky, where the rain comes in. The holes are small—that's why rain is thin." (8+) See HUMOUR

Milne, A. A. *Winnie-the-Pooh* (1926) ★ ✄ ▣
This clumsy, greedy and lovable bear has been bumbling his way into children's affections for more than half a century. Timeless; enchanting. (6+) Also: *The House at Pooh Corner; When We Were Very Young; Now We Are Six*, etc

Montgomery, L. M. *Anne of Green Gables* (1908)
In her heyday, Montgomery was read by politicians and housemaids; her Canadian orphan, Anne, still retains especial charm for teenage girls. (12+) Also: *Anne of Avonlea*

Nesbit, E. *The Railway Children* (1906)
After their father goes to prison, the children live in a dilapidated cottage near the railway and spend much of their time watching the line and indirectly bringing about their father's release. (10+) Also: *Five Children and It; The Story of the Treasure Seekers*, etc

Norton, André *Knave of Dreams* (1976)
Ramsay, the Knave, transported to a parallel time as a tool to destroy an evil ruler, has to adjust to a wholly new way of life, for there is no returning to his own time. (12+) Also: *Moon of Three Rings; Breed to Come*, etc

Norton, Mary *The Borrowers* (1952)
The Borrowers are miniature people who inhabit old houses and live by borrowing. If they are discovered they must move. But Arrietty has broken the rules and made friends with a human boy—which is how Mrs May comes to tell Kate everything. (7+) Also: *Bedknobs and Broomsticks*, etc

Pearce, Philippa *Minnow on the Say* (1955)
Boys messing around in a canoe on a sunny river, a hunt for lost treasure and the restoration of family fortunes provide the ingredients for this friendly, uncomplicated story. (9+) *Tom's Midnight Garden* older, tougher: discovery of the past leads to discovery of self. (11+) Also: *A Dog So Small*, etc

Perrault, Charles *The Fairy Tales of Charles Perrault* (1697) ★ ✄
Some of the best-loved of all fairy tales (Sleeping Beauty, Little Red Riding Hood, Beauty and the Beast, etc), well written and pleasingly unsentimental. Edition by Angela Carter (1967) recommended. (6+)

Peyton, K. M. *Flambards* (1967)
Horses and flying machines; nostalgic romance set in decrepit English Edwardian country house. Novelettish plot is redeemed by sensitive characterization and witty style. (12+) Also: *Thunder in the Sky; Pattern of Roses*

Potter, Beatrix *The Tale of Peter Rabbit* (1900) ★ ✄ ▣
Although Potter's animals are anthropomorphized, they never suffer from the coy sentimentality displayed by less able executants. Her down-to-earth directness makes no concessions to "childish" vocabulary or tender emotions: Peter's father was "put in a pie and eaten". (2+) Also: *The Tale of Mrs Tiggywinkle; The Tale of Benjamin Bunny*, etc

Prøysen, Alf *Little Old Mrs Pepperpot and Other Stories* (1958) 🔔 ✄
Old woman wakes up one morning, finds herself size of a pepperpot, loses no opportunity to take full advantage. Witty slapstick, like updated folk-tales. (6+)

Ransome, Arthur *Swallows and Amazons* (1931)
Ransome's true motives and popularity have been questioned; but there is no doubt that for many readers his stories of children messing around in boats or prospecting for gold in the English Lake District hold an imaginative reality equalled only by Sherlock Holmes. (8+) Also: *Coot Club*; *Winter Holiday*; *Old Peter's Russian Tales*, etc

St Exupéry, Antoine de *The Little Prince* (1943)
Written for children "because adults don't understand anything", this story of a downed aviator and his friend, a prince from a far-off star, has surface beauty, emotional profundity. (9+)

Scarry, Richard *Best Rainy Day Book Ever* (1974)
In a dozen bright, comic-strip picture-books, Scarry creates a colourful world of anthropomorphic animals (Sam Pig, Huckle Kitten, Lowly Worm). Exuberant detail: the books are notable for clear, accurate drawings of how things work: electricity, water supply, hospitals, travelling on a bus. Blend of fantasy and the everyday, and terrible jokes, may seem arch to some adults; but this is the kindergarten world (and the world through kindergarten eyes) exactly caught.

Sendak, Maurice *Where the Wild Things Are* (1970)
Original, imaginative picture book: little boy can tame wild things simply by staring at them. Especially good with young children who suffer from nightmares about wild animals and monsters. Also: *In the Night Kitchen*, etc

Sharmat, Marjorie *Getting Something on Maggie Marmelstein* (1971)
Splendid saga of life at American Junior High School. Thaddeus Gideon Smith V has a worst enemy, Maggie Marmelstein, who Knows Something Terrible about him. He sets out to restore the balance of the sex-war by playing Frog to her Princess in the school play. (9+) Also: *Goodnight Andrew, Goodnight Craig*; *Gladys Told Me to Meet Her Here*, etc.

Stevenson, Robert Louis *Treasure Island* (1883)
The very model of an adventure story—buried treasure, secret maps, pirates, mutiny on the high seas. (10+) See FICTION/SHORT STORIES

Sutcliff, Rosemary *Eagle of the Ninth* (1954)
The fortunes of a family of Roman settlers in Britain. Splendid story concerns the fate of the Ninth Legion, which mysteriously disappeared beyond "the Wall" at the height of the Empire. Subsequent volumes follow the family through "the decline and fall" in Britain, to the coming of Arthur and the Danes. (10+)

Tolkien, J. R. R. *The Hobbit* (1937)
Hobbits are small, home-loving creatures; Bilbo's uncharacteristic expedition with the dwarfs to find dragon treasure leads, among other things, to finding the fateful ring which, in later (adult) *The Lord of the Rings* trilogy, leads his nephew Frodo to the edge of Mordor and the destruction of its dark powers. Brevity and unpretentious narrative strength make this book one of Tolkien's best. (8+)

Treece, Henry *The Dream Time* (1967)
Treece interprets scant evidence with sincerity and his fundamental theme—the rejection of change—is as valid today as it was in the early tribal society he describes. A fine book by a poet and major children's novelist. (11+) Also: *Man with a Sword*; *Viking's Dawn*, etc. See FICTION/NOVELS

Uden, Grant *A Dictionary of Chivalry* (1968)
Alphabetical tour of the medieval knight and his world, from "Abatements of honour" to "Zutphen, Battle of". Should be specialist, dry; is witty, fascinating. Good illustrations in period style. (11+)

White, E. B. *The Trumpet of the Swan* (1970)
Voiceless Trumpeter Swan, with help of small boy and advice from old cob, his own father, learns reading, writing, and ultimately happiness and self-respect. White's is a rare voice, of great distinction: beauty and "the tears of things" have seldom been better caught. (7+) Also: *Charlotte's Web*; *Stuart Little*. See DIARIES (Garnett, White); HUMOUR; REFERENCE (Strunk)

White, T. H. *The Once and Future King* (1958)
Compendious (700-page) fantasy on the life of King Arthur. White's combination of slapstick and erudition is unique—as if Laurel and Hardy were set down in a Middle Ages accurate to the last detail. Nearest analogy is Tolkien (qv); but White writes better, and his mode is historical rather than imaginative fantasy. (10+) See MYTHOLOGY (Malory)

Wilder, Laura Ingalls *The Little House in the Big Woods* (1932)
In this and other "Little House" books the author wrote about her own childhood in 19th-century pioneer America. Warmth and sincerity have endeared these stories to generations of children. (8+) Also: *Little House on the Prairie*, etc

Williamson, Henry *Tarka the Otter* (1927)
Outstanding, non-anthropomorphic story of otters. (10+)

Zindel, Paul *The Pigman* (1968)
Sensitive novel about relations between old and young: two teenagers befriend an old man and then wreck his home while he is in hospital. There is a rich school of teenage fiction in current American writing; this novel shows it at its serious best. (12+) Also: *My Darling, My Hamburger*, etc

Diaries and Letters

For the reader, diaries and letters offer the voyeur's pleasure of a peep into other people's (more or less) unguarded lives; for the writer, anticipating this reaction, they are often a carefully contrived and artfully autobiographical form. The books on this list are of three kinds: those written from the start with publication in mind; those arranged, more or less cosmetically, for publication by the writers themselves; and (a rare few) intimate, personal documents intended for the writers' use alone.

See ART (Delacroix, Haydon, Pisarro); DRAMA (Redfield); FEMINISM (Rosen); HISTORY/ASIAN (Preble); HUMOUR (Grossmith); LITERARY CRITICISM (Keats); MEDIA (King, Nowell-Smith); NATURAL HISTORY (Banks, Douglas-Hamilton, Holden, White); OCCULT (Reyner); RELIGION (Bonhoeffer, Weil); TRAVEL (Cook, Lewis)

Anderson, Emily (ed) *The Letters of Wolfgang Amadeus Mozart* (1966) ★

Mozart and his father were devoted letter-writers; this collection of over 600 letters gives an absorbing insight into Mozart's life, character, opinions and views on music. Also: *The Letters of Beethoven.* See MUSIC (Einstein)

Barrett, E. and **Browning, R.** *The Letters of Robert Browning and Elizabeth Barrett, 1845–46* (1897) ♀

Love letters can make boring reading, unless you happen to be the recipient. However, these are extraordinary. A bizarre, intriguing literary courtship. See Heyden; BIOGRAPHY (Pickering); POETRY (Browning)

Baudelaire, Charles *Intimate Journals* (1920) ♀

As a young poet in Paris Baudelaire was the fashionable dandy *par excellence*: eccentric, outrageous, abandoned. Most of this brief but powerful journal was written in Brussels after 1857, when he was miserably in debt, reviled as a pornographer and dying of syphilis. Disturbing account of a personal descent into hell. See ART; BIOGRAPHY (Starkie); POETRY

Bennett, Arnold *The Journals of Arnold Bennett, 1896–1928* (1932–33)

Thousands of words a week: what he ate, what he did in the evenings, how late the trains were, how many words he wrote and what he was paid for them. Also: *Letters.* See FICTION/NOVELS

Boswell, James *Boswell's London Journal* (1763) ♀

Disarmingly candid, it charts the keen young Scotsman's attempts to become both a fully-fledged libertine—tumbling whores in St James's Park—and a member of the most respected literary salons; sparkling verbatim conversations with Garrick, Goldsmith and, of course, Dr Johnson. 1950 edition recommended. Also: *A Journal of a Tour to the Hebrides with Dr Samuel Johnson* (Scotland as dystopia—not to be missed). See BIOGRAPHY

Burney, Fanny *Diary* (1846) ★

Daughter and unofficial secretary of Charles Burney, the musicologist; fashionable novelist; lady-in-waiting to Queen Charlotte; wife of French army officer during the Revolution and later under Napoleon—Burney lived a full life, and spent much of it writing letters and the famous diary. Fresh; intimate; stylish; as domestic and as witty as *Pride and Prejudice*. Original seven volume edition rarely flags. For a sample, try Lewis Gibbs' one-volume selection (1940). Also: *Memoirs of Doctor Burney*, etc

Byron, Lord *Letters and Journals* (1898)

Among the most famous of English letters. Full, charismatic impact of Byron the man dramatically revealed in direct, vivid and astonishingly modern tones. See BIOGRAPHY (Marchand, Trelawny); POETRY

Carlyle, Thomas (ed) *The Letters and Speeches of Oliver Cromwell* (1845) ♀

Cromwell's letters, and even more his speeches, are vivid evidence for the revolutionary puritan conscience, the zealot as self-inventor, denier of self. Carlyle supplies idiosyncratic running commentary, making points of his own about mid-19th-century British society. Two revolutionaries, in action and thought, in endlessly fascinating juxtaposition. See BIOGRAPHY (Froude); LITERARY CRITICISM

Chesterfield, Lord *Letters to His Son* (1774) ♀★

Letters from statesman father to beloved bastard son; actually short essays in beautifully-poised 18th-century prose on manners, morals, politics, the way of the world. Definitive sketch of a gentleman of honour in the Age of Elegance—and personal and intimate too.

Cicero, Marcus Tullius *Letters* (1st century BC) ✆
Cicero, the great lawyer-politician of late Republican Rome, was a contemporary of Julius Caesar, and was intimately concerned in the upheavals of the Civil War and the manoeuvrings which led to Caesar's assassination in 44 BC. His more than 900 private letters reflect the cares and anxieties of a sensitive, honourable public man, and are particularly revealing of the clash between public and private political morality. Good translation by Shackleton Bailey.
See AUTOBIOGRAPHY (Caesar); HISTORY/ANCIENT (Selzer)

Cowper, William *Selected Letters* (1926)
Numerous collections have appeared of the graceful, charming intimate letters of this most domestic of English poets, who alternated between long periods of country calm and savage bouts of insanity which finally killed him. Much read in his day, his poetry is no longer greatly regarded, but the letters remain, their careful observation and transcendent sweetness ensuring Cowper's fame.

Crèvecoeur, Hector St John de *Letters of an American Farmer* (1782)
"Here individuals of all nations," Crèvecoeur wrote, "are melted into a new race of men, whose labors and posterity will one day cause great change in the world." Published in London, these letters fired the imaginations and hopes of a generation of British emigrants to the New World.

Crossman, Richard *Diaries of a Cabinet Minister, 1964–70*
(3 vols, 1975–77) ✆ ∥ ▦
Greeted on publication with much brouhaha and attempts to get them censored, Crossman's censorious diaries turned out to be something of a let-down. Nonetheless they remain far and away the best account of how modern British government actually works. Fascinating to compare it with "insider accounts" of earlier politics, such as those of Cicero (qv) and Greville (qv).

Dali, Salvador *Diary of a Genius* (1966) ✆ ∥
Weird, wonderful, near-certifiable musings; a true companion to his paintings—effectively explains such phenomena as burning giraffes, swarming ants and auto-sodomized virgins. Anti-memoirs? Could be. Also: *The Unspeakable Confessions of Salvador Dali*

Durrell, L. and **Miller, H.** *Lawrence Durrell, Henry Miller: A Private Correspondence* (1963) ✆
Exchange began when Durrell (aged 23) wrote Miller (43) a fan-letter about *Tropic of Cancer*; it continued over several decades. Energetic, ego-brimming letters, full of spontaneity and trail-blazing self-evaluation. See CHILDREN'S BOOKS (Durrell, G.); FICTION/NOVELS (Durrell); POETRY (Durrell); SEX (Miller); TRAVEL (Durrell)

Edgeworth, Maria *Letters from England, 1813–44* (1971) ▣ ∥
Personal letters of English novelist (1767–1849). Her circle of friends and acquaintances included Wedgwood, Darwin, Byron and Walter Scott; but her most delightful letters are those to her numerous family, on landscape, town life and above all human foible, viewed with unaffected warmth and wit. This selection by Christine Colvin recommended. Its introduction, notes and index are models of thoroughness and tact.

Evelyn, John *The Diary of John Evelyn* (1818) ✆ ★
Posterity-conscious diary contains brilliant portraits of Restoration figures. Evelyn was a wholly different man from his friend Pepys, who remarked of him, "A most excellent person, and must be allowed a little for his conceitedness." Worth reading in conjunction with Pepys (qv), and with Aubrey's *Brief Lives* (herewith recommended).

Fitzgerald, F. Scott and **Perkins, Max** *Dear Scott, Dear Max* (1971)
Fascinating exchange of letters between celebrated writer and equally well-known editor. Intriguing exposé of a working relationship that illuminates the nuts and bolts, dollars and cents, of being a famous novelist. Compare with Bennett (qv) and (for private agonies of authorship) Simenon (AUTOBIOGRAPHY) and Steinbeck (qv). See BIOGRAPHY (Milford); FICTION/NOVELS; FICTION/SHORT STORIES; FILM (Latham); MEDIA (Berg)

Flaubert, Gustave *Selected Letters* (1953) ★
Lively literary letters (edited by Francis Steegmuller) from the period when Flaubert was writing *Madame Bovary* and many deal with the problems of creating that work. Flaubert is hardly a genial genius but is none the less fascinating for that. See Goncourt; FICTION/NOVELS; FICTION/SHORT STORIES

Frank, Anne *The Diary of Anne Frank* (1947) ★ ∥
Difficult to avoid words like "deeply moving" and "unique" in relation to this justly famous diary, a rare document of the unsullied, untarnished human spirit. See Tuttle.

Garnett, David *The White/Garnett Letters* (1968)
Poised, elegant correspondence between E. B. White and David Garnett: two high-class literary craftsmen striking amiable sparks from each other. Great fun. See White; CHILDREN'S BOOKS (White); HUMOUR (White); REFERENCE (Strunk)

Ginsberg, Allen *Journals Early Fifties Early Sixties* (1977)
Ginsberg can sometimes seem a pain in the neck, but these journals are
fascinating chronicles of the "beat generation": a motley collection of variously
talented writers, junkies, Buddhists, manic depressives and homosexuals whose
never dull brand of naïve decadence defined their era. See BIOGRAPHY
(Charters); FICTION/NOVELS (Kerouac)

Goncourt, E. and **J. de** *The Goncourt Journal* (1887–96)　　　　★
"Dinner with Flaubert . . .", "Zola was in a talkative mood . . .", "We discussed
the question of Mme Sand's love affairs . . ."—the Goncourt brothers' engagingly
jaundiced eyes evaluate their celebrated contemporaries with scant regard for
their public image. Shortened edition by Baldick recommended. See Flaubert;
FICTION/NOVELS (Flaubert, Zola); FICTION/SHORT STORIES (Flaubert)

Gorki, Maxim *Fragments from My Diary* (1924)
Gorki consciously modelled his themes and style on Tolstoy—with the crucial
change that he replaced what Marxist critics saw as "decadent" themes (eg the
morbid love affair in *Anna Karenina*) with a framework of dynamic social realism
(eg the revolutionary fervour of *Mother*). Some Western critics, preferring their
own dogma, have accordingly dismissed him. But he is a great novelist, no more
propagandist than Dickens or Mann. These diary fragments make an excellent
introduction to his complex, thoughtful work, shamefully neglected in the West.
Also: *The Confession* (autobiography); *Foma Gordeyev* (novel)

Green, Julien *Diary, 1928–1957* (1964)　　　　℗
Green, an American, made his reputation as a French novelist. Diary provides an
outsider's view of French intellectual society but is also a quiet, reflective record
of a writer's life. Comparison with Bennett (qv) is revealing and fascinating—and
then compare Kafka (qv) and Joyce (qv).

Gregory, Kenneth (ed) *The First Cuckoo* (1976)
Are the British the sanest or the dottiest race on earth? Prove both contentions
conclusively with this selection of letters to *The Times*. Ciceronian, barbed,
pungent: the literate British performing party tricks.

Hall, Ruth (ed) *Dear Dr Stopes* (1978)
Edited compilation of letters written to the great 1920s British sex liberationist,
Marie Stopes, between 1918 and 1928, after the publication of her book *Married
Love*. Some of her sane, helpful replies are included. Ghastly first-hand evidence
of human sexual and compassionate failure: implicit indictment of the medical
profession and churchmen of the time. Have we really changed *that* much?

Heyden, P. and **Kelley, P. (eds)** *Elizabeth Barrett Browning's Letters to
Mrs David Ogilvy* (1973)
Intimate letters to a close friend (and fellow poetess), on family matters (chiefly
children) and on literary life. Newly discovered in 1971, these letters are
unforced, affectionate and reveal what an unexpectedly *witty* woman EBB could
be. See Barrett; BIOGRAPHY (Pickering)

James, Henry *The Letters of Henry James* (1969)
James dwelt as lovingly over a phrase in his many letters as he did in his novels and
these (edited by Percy Lubbock)—or the letters selected by Leon Edel, James's
biographer (1955)—are eminently worth reading for their insights into the man
as well as their comments on life and literature. See BIOGRAPHY (Edel, James);
FICTION/NOVELS; FICTION/SHORT STORIES; LITERARY CRITICISM

Joyce, James *The Collected Letters of James Joyce* (1957)　　　　℗
In these letters the private Joyce breaks out of the citadel of doctoral theses and
critical monographs in which he is nowadays enclosed—and nowhere more so
than in the astonishing exchange of torrid love letters that passed between Joyce
and his wife when they were temporarily separated in 1904. Full collection in
three volumes; one-volume selection also issued. See BIOGRAPHY (Ellmann);
FICTION/NOVELS; FICTION/SHORT STORIES

Kafka, Franz *The Diaries of Franz Kafka, 1910–1923* (1948)　　　　℗
Rapid access to the mind and personality of one of the most extraordinary writers
of the 20th century; invaluable source for many of his acclaimed stories and
literary themes. See FICTION/NOVELS; FICTION/SHORT STORIES

Kierkegaard Søren *The Last Years* (1865)　　　　℗
Kierkegaard—the "depression over Denmark"— was the father of both secular
and religious existentialism. These diaries and their brilliant introduction make a
good beginning to his thought. Also: *The Present Age*. See PHILOSOPHY

Kilvert, Francis Thomas *Kilvert's Diary* (1938–40)　　　　🏛 ▦
Diary of 1870s country curate in a remote Welsh community. Kilvert's
admirable, unselfconscious personality shines undiminished from its pages; book
is also a bleak testimony to the nasty, brutish and short lives many people led in
rural Victorian Britain. See Woodeforde.

Lawrence, D. H. *The Collected Letters of D. H. Lawrence* (1932)　　　　℗
Lawrence used his letters like weapons: often scathing and always stimulating, he
berated friends and intellectuals, attacked established dogma and passionately
propagated his own. See FICTION/NOVELS; FICTION/SHORT STORIES;
HISTORY/EUROPEAN; LITERARY CRITICISM; POETRY; TRAVEL

Lincoln, Abraham *Speeches and Letters* (1919)　　　　　　　　🏛
Numerous collections of Lincoln's writings—mostly speeches and letters, both
formal and informal—have been published, and this (edited by Angle) is an
especially pleasing one. Lincoln was an extraordinary writer, even in the most
ephemeral letters and notes—no politician surpasses him for his power over
words. As he lived in a time of great events, the combination is explosive. See
BIOGRAPHY (Sandburg)

Mansfield, Katherine *The Journal of Katherine Mansfield* (1927)　　　♀
Another Bloomsbury journal that reveals best and worst of the movement: arch
self-consciousness coupled with memorable observation. For example,
Mansfield on E. M. Forster, he "never gets any further than warming the teapot.
Feel this teapot. Is it not beautifully warm? Yes, but there ain't going to be no
tea." See FICTION/SHORT STORIES

Montagu, Lady Mary Wortley *Complete Letters* (1965–67)　　　　　♀
Sense and sensibility: the upper-class life of Georgian Britain discussed in cool,
elegant prose.

Nicolson, Harold *Diaries, 1930–62* (1966–68)　　　　　　　　📖
Highly literate, effortlessly readable, semi-private account of a life rich in literary
and political insights and in-fights. See BIOGRAPHY

Pepys, Samuel *The Diary of Samuel Pepys* (1825)　　　　　　　♀★
Perhaps the most celebrated of all English diaries. Splendid historical document
covering the years 1660–69 but even more compelling for the self-portrait of
Pepys: an engaging, hard-working, sensuous man. Of attractive women he notes,
a little regretfully that it "is a strange slavery that I stand in to beauty, that I value
nothing near it." The complete nine volumes have recently been published—a
hefty read, but there are several good abridgements.

Pliny the Younger *Letters* (2nd century)　　　　　　　　　　★
Pliny does for his age what Pepys (qv) does for his. His letters reflect the private
life of a public man (he was a distinguished lawyer-statesman). Evocative
accounts of villas, meals, journeys, literary and political occasions, the gossip and
daily life of aristocratic Rome. Urbane; ironic; cool—a Renaissance humanist
before his time.

Pope John XXIII *Letters to His Family, 1901–62* (1968)

Rilke, Rainer Maria *Letters to a Young Poet* (1954)
One of the great poets of the 20th century, Rilke paid careful heed to his
voluminous, masterful correspondence with friends all over the world. This
selection (translated by Norton) is a fine one. See POETRY

Sacco, N. and **Vanzetti, B.** *The Letters of Sacco and Vanzetti* (1928)
Atheists, anarchists, draft dodgers, Sacco and Vanzetti appeared enormously
threatening to most Americans in the 1920s, even though they probably did not
commit the armed robbery and murders for which they were finally executed in
1927. The long years of protests and counter-protests, as well as court
manoeuvres, produced many remarkable and moving letters from these nearly
illiterate but enormously articulate men.

Seneca, Lucius Annaeus *Letters from a Stoic* (1st century)　　　　♀
Seneca, banker-statesman, tutor to the young Nero (no sinecure), wrote a series
of "letters" at the end of his life. They are really essays on aspects of Stoic
philosophy. For modern readers, the interest is twofold: in Stoicism itself (closely
akin to Pauline Christianity in ethical and moral arguments), and in Seneca's
lively pen-portraits of life in Rome, the noisy capital of the world, and on his
peaceful country estates.

Steegmuller, Francis (ed) *Your Isadora* (1974)　　　　　　　🏛✓
The love story of Isadora Duncan and Gordon Craig, told through breathless
romantic letters and diaries. Warm, intimate, often very funny: the grandest of
grand passions, a three-handkerchief read. See BIOGRAPHY

Steinbeck, John *Journal of a Novel* (1970)　　　　　　　　　♀
Steinbeck used this journal to write himself out of a creative block and to "warm
himself up" for *East of Eden*. Honest, revealing; may even outlast the novel.
Also: *Letters*; *A Life in Letters* (ed Elaine Steinbeck). See FICTION/NOVELS;
TRAVEL

Teilhard de Chardin, Pierre *Letters to Two Friends, 1926–52*
(1968)　　　　　　　　　　　　　　　　　　　　　　　　★
The great religious thinker and philosopher wrote these letters as a kind of
spiritual journal: they cover external events, but are mainly concerned with
charting his inner life, and in particular the crucial evolution in his thinking from
early palaeontological studies to the programmatic certainties of his later years.
The dark night of the soul, and the bright dawn of hope, movingly described. See
RELIGION

Thomas, Dylan *The Letters of Dylan Thomas* (1966)
Thomas worked on his letters with almost the same diligence that he devoted to
his poems; his regular unscrupulous sponging also prompted feats of
penmanship: the begging letters are masterpieces of flattering cajolery and
artistic bombast. See POETRY

Tuttle, Andrew (ed) *The Journal of Andrew Bihaly* (1972)   ♀ ✳
Bihaly's story is as harrowing and poignant as Anne Frank's (qv). He was eight when his parents left him in a monastery housing delinquent boys, with a forged birth certificate concealing his Jewishness. Shortly afterwards both his mother and father died in Hitler's concentration camps; Andrew himself was raped and brutalized by his companions. He later escaped to the USA—and this journal is an account of how he tried to come to terms both with the horrors in his own soul and the life of a drop-out in the Manhattan slums of the late 1960s (Vietnam, the Peace Corps, drugs and communes). An essential text for anyone trying to understand the roots of alienation in our own torn era—and a moving document of a ruined human soul.

Van Gogh, Vincent *The Letters of Van Gogh* (1927)   ♀
Moving account of Van Gogh's struggles against encroaching mental illness and artistic neglect; but full of the sharp irony that hindsight brings: "I dare swear to you," he writes towards the end of his life, "that my sunflowers are worth 500 francs".

Wagner, Cosima *Letters and Diaries* (1979)   ★
No less an autocratic, inspired bully than her husband, Cosima Wagner was the Iron Lady of Bayreuth in its founding years, and for a generation after. Everyone knows Wagner was intolerable as a man—however did she live with him? These letters and notebooks tell—and now, we wonder, however did he live with *her*? See MUSIC (Newman, Wagner)

Walpole, Horace *Letters* (1920)   ▣
Walpole turned on an elegant style like water from a tap; he saw letters as the epitome of his urbane age, and used them to reflect on everything, from political scandals to ladies' bonnets and the merits of sea bathing. He was called (by Walter Scott) the finest letter-writer in English, and the four volumes of his correspondence are full of endless delights. For those with less leisure than he had, Hadley's one-volume selection (1926) supplies the cream.

Warren, Nella *The Letters of Ruth Draper, 1920–56* (1979)   🔒
Ruth Draper's monologues "peopled the stage with characters"; these personal letters have the same bustling energy, wit and perception of the eccentricities and delights of humanity. Life as a game, and savoured—a welcome, unbitchy addition to the showbusiness shelves.

White, E. B. *The Letters of E. B. White* (1976)   ★
No American journalist ever wrote better than E. B. White—or no American writer was a better journalist. His essays and comments for the *New Yorker* and for other magazines are rightly famous, but his letters make equally fascinating reading. See Garnett; CHILDREN'S BOOKS; HUMOUR; REFERENCE (Strunk)

Wilde, Oscar *The Letters of Oscar Wilde* (1962)
Wilde's mercurial career encapsulated in his own words, from international literary fame to public obloquy, destitution and neglect. Full text included of the famous *De Profundis* letter to Lord Alfred Douglas; bitter, poignant reading: "I thought life was going to be a brilliant comedy . . . I found it to be a revolting and repellent tragedy." See BIOGRAPHY (Hyde); DRAMA; FICTION/NOVELS

Wilson, Edmund *Letters on Literature and Politics, 1912–72* (1977)   ★
America's nearest thing to Dr Johnson, but less polysyllabic, Wilson was an opinionated, opinion-forming critic who, almost single-handed, tried to make writing an important part of American life and sought, successfully, to be its monitor and prize-giver. The letters should be supplemented by his memoirs, eg *The Twenties.* See HISTORY/AMERICAN; LITERARY CRITICISM; POLITICS

Woodforde, James *The Diary of a Country Parson, 1758–1802* (1924)   ★▣
Kilvert's (qv) great rival, and a worthy one. Gossipy, self-indulgent account of the author's remarkably secular life and his obsession with food. Vivid illumination of English village life: "Poor Tom Cary died this morn' of a violent fever . . . His parents almost distracted . . . a very good-natured, inoffensive man. At cribbage this evening with Nancy won 0–6." See Kilvert.

Woolf, Virginia *A Writer's Diary* (1953)   ♀
Possibly the best of the Bloomsbury diaries, though the standard is generally high. Woolf emerges as at once sympathetic and awesome, with a nice line in dismissive bitchery. Interesting to compare Mansfield (qv). Also: *Letters.* See BIOGRAPHY (Bell, Woolf); FEMINISM (Woolf); FICTION/NOVELS (Woolf)

Wordsworth, Dorothy *The Alfoxden and Grasmere Journals* (1941)   ★
Vivid, unaffected account of Wordsworth's friendship with Coleridge and his daily life in the Lake District during one of his most creative periods. See BIOGRAPHY (Coleridge, De Quincey, Lefebure); POETRY (Coleridge, Wordsworth)

Drama

A selective list, covering a huge and varied field. Crucial play-wrights, with typical (or best introductory) works; standard guides and works of criticism, especially those that explain or define a vital area; a few biographies and memoirs for fun. The interested reader will want to explore the heights (and crevasses) for himself—this list provides a base camp and a survival kit.

See DIARIES (Warren); HISTORY/BRITISH (Strong); HUMOUR (Green); LITERARY CRITICISM (Bradley, Johnson, Stendhal)

Aeschylus *The Oresteia* (458 BC) ◘
First and one of the greatest of all tragedians, Aeschylus was for long regarded as influential but unstageable, a reader's dramatist. Recent productions have proved this false: his work is as accessible (and as fine) as Shakespeare's. *The Oresteia* is magnificent with theatrical energy, its poetry as resonant and comprehensible as that of *Hamlet*. Good translations by Roche (*The Orestes Plays of Aeschylus*, 1962) and by Raphael and McLeish (*The Serpent Son*, 1979). Also: *Prometheus Bound*, etc

Albee, Edward *Who's Afraid of Virginia Woolf?* (1961)
Albee is one of the best post-war American dramatists; this is his most successful play. Raucously witty, agonized dissection of campus marriage; a bravura piece for bravura actors. Also: *The Zoo Story*; *A Delicate Balance*, etc

Anouilh, Jean *Ring Round the Moon* (1950)
Strong on character and theatricality, Anouilh is not as fashionable, but is certainly as entertaining as Miller (qv), and at times (eg this play) as good as Shaw (qv). This, or *Antigone* (reworking of Sophocles (qv) in modern terms) are the best introductions to a lively, graceful playwright. Also: *Traveller without Luggage*; *Waltz of the Toreadors*

Arden, John *Sergeant Musgrave's Dance* (1959) ♀
Sergeant and three soldiers descend on a small town, ostensibly seeking recruits. They are in fact deserters, obsessed with a feverish mission to awaken their countrymen to the futility and cruelty of war. Arden's tendency to write tracts is here offset by a sharp plot and vivid theatricality. An important heterodox dramatist. Also: *The Workhouse Donkey*; *The Waters of Babylon*, etc

Aristophanes *Women in Power* (4th century BC) ★
First and one of the greatest comic dramatists, Aristophanes is still fresh and funny today. Style is like modern Absurd drama crossed with Laurel and Hardy. This play (original title *Ecclesiazusae*) is a satire on communism, women's rights and sex (hilarious music-hall finale on the theme "the ugliest shall be first"): topical, timeless, vigorous. Good English translations by Parker (*The Congresswomen*, 1967) and by McLeish (in *Aristophanes' Clouds, Women in Power, Knights*, 1980). Also: *Lysistrata*; *The Frogs*; *The Birds*, etc

Arnott, Peter *The Ancient Greek and Roman Theatre* (1971) **a** ✓ *♪*
Short, crisp, non-specialist introduction. For fuller treatment (standard works accessible to the layman) see Kitto's *Greek Tragedy* (1939), Dover's *Aristophanic Comedy* (1972) and Duckworth's *The Nature of Roman Comedy* (1952).

Artaud, Antonin *The Theatre and Its Double* (1938) ♀
Artaud (1896–1948) was the leading theoretician of modern "experimental theatre". Believing that the theatre of his day lacked any kind of authentic correlative, he advocated a theatre that would replace naturalism and realism with the old "magical" elements of myth and ritual. This collection includes the seminal manifesto on the Theatre of Cruelty and also the controversial article "Seraphim's Theatre" on the actor's craft and his role in society.

Auden, W. H. and **Isherwood, C.** *The Ascent of F6* (1936)
Supreme example of high camp at high altitudes; straightfaced *jeu d'esprit* which deserves its place in the margin of English expressionist drama. Also: *The Dog beneath the Skin*. See FICTION/SHORT STORIES (Isherwood); LITERARY CRITICISM (Auden); POETRY (Auden)

Beckett, Samuel *Waiting for Godot* (1952) ★
One of the seminal texts of contemporary theatre. Two tramps (play originally conceived for Laurel and Hardy in old age) wait by the roadside for arrival of Godot, whoever he may be. Their crosstalk, with interruptions, is like a sketch from an existentialist, esoteric revue. Also: *Krapp's Last Tape*; *Endgame*, etc. See Esslin; FICTION/NOVELS; FICTION/SHORT STORIES; LITERARY CRITICISM

Braun, Edward *The Theatre of Meyerhold* (1979) ♀
Taught by Stanislavski (qv), Meyerhold was one of the first to grasp the significance of the grotesque for modern theatre. After the Russian Revolution he committed himself to the Bolshevik cause, and became the first exponent of agitprop theatre. He is a major influence; this book gives his essence, well. Also: *Meyerhold on Theatre.*

41

Brecht, Berthold *Mother Courage* (1939) ★
However alienated we have been by the "alienation-effect", Brecht here displays
that indisputable theatrical sense which made his Berliner Ensemble the eye-
opening force that it was in the 1950s. The cyclic futility of war parades before us,
spiked with marvellous moments (eg that when Mother Courage must deny, with
a smile, that she recognizes the corpse of her own son) that make nonsense of
theatrical ideology. Also: *The Caucasian Chalk Circle*; *Galileo*; *The Resistible
Rise of Arturo Ui*, etc. See Heilman.

Brook, Peter *The Empty Space* (1968) 🔖♀✳a
Personal statement of intent by one of best–respected, most influential of British
experimental directors. Book (and Brook) something of a cult; but his theories
are important and challenging.

Chekhov, Anton *The Cherry Orchard* (1904) 📖
"It has turned out not a drama," said Chekhov, "but a comedy, in parts a farce."
Much is amusing; but (as always with Chekhov) on the splinter-edge of tears. The
cherry orchard falls; the old life, the old Russia pass with it. Also: *The Seagull*;
Three Sisters; *Uncle Vanya*. See FICTION/SHORT STORIES

Cibber, Colley *An Apology for the Life of Mr Colley Cibber, Comedian*
(1740) 🏛
18th-century dramatist, actor, inferior poet laureate, butt of Pope (in *The
Dunciad*), Cibber in these memoirs discursively and amiably describes, defines
the vigorous theatre of his time. Book contains among other things, a famous
description of Thomas Betterton's performance as Hamlet.

Clurman, Harold *The Naked Image: Observations on the Modern
Theatre* (1966) 📐
One of the founders of Group Theatre, which in the rosy dawn of the New Deal
tried to bring community theatre to 1930s New York, tells of the trials and real
achievements that brought to light Clifford Odets, and to bright lights men like
Franchot Tone who finally succumbed, graciously but inevitably, to Hollywood.
See McCrindle.

Congreve, William *The Way of the World* (1700) ★
Superb comedy, in which plot is to wit (in words of play) "as a dead whiting's eye
to a pearl of orient". The prose rhythms are what matter, their lift and sway, the
tumble of characters from the cheerful disorderly house of Restoration theatre.

Coward, Noël *Private Lives* (1930)
Definitive Coward comedy, perhaps his best play. Clipped, brittle dialogue is all.
Coward is as dazzling (though not as rhetorical) as Wilde (qv), as sparkling
(though not as warm) as Travers (qv). Also: *Hay Fever*; *Blithe Spirit*, etc

Eliot, T. S. *Murder in the Cathedral* (1935) 📖
Eliot's play on the murder of Thomas à Becket (in a 20th-century
reinterpretation of Greek classic style) is a masterpiece of modern theatre: fine
dramatic verse, measured argument, a noble exposition of the nature of
saintliness. This is his most accessible and resonant play: the others are elliptical,
mannered, sometimes tedious. Also: *The Confidential Clerk*; *The Family
Reunion*; *The Elder Statesman*. See LITERARY CRITICISM (Eliot, Gardner);
POETRY

Esslin, Martin *The Theatre of the Absurd* (1961) 🏛📘a
Absurd (meaning "at odds with the surroundings" rather than "ridiculous")
drama is the dominant, most fruitful style of post-war theatre: it has influenced
other arts (notably film and the novel), and partly helped shape social attitudes
and manners at large. This book is a finely written account of the theories, and a
guide to the work of major figures (Adamov, Beckett, Genet, Ionesco and a
dozen followers such as Grass, Pinter and Kopit).

Euripides *The Bacchae* (405 BC) 📘
Euripides is the most controversial of the great Greek tragedians; raw ideas ride
through his plays, invested with superb theatrical power. *The Bacchae* (religious
ecstasy and the tearing apart of the king who opposes it) is his most
"contemporary" play: resonance (eg for drug culture) remarkable; action
horrific, irresistibly in the theatre-of-cruelty mode. Good translation by
Volanakis in Corrigan (ed): *Laurel Classical Drama: Euripides*, 1965. Also:
Medea; *The Trojan Women*; *Hippolytus*

Farquhar, George *The Beaux' Stratagem* (1707)
One of the most revived of 18th-century plays, this marks the end of Restoration
drama and the beginning of modern dramatic sensibility. Farquhar died at 28;
this, his last play, makes one wonder what he might have accomplished if he had
survived into a new age. Also: *The Recruiting Officer*

Fitzsimons, Raymund *Edmund Kean: Fire from Heaven* (1976)
Kean was one of the greatest actors in 19th-century British theatre. Hazlitt said
"He bore on his brow the mark of the Fire from Heaven"; Coleridge, "To see him
act is like reading Shakespeare by flashes of lightning". This biography is vivid,
relaxed, readable—interesting to compare with Sartre's (qv) play (where Kean is
an existential mirror-man, only himself when performing). Also: *The Charles
Dickens Show*

Frisch, Max *The Fire–raisers* (1959)
Brechtian fable: bourgeois household invaded by endlessly talkative terrorists
intent on destroying it. Absurd comedy, or black parable of Europe in decline?
Either way, it brings the house down. Also: *Andorra*. See Heilman.

Gascoigne, Bamber *World Theatre* (1968)   🏛📖★✓♫
Scholarly, zestfully written history of "drama" from Stone-Age ritual to theatre
of the absurd.

Giraudoux, Jean *Tiger at the Gates* (1935)
Marvellous retelling of Homer showing in a modern context how the Trojan War
had to take place although nobody wanted it—political parallels in the 1930s
were clear and compelling. *The Mad Woman of Chaillot* (1946) was Giraudoux's
post-war comment on the idiocy of the intervening years.

Goethe, J. W. von *Faust* (1808)   📁
It sometimes escapes notice that this play, which influenced so many subsequent
19th-century creative minds, also exists in its own powerful right. Good
translations: C. F. MacIntyre; A. Raphael. See POETRY

Goldoni, Carlo *The Servant of Two Masters* (*c.* 1750)
Goldoni is underrated in the English-speaking world (possibly because of scarce,
poor translations). He is as funny as Molière (qv) or Beaumarchais; a master of
farcical comedy, with a warmth like that of (say) Goldsmith's *She Stoops to
Conquer*. Also: *The Campiello*, etc

Goldsmith, Oliver *She Stoops to Conquer* (1773)
Perennial stage favourite; classic upstairs-downstairs comedy, with the
downstairs characters having rather the better of it.

Granville-Barker, Harley *The Madras House* (1910)
In *The Madras House* (the name of a London dress shop) Granville-Barker, the
leader with Shaw of the Edwardian theatre of ideas, examined feminine
repression and, in general, the state of women and their future. Best remembered
now for his fine 3-volume *Prefaces to Shakespeare* (herewith recommended), he
was also a powerful, Ibsenish dramatist. Also: *The Voysey Inheritance*; *Waste*, etc

Grotowski, Jerzy *Towards a Poor Theatre* (1968)
Grotowski created the Theatre Laboratory in Poland in 1959, a company as
revolutionary and as influential for contemporary drama as Stanislavski's (qv)
Moscow Arts Company was at the beginning of the century. This book records
the company's methods and discoveries, a seminal text for those who seek a
philosophical basis for theatre of today.

Hampton, Christopher *Savages* (1974)
Kidnapped by guerillas and kept in a cell while his ransom is negotiated, an
ineffable English diplomat provides the backbone of a play which sets out to do
nothing less than indict Western man for his wholesale murder of a tribe few, if
any, of us have ever heard of. Hampton was a new, disturbing voice in the
1970s—dazzling theatrical style, uncomfortable messages.

Hartnoll, Phyllis *Concise History of Theatre* (1968)   🏛📖★♫
Heilman, Robert E. *The Iceman, the Arsonist and the Troubled Agent*
(1973)
Excellent study of "tragedy and melodrama on the modern stage". Balances
O'Neill, Williams and Miller against three Europeans, Brecht, Frisch and
Durrenmatt. Useful scholarly adjunct to Esslin (qv) and Taylor (qv).

Hethman, Robert H. (ed) *Strasberg at the Actors' Studio* (1965)
The home of American Method acting: tape-recorded sessions transcribed, with
commentary by Strasberg and his colleague-pupils. Fascinating first-hand
account of a central development in modern acting.

Ibsen, Henrik *Ghosts* (1881)   📖
One of the group of plays on a favourite Ibsen theme: the way we are haunted,
dominated by the past, the way (as he put it) "We sail with a corpse in the cargo".
Good translation (of complete plays) by Michael Meyer, whose biography of
Ibsen is also the standard account. Also: *The Wild Duck*; *Hedda Gabler*, etc

Ionesco, Eugène *The Bald Prima Donna* (*The Bald Soprano*)
(1948)   ★
Surreal parody of drama itself; hilarious surface masks bleak philosophy—"I
imagined I had written something like the tragedy of language", he later wrote of
it. Also: *Rhinoceros*; *Walking on Air*; *The Chairs*, etc. See Heilman.

Johnson, Pamela Hansford *Six Proust Reconstructions* (1958)
A *bonne bouche*: Hansford Johnson has extended and "improved" Proust in a
radio sequence which at once criticizes (affectionately), embellishes and reveals
his world: Marcel air-waved *à la mode*. See BIOGRAPHY (Painter, Pickering);
FICTION/NOVELS (Proust); LITERARY CRITICISM (Beckett)

Jonson, Ben *The Alchemist* (1610)   📁
One of the best plays (and certainly the easiest to begin with) by Jacobean
dramatist and poet second only to Shakespeare. The "quick theatre-stuff" of his
plays carries all the "humours" of Jacobean London. Absurd drama, 17th-
century style: like Aristophanes (qv) crossed with a dictionary of antique slang.
Also: *Volpone*; *Bartholomew Fair*, etc

Lorca, Frederico García *The House of Bernarda Alba* (1936)
Lorca was murdered by Fascist gunmen at age of 37. (See Ian Gibson's *The Death of Lorca*, 1957.) This play is a parabolic comment on 1930s Spain—the tyranny of the central female character paralleling that of Franco. He is a great poet of the theatre; Synge or Yeats with dark Iberian overtones. Also: *Blood Wedding*; *Yerma*

McCrindle, Joseph F. (ed) *Behind the Scenes* (1971)
Outstanding theatre and film interviews from the *Transatlantic Review*. Littlewood, Kopit, Stoppard, Orton, Tynan, Fellini, Clurman, Marceau, Pinter, Vidal, and dozens more. Should be on every theatre-lover's shelf.

Marlowe, Christopher *Tamburlaine the Great* (1590)   ★
At its best, Marlowe's poetry approaches Shakespeare's; his plays are like magnificent symphonies of language. But they are loosely structured and often fall into rant and obscurity. *Tamburlaine* shows these qualities, all of them, at peak; better seen, perhaps, than read; unforgettable. Also: *Dr Faustus*; *The Jew of Malta*, etc

Masefield, John *William Shakespeare* (1911)   a
Good general introduction. Masefield's style is direct as a Roman road; he never wastes a word. Almost everything one needs to know; no fruitless speculation; well-judged quotations. See Granville-Barker; Shakespeare; Van Doren; CHILDREN'S BOOKS; LITERARY CRITICISM (Bradley, Johnson, Knight, Stendhal); POETRY (Shakespeare)

Maugham, W. Somerset *For Services Rendered* (1932)
Maugham, precise storyteller, can be an over-estimated dramatist; but this play is likely to last. A picture of the chaos brought by war, symbolized by events in a small Kentish household. Also: *Collected Plays* (3 vols); *Theatre* (a novel). See AUTOBIOGRAPHY; FICTION/CRIME; FICTION/NOVELS; FICTION/SHORT STORIES

Miller, Arthur *The Crucible* (1953)   ★
Miller is one of finest American tragedians of the century: clear prose, good characterization, rock-solid theatricality. This play (on witchcraft trials in Salem, Massachusetts in 1692) discusses freedom of conscience, and develops it so as to draw parallels with the 20th century (the play was produced shortly after the McCarthy scandal, in the early 1950s). Also: *Death of a Salesman*; *A View from the Bridge*, etc. See Heilman.

Molière, Jean Baptiste Poquelin de *The Misanthrope* (1666)   ▯
Rhymed verse not being too popular on the English-speaking stage, Molière is often represented by shoddy translations which capture plot but nothing of style or atmosphere. This may account for his comparative neglect. Read him (or see him) in French if possible; there is a tolerable English translation by Tony Harrison (1975), and even that is sometimes arch, over-sophisticated and false. Also: *The Miser*; *Le Bourgeois Gentilhomme*, etc

O'Casey, Sean *The Silver Tassie* (1928)
Poignant, tragic play on war and its aftermath, free of the surface Irish whimsy that can disfigure even O'Casey's best work. Also: *The Shadow of a Gunman*; *Juno and the Paycock*; *The Plough and the Stars*

O'Neill, Eugene *The Iceman Cometh* (1946)   ★
At his worst, O'Neill is portentous and bombastic; at his best (as here) he earns the extravagant praise once heaped on him ("greatest genius of American theatre"). In a cheap tavern, craven dreamers are startled into action by a travelling salesman—in effect a salesman of death. Also: *Anna Christie*; *Mourning Becomes Electra*; *Long Day's Journey into Night*. See Heilman.

Osborne, John *Look Back in Anger* (1956)   ▮
Resolute, over-praised play ("Love it or leave me," said Tynan), whose peevish, ranting anti-hero set a long trend in snappy nihilism. It now seems dated, pat and over-emphatic. But it has energy and dramatic power—the main qualities of Osborne's later, increasingly misanthropic output. Also: *Luther*; *The Entertainer*; *Inadmissible Evidence*

Pinero, Arthur W. *The Second Mrs Tanqueray* (1893)
Drawing-room Ibsen: urbanely concerned and wittily reflective. Pinero was overshadowed (not to say eclipsed) by early Shaw, but is a solid craftsman producing enjoyable evenings in the theatre. Also: *Trelawny of the "Wells"*; *The Magistrate*, etc

Pinter, Harold *No Man's Land* (1975)   ★
Paranoid despair expressed in ambiguous, poetic prose: the rhythms of ordinary speech given elusive, unnerving hardness. Also: *The Caretaker*; *The Homecoming*; *The Birthday Party*, etc. See Esslin; McCrindle.

Pirandello, Luigi *Six Characters in Search of an Author* (1921)   ★
A company of six characters appears during a rehearsal, announces that it is the incomplete, unused creation of the author's imagination, and demands to be allowed to perform the drama that was never written for them but is implied in their lives. Also: *Henry IV*; *Tonight We Improvise*, etc. See FICTION/SHORT STORIES

Racine, Jean *Phaedra* (1677) ★
Pellucid, civilized verse, grave and sonorous, animates gory human dilemmas
(incest, parricide, assassination) from the mythology and history of Greece and
Rome. Like Molière (qv), Racine is not notably well served in English
translation: best enjoyed in French. This play is an exception: Robert Lowell's
translation (1963) is dignified and fine, poet matching poet line for line. Also:
Berenice; *Andromache*; *Athaliah*, etc. See LITERARY CRITICISM (Stendhal)

Rattigan, Terence *The Winslow Boy* (1946)
Switchback critical reputation; but Rattigan's best work (this play; *The Deep Blue
Sea*; *Separate Tables*) will last. He is a first-class dramatist of the second rank, the
Galsworthy of drama (except that Galsworthy got there first).

Redfield, William *Letters from an Actor* (1966) 🏛
When Gielgud and Burton toured *Hamlet* in America in 1964, Redfield played
Guildenstern. Throughout, he wrote letters describing the preparation,
performance and reception; then worked the letters up into this enjoyable,
informative book.

Roberts, Vera M. *The Nature of Theatre* (1971) 📘 a ★ ✓ ∥
Magnificent book on the aesthetics and practicalities of drama: what comedy,
tragedy, melodrama are; the role of the audience in "creating" a performance;
the function of spectacle. Accessible, compendious, important.

Sartre, Jean-Paul *Crime Passionel (Les Mains Sales)* (1948)
Probably the best political play of the post-war period, embraced by cold warriors
as an exposé of Communist opportunism—the plot hinges on a change in the
Party "line"—and as often disowned by Sartre because he felt he had betrayed
the cause he intermittently endorsed. Also: *Nekrassov*; *Kean*; *The Flies*; and
(again, superb theatre) *Vicious Circle (Huis-clos)*. See BIOGRAPHY;
FICTION/NOVELS; PHILOSOPHY

Sayers, Dorothy, L. *The Man Born to Be King* (1943)
Dated but exemplary version of the Gospels, simplified but never falsified
(especially for those who greet the news as genuinely good). Radio drama is a
relatively neglected field; Sayers was a pioneer and a masterly popularizer. See
FICTION/CRIME

Shaffer, Peter *Royal Hunt of the Sun* (1964)
Mannered, stylish, theatre-of-spectacle mixed with Rattiganesque private
agonizing, this stunning play charts the relationship between the conquering
Pizarro and the Incas of Peru in 1533. A healing friendship: they adopt, invest
each other. Also: *Equus*; *Five Finger Exercise*, etc

Shakespeare, William *Othello* (*c*. 1604) 📗
What can one say? He is an Everest, and all other dramatists stumble in his
foothills; the poet of poets, the man of men? All of that, and none of that: he is
unique. *Othello* is one of the most accessible of his greatest plays: poetry, form
and spectacle are kept in perfect balance. For readers, the excellent Arden
edition is recommended for good text, interesting and useful notes. Also:
Complete Works. See Granville-Barker; Masefield; Van Doren; LITERARY
CRITICISM (Bradley, Johnson, Knight, Stendhal); POETRY

Shank, Theodore J. (ed) *A Digest of 500 Plays* (1963) 📘
Compact guide: outline of plots, difficulties and production requirements of
significant plays from Aeschylus' *Persians* to Wouk's *The Caine Mutiny Court
Martial*.

Shaw, George Bernard *Saint Joan* (1924) ★
Shaw's unsentimental, unfussy drama at its best. Prose has poise and point;
arguments lucid, not too wordy; stage action compelling; portrait of clear-headed
young girl (a recurring theme in Shaw's work) persuasive and warm. Also: *Our
Theatres in the Nineties* (critical writings)

Sheridan, Richard B. *The School for Scandal* (1777) ★
One of the most enduring comedies in English: funny dialogue, in graceful
18th-century prose; razor characterization; fast action. For grace and speed,
matched by his other most enduring play, *The Rivals*, a generally tighter, less
prismatic piece. Also: *The Critic*, etc

Sophocles *King Oedipus* (*c*. 430 BC) 📗
One of the rocks on which all later European drama is founded. Formal, elegant
poetry: for grandeur of themes, Sophocles is matched only by Shakespeare (qv);
for limpidity of style, by Racine (qv). His work resists translation: good English
versions are by Kitto (*Sophocles: Three Tragedies*, 1962—plain), and by Roche
(*The Oedipus Plays of Sophocles*, 1958—fancy). Pound's magnificent *The
Women of Trachis* (1956) is one of the crankiest translations ever made. Also:
Antigone; *Electra*, etc

Soyinka, Wole *Death of the King's Horseman* (1972) ★
The greatest play of the greatest African playwright. Based on a true story of the
jarring conflict between old ways and new, between tribal mores and the imposed
ways of the British resident, in southern Nigeria at the end of World War II.
Soyinka has some of the power and eloquence of the Greek tragedians, though he
lacks their poetry. An extraordinary and forceful play.

Stanislavski, Constantin *Building a Character* (1950) ▮♀
Greatest single influence on 20th-century acting technique, Stanislavski was responsible for the school of "method acting", advocating intense inward preparation for the physical realization of character on stage. Also: *An Actor Prepares*

Stoppard, Tom *Travesties* (1972)
Considers wittily what might have happened if Lenin, Joyce and the Dadaist poet Tzara (all living in Zurich simultaneously during World War I) had met each other. Stoppard's passion is the interplay of intransigent philosophies; his method is a cold cascade of words. Also: *Rosencrantz and Guildenstern Are Dead*; *Jumpers*; *Night and Day*, etc. See McCrindle

Synge, J. M. *The Playboy of the Western World* (1907)
Magical Irishness, about a stranger arriving at a remote Mayo inn (the Iceman cometh?); whimsical surface with skeleton of steel. Also: *Riders to the Sea*; *The Well of the Saints*, etc

Taubman, Howard *The Making of the American Theatre* (1965) ▦▮
Lively history of the growth of the theatre in 19th-century America. For some, first nights in Boston and New York; for others, touring in covered wagons, treading the dusty trail, bringing theatre like water to thirsty desert land. Great fun.

Travers, Ben *Rookery Nook* (1926) ★
Travers' Aldwych farces are definitive works: warmer and more humane than Feydeau or Coward (qv), full of ingenious twists of plot and language. His stature increases with time; his plays are sure to last. Also: *Thark*; *Plunder*; *The Bed before Yesterday*, etc

Van Doren, Mark *Shakespeare* (1939) ▦ ⫽
Trenchant essays on each of the plays by a well-known American poet-teacher. Influential on production style in the 1940s and 1950s; full of insight and good sense, in a fluent and graceful style. Also: *Don Quixote's Profession*. See Granville-Barker; Masefield; Shakespeare; LITERARY CRITICISM (Bradley, Johnson, Knight, Stendhal); POETRY (Shakespeare)

Webster, John *The White Devil* (1612) ♀
T. S. Eliot said that Webster "saw the skull beneath the skin", and this is certainly true of the two "revenge" tragedies on which his reputation rests. Violent and macabre; all-pervasive evil and darkness relieved by passages of fiercely brilliant poetry. Also: *The Duchess of Malfi*, etc

Wilde, Oscar, *The Importance of Being Earnest* (1895) ▯
Cool as a cucumber sandwich, reasonable as Euclid, this famous farce avoids the melodrama that often flaws Wilde's other work. Also: *Lady Windermere's Fan*, etc. See BIOGRAPHY; DIARIES; FICTION/NOVELS

Wilder, Thornton *Our Town* (1938) ▯
By now *the* American classic, revived almost every year in almost every American town. The play deserves this fate, being utterly simple and basic, about birth, love, life, death, the immemorially important dramatic themes. Also; *The Skin of Our Teeth*; *The Matchmaker*

Williams, Raymond *Drama in Performance* (1954)
Brilliant recreations of first audiences' experience of Greek theatre (Sophocles' *Antigone*), English medieval drama (*Everyman*), Shakespeare (*Antony and Cleopatra*), Restoration theatre, Stanislavski (Moscow Arts' *The Seagull*), modern experimental theatre (Eliot, Brecht, Beckett) and film (Bergman's *Wild Strawberries*). Analyses the relationship between text and performance, a neglected, vital subject. Revised edition (1968) recommended. Also: *Drama from Ibsen to Eliot*. See MEDIA

Williams, Tennessee *A Streetcar Named Desire* (1947)
Theatre of magnolia-scented exoticism. Set in the French quarter of New Orleans, with characters and dialogue as lush and exuberant as the place itself. Williams' stature is hard to assess; the theatrical power of his plays is undeniable. Also: *Cat on a Hot Tin Roof*; *Sweet Bird of Youth*, etc. See Heilman.

Wycherley, William *The Country Wife* (1675) ▦
Savage but nonetheless comic satire of Restoration—and human—foibles. This was the first great stage success after the return of the English court from exile in France, and is still a successful theatrical piece. Important for brilliant comic dialogue, unheard of on the English stage before. Also: *The Plain Dealer*

Yeats, W. B. *The Countess Cathleen* (1892) ♀
Yeats' plays (really dramatic poems) display a mixture of influences, treating Gaelic legend in styles adapted from Greek and Japanese theatre. Unstageable; unique; unforgettable. See POETRY

Economics

Watching economists tear at one another's throats, and reflecting on the holes in his own pockets, the layman might be forgiven for wondering, cynically, just how relevant this subject is to human life. The books in this list (an unpolemical, undogmatic selection) may go some way to providing an answer, or answers. "You pays your money . . ."

See ANTHROPOLOGY (Dalton); MEDICINE (Fuchs); PHILOSOPHY (Ortega y Gasset); POLITICS (Schumpeter); SOCIOLOGY (Weber)

Barber, William J. *A History of Economic Thought* (1967) ♀ **a**
Introduction to the work of Smith, Ricardo, Mill, Marx, Marshall, Keynes. Critical outline of their theories, set in the context of the particular economic problems they were trying to solve.

Beckerman, Wilfred *In Defence of Economic Growth* (1974) ♀
Reply to Mishan (qv) and the Club of Rome, making a strong case that the hidden costs of growth *can* be accounted for, and that economic growth that takes these into account will still show a net gain in welfare.

Donaldson, Peter *Economics of the Real World* (1973) **a**
A concise introduction, in accessible language.

Drucker, P. F. *The Age of Discontinuity* (1969) **a**
Lucid discussion of the wider issues at the heart of the new economy: micro-technology, industrial pluralism, mass leisure, the multinational economic state. Full of theories and programmes for action—still (a dozen years after the book was written) relevant, essential and largely unfulfilled. Ideal reading for those baffled by today's economic headlines. Also: *Landmarks of Tomorrow*; *The Future of Industrial Man*, etc

Friedman, Milton *Capitalism and Freedom* (1962) ♀ ★
The Samuel Smiles of the "New Monetarism" shows the relationship between his brand of *laissez-faire* economics and his ideology. Read it to understand the wider—or narrower—significance of the current fashion for monetarist economic policies. Also: *Essays in Positive Economics*, etc

Galbraith, J. K. *Economics and the Public Purpose* (1974) ★
Galbraith was the first to draw widespread attention to the paradox of private affluence and public squalor, and to recommend measures to deal with it. Roughly handled by critics, he remains one of the best starting points for exploring contemporary economic concerns. Also: *The Affluent Society*; *Money: Whence It Came Where It Went*; *The New Industrial State*, etc

Gamble, A. and **Walton P.** *Capitalism in Crisis: Inflation and the State* (1976) ✻
Clear, uncomplicated polemic (with left-wing bias) about what has gone wrong with economic theories and the British economy.

Glynn, A, and **Sutcliffe, R.** *British Capitalism, Workers and the Profits Squeeze* (1972) ★
A Marxist view of the crisis which has been developing in British industry since the 1960s. Compelling alternative to the monetarist analyses and nostrums which are our daily fare.

Harrison, John *Marxist Economics for Socialists* (1978) ✻ **a**
Short, readable account of Marxist economics. Wide scope; clear style.

Harrod, Roy *Towards a Dynamic Economics* (1949) ♀
Significant (though now dated) first attempt for over a century to see the economic system as a fluid, not static phenomenon. Also: *The Trade Cycle*

Heilbroner, R. L. *The Worldly Philosophers: The Lives, Times and Ideas of the Great Economic Thinkers* (1967) **a**
Exceptionally useful—it replaces reading thousands of pages of impossible learned prose.

Hicks, John *Capital and Time* (1973) ♀
Good example of solid workmanship, honest critique of the idiocy of last year's ideas.

Hirsch, Fred *Social Limits to Growth* (1977) ♀
At the present level of development of rich economies, individual decisions become less effective in allocating resources. To save capitalism again (shades of Keynes, qv) a more collectivist approach is required.

Keynes, John Maynard *The General Theory of Employment, Interest and Money* (1936) ❢ ▮ ♀
Influential classic: a dialogue by Keynes with other economists and with his own past. Also: *The Economic Consequences of the Peace*; *Essays in Biography*, etc

Kidron, Michael *Western Capitalism since the War* (1968) ✻
Kidron's major thesis (that the world economy has been kept going by the arms

race—a view he has since radically revised) was highly debatable; his book nevertheless applies a Marxist analysis to the problems of today with vigorous conviction. Also: *Capitalism and Theory*

Kuznets, Simon *Six Lectures on Economic Growth* (1959) ♀
Kuznets allies a strong sense of realism with humour and delicacy. Accessible specialist book. Also: *Economic Growth of Nations*; *Modern Economic Growth*; *Capital in the American Economy*

Machlup, Fritz (ed) *Essays on Hayek* (1976) ♀
Hayek was an innovative force in the establishment of a critical rationale and methodology for the social sciences. These essays (by several leading US economists and economic journalists, including Buckley, Friedman and Dietz) discuss his contribution to economics both as an academic study and as a programme for social change. Technical but accessible.

Marshall, Alfred *The Principles of Economics* (1890) ★
Useful, brilliant, essential.

Marx, Karl *Capital* (1867) ❗✳★✓
Magnificent sweep of excitement, raises profound questions about the workings of industrial society. See POLITICS; SOCIOLOGY

Mill, John Stuart *Principles of Political Economy* (1848) 🏛 a
Characteristically clear, fair and liberal. See FEMINISM; PHILOSOPHY; POLITICS

Mishan, E. J. *The Costs of Economic Growth* (1967)
Economist's contribution to the case being made at the time by ecologists and conservationists. Sets out the hidden costs, in terms of social and environmental effects, of continuing increases in current patterns of production and consumption. Also: *21 Popular Economic Fallacies*

Myrdal, Gunnar *Asian Drama: An Enquiry into the Poverty of Nations* (1968) ♀
Enormous study of the economic and social structures of southern Asian countries, demonstrating how the experiences of developed countries are irrelevant for helping countries such as India escape from the teeming consequences of their own population growth.

Norris, K. and **Vaizey, J.** *Economics for Everyone* (1973) a
Makes other introductions redundant; elicits the minimal level of belief necessary if economics is to be believed at all.

Robinson, Joan *Economic Philosophy* (1962) ♀
Dismal state of a dismal science seen through the eyes of one of its few honest practitioners. Clear-headed; funny; gutsy. Also: *Accumulation of Capital*; *Collected Economic Papers* (4 vols); *Imperfect Competition*

Rostow, W. W. *How It All Began: Origins of the Modern Economy* (1975) a ★
How did the world survive until the 18th century without a modern economy? What is economic sense, and can it be restored? These and other awkward questions are brilliantly discussed in a book which should be as mortifying for orthodox monetarists as it is fascinating for the rest of us—it's reassuring to find a professional so undogmatic and open-minded about his speciality. Hawkish Rostow became enmeshed in the politics of the Vietnam War; this book reverts to the pure economics of his distinguished earlier career. Also: *The Process of Economic Growth*; *The Stages of Economic Growth*; *Politics and the Stages of Growth*, etc

Samuelson, Paul A. *Economics: An Introductory Analysis* (1948) ❚♀
For those wanting, or needing, a solid basis in formal economics theory, this is the text book several generations of students have cut their teeth on. Heavy, but authoritative.

Schumacher, E. F. *Small Is Beautiful* (1973) ★
You've heard the short slogan: now read the long book. Study of the requirements of an economic system based on meaningful work, small-scale organization and respect for the environment.

Smith, Adam *The Wealth of Nations* (1776) ❗★
Jolly Smith was an early advocate of not-so-jolly *laissez-faire*. Influential—some say catastrophic—and essential. Also: *Theory of the Moral Sentiments*

Stigler, George *The Theory of Price* (1966) ♀
Classic statement of the case for believing that the market is the analogue by which any actual economy works.

Westergaard, J. and **Resler, H.** *Class in a Capitalist Society* (1975)
Authors' thesis is that economics is not about the balance of payments but about power: control of institutions and the distribution of wealth and privilege. Analysis is more impressive than the evidence; the book will be replaced by better ones; until then, it's merely indispensable.

Feminism

Feminist literature dates back to the 18th century, but there have been intervals of quiescence, during which writers devoted their energies more to the novel and to social reform. The earliest examples of the genre tended to formal rectitude, despite the vigour of the political argument. More recently, the tone has become personal, at times violently polemical. The American women's movement has been especially vociferous. However, a comparison of, say, Mary Wollstonecraft with Germaine Greer suggests that women's grievances remain much the same, as do basic attitudes on both sides of the sexual divide. Natural history or indoctrination? It remains true that despite the considerable economic and social changes in Western society, the repression of women has had and continues to have ugly effects all round. We have limited ourselves to books worth reading for their originality and vigour as well as for their socio-historical importance. We hope that this list may soon be scrapped—for the battle will have been won at last.

See ANTHROPOLOGY (Kitzinger); AUTOBIOGRAPHY (Brittain, Mead); BIOGRAPHY (Tomalin); HISTORY/AMERICAN (Krantor); MEDICINE (Boston Women's Collective); MYTHOLOGY (Slater); RELIGION (Warner); SEX (Hite); SOCIOLOGY (Mead)

Beauvoir, Simone de *The Second Sex* (1949) *!♀★*
Wordy "philosophical" analysis of the condition of women; historical, biological and literary perspectives. Rational, erudite, convincing. Also: *Memoirs of a Dutiful Daughter.* See FICTION/NOVELS

Bird, Caroline *Born Female* (1970)
Eloquent review of the physical and psychological make-up of the female human being. Dispels many myths. Revised edition (1971) recommended.

Brownmiller, Susan *Against Our Will: Men, Women and Rape* (1975) ♀
Main, chilling argument is that rape is about male-female power politics.

Evans, Sara *Personal Politics* (1979) ♀
Vital for understanding the roots of women's liberation in the USA. Author traces the connections between the civil rights movement and the New Left in the emergence of an autonomous feminist movement.

Figes, Eva *Patriarchal Attitudes* (1970) ★
Basic premise is that over the centuries women have fulfilled a role cast for them by men and that the way women are is not given in nature but a product of society. The author discusses ideas of women in such diverse and influential sources as religion, Schopenhauer and Freud, and suggests possibilities for change.

Flexner, Eleanor *Century of Struggle: The Woman's Rights Movement in the United States* (1959) 🖿
Excellent historical overview. 1979 revision brings it up to date.

Friedan, Betty *The Feminine Mystique* (1962) *!*
This book inspired the emergence of the women's liberation movement in the USA. About "the problem that has no name": the denial of the humanity of women in American society; concluding chapters explain ways to escape the trap.

Greer, Germaine *The Female Eunuch* (1970) *!★*
Witty, entertaining attack on the absurdities of the female condition, with a convincing analysis of how they arose. Makes stylish mincemeat of the charge that feminists are humourless. Also: *The Obstacle Race* (on women artists)

Hiley, Michael *Victorian Working Women* (1979)
Everyday lives, photographed and described in dispassionate detail by Arthur Munby, a leading 19th-century barrister. Alternately horrifying and uplifting, the triumph over circumstance of the human spirit. See Munro; BIOGRAPHY (Hudson); SOCIOLOGY (Chesney, Reeves)

Hufstedler, S. M. *Women and the Law* (1977) 🖿
Judge Hufstedler reviews the general field of American women's rights—and obligations—under the law. They are different from men's although not in all respects: women, like men, are not allowed to commit murder, although as a general rule it is still easier for a man to get away with killing a woman than vice versa.

Janeway, Elizabeth *Man's World, Woman's Place: A Study in Social Mythology* (1971) ★
The title says it all. This is one of the best feminist books—measured, eloquent, overwhelming for all of good will.

Kollontai, Alexandra *Selected Writings* (1977)   ♀
First major collection (ed Alex Holt) of famous Russian revolutionary's writings
to be published in English. Kollontai raises still relevant questions about the
family, morality and love. The publisher, Virago (London), is doing notable work
in republishing works of revolutionary and feminist interest, many from the late
19th and early 20th centuries.

Mill, John Stuart *The Subjection of Women* (1869)   ★
Argues strongly that both sexes have lost out because of the political and legal
subjection of women. Stresses mutal support and the importance of a "just"
society. Inspiring, influential. See ECONOMICS; PHILOSOPHY; POLITICS

Millet, Kate *Sexual Politics* (1969)
How women have been and are portrayed by historians, sociologists, politicians,
psychologists and writers. A revelation to anyone who remains unimpressed by
the validity of feminism. Her attacks upon Mailer, Lawrence *et al* (if flawed)
make one shout for joy. Also *Sita; The Prostitution Papers*

Mitchell, Juliet *Woman's Estate* (1971)   a
From within the politics of women's literature Mitchell defines the specific areas
of oppression and describes current attempts to break the pattern of repression
imposed on women. Useful summary of the debate between feminists and
Marxist-socialists on the nature of oppression.

Munro, Alice *Lives of Girls and Women* (1973)
Sensitive description of growing up in small-town Canada. Brilliant descriptions
of agonies of "first-dates" and the sex-versus-intellect debate which presented
itself to many 18-year-olds. Strikes many right notes; delightful, insightful read.

Norris, Jill and **Liddington, Jill** *One Hand Tied Behind Us* (1978)   ★
A study of interconnections between trade unionism, suffrage and socialism in
Lancashire in the late 19th and early 20th centuries. Moving accounts of those
radical suffragists' personal lives and political views—partly gleaned from
interviews.

Pomeroy, Sarah B. *Goddesses, Whores, Wives and Slaves* (1975)
Fascinating study of women in classical antiquity. "The hand that rocks the cradle
rules the world"—a comfortable (male) view, definitively examined. Lucid,
elegant, shocking.

Porter, Cathy *Fathers and Daughters* (1976)   ♀
Women as political and social activists in the reign of Tsar Alexander II
(1855–81). The *real* Revolution began here. Also: *Alexandra Kollontai*. See
Thomas.

Ramelson, Marian *The Petticoat Rebellion* (1967)   a
Moving general account of various strands in the women's movement in Britain
from the late 18th century to the early 20th century.

Rosen, R. and **Davidson, S. (eds)** *The Maimie Papers* (1979)
Maimie Pinzer, a Philadelphia prostitute at 20, a drug addict at 25, began at 30 a
correspondence with Fanny Quincey Howe, a rich Boston feminist, reformed,
and devoted her life to rehabilitating prostitutes, and to feminist causes. Warm,
raucous, passionate, she is full of good sense, full of the true life force.

Rossi, Alice *The Feminist Papers* (1973)   a
Comprehensive anthology of major feminist writings from the late 18th century
to Simone de Beauvoir (qv).

Rowbotham, Sheila *Women, Resistance and Revolution* (1972)
Wide-ranging survey of the roots of inequality from the 17th century to the
present. As the author says, "feminism and Marxism come home to roost". They
cohabit somewhat uneasily, being at once incompatible and in need of each other.
Essential for those not convinced of this mutal dependence.

Russell, Dora *The Tamarisk Tree* (1975)
Links the British new feminism of the 1920s and socialism in the Independent
Labour Party with intellectual and political movements, progressive education
and sex reform. Social change seen in terms of the personal quest of one woman
"for liberty and love," first stimulated and then overshadowed by "Bertie's
(Bertrand Russell's) genius." Also: *Hypatia, or Woman and Knowledge*, etc

Thomas, Edith *The Women Incendiaries* (1963)   ★
Moving description of the role of women in the Paris Commune of 1871, women
on the barricades persuading the soldiers not to shoot, standing in bread queues,
speaking in the revolutionary clubs, killed and imprisoned after the fall of the
Commune.

Wollstonecraft, Mary *Vindication of the Rights of Women* (1792)
One of the first British feminists was also Mary Shelley's mother and married to
the anarchist philosopher, William Godwin. Her arguments for the liberation of
women are still relevant. See BIOGRAPHY (Tomalin)

Woolf, Virginia *A Room of One's Own* (1929)
Long essay on the need for women to have economic independence to fulfil their
potential. Beautifully written, though now (dated by the changes it helped to
bring about) seems rather ladylike. See BIOGRAPHY (Bell, Woolf); DIARIES;
FICTION/NOVELS

Fiction

The story, it has been argued, is finally all that men can contrive to leave behind them, their only personal immortality. Their riches are perishable (unless they become the stuff of museums or vaults), but a man's story is his true legacy, the ghost through which we see him forever. But man is not only a speaking and a writing animal: he is unique in being a lying animal as well. His fictions are made of the same stuff as truth and if truth is stranger than fiction, fiction is sometimes truer. Thus though common sense may assert that the novel is merely a narrative form and that "creative writing" is but entertainment, we have a persistent feeling that novelists have more to tell us about life than all the psychoanalysts and sociologists. When all has been said and done, there is one more thing to say and do: write and tell stories, read and recommend and pass them on.

The books recommended here are chosen not only to entertain, but also to give a cross-section—including a fair proportion of masterworks—of a form of literature in which everyone will have his own taste. Some great books have, no doubt, been omitted (especially if they are not in English), sometimes because (as in the case of, say, Doeblin's *Alexanderplatz*) no reliable translation yet exists. Classics have tended to prevail over contemporary work, not least because it would have been ridiculous to leave them out. Only a Cretan would claim that *all* the best novels and short fictions are contained here, and Cretans, as we all know, are renowned for telling stories.

Crime Fiction and Thrillers
See CHILDREN'S BOOKS (Buchan, Haggard, Stevenson)

Allingham, Margery *The Tiger in the Smoke* (1952) ★
Allingham has been described as "sensitive enough to make human beings out of victim, criminal and detective alike." Secure plotting; magnificent feel for poetry of place. Also: *More Work for the Undertaker; Mystery Mile; The Beckoning Lady*

Ambler, Eric *The Mask of Dimitrios* (1939)
Astringent, unromantic, meticulously detailed, Ambler introduced a new and radical approach to the novel of espionage. Buchan-style yarns told with icy irony. Also: *The Dark Frontier; Dirty Story; Dr Frigo*, etc

Bardin, John Franklin *The Deadly Percheron* (1946)
With his rediscovery in 1976, Bardin's particular brand of surreal imagination and obsession with morbid psychology have brought him new recognition. Flawed but interesting minor master. Also: *The Last of Philip Banter; Devil Take the Blue-Tailed Fly*

Canning, Victor *The Golden Salamander* (1947)
Canning's inventiveness, his sense of pace and humour compensate for a certain implausibility in the plotting. Also: *Birdcage; The Rainbird Pattern*

Chandler, Raymond *The Big Sleep* (1939) ▣
It was not until his forties that Chandler began to write pulp novelettes for *Black Mask*. This apprenticeship produced the most famous private eye of them all—Philip Marlowe. Chandler's desire to make him a modern knight-errant is redeemed by a sardonic wit that salts the sentimentality. Also: *Farewell, My Lovely; The Long Goodbye; The Little Sister*

Christie, Agatha *The ABC Murders* (1936)
The dapper little master detective, Hercule Poirot, took his first bow in 1915, and thanks to those phenomenal "little grey cells", never failed to unravel puzzles of murderous duplicity. Simplistic, irritating prose-style; every other hair in place. Also: *The Murder of Roger Ackroyd; Ten Little Niggers* (sometimes *Indians*); *Curtain: Poirot's Last Case*, etc

Collins, Wilkie *The Moonstone* (1868) ♀★
T. S. Eliot called this "the first, the longest and the best of modern English detective novels." Also: *The Woman in White*

Crispin, Edmund *The Moving Toyshop* (1946) ⚱
Crispin's highly-wrought, suave mysteries, starring the eccentric and erudite Oxford professor, Dr Gervase Fen, delight in bizarre bafflement. Also: *The Case of the Gilded Fly; Love Lies Bleeding; The Glimpses of the Moon*

Davidson, Lionel *Making Good Again* (1968)
Davidson is not strictly a crime novelist, but rather a writer of vivid and atmospheric high adventure. This book and *Smith's Gazelle* (1971) are serious

novels, badged with the pace and narrative excellence of his other work. Also; *A Long Way to Shiloh*; *The Night of Wenceslas*, etc

Deighton, Len *Spy Story* (1974)
Scrupulously researched, often iconoclastic writing; "a kind of poet of the spy novel" (Julian Symons). Working-class, laconic hero—a rare treat in a generally snobbish, middle-class-oriented genre. Cracking style and pace. Also: *The Billion Dollar Brain*; *Yesterday's Spy*

Dickinson, Peter *The Poison Oracle* (1974)
After five books unglamorous, elderly but crafty copper's copper, Superintendent Pibble, was obliged to retire from Scotland Yard. Dickinson's range is now wider—stylish mysteries fizzing with bizarre invention. Also: *The Lively Dead*; *Sleep and His Brother*, etc. See CHILDREN'S BOOKS

Doyle, Sir Arthur Conan *The Memoirs of Sherlock Holmes* (1894)   📖
Despite time, competition and the Reichenbach Falls, Holmes survives as the greatest, most famous detective in literature, an enduring part of popular mythology. Also: *The Adventures of Sherlock Holmes*; *The Hound of the Baskervilles*; *His Last Bow*, etc

Ellin, Stanley *The Blessington Method* (1964)
Despite a number of fine and varied novels Ellin is best-known for his short stories. He writes with a compressed imaginative intensity that transcends the genre. Also: *The Speciality of the House and Other Stories*; *The Eighth Circle*, etc

Forsyth, Frederick *The Day of the Jackal* (1971)
It is a tribute to Forsyth's dramatic skill that the threat to assassinate General de Gaulle remains nailbitingly tense and convincing, despite our knowledge that the attempt is doomed from the outset. Later books less good; this one excellent.

Francis, Dick *Bonecrack* (1971)
An ex-champion jockey, Francis knows the value of a good start. He hooks you on the first page and never lets go. His intimate knowledge of horse racing has provided background for a series of tautly written adventure stories, consistent winners. Also: *Dead Cert*; *Nerve*; *For Kicks*, etc

Freeling, Nicolas *Criminal Conversation* (1965)
After killing off Van der Valk, Freeling has not quite managed to replace the complex Dutch Inspector with the (not unsympathetic) Frenchman Castang. An original writer, he sometimes allows philosophical ramble to obscure narrative drive. Also: *Love in Amsterdam*; *Gun before Butter*; *Because of the Cats*, etc

Gilbert, Michael *The Night of the Twelfth* (1976)
At one time, Gilbert was Raymond Chandler's legal adviser, and even drew up his will. His classic mystery, *Smallbone Deceased* (1950), has a corpse discovered in a safe deposit box. Unfailingly accomplished. Also: *The Crack in the Teacup*; *Game without Rules*

Haggard, William *The Scorpion's Tail* (1975)
"Haggard is a right-wing romantic of the Buchan school . . . who has an agreeable streak of realism" (Julian Symons). Politics intrusive at times; but pace and invention rarely flag. Also: *The Doubtful Disciple*; *The Telemann Touch*; *The Powder Barrel*

Hammett, Dashiell *The Maltese Falcon* (1932)   📖
Tougher and more uncompromising than Chandler, Hammett's spare, cynical, unglamorized stories looked hard at violence, crooked police and urban corruption. Also: *The Glass Key*; *The Dain Curse*; *Red Harvest*; *The Thin Man*. See AUTOBIOGRAPHY (Hellman)

Highsmith, Patricia *The Talented Mr Ripley* (1955)   ★
Since her success with *Strangers on the Train* (1950), Highsmith has explored criminal psychology with dark and imaginative insight. Also: *Ripley under Ground*; *The Two Faces of January*; *A Dog's Ransom*, etc

Hornung, E. W. *Raffles, the Amateur Cracksman* (1899)
Raffles is the perfect English gentleman—finest slow-arm bowler of his generation, and a highly successful burglar. Also: *A Thief in the Night*; *Mr Justice Raffles*

Household, Geoffrey *Rogue Male* (1938)
Classic chase story, where the hunter, an English aristocratic sportsman, becomes the hunted. Suspense never slackens. Also: *Watcher in the Shadows*

Innes, Michael *Hamlet, Revenge* (1936)   🛏
Apotheosis of "don's delight" escapist detective fiction. Suave John Appleby solves the most obscure cases as he would a Sunday crossword. Also: *The Journeying Boy*; *Lament for a Maker*; *From London Far*

James, P. D. *The Black Tower* (1975)
Brooding, atmospheric style, and a sensitive sleuth in Adam Dagleish. Also: *A Mind to Murder*; *Death of an Expert Witness*, etc

Keating, H. R. F. *Inspector Ghote Trusts the Heart* (1972)
Gentle, intelligent stories, whose chief joy is the endearing and bumbling character of the little Inspector. Non-Ghote novels are underrated, but funnier, more tightly plotted, sparkling with bizarre events. Also: *A Rush on the Ultimate*; *Death and the Visiting Firemen*; *Zen There Was Murder*, etc

Kemelman, Harry *Wednesday the Rabbi Got Wet* (1976) 🏛
Starting with *Friday the Rabbi Slept Late* (1964), Kemelman has now reached the end of a packed week. Whilst mystery elements have become subservient to suburban American synagogue politics, that interesting but unlikely detective, Rabbi David Small, has a sneaky advantage neither Holmes, Spade nor Maigret ever had—Talmudic logic. Also: *Thursday the Rabbi Walked Out*, etc

Lathen, Emma *Murder against the Grain* (1967) 🏛
Behind the pseudonym lurk two Boston businesswomen who have made Wall Street synonymous with murder and mayhem. Also: *When in Greece*; *The Longer the Thread*; *By Hook or by Crook*, etc

Le Carré, John *The Spy Who Came in from the Cold* (1963); *The Naïve and Sentimental Lover* (1971) 🏛
Le Carré's achievement has been wildly exaggerated, and his work can be repetitive, hermetic and as dull as the routine he so lovingly dissects. But at his best, he is grippingly good: in *The Spy Who Came in from the Cold* he created a true mirror of our distracted times, and in *The Naïve and Sentimental Lover*, he found a warmth, a depth and a dignity his other bleak visions signally lack.

McBain, Ed *Cop Hater* (1956) ★
Versatile, prolific, consistent, McBain has written a string of pacey police procedurals. His detectives, Steve Carella, Cotton Hawes, Meyer Meyer get regular feature spots, but unusually it is the 87th Precinct itself that has retained the limelight. Also: *The Mugger*; *Like Love*; *Give the Boys a Great Big Hand*, etc

Macdonald, Ross *The Goodbye Look* (1969) ★
Lew Archer started life as a Marlowe imitator, but Macdonald's exuberant relish for story telling has helped his sleuth acquire a precise personal identity. Also: *The Far Side of the Dollar*; *The Moving Target*; *Sleeping Beauty*, etc

Maugham, W. Somerset *Ashenden, or the British Agent* (1928) ★
With these crisp short stories, Maugham not only pioneered the modern novel of espionage, but also introduced a new kind of anti-hero with the downbeat character of Ashenden. See AUTOBIOGRAPHY; DRAMA; FICTION/NOVELS; FICTION/SHORT STORIES

Poe, Edgar Allan *Tales of Mystery and Imagination* (1850) 📃
Poe may not have held his "tales of ratiocination" in the highest esteem, but these stories alone earned him the title of "the father of detective fiction". Even Holmes took lessons from C. Auguste Dupin. See FICTION/SHORT STORIES

Price, Anthony *Other Paths to Glory* (1974)
With cool intelligence, Price has added new polish to a sometimes tarnished genre. British right-wing upper-class heroics again—and none the worse, perhaps, for that. Also: *The Labyrinth Makers*; *The October Men*, etc

Sayers, Dorothy L. *Murder Must Advertise* (1933) 📃
Sayers claimed she wrote Wimsey stories only for money. But her inspired aristocratic detective still has few rivals. See DRAMA

Simenon, Georges *My Friend Maigret* (1949) 📃
How Simenon managed an output of six short novels a year coupled with an endless series of amorous conquests is a subject for the record books. Best read in French: English translations (even those by Baldick, the best) are slapdash and unstylish. Also: *Maigret and the Enigmatic Lett*; *Maigret's Memoirs*; *Maigret Meets a Milord*, etc. See AUTOBIOGRAPHY

Sims, George *Sleep No More* (1966)
A thriller writer with a touch of class and an edge of anger, Sims manages to combine high-octane excitement with plausible incident and an insider's knowledge of the antique and book trade. Succinct but never mannered, Luciferian heroes on the side of the angels. Also: *End of the Web*, etc

Stout, Rex *Fer-de-Lance* (1934) 🏛
Who weighs one seventh of a ton, is nearly six feet tall, grows orchids, lives in a brownstone in New York, and is a self-confessed genius? The answer is Nero Wolfe, who with his laconic legman, Archie Goodwin, forms one of the most entertaining double acts in detective fiction. Also: *The League of Frightened Men*; *The Silent Speaker*; *A Family Affair*, etc

Symons, Julian *The Man Who Lost His Wife* (1970)
Symons's reputation and influence in the field of crime fiction have rested more with crusading criticism than with novels. His mordant wit, psychological probing and clever plotting deserve a large audience. Also: *The Man Who Killed Himself*; *A Three-pipe Problem*; *The Blackheath Poisonings*, etc

Tey, Josephine *The Daughter of Time* (1951)
A perennial seller, this historical detective story confines Tey's Scotland Yard Inspector Grant to his sickbed. To relieve the boredom, Grant delves into the mystery of the murdered Princes in the Tower and absolves Richard III of guilt. A curio. Also: *The Franchise Affair*; *The Singing Sands*, etc

Wahloo, Per and **Sjowall, Maj** *The Laughing Policeman* (1970)
Police procedurals, featuring the lugubrious Martin Beck, take a hard and abrasive look at Swedish society. Gloomily compulsive. Also: *The Abominable Man*; *The Locked Room*; *Cop Killer*, etc

Novels

See CHILDREN'S BOOKS (Tolkien, White, Williamson); HUMOUR (Chevalier, Dennis, Frayn, Jerome, Loos, Petronius, Queneau, Smith, Tinniswood, Twain, De Vries, Westlake, Wodehouse); MYTHOLOGY (Mitchison); SEX (Cleland, Genet, Haddon, Laclos, Miller, Nin, Reage, Sade, Southern)

Achebe, Chinua *Things Fall Apart* (1958)
Wry African view of comedy and scandal of independence in a Nigeria at once debauched by its one-time masters and thrust, by their departure, into a parody of their vanities. Also: *No Longer at Ease*; *A Man of the People*

Alain-Fournier *The Lost Domain* (*Le Grand Meaulnes*) (1913)
School and adolescence in the French countryside: lost love rendered poignant by the author's death in the Great War, which elevates his memory—book is surprisingly based on "reality"—into legend.

Algren, Nelson *The Man with the Golden Arm* (1972)
Determinedly tough and wrong-side-of-the-trackish, Algren is of the Chicago school which refuses to make overtures to (or accept them from) the literary establishment. His writing lacks conscious grace, but is consciously disgraceful instead: this novel was one of the first to deal boldly, melodramatically perhaps, with drugs, and it has a typically rough, diamantine quality. Algren is portrayed in Beauvoir's (qv) *The Mandarins*.

Amado, Jorge *Gabriela, Clove and Cinnamon* (1958)
Ilhéus, a port city in the Brazilian province of Bahia, comes alive when beautiful Gabriela from the backlands is hired as a cook by Nacib, owner of the town's most popular café. An enchanting novel teeming with Brazilian folklore and humour.

Amis, Kingsley *Lucky Jim* (1954)
Amis' first book grows ever slighter, more enduring; Jim Dixon, English grammar school-educated academic, has had a thousand irreverent successors, none with quite his anarchic eye for the main chance.

Austen, Jane *Sense and Sensibility* (1815)
The determination of orthodox criticism to find in Jane Austen the virtue of moral sensitivity tends to make furtive the view that her books maintain their vitality because they are about what interests readers: love and money. Her novels' view of life is alert to form and to reality; from that shaping tension comes classic quality. Also: *Pride and Prejudice*; *Emma*; *Northanger Abbey*, etc

Ayrton, Michael *The Mazemaker* (1967)
Myth of Daedalus relived by an artist as protean as the legendary Cretan craftsman; less a historical novel than a personalized view of the relationship between power and art, grit and oyster.

Baldwin, James *Another Country* (1963)
Much better than *Giovanni's Room*—trash which brought him fame. American expatriates in 1950s and early 1960s search for sexual and emotional liberation. Black and white, "queer" and "straight", matched with convincing sympathy and urgency. Also: *Go Tell It on the Mountain*; *The Fire Next Time* (polemic), etc

Balzac, Honoré de *Old Goriot* (1834)
Old Goriot—a bourgeois King Lear living in a *pension*—is but one panel in *The Human Comedy*, and a good introduction to its brilliant pageant of realism and fantasy, of observation and monstrous fancy. Also: *Cousin Bette*; *Eugènie Grandet*, etc. See BIOGRAPHY (Zweig)

Barth, John *The End of the Road* (1962)
Best, early work of later logorrhoid; campus life with the blinds rolled up; scabrous tenderness illuminates characteristic 1950s American milieu.

Beauvoir, Simone de *The Mandarins* (1954)
Lacking wit, by a process of earnest accumulation and resolute seriousness de Beauvoir analyses post-war French intellectuals—Sartre, Camus *et al*—in a book both seductive and self-indulgent. See FEMINISM

Beckett, Samuel *Molloy* (1950)
The novel reduced to literature; the skeleton as flesh; the flesh made words; words in a state of decomposition. Also: *Murphy*; *Malone Dies*; *Watt*. See DRAMA; FICTION/SHORT STORIES; LITERARY CRITICISM

Beerbohm, Max *Zuleika Dobson* (1911)
Beerbohm's dandyism kept his literary wardrobe slim and neat. *Zuleika Dobson* is perhaps the most elegant bad example ever set to the young; idle, gilded Oxford epitomized.

Bellow, Saul *The Victim* (1947)
Tense study in paranoia in which forces of self-destruction and external menace are artfully balanced; one of his good early books—*Dangling Man* (1944) is another—before *The Adventures of Augie March* (1953) led to fame and fat.

Bennett, Arnold *The Old Wives' Tale* (1908)
Lives of two sisters from one of Bennett's "Five Towns" (industrial Midlands of Britain, Victorian style), from girlhood to grave; memorable scenes of Paris under siege in 1870. "Arnold has written a masterpiece," said Maugham. Also:

Anna of the Five Towns; *Clayhanger*; *Buried Alive*, etc. See DIARIES

Brontë, Charlotte *Jane Eyre* (1847) 📖
"Realistic" wish-fulfilment in which the wish-bone sticks in the heroine's throat until a happily painful operation gives her the stars while denying her the moon. See Jean Rhys' *Wide Sargasso Sea* (1966) for a recension of the life of Mrs Rochester. See BIOGRAPHY (Gaskell, Gérin)

Brontë, Emily *Wuthering Heights* (1847) 📖
The supreme Romantic fiction, archetypal and idiosyncratic for passion and for surging, self-justifying conviction; no parody can match its hysterics, but Heathcliff continues to lord it over his detractors, both in the story and without. See BIOGRAPHY (Gérin)

Burgess, Anthony *The Malayan Trilogy* (1956–59)
Best, least ostentatious early work of prolific man of letters; conscript life in the oriental twilight of empire reported in plain but personal style.

Butler, Samuel *The Way of All Flesh* (1903); *Erewhon* (1872) ★
Creepy classic of the relationship between a British Victorian father and his floundering, rationalist son, *The Way of All Flesh* is a consummate example of the novel-as-revenge. *Erewhon* is elegant satire: illness as social crime, crime as illness have unhappily manifold modern reverberations. On father-son theme, see AUTOBIOGRAPHY (Gosse)

Butor, Michel *Second Thoughts* (*La Modification*) (1957) ♀
Regarded by Sartre as the best living French novelist, Butor is a *nouveau romancier* whose experiments still leave us with a story. *Second Thoughts* is an innovative sequence of presents, urgent with traditional themes of personality, love and redemption. More profound, though less readable, than Robbe-Grillet (qv).

Camus, Albert *The Outsider* (*L'Étranger*) (1942); *The Plague* (1948) ♀📖
In *The Outsider* (also translated as *The Stranger* and *The Bystander*) Camus eliminated formal conditions of "character" and, in Meursault, "invented" a hero without heroic attributes or psychological coherence. *The Outsider* has cinematic terseness; *The Plague* is a denser, more pretentious book: the apocalypse in Oran, foreshadowing the Algerian bloodbath.

Cather, Willa *The Song of the Lark* (1875)
The story of an ambitious girl from middle America who will not be silenced either by lack of opportunity or the prejudice of family and neighbours. Her journey from prairie farm to the Metropolitan Opera is emblematic of the American Way at its optimistic best. Also: *My Antonia*; *Death Comes for the Archbishop*, etc

Cervantes, Miguel de *Don Quixote* (1605) 📖
Don Quixote, a gaunt country gentleman crazed by reading books of knight-errantry, sets out to redress the evils of the 17th-century world.

Cheever, John *Falconer* (1977)
A Kafkaesque study of an intellectual, sensitive and savage, reduced (or promoted) to the level of his fellow-convicts in an American "correctional facility", a prison where homosexuality is the rule. A sly, wished-for book with something of Malaparte's dandyish *nostalgie de la boue*. See FICTION/SHORT STORIES

Clavell, James *Shogun* (1975)
An extraordinarily imaginative evocation of life in medieval Japan by a writer who previously specialized in potboilers. Here Clavel found his subject, and treated it with range and skill.

Colette *Chéri* (1920) 📖
No single work of Colette's is "great", but, in the tradition of French writing, the entire works constitute the achievement. Language weakened in translation. Also: *Claudine*; *The Vagabond*; *The End of Chéri*, etc

Compton-Burnett, Ivy *Mother and Son* (1955) ♀★
The hypnotic tone and knotty style of Compton-Burnett's novels are notorious. Their grave absurdity and regular wit—they are all style, with little action—can seem merely ingenious; but stringent perceptiveness is at work throughout. The Edwardian English "domus system" never had a more searching obituary. Also: *A God and His Gifts*, etc

Conrad, Joseph *Nostromo* (1904); *The Secret Agent* (1907) ★
Set in an imaginary South American republic, *Nostromo* is a study of adventure and the temptations of power. The "South American novel" originates and flowers here. *The Secret Agent* once seemed grotesque melodrama, but modern urban terrorism has its roots in Mr Verloc's nihilistic mania and, perhaps, domestic despair. Useful biography: Karl's *Joseph Conrad: The Three Lives*. See FICTION/SHORT STORIES

Cooper, William *Scenes from Provincial Life* (1961)
Neat and humorous tales, understated but never etiolated, of English adolescent life before television and jeans. The school of Amis and Larkin was equalled and perhaps preceded by Cooper's nicely scathing, affectionate study.

Defoe, Daniel *Robinson Crusoe* (1719); *A Journal of the Plague Year* (1722)   ◖

Virtues of forthright style are seldom virtuous in critical circles, but Defoe's capacity for creating suspension of disbelief bypasses aesthetics. *Robinson Crusoe* is an early example of the creative use of "news stories"—it was suggested by an actual marooning—just as *A Journal of the Plague Year* brilliantly impersonates an eye-witness account.

Dickens, Charles *Great Expectations* (1860–61)   ◖

Dickens was a master of sentimental, savage Victorian journalism, the anatomist of his gory age; but plots, wit and warm characterization triumph over particularity, and render him a timeless joy. *Great Expectations* is his masterpiece, autobiography transmuted into art; but *Oliver Twist, The Pickwick Papers* and above all *Bleak House* make almost equal claims. See BIOGRAPHY (Zweig)

Dos Passos, John *Three Soldiers* (1922); *Manhattan Transfer* (1925); *USA* (1932–36)

Three Soldiers is a conventional but innovative study of Americans at war in 1917; *Manhattan Transfer* a montage of 1920s life; *USA* an impressive attempt to manage a large, politically committed theme.

Dostoyevsky, Fyodor *Notes from the House of the Dead* (1861); *Crime and Punishment* (1866)   ◖

Tolstoy's rival (according to the critic George Steiner), journalistic ranter (according to Nabokov, qv), Dostoyevsky's capacity to dramatize deadly, comic dilemmas of Russian life under the Tsars makes him the master whose *Crime and Punishment* is the best introduction. *Notes from the House of the Dead*—based on Dostoyevsky's life in Tsarist prisons—presages the Gulag. Also: *The Brothers Karamazov; The Idiot; The Devils*, etc. See BIOGRAPHY (Zweig)

Drabble, Margaret *The Millstone* (1970)

A characteristically sixties study (a milestone it ain't) of young motherhood, unsentimental, caustic and socially aware, though with a strong sense of privilege (the unmarried mother is a scholarship girl). Drabble's fiction is self-conscious and less well written than her reputation might imply, but if it is inclined to insularity, it is always at least aware of the deep water beyond the smug island.

Dreiser, Theodore *An American Tragedy* (1925)   ♀

Inelegant, Zolaesque, Theodore Dreiser heaped up authenticity like a scrap merchant making his pile. Earnest anger makes his social-climber hero's "murder" of his working class fiancée a "tragedy" of sentimental ruthlessness in the heyday of rugged individualism. Also: *Sister Carrie*

Durrell, Lawrence *The Alexandria Quartet* (1957–60)

Grandiose composition, supposedly Einsteinian in its literary "relativity"; gaudy, often splendid style. The outrageous Scobie wittily homonymous with the dull hero of Graham Greene's (qv) *The Heart of the Matter*. As often with Durrell, topography wins. See DIARIES; POETRY; TRAVEL

Eliot, George *Middlemarch* (1871); *Daniel Deronda* (1874)   ◖

Outspokenness in sexual and social matters was never better combined with literary decorum than in *Middlemarch*. We know everything about Casaubon and Dorothea's terrible marriage without ever entering their bedroom; we see Lydgate's early flame doused by his own passion and can infer his shortcomings; morality without Christian affectations. *Daniel Deronda* is prolix but acute on Victorian attitudes to the Jewish problem. Also: *Silas Marner, Adam Bede*, etc

Ellison, Ralph *Invisible Man* (1952)

Negro life in the USA: somewhat overtaken, despite its controlled rage, by black literature of 1960s and 1970s; honoured more in pantheon than library; but truthful, literate narrative.

Enright, D. J. *Academic Year* (1955)

A dry, witty corrective to the lay-it-on-with-a-trowellishness of Lawrence Durrell (qv) is this study of studies in Alexandria, an exquisitely deft and astringent early entrant in the long list of campus novels, by a poet and critic who is not in the habit of letting people off.

Faulkner, William *Light in August* (1932)   ★

Faulkner's style echoed European models—especially Joyce—but remained, not always happily, massively "personal" in its experimental industry. *Light in August* combines swift story-telling with brilliant, multi-faceted presentation of the semi-literate. Also: *Sartoris; As I Lay Dying; Sanctuary*, etc. See FICTION/SHORT STORIES

Fielding, Henry *The History of Tom Jones, a Foundling* (1749); *Jonathan Wild the Great* (1743)   ♀◖

The History of Tom Jones is long for modern taste: lacking in "development", a gallery of rogues and rips, it demands to be read at a gallop. *Jonathan Wild the Great* is a knowing, low-life satire with a notorious criminal as "King". "The prose Homer of human nature," said Byron of Fielding.

Firbank, Ronald *Caprice* (1916)   ▲

Firbank flavours a distinct area of modern fantastic fiction—Waugh (qv),

Nabokov (qv), Powell (qv) all have debts to pay—a scandalous pointillist world of gay abandon; his novels are brilliantly coloured scatter cushions dangerous with hidden pins. Also: *Valmouth*, etc

Fitzgerald, F. Scott *The Great Gatsby* (1925)   ★
The Great Gatsby is memorial enough to Fitzgerald's self-destructive genius; quibbles concerning the narrator's shadowy personality cannot bruise the flawless, original image of the jazz age, its charm and its corruption. See BIOGRAPHY (Milford); DIARIES; FICTION/SHORT STORIES; FILM (Latham)

Flaubert, Gustave *Madame Bovary* (1857); *Salammbô* (1862)   📖
Madame Bovary is the classic novel, narrative as art. "*Madame Bovary, c'est moi*" said Flaubert, claiming fiction as his kingdom. *Salammbô*, his "failure", is a terrific case of historical verbosity (life in old Carthage): overwritten, magnificent. See DIARIES (Flaubert, Goncourt); FICTION/SHORT STORIES

Ford, Ford Madox *Parade's End* (1957)   🏛
Ford is maddening to certain tastes; morosely punctuated with dots and dashes; but the collapse of English society during the Great War has never been more passionately depicted than in his touching account of marriage and betrayal among the upper middle classes. Also: *The Good Soldier*, etc

Forster, E. M. *A Passage to India* (1924)
Time is not being kind to Forster's essentially genteel muse but *A Passage to India* is a brave, liberal view of British India at its confident, uncertain zenith. See also *The Hall of Devi* (1953) on Forster's own Indian visits.

Fowles, John *The Magus* (1966, revised 1976)
Long, complex "novel of adolescence written by an adolescent" (Fowles in his introduction). Owes debts to *Le Grand Meaulnes*, to *Bevis*, to *Great Expectations* and to such contemporary novelists as Durrell (qv), Bellow (qv) and Marguerite Duras (q non v). Convoluted games on a mesmeric Greek island: tries to provide "an experience beyond the literary" and certainly dishes up a rich and stimulating brew. Also: *The French Lieutenant's Woman*; *Daniel Martin*, etc

Galsworthy, John *The Forsyte Saga* (1905–22)
Begins as a readable indictment of English Edwardianism; ends as a mausoleum. First volume, *The Man of Property*, is the best and most honest, with Soames and Irene superbly contrasted in a light which favours now one now the other and leaves neither gilded nor damned.

Gaskell, Elizabeth *Cranford* (1853)   📖
Life in an early-19th-century English country town. Gaskell lacks the grand scale and intellectual fire of George Eliot (qv), but has an ironic eye for suffering and for conceit. Witty mirror-image of Brontë, Haworth and those uncouth, insufferable moors. See BIOGRAPHY

Gide, André *The Immoralist* (1902)   ♀
Proselytizing account of self-discovery by homosexual authoritative figure. Gide's fiction is datedly daring, innovative, old hat. Also: *The Counterfeiters*, etc

Glanville, Brian *Along the Arno* (1956); *The Bankrupts* (1958)
Along the Arno sees British expatriate life, *The Bankrupts* London Jewish life without illusions; tenderness wars with derision in both.

Gogol, Nicolai *Dead Souls* (1842)   📖
Unfinished, like the maze it depicts, *Dead Souls* is a satire of desperation in which the lost millions—the serfs of imperial Russia—are "redeemed" by the scurrilous, picaresque, activities of an archetypal confidence man. Good translation: Magarshack (1961). See BIOGRAPHY (Nabokov)

Golding, William *Lord of the Flies* (1954); *Pincher Martin* (1956)
Lord of the Flies is a devilish *Coral Island*: British prep schoolboys marooned on a desert island, a classic of malign vision by Catholic apologist. *Pincher Martin* is a *tour de force* about a drowning sailor: melodramatic notions redeemed by fastidious imagination.

Gordimer, Nadine *Guest of Honour* (1977); *The Late Bourgeois World* (1966)   ♀
Gordimer's brave attempts to find moral orientations in an apartheid state give her dignity and seriousness, but she lacks literary grace. *Guest of Honour* is about a "good" Briton returning to a recently decolonialized land; *The Late Bourgeois World* is a love story between black and white in South Africa. Also: *Burger's Daughter*

Grass, Günter *The Tin Drum* (1959)   ♀
Inventive, patchy disquisition (as if by a German Laurence Sterne) on the Hitlerian legacy as seen by an "autobiographical" dwarf. Grass is strident, coarse, very subtle. Also: *The Flounder*

Graves, Robert *I, Claudius* (1934); *Claudius the God* (1934); *Count Belisarius* (1938)   📖
Pioneering "autobiographies" of the stammering emperor, at once clean and scabrous. Graves claimed to write fiction to subsidize his poetry; but *Count Belisarius*, with its assured use of Byzantine background, deserves more than a pot-boiling reputation. See AUTOBIOGRAPHY; HISTORY/ANCIENT (Procopius, Suetonius); MYTHOLOGY; POETRY

Green, Henry *Living* (1929); *Loving* (1945)
Henry Green worked as a factory manager but was also an upper-class
contemporary of the slightly envious Waugh (qv); he wrote unpatronizingly
tender, comic and economical studies of British life.

Greene, Graham *The Power and the Glory* (1940) ★
Paradoxes of Catholic faith teasingly, sometimes superbly anatomized. *The
Power and the Glory* is a schematic masterpiece of a whisky priest in Mexico. The
anti-Catholic case is consistently trivialized throughout his work. Later work
smacks of self-parody, eager at once to shock and to please. Also: *Brighton Rock*;
The Heart of the Matter; *The Confidential Agent*, etc. See TRAVEL

Hardy, Thomas *Far from the Madding Crowd* (1874); *Tess of the
D'Urbervilles* (1891); *Jude the Obscure* (1895)
Hard to deny Hardy classic status, hard to grant it whole-heartedly on account of
his clotted style, glum philosophy. *Far from the Madding Crowd* earliest, liveliest
masterpiece: Bathsheba Everdene is a new woman in an old Wessex setting; *Tess
of the D'Urbervilles* is full of memorable images, flawed by Hardy's appetite for
rigged doom; *Jude the Obscure*'s scandalous reception turned Hardy from fiction
to poetry. Also: *The Mayor of Casterbridge*; *Under the Greenwood Tree*, etc. See
POETRY

Hartley, L. P. *The Shrimp and the Anemone* (1944, trilogy with *The
Sixth Heaven*, 1946, and *Eustace and Hilda*, 1947); *The Go-Between*
(1953)
The Go-Between charts the emotional deadening of an insecure small boy used as
a go-between by lovers of different classes in Edwardian rural England: powerful
portrait of the period and of repression. The trilogy concerns a brother and sister
from cradle to maturity in England between-the-wars.

Hašek, Jaroslav *The Good Soldier Švejk* (1922) 📖
Endearing, caustic satire on war and the lunatic proceduralists who wage it. Švejk
himself conceals intelligence under a veneer of slavish obedience to
authority—and pretentious officials are revealed for the sterile fools they are.
Epic masterpiece, of the quality of Gogol (qv) or Rabelais (qv). The definitive,
unexpurgated translation by Parrott (1973) recommended.

Hawthorne, Nathaniel *The Scarlet Letter* (1850) ★
No need to continue to seek the Great American Novel; this was it. Hester
Prynne's search for freedom from the prison of society is the archetypal
American story—and it ends in the same way, with a retreat, or flight, into the
wilderness, where all men are, or seem to be, free. See FICTION/SHORT STORIES

Hayes, Alfred *In Love* (1954)
New York in the 1940s; love affair between a model and an older man; terse,
emblematic, ironic. Hayes' post-Hemingway brevity is also seen in stories of Italy
under US occupation: *The Girl on the Via Flaminia*.

Heller, Joseph *Catch 22* (1961) 📖
Title proverbial; book longer than witty, though very witty. Bravura passages of
anti-war farce laced with blood; Yossarian a memorable protagonist, what one
can remember of him.

Hemingway, Ernest *The Sun also Rises* (*Fiesta*) (1926); *A Farewell to
Arms* (1929); *For Whom the Bell Tolls* (1940) 📖
Development of character was alien to Hemingway. *A Farewell To Arms* is the
most integrated of his longer works, stained with lost love and the blood of
Caporetto; a tendency to self-ennobling postures deforms both *The Sun also
Rises* and *For Whom the Bell Tolls* but their virtues of narrative tautness and
sensational pointillism easily justify his place in the modern pantheon. See
BIOGRAPHY (Baker); FICTION/SHORT STORIES

Hersey, John *The Wall* (1962)
A vivid, highly effective account of the Warsaw Ghetto, its vicious encirclement
and isolation from the rest of the world. A documentary with a strong sense of
indignation checked by a cool head. Hersey (whose *Hiroshima* was a classic
account of the bombing and its aftermath) proves that fiction remains an
honourable tool in the reporting of life, and death.

Hesse, Hermann *Steppenwolf* (1927) ★
Shambling, repugnant yet touching figure of the artist as "outsider" in a smug,
bourgeois world is a representative symbol of Hesse's alert, romantic spirit. Also:
Rosshalde; *Siddhartha*; *The Glass Bead Game*, etc

Hope, Anthony *The Prisoner of Zenda* (1894); *Rupert of Hentzau*
(1898)
Supreme romantic *mittel-Europan* escapism, not without wit and spirit; sequel as
good as famous original.

Huxley, Aldous *Point Counter Point* (1928); *Brave New World*
(1932) 🏛
Ostentatiously "libellous", *Point Counter Point* retains interest as a portrait of
1930s *galère* (D. H. Lawrence *et al*). Prurience and wit are lively and sustaining.
Brave New World is an early example of modish dystopianism: the future as awful
warning. Also: *Chrome Yellow*; *Antic Hay*; *Eyeless in Gaza*, etc

Jacobson, Dan *A Dance in the Sun* (1956)
A short novel set in the South African *veldt* which, without rhetoric or accusation, marvellously catches the dogged spirit of the Afrikaaner. Jacobson's later books, including *Tamar* and *The Life of Joseph Basz*, are often ingenious and astringent, but their literary quality cuts against the dry realism which dignified the early book.

James, Henry *The Portrait of a Lady* (1880); *The Golden Bowl* (1904) ▯
The master of novel-as-art. *The Portrait of a Lady*, the most accessible, if long-drawn-out, describes Isabel Archer, an American heiress, and her fortunes in Europe. *The Golden Bowl* is a 21 carat, dense, abstruse evocation of sexual guilt and innocence. Also: *The Europeans*; *The Bostonians*; *Washington Square*, etc. See BIOGRAPHY (Edel, James); DIARIES; FICTION/SHORT STORIES; LITERARY CRITICISM

Jarrell, Randall *Pictures from an Institution* (1954) ▯
American academic life satirized by poet. Particularly spicy for those able to unlock *à clef* elements, but rises above malice to elegance. See LITERARY CRITICISM; POETRY

Jones, James *From Here to Eternity* (1951)
Another novelist promoted to impotence by early success; Jones's ponderous compendium of service life before and after Pearl Harbour is memorable for furious honesty, at least. Also: *The Thin Red Line*; *Some Came Running*

Joyce, James *Portrait of the Artist as a Young Man* (1914); *Ulysses* (1922) ▯
Portrait of the Artist as a Young Man is a "conventional" narrative of Stephen Dedalus's Dublin adolescence at the turn of the century, branded by Catholic bigotry; increasingly less "difficult" in the light of its derivatives. *Ulysses*, once scandalous, now classic account of one day in the life of Leopold Bloom, a Dublin Jew, doubling for wily Odysseus. Joyce was a master of pastiche and verbal ingenuity, sometimes committed to protracted (and wearisome) experiment; thus *Finnegan's Wake* is more interesting as a text for academic exegesis than for its own sake. See BIOGRAPHY (Ellmann); DIARIES; FICTION/SHORT STORIES

Kafka, Franz *The Trial* (1925); *The Castle* (1926); *America* (1927) ▯
The Trial concerns Josef K's arrest and degradation, "although he had done nothing wrong"; it is a supreme creation of prognostic and literary imagination. *America* is a comedy of the immigrant Kafka never was (he never saw America). *The Castle* is a superb comic chiller of the search for a spiritual keep. See DIARIES; FICTION/SHORT STORIES

Karp, David *The Day of the Monkey* (1955)
Prescient vision of colonial crack-up, impressively *avant la lettre*, it foresaw the Mau Mau "emergency" in Kenya and the emergence of a new, savagely implacable African spirit. Karp writes unhysterically (far better than Ruark in *Something of Value*) and looked like becoming a major writer. His *One* is a better dystopian novel than more recent additions to the genre—as nasty and as memorable as Nabokov's (qv) *Bend Sinister*.

Keneally, Thomas *The Confederates* (1970)
An excellent, chop-licking account of Stonewall Jackson and his more or less all honourable men in the service of a dishonourable cause (but compare Warren, qv). A memorable evocation of the sexual urgency that accompanies war, vivid set pieces that stir the blood while always reminding one of the virtuosity of a basilisk-eyed author.

Kerouac, Jack *On the Road* (1957) ℘
Maddening "bible" of the Beat generation. Starry-eyed search for the Wide Blue Yonder was (and is) an American dream; Kerouac's sentimental attitude to sex and to drugs was to see its apogee in a nadir called Manson. See BIOGRAPHY (Charters); DIARIES (Ginsberg)

Koestler, Arthur *Darkness at Noon* (1940) ★
Darkness at Noon is a convincing analysis of the self-inculpation of an old Bolshevik arrested by Stalin: Rubashov, innocent, finally agrees to plead guilty "for the good of the Party". (But compare with Victor Serge, qv). See MATHEMATICS; NATURAL HISTORY; OCCULT

Kosinski, Jerzy *The Painted Bird* (1968)
The first and best book of a talent increasingly seduced by his own capacity for sex'n'violence. The painted bird is a young Jewish child turned loose among the peasants of Poland when the Germans overrun the country. Kosinski keeps his "surrealistic" impulse superbly in place here and the unwilling pilgrim's progress through a godless world is a text for our time, alas.

Lagerkvist, Pär *The Sibyl* (1958)
Memoirs of a poor village girl elected to act as Sibyl at Delphi, to experience the torment and ecstasy of possession by Apollo. Bare, bony, Bergmanesque; Scandinavian Beckett (qv). Don't be misled by the awful epic film of Lagerkvist's *Barabbas*: he's a major writer, a subtle, poetic stylist, as cool as spring water. Also: *The Guest of Reality*; *The Dwarf*

Lawrence, D. H. *Sons and Lovers* (1913); *The Rainbow* (1915); *Women in Love* (1920) ★

Lawrence has been less admired since the rise of militant feminism, yet *Sons and Lovers*, as a particular case (if not "philosophy"), is unrivalled: Paul Morel's working class youth is thick with sensitive pain and observed life. *The Rainbow* and *Women in Love* form a diptych; two sisters and their married destinies against the background of Nottingham farming and mining life. See DIARIES; FICTION/SHORT STORIES; HISTORY/EUROPEAN; LITERARY CRITICISM; POETRY; TRAVEL

Lessing, Doris *The Golden Notebook* (1962)

Lessing was a pioneer of the unsmiling stance of modern feminism; her language is the mundane consequence of the rejection of wit. *The Golden Notebook* is solemn with determination to give a full account of Modern Woman at the end of her tether. Also: *Children of Violence* (5-novel sequence)

Lewis, Sinclair *Babbitt* (1922); *Elmer Gantry* (1927)

Documentary novelist of the 1920s portrayed non-metropolitan post-Woodrow Wilson USA. *Babbitt* is a loving, never sentimental portrait of a small-town businessman; *Elmer Gantry* debunks religious revivalism through the person of one phoney preacher. Also: *Main Street*, etc

Lewis, Wyndham *The Apes of God* (1930); *The Human Age* (1955) ℘

Lewis is regarded as a genius by some; his polemicism sent him to war with all the available targets. *The Apes of God* is a rampantly comic satire on his pet 20s hates, especially Bloomsbury. *The Human Age* (tetralogy) is apocalyptic, vast; an epic masterpiece or the apotheosis of turgidity, his most important work. Also: *Blasting and Bombardiering* (memoirs)

Lodge, David *Changing Places* (1975)

Home and away version of Bradbury (qv), the American and British campus as seen by a pair of visiting professors who take over each other's unfinished lives during the course of teaching each other's courses. Some slickness in the carpentered dove-tailing, but a sense of pity lends life to schematic example of the don-it-yourself school.

Lowry, Malcolm *Under the Volcano* (1947) ℘

Malcolm Lowry as a lost genius is a stock figure in literary circles. *Under the Volcano* (anatomy of British consul in pre-war Cuernavaca, Mexico) is a drunken, lachrymose alternative to Joyce's (qv) Bloom; a whole life revealed in a day or two of alcoholic despair.

McCarthy, Mary *The Group* (1963)

Bitchiness as method marks Mary McCarthy's work, but malice is a piquant ingredient for a novelist and she rarely spares herself in a clever pastiche of life-styles among well-heeled female graduates in the thirties and onwards. The *à clef* elements lend piquancy to the paying off of old scores among New York Trotskyites, intellectuals and climbers.

McCullers, Carson *The Heart is a Lonely Hunter* (1940); *The Member of the Wedding* (1946); *The Ballad of the Sad Café* (1951) ▣

The "Southern" theme—sexual ingrowth, social decay—repossessed by narrow, self-centred, inventive talent; restraint and melodrama work together to unnerving effect in studies of loneliness and jealousy.

Mackenzie, Compton *Sinister Street* (1913)

Mackenzie was a scholar, wit, Scottish nationalist. *Sinister Street* concerns Stephen Fane's adolescence at St Paul's School, London, before World War I.

Mailer, Norman *The Naked and the Dead* (1948)

Tour de force of an enforced tour of duty by riflemen in the South Pacific in World War II; the sexual obsessiveness of frightened soldiers counterpoints the power-madness of their commanders. The individual, and the American system, thrillingly, sensationally slit open like a bag of guts. See BIOGRAPHY

Malamud, Bernard *The Assistant* (1957)

The Jewish theme made over for inter-denominational consumption, is Malamud's speciality. *The Assistant*: Gentile New York shop assistant converted to Judaism, circumcision and all, by love.

Malraux, André *Man's Estate (La Condition Humaine)* (1933)

Malraux's obsessive wish to live at the centre of history can seem rhetorical and suspect, but he had a way of being there. Like all writers, he gilded the occasion; but the collapse of the Chinese Empire, the triumph of Kuomintang and the savage repression of Communist allies in Shanghai in 1927 are all marvellously realized, sentimental callousness notwithstanding. Also translated as *Man's Fate* (Macdonald, 1948).

Mann, Thomas *The Magic Mountain* (1924); *Joseph and His Brethren* (1933–43); *The Confessions of Felix Krull* (1954) ▯

Mann is sometimes said to have been, *à la* Victor Hugo, "the greatest living novelist—alas". The theme of the artist as "neurasthenic" haunts his long *oeuvre*, but brilliant variations are played on it. His thought evolved from Nietzschean to orthodox liberal, of which *The Magic Mountain* is the first, towering inkling—life in a sanatorium symbolically standing for the European predicament. *Joseph and His Brethren* is a monumental "recovery" of ancient Palestine and Egypt, badged with ingenious research and psychological slyness; *The Confessions of Felix Krull* is a marvellous work of old age, unfinished but sappy with iconoclastic vigour. Also: *Buddenbrooks*; *The Holy Sinner*, etc. See FICTION/SHORT STORIES

Márquez, Gabriel Garcia *One Hundred Years of Solitude* (1967)
The rich, lusty story of the rise and fall of the Buendia family in the imaginary town of Macondo, Brazil.

Maugham, W. Somerset *Of Human Bondage* (1915); *Cakes and Ale* (1930)
Cakes and Ale is Maugham at his terse, malicious best. *Of Human Bondage* is a ponderous, readable *bildungsroman*: club-footed Philip Carey, glum but convincing *alter ego* for the young Maugham, progresses through arty Paris and grim Victorian London. See AUTOBIOGRAPHY; DRAMA; FICTION/CRIME; FICTION/SHORT STORIES

Mauriac, François *Thérèse Desqueyroux* (1927)
Melancholy family life among the richer inhabitants of the Bordelais is the main theme of Mauriac's fiction, of which Sartre said that it denied freedom to its characters. Since Mauriac's Catholicism saw mankind tainted by distance from God and doomed to suffering, this charge is both true and irrelevant, though Mauriac's Jansenism reduces all except perhaps Thérèse, the murderess, to insignificance. Also: *The Nest of Vipers*, etc

Melville, Herman *Moby Dick* (1851)
Pursuit of the white whale by Captain Ahab has the elemental, symbolic force demanded of the Great American Novel; this book is often held to be just that. Erudite with whaling lore, grandiosely stocked with archetypes, it commands the memory more than the attention.

Mitchell, Margaret *Gone With the Wind* (1936) ★
Quintessential, 1,000-violin romantic novel. Rhett and Scarlett unforgettable.

Moravia, Alberto *The Woman of Rome* (1947)
Moravia's clear style and cocky assurance has made his Rome stand for the whole Italian imbroglio. *The Woman of Rome*, full of somewhat literary realism, recounts the degraded but "noble" life of a prostitute in Fascist times; never as crude as Moravia's later, more hotly sophisticated work. Also: *The Conformist*

Murdoch, Iris *Under the Net* (1954); *A Severed Head* (1961)
Under the Net, first novel, contains a memorable made-over portrait of Wittgenstein. Murdoch is a professional philosopher; her novels are often fables of existential ethics, florid with imagery and sensuality. *A Severed Head* is a sexual quadrille, "wish fulfilment" bristling with wit and unnerving observation. Also: *The Bell*; *The Black Prince*, etc

Musil, Robert *The Man without Qualities* (3 vols, 1930–43)
Overlong, but influential and informative study of a Viennese intellectual just before the Kaiser's war. The hero's attempt to define himself, against the decline of the Hapsburgs, issues in a definition coterminous with the novel itself—punishment without crime, as it were.

Myers, L. H. *The Near and the Far* (1929)
One of the purportedly great "lost" novels of the interwar years; one of a tetralogy dealing with the era of Akbar, the great 16th-century Mogul emperor. Grandiose, sometimes impermeably philosophical; but majestic and painful with erudition.

Nabokov, Vladimir *King, Queen, Knave* (1928)
Nabokov stands alone in the modern canon, the idiosyncratic instance of an artist jealous of his own uniqueness. Kafka and Joyce inspire work of sometimes maddening involution and conceit (in every sense); but his variety, wit and teasing literary iconography make Nabokov both nightmare and addiction. Also: *The Real Life of Sebastian Knight*; *Laughter in the Dark*; *Pale Fire*, etc. See AUTOBIOGRAPHY; BIOGRAPHY; CHILDREN'S BOOKS (Carroll); POETRY (Pushkin)

Nye, Robert *Falstaff* (1974)
The memoirs of Sir Jack Falstaff, as dictated in his swaggering Rabelaisian old age. A rich tapestry, the Middle Ages made sack-soaked, sucks-to-Shakespeare flesh. Also: *Merlin*; *Tales I Told My Mother* (short stories)

O'Hara, John *Appointment in Samarra* (1934)
O'Hara's Middle-America became an imaginary province stocked with closely observed and remembered figures, a heartland, lovingly overdrawn. His dialogue, prolix with innuendo, is often superb. Also: *Butterfield 8*. See FICTION/SHORT STORIES

Orwell, George *Animal Farm* (1945); *1984* (1949) ★
Animal Farm, denounced by pro-Soviets in 1944, rejected by publisher Gollancz, is a Swiftian fable of the Russian Revolution and its perversions; *1984* a glum warning of future militant banality, institutionalized "left" repression, Big Brother, Newspeak and all. Orwell's passion for decency pumps blood into stony themes. See HISTORY/BRITISH; LITERARY CRITICISM; POLITICS

Peacock, Thomas Love *Nightmare Abbey* (1818)   ▲
Peacock's satire sheathed its sharpness in amiable brevity. *Nightmare Abbey* is a piquant, uncensorious skit on Byron, Coleridge and the gloomy Romantic movement, from a detached "classical" standpoint. Peacock's derision has influenced English satirical posture—compare Anstey, Wodehouse etc—towards "enthusiasms" of all kind.

Potok, Chaim *The Chosen* (1967)
Intense, powerful story of an orthodox Jewish youth in Brooklyn, the son of a noted rabbi, who offends his father and is punished by silence for years. The boy survives, prospers, becomes a great scholar: his extraordinary education in Talmudic studies is described in fascinating detail in the book.

Powell, Anthony *Venusberg* (1932); *From a View to a Death* (1933); *The Music of Time* (1951–1977)
The last is a sequence of twelve novels. Englishmen, often of extremely etiolated temperament, are shown in revealing postures of upperclass—1920s onwards—embarrassment. *The Music of Time* is greatly admired for its evocation of wartime England—and for those in the know, especially spicy. The early novels are sharp with wit, a good apéritif to the main 12-course meal. Also: *What's Become of Waring?*

Powys, John Cowper *A Glastonbury Romance* (1933)   ♀
Neglected genius, some say. Mythopoeic grandiloquence—the Holy Grail is the theme of *A Glastonbury Romance*—renders him suspect in circles happier with understatement; but his force and vision are undeniable. Also: *Wolf Solent; Maiden Castle; The Brazen Head*, etc

Proust, Marcel *Remembrance of Things Past* (12 vols, 1912–27)   ▯
Not so much a novel as a library; the experience of a lifetime examined, expanded, imaginatively revived and finally restored to life in art. Great characters—and minor—swim in translucent jelly, the narrator's consciousness and conscience rendered prose, and the emulous nature of both social ambition and sexual desire become, in these slow and tremendous pages, the psychoanalysis of France itself. Definitive English translation by Moncrieff and Hudson (1922–1931). See BIOGRAPHY (Painter, Pickering); DRAMA (Johnson); LITERARY CRITICISM (Beckett)

Rabelais, François *Pantagruel* (1532); *Gargantua* (1533)   ▯
Relish for excess, the French appetite, is here displayed at its most gluttonous, not only for food and sex but for ideas and display of rhetorical virtuosity; the 16th century is anatomized literally and metaphorically—though at a length which inclines one (to one's loss) to make a chapter or two stand for the whole. Urquhart's English translation (1653, 1693) is that very rare thing: a translation as great as, or greater than, the original.

Raphael, Frederic *Lindmann* (1962); *California Time* (1976)
Lindmann is a passionate, compassionate examination of one man's guilt, and racked conscience, for the sinking of a refugee-ship in World War II; *California Time* is a witty experiment, the movie novel (the novel *as* movie) to end them all. Also: *April, June and November; The Glittering Prizes; Sleeps Six* (short stories), etc. See DRAMA (Aeschylus); POETRY (Catullus)

Raven, Simon *Bring Forth the Body* (1974)
The best sample for those unfamiliar with the scapegrace sequence entitled *Alms for Oblivion* in which old scores are paid off, old sores re-opened by a writer who combines hedonism with a certain callous sense of justice and honour. Charterhouse, the Army, Cambridge and high-class low life are cynically concocted into dishy, anti-feminine fare.

Rhys, Jean *Voyage in the Dark* (1934)   ★
The "Jean Rhys Woman", loyal, betrayed, loving and unloved, inhabits, with sly variations, all the stories; unselfpityingly distanced, the writing is exemplary, though an example too few have followed. Also: *After Leaving Mr Mackenzie; Good Morning Midnight; Quartet*. See Brontë, C.

Richardson, Samuel *Clarissa* (1748)
Can we refuse recognition to a founding work? No; but can we still read it? Clarissa's solemn moralizing marked the English novel, led to a thousand works in which men confidently depicted female characters—and so helped, consciously or not, to alienate women from their own feelings and "truth".

Robbe-Grillet, Alain *Jealousy* (1957)   ♀
Quintessential example of the *nouveau roman*, of which Robbe-Grillet was both pioneer and publicist. The attempt to remove the psychologizing fetish from fiction is superbly realized—though the "objectivity" with which a husband sees his wife's suspected infidelity is only an iota away from being "symbolic". But forget theory: the book, especially for those who enjoyed the film *Last Year in Marienbad*, scripted by Robbe-Grillet, is a pleasure to read.

Roth, Henry *Call It Sleep* (1934)   ♀
Roth's only published novel: "Oedipal" childhood in immigrant New York's Lower East Side. It has been likened to a Jewish *Sons and Lovers*, as seminal to Jewish writing in the USA as Ellison's (qv) *Invisible Man* to black.

Roth, Philip *Goodbye, Columbus* (1959); *Letting Go* (1963); *Portnoy's Complaint* (1969) ★
Written by a Gentile, Roth's work would be anti-Semitic; by a Jew, it holds a note of furious affection. *Goodbye, Columbus* is a fine novella (published with stories); *Letting Go*, a long, serious study of graduate life, is possibly Roth's finest book; *Portnoy's Complaint* is a "confessional"—set-pieces of irresistibly comic anguish by the conscientious masturbator, Portnoy. Also: *The Professor of Desire*

Salinger, J. D. *The Catcher in the Rye* (1951) 🖃
New, liberating tone made *The Catcher in the Rye*'s Holden Caulfield an American archetype—puzzled yet outspoken with a jargon ("big deal") still comic and current. Later work, about the Glass family—*Franny and Zooey*, etc—highly rated but incestuously self-involved.

Sartre, Jean-Paul *The Roads to Freedom* (1945–49) ♀
Impressive, unremittingly glum "philosophical" study of left-bank Parisians under pressure, 1938–40. À *clef* elements lend spice, but this novel of manners is self-justifyingly taken to melodramatic, hard-headed extremes. See
BIOGRAPHY; DRAMA; PHILOSOPHY

Schulberg, Budd *What Makes Sammy Run?* (1961)
Sammy Glick knows many imitators but stands supreme, a Rastignac who confronts Hollywood with an "*À nous deux*" and fights it to a standstill. The legendary plagiarizer and hustler was based, it is said, on Jerry Wald, but many real Hollywood *arrivistes* have surely based themselves on Sammy. It is not only art that life imitates.

Scott, Paul *Staying On* (1977)
A pendant to his impressive, lengthy trilogy about the British in India, *Staying On* is about the pensioners of the Raj, a delicate study in sunset colours, though stronger on detail than on literary grace.

Serge, Victor *Men in Prison* (1931); *The Case of Comrade Tulayev* (1948) ★
Serge lived revolution and imprisonment; his novels are etched with authenticity; but despite suffering and disillusionment he was capable of lyrical and intense flights of generous imagination. *The Case of Comrade Tulayev* is arguably a truer picture of Stalinism than either Koestler's (qv) *Darkness at Noon* or Trotsky's "historical" accounts. *Men in Prison* arises from Serge's own experiences in France where he served five years for "terrorism".

Shelley, Mary *Frankenstein, or the Modern Prometheus* (1818) 🖃
Unlikely winner of a competition for gothic tales in which Byron and Shelley dead-heated for the wooden spoon, Mary Shelley's shocker is thrillingly written, full of plausible implausibilities. Pregnant with Freudian clues, the monster's story is a true original among imitations.

Sillitoe, Alan *Saturday Night and Sunday Morning* (1958)
Marvellously fresh, loving and yet clear-eyed vision of working class life in early post-war England. A classic and honest claim for the vitality of the provincial hero, yet well aware of the transitory nature of sappy happiness.

Sinclair, Upton *The Jungle* (1906)
Classic realistic—compare Frank Norris' *The Pit*—exposé of Chicago stockyards during the heyday of union-bashing beef barons. "Documentary" as socialist polemic. Also: *World's End*

Singer, Isaac Bashevis *The Family Moskat* (1950); *The Magician of Lublin* (1960); *The Slave* (1962) 🖿
Yiddish novelist of cosmic scope and vision, Singer exhibits "traditional" motifs and psychological acuity, Dickensian detail; *The Family Moskat* deals, with Tolstoyan range and certainty, with a ghetto family and its slow disintegration and advance into (1939) modernity; *The Magician of Lublin* and *The Slave* are less "modern" in tone, but are both specific in their Eastern European setting and "mythic" in timeless morality. The "foreignness" of Singer's world seems opaque at first but soon yields images and scenes of dramatic clarity and force. See
FICTION/SHORT STORIES

Smollett, Tobias *The Expedition of Humphrey Clinker* (1771) 🖃
Smollett's medical training is visible in the scatological frankness of this amiably robust epistolary novel. Humphrey is an ostler—prefiguring Dickens' Sam Weller—attendant on a family journeying through England and Scotland.

Snow, C. P. *The Masters* (1951)
Jewel in a sometimes wooden crown, *The Masters* is part of Snow's sequence, *Strangers and Brothers*, but stands happily independent as a solemn but convincing account of the struggle to succeed the Master of a Cambridge college.

Spark, Muriel *Memento Mori* (1959); *The Prime of Miss Jean Brodie* (1961) 🏛
Febrile with tart phrases, Spark's work glitters with unnerving, sometimes chilling ironies. Catholic ideology informs satirical fables. *Memento Mori* concerns old people seeking to forget—and being reminded of—the inevitable; *The Prime of Miss Jean Brodie* famously, if thinly celebrates a sacred monster of a school teacher and her girls in 1930s Edinburgh.

Stead, Christina *House of All Nations* (1938)
Mammoth compendium of characters and cases, of swindlers and swingers in the world of a private bank in Paris between the two wars, with hints of Stavisky and other scandals. A curious and often facile, even Fascistic attitude towards the financial establishment sours but cannot spoil a talent furious at human duplicity and shallowness. The novel as mural.

Steinbeck, John *The Grapes of Wrath* (1939)   ★
This masterpiece easily transcends its melodramatic crudities. The Joad family's desperate emigration from the dust-bowl to California opened eyes to the plight of the "Okies", poor farmers; retains vividness and heartfelt warmth. See DIARIES; TRAVEL

Stendhal *The Red and the Black* (1830); *The Charterhouse of Parma* (1839)
Rise and fall of Julien Sorel makes a great novel of ambition in a France open to all talents, including shameless romantic premeditation. *The Charterhouse of Parma* has a more splendid hero in Fabrizio del Dongo and though less readable is luminous with political fireworks and contains a puncturingly "modern" passage describing the Battle of Waterloo. Good translations: *The Red and the Black* by Shaw (1953); *The Charterhouse of Parma* by Blair (1960). See LITERARY CRITICISM

Sterne, Laurence *The Life and Opinions of Tristram Shandy* (1760–67)
Sterne, a bucolic vicar, scandalized Dr Johnson, Goldsmith and others, with *Tristram Shandy*; modern readers may wonder why. Picaresque; long; idiosyncratic; a maverick to be enjoyed piecemeal, save by addicts of Irishness or the picaresque. See TRAVEL

Storey, David *This Sporting Life* (1960)
A seminal work in the emancipation of the English post-war novel from a largely metropolitan and intellectual ambience. The use of rugby league football as a metaphor for the life-struggle presages the sports-mad sixties and seventies. A tendency to live in the shadow of D. H. Lawrence renders this and Storey's later work somewhat sunless.

Styron, William *The Long March* (1962); *The Confessions of Nat Turner* (1967); *Sophie's Choice* (1979)
The Long March is the shortest and best of Styron's occasional, ponderous work. It describes the conflict between the liberal and the authoritarian through the image of a training march in which the liberal seeks to prove himself through self-destructive endurance. The other two novels deal with Big Issues—race and Auschwitz—with a discursive thoroughness that attempts to rehabilitate the Novel With A Purpose. Blacks resented the one, Jews described the other as "Auschwitz meets Playboy magazine". Styron is earnest and sexy, and earnestly sexy.

Svevo, Italo *As a Man Grows Older (Senilità)* (1898); *The Confessions of Zeno* (1923)   ★
Wry, self-deprecating satires of provincial life: Zeno's confessions are prompted by a desire to give up smoking. Svevo died in a road accident in 1928, asking in vain for a smoke. "That really would have been a last cigarette," he said, and died, a character of his own creation.

Swift, Jonathan *Gulliver's Travels* (1726)
Is *Gulliver's Travels* a novel? Can you play chess without the queen? Cardinal example of satire fully realized as fantasy, or scorn gilding witty imagination; self-justifying world of big and small unfolded and decorated to the point where a political tract of trenchant ferocity can serve as a children's classic. For grown-ups, its bite may be more obvious.

Thackeray, William Makepeace *Vanity Fair* (1847); *The Newcomes* (1853)
Vanity Fair is Thackeray's masterpiece, with Becky Sharp a superbly seductive villainess, the whole glamorous tale as sharp as she with satirical energy. *The Newcomes* is more tender, but lacks Dickens' exuberant sentimentality.

Tolstoy, Leo *War and Peace* (1866); *Anna Karenina* (1875–77)
Two great novels, one flawed by its scope, the other by its schematic morality, both instinct with genius. Much is said to be lost in translation; a world remains. *War and Peace* is a masterpiece of realism, sparkling with characters and only occasionally rendered tedious by the philosophical special pleading of which Tolstoy became a compulsive victim. Though *Anna Karenina* is unbalanced by the sentimental falseness of the relationship between the Levins (to which Tolstoy's flight from marriage in old age is a sort of bitter pendant), Anna's beauty and fineness of character, Vronsky's heartless tenderness and the odious, touching Karenin constitute a triangle for eternity. See BIOGRAPHY (Troyat); LITERARY CRITICISM

Treece, Henry *Electra* (1963)
Superb evocation of the dust and cruelty of ancient Greece, a vision unadorned with marbled afterthoughts; inspired empathy with a wild girl who imagines herself Electra. See CHILDREN'S BOOKS

Trilling, Lionel *The Middle of the Journey* (1947) ✱
Sole novel by pundit of American liberalism. Famous fictionalization of
Whittaker Chambers (accuser of Alger Hiss); lucid analysis of intellectual and
political postures in the thirties. See LITERARY CRITICISM

Twain, Mark *Huckleberry Finn* (1885) 📖
Huckleberry Finn is no more a children's book than is *Gulliver's Travels*, although
children read and love both. The freedom Huck seeks—like the hero of every
Great American novel—is found not in the wilderness, the West, but on the
smooth free-flowing river, the Mississippi, down which he journeys on a raft with
the escaped slave, Jim. By adults, Twain is as underrated as Swift. See
FICTION/SHORT STORIES; HISTORY/AMERICAN; HUMOUR; TRAVEL

Updike, John *Couples* (1968); *Rabbit, Run* (1961)
The sexual *malaises* and *mêlées* of middle-class New England have provided
Updike with his narrow world, which he details with merciless, narcissistic
pointillism. He is a literary dandy, in the Nabokov tradition, whose *Couples* is a
display of shameless virtuosity. The *Rabbit* books show that he can play equally
well away from home, in the lower middle class world of Rabbit, a randy failure.

Voltaire *Candide* (1759) 📖
Not a novel? Then so much the worse for the novel. Dr Pangloss is the great,
absurd antidote to chiliastic and Leibnitzian optimism. The gardener's supreme
licence ("Cultivate!") begins here. See BIOGRAPHY (Mitford)

Warren, Robert Penn *Night Rider* (1938)
Poet and Southern agrarian, Warren deals with scandals—of violence and
corruption, with neat sexual twists—but in a formal, didactic style where literary
skill contrives an inadvertent apology for depicted guilt. Also: *All the King's Men*

Waugh, Evelyn *Decline and Fall* (1928); *A Handful of Dust* (1934);
Brideshead Revisited (1945); *Sword of Honour* (3 vols, 1952–55) ★
Waugh's pre-war novels are ruthless romps; *Sword of Honour* attempts more
serious socio-political appraisal, but is more memorable for Ritchie-Hook and
the thunderbox than for "mature" passages, though it contains a notable account
of cowardice and collapse in Crete. *Brideshead Revisited* is a lushly-written
encomium on old Catholic British families and Waugh's Oxford generation,
teddy-bears and all.

Weidman, Jerome *Fourth Street East* (1971)
Weidman's characters began life as poor immigrant Jews in 1920s New York;
now, as affluent, compromised and compromising adults, they look back at their
past with rose-tinted spectacles and notably beady eyes. A prolific, consistent
novelist of wit and charm. Also: *I Can Get It for You Wholesale*; *The Enemy
Camp*; *Other People's Money*, etc

Wells, H. G. *Kipps* (1905); *The History of Mr Polly* (1910)
Wells, in his own estimation, was always journalist, never Jamesian artist. He
wrote quickly, but his accounts of lower middle-class British life at the turn of the
century are cheeky and truthful. See FICTION/SF; HISTORY/WORLD

Welty, Eudora *Delta Wedding* (1946)
Decorous, scintillating portrayal of Mississippi aristocratic family in the 1920s.
Nobody is better at capturing Southern dialogue and mannerisms. The Jane
Austen of the South?

West, Nathanael *Miss Lonelyhearts* (1933); *The Day of the Locust*
(1939) ★
Terse, mordant satires on American life. *Miss Lonelyhearts* lampoons the bogus
sympathy of newspapers for readers' agonies; *The Day of the Locust* depicts
Hollywood as a sumptuous hell. West matches Fitzgerald for sharpness, beats
him for sophistication.

Wharton, Edith *The Custom of the Country* (1913); *The Age of
Innocence* (1920) ★
Put down as a clumsy Henry James (qv), Wharton's uncertain origins stoked her
prodigious snobbery, but made her an acute observer of "old New York"
families. *The Custom of the Country* is a readable, cunningly plotted portrait of a
less than ladylike adventuress, sharply funny; *The Age of Innocence* looks
engagingly back on childhood among grand families in "Edwardian" New York.
Also: *The House of Mirth*

White, Patrick *Voss* (1957); *Riders in the Chariot* (1961)
The Australian novelist, with *Voss*—an account of a doomed explorer crossing
the continent in the 1880s—his masterwork; *Rider in the Chariot* attempts
grandiloquently and majestically to grapple with anti-Semitism.

Wilde, Oscar *The Picture of Dorian Gray* (1891) 📖
Wilde said he put genius into life, talent into work. *The Picture of Dorian Gray* is a
talented shocker, ridiculously brilliant with epigrams but haunted by a sense of
doom which, with cruel punctuality, was later to ruin Wilde's own life. See
BIOGRAPHY (Hyde); DIARIES; DRAMA

Wolfe, Thomas *Look Homeward, Angel* (1929) 📖
Logorrhoeic Great American Novel. Standard themes of boyhood—in North
Carolina—and escape into more worldly circles, decorated with interminably

brilliant dialogue and nostalgia for exuberance of a once suffocating family and provincial life. Wolfe's autobiographical novels repeat these themes with surfeiting effect. Also: *You Can't Go Home Again*, etc

Woolf, Virginia *Mrs Dalloway* (1925); *The Waves* (1931) ◗ ★
Boom in crying Woolf makes her essential if less mysterious reading now than when her "envelopes of consciousness" seemed filled with some rarer sense of life than any common reader could contrive. *Mrs Dalloway* echoes Joycean innovation and, like *Ulysses*, covers one day in its heroine's life. *The Waves* is marvellous: a richly brocaded poetic tapestry, close-patterned with Bloomsbury figures. Also: *To the Lighthouse*; *The Voyage Out*; *Night and Day*, etc. See BIOGRAPHY (Bell, Woolf); DIARIES; FEMINISM

Wright, Richard *Native Son* (1940)
Classic of Negro life in Chicago slums seen, through the life of Bigger Thomas, without sentiment or apology; implied indictment of white world. Wright's later work is explicitly polemical; *Native Son*, with *Invisible Man* (Ellison, qv), is a crucial novel in the statement of the black claim.

Yourcenar, Marguerite *Memoirs of Hadrian* (1959)
The Emperor Hadrian had Greek sensitivity in a Roman mind, Christian aspirations in a pagan soul. He is the bridge between the ancient world and ours. Yourcenar's novel "ghosts" his memoirs in fine French style.

Zola, Émile *Nana* (1880); *Germinal* (1885) ★
Nana is a sensational, purportedly "naturalistic" account of the *belle époque* in Paris as revealed by the lurid career of a striptease artist who strips more than she teases. Its sexual frankness shocked and delighted readers less enchanted with *Germinal*, a much better book, which portrayed with terrible, wilful and "scientific" honesty the life of a mining village in the great age of unrestricted capitalism. See DIARIES (Goncourt)

Science Fiction

Aldiss, Brian *Hothouse* (1962)
Interesting dramatization of major science fiction theme; what happens when elements that man takes for granted are turned topsy-turvy. In this case the earth's atmosphere becomes overheated and mankind has to sweat it out. Also: *Billion Year Spree* (history of the genre); *Frankenstein Unbound*; *The Malacia Tapestry*, etc

Asimov, Isaac *The Foundation Trilogy* (1951) 📖
Asimov is one of the great names in modern science fiction; his enormous output tends to slapdash chatter in later books, but here he was at full stretch. Also: *Nightfall and Other Stories*; *The Gods Themselves*; *The Caves of Steel*, etc. See MATHEMATICS

Ballard, J. G. *The Terminal Beach* (1964) 🐚
These stories, by Britain's master of SF alienation and disaster, have the clarity of obsession which is more diluted in his other work. Also: *The Atrocity Exhibition*; *The Drowned World*; *Vermilion Sands*, etc

Bester, Alfred *Tiger! Tiger!* (1957) ★
Also known as *The Stars My Destination*. One of the cult books of the field. Lurid adventures and vengeance of Gully Foyle, bane of the 24th century. Ingenious, surrealist fun. Also: *The Demolished Man*

Blish, James *A Case of Conscience* (1958) ★
Sense of morality perfectly matches SF ideas: Blish invents an alien race with no sense of good or evil and therefore considered "in a state of sin" by religious zealot, very disturbing. Also: *And All the Stars a Stage*; *The Day after Judgement*; *Cities in Flight*, etc

Bradbury, Ray *The Martian Chronicles* (1950)
Although Bradbury's prose sometimes seems empurpled, his consistent sense of the poetry of man's search for new frontiers, both inside and outside himself, has attracted many who might not consider themselves SF readers. Also: *Fahrenheit 451*; *The Golden Apples of the Sun*; *The Illustrated Man*, etc

Clarke, Arthur C. *Childhood's End* (1953) ★
Clarke's vision of humanity eventually becoming godlike reached its ultimate in the film *2001: A Space Odyssey*. But *Childhood's End* expresses this view with even more coherence; it is remarkable for its compassion. Also: *Imperial Earth*; *Rendezvous with Rama*; *Fountains of Paradise*, etc. See MATHEMATICS

Dick, Philip K. *The Man in the High Castle* (1962) ★
Beautifully organized novel postulating an alternative world in which the Axis powers won World War II. One of modern SF's great books. Also: *The Three Stigmata of Palmer Eldritch*; *Martian Time-slip*; *A Scanner Darkly*, etc

Harrison, Harry *Make Room! Make Room!* (1966)
Prolific (and variable) author's best if not funniest novel, later filmed as *Soylent Green*. Set in a teeming New York, where people, regardless of the pressure of space, will not stop reproducing. Also: *Bill: The Galactic Hero*; *The Technicolor Time Machine*; *The Stainless Steel Rat*, etc

Heinlein, Robert A. *Stranger in a Strange Land* (1961)
Heinlein is the guru of SF conservatism, yet this book (preaching what appeared to be free-choice and free-love) was adopted by the hippies of the 1960s, even becoming a "bible" for killer Charles Manson and his family. The message, though, was much more rigorous than they thought. Also: *Starship Troopers*, etc
Herbert, Frank *Dune* (1965)
Dune is a planet in a far off time and a far off system on the extreme edge of aridity—water is more precious than diamonds; an entire culture is based on water scarcity rather than on water plenty. Technically superb in its details, the book is also a masterful thriller.
Le Guin, Ursula K. *The Left Hand of Darkness* (1969)
Le Guin has a poetic sensibility; this study of a world called "Winter" and the sexual life of its inhabitants is a stunning creation. Also: *The Lathe of Heaven*; *Planet of Exile*; *The Dispossessed*. See CHILDREN'S BOOKS
Lem, Stanislaw *Solaris* (1971)
Story of a planet which is a sentient creature, capable of creating duplicates from the memories of the earth people who visit it; made into a haunting film. Also: *The Cyberiad*; *The Invincible*
Lewis, C. S. *Out of the Silent Planet* (1938)
One of Lewis's attempts to charge SF ideas with Christian principles. Not always liked by SF buffs, its popularity has nevertheless brought many readers into the fold (of the genre). Also: *Perelandra*; *That Hideous Strength*. See CHILDREN'S BOOKS; RELIGION
Miller, Walter M., Jr. *A Canticle for Leibowitz* (1960)
Awesome account of post-apocalypse world and the Second Coming, immaculately conceived in SF terms; postulates the Church as a repository of technological secrets from a past civilization now regarded as sacred writings. Also: *Conditionally Human*
Moorcock, Michael *The Final Programme* (1968)
The "wild man" of British science fiction, claims that the apocalypse is now. One of many novels starring Moorcock's anti-hero Jerry Cornelius. Also: *The English Assassin*; *A Cure for Cancer*; *Gloriana*, etc
Pohl, F. and **Kornbluth, C. M.** *The Space Merchants* (1953)
The authors were exercised about how consumers are manipulated by conglomerates. In this novel, Venus is being carved up by advertising agents. Madison Avenue lives—out there! Also: *Slave Ship*; *Drunkard's Walk*; *Gateway* (all by Pohl)
Stapledon, Olaf *Last and First Men* (1930)
Stapledon had vast ideas; this account of the human species swings through millennia as though they were skittles. Also: *Sirius*; *Odd John*; *Star Maker*, etc
Van Vogt, A. E. *The Voyage of the Space Beagle* (1950)
Van Vogt's apocalyptic prose is easily parodied; but his ideas, as in this episodic story of a space ship threading through space, are fascinating. Also: *The Weapon Shops of Isher*; *The World of Null-A*
Verne, Jules *Journey to the Centre of the Earth* (1864)
One of the great precursors of modern SF takes one of the great precursory themes, despatching his explorers on a trip which includes Atlantis, Iceland, prehistory and a packet of lecturing. Also: *From the Earth to the Moon*; *20,000 Leagues under the Sea*; *Around the World in Eighty Days*
Vonnegut, Kurt, Jr. *The Sirens of Titan* (1959)
Cascade of elegantly loony invention, set on more than one heavenly body. Cynical explanations for just about everything (including Stonehenge and the Great Wall of China) well-wrapped in a neat plot. Hellishly funny—Vonnegut before he was taken up by everyone and went soft. Also: *Player Piano*; *Cat's Cradle*; *Slaughterhouse 5*, etc
Wells, H. G. *The Time Machine* (1895)
This marvellous story contains much of Wells' genius; science made plausible and shaped to the needs of mankind. Also: *The Invisible Man*; *The Shape of Things to Come*; *The First Men in the Moon*. See FICTION/NOVELS; HISTORY/WORLD
Wyndham, John *The Day of the Triffids* (1951)
Through mankind's negligence—not to mention sudden world-wide blindness—large perambulating hunks of vegetation take over the British Isles. Fine example of the English Cosy Catastrophe School. Also: *The Kraken Wakes*; *The Midwich Cuckoos*; *The Crysalids*

Short Stories

See HUMOUR (Daudet, Lardner, O'Brien, Runyon); MUSIC (Wagner); MYTHOLOGY (Feldman, Gantz, Hatto, Malory, Sandars, Thomas); SEX (Boccaccio, Nefzawi)

Aesop *Fables* (6th century BC)
Aesop was a slave on the Greek island of Samos; either as moral metaphors or as "absurdities" his fables are unsurpassed.

Agnon, S. Y. *The Bridal Canopy* (1922)
Bleak, dark visions: purgation of emotions by pity and despair. Nonetheless, fine, springing prose. Also: *Two Tales*; *And the Crooked Shall Be Made Straight*; *In the Heart of the Seas*, etc

Anderson, Sherwood *Winesburg, Ohio* (1919)
Anderson, one-time manager of an Ohio paint factory, knew his material inside out. These 23 stories present, in straightforward, intense style, moments in the lives of inhabitants of the kind of small town in which he grew up. Also: *Poor White*; *Death in the Woods*; *The Memoirs of Sherwood Anderson*

Babel, Isaak *Collected Stories* (1957)   🏛
Babel, born in the Odessa ghetto, died in one of Stalin's concentration camps. His stories are brief and vivid, his viewpoint that of a Jew "with spectacles on his nose and autumn in his heart".

Beckett, Samuel *More Pricks than Kicks* (1934)   ℘
Beckett's first work of fiction consists of ten stories. Most are laboriously overwritten, as early work by important writers often is, but *Dante and the Lobster* is brilliant, and there is grim humour in several of the others. See DRAMA; FICTION/NOVELS; LITERARY CRITICISM

Bierce, Ambrose *Tales of Soldiers and Civilians* (1891)
Bierce disappeared into Mexico in 1913—in search, he said, of "the good, kind darkness". Reasons for such a wish can be found here: sardonic wit barely conceals despair. Also: *Can Such Things Be?*

Borges, Jorge Luis *Fictions* (1944)   ℘ ★
Terse, teasing, sometimes intriguing *jeux d'esprit* by a writer whose favourite joke is the reader. Also: *Labyrinths*; *Dreamtigers*; *Selected Poems, 1923–1967*

Bowles, John *Collected Short Stories* (1980)
Unnerving, mannered but savagely effective tales of violence at the boundary between civilization and its discontented neighbours. The interface of love and lust, impotence and insolence, exhaustion and delirium is charted with a terrible relish and conviction.

Cheever, John *The Stories of John Cheever* (1978)   🏛
Evocative stories about quietly desperate New York commuters: wives meeting the train with a double Martini in the hand; children, all-knowing, concocting fiendish plots. Somehow the stories have coloured everyone's concept of the suburban life of all America, even though most Americans don't live that way.

Chekhov, Anton *The Schoolmistress and Other Stories* (1894)   📖
Chekhov wrote over 1,000 stories. Mood, atmosphere, "the unforgettable flash of life in its perpetual flow"—no short story writer ever caught these things better. See DRAMA

Chesterton, G. K. *The Father Brown Stories* (1947)   🏛
Chesterton's Father Brown stories are outstanding in an uneven *oeuvre*—his one escape from being what Wyndham Lewis (justly) called him, "the dogmatic Toby–jug". Also: *The Man Who Was Thursday*

Conrad, Joseph *The Heart of Darkness* (1902)   ★
Conrad's most compelling short story, flawed by melodramatic adjectives but still alive and horrifying. See FICTION/NOVELS

Dinesen, Isak *Seven Gothic Tales* (1934)
Sophisticated entertainments, with appealing irony implicit in deliberately old-fashioned narrative method. Also: *Out of Africa*; *Winter's Tales*; *The Angelic Avengers*, etc

Faulkner, William *Collected Stories* (1950)   ★
There is a story that Sherwood Anderson, having read some would-be sophisticated dialogue in one of Faulkner's earliest novels, told him to forget all that smart stuff and concentrate on cultivating his own garden, the little patch of Mississippi he knew to the bone. The result was the major novels, and the best stories in this book, *The Bear* and *The Barn Burning*. See FICTION/NOVELS

Fitzgerald, F. Scott *The Stories of F. Scott Fitzgerald* (1951)   🏛
Fitzgerald himself once commented (looking sideways at his friend and rival, Hemingway): "I talk with the authority of failure." He wrote good stories all his life—along with many bad ones for magazines, to pay debts. Among lesser-known stories, *Outside the Cabinet-Maker's* is well worth seeking out. See BIOGRAPHY (Milford); DIARIES; FICTION/NOVELS; FILM (Latham)

Flaubert, Gustave *Three Tales* (1877)   🏛
Twenty years after *Madame Bovary*, Flaubert published these stories. *The Legend of St Julian Hospitator* is the most remarkable—an exploration of the medieval mind, inspired by a stained-glass window in Rouen Cathedral. See DIARIES (Flaubert, Goncourt); FICTION/NOVELS

Grimm, Jacob and **Wilhelm** *Household Tales* (1812–15)   ★
The brothers Grimm were a well-matched pair; from their two heads came the right balance to make sense of something in the German character that takes in *The Bremen Town Musicians*, *The Twelve Dancing Princesses* and the glorious ghastly death of *Rumpelstiltskin*. Best collection for adults: Penguin Classics. Best for children: *The Juniper Tree and Other Tales* (Segal and Sendak, 1973).

Hawthorne, Nathaniel *Twice-told Tales* (1837) 🗿
Thirty-nine early stories, some mannered and boring, but the best— *The Ambitious Guest* and *Howe's Masquerade*—foreshadowing *The Scarlet Letter* in their preoccupation with guilt and secrecy and in their obsession with the effects of New England Puritanism. Also: *House of the Seven Gables*; *Tanglewood Tales*, etc. See FICTION/NOVELS

Hemingway, Ernest *In Our Time* (1925) ★
Hemingway's first book—fifteen stories with linking vignettes. The stories describe life in the American Middle West; vignettes describe war in Europe and bullfights. Hemingway before the rot set in. Also: *Men without Women*; *Winner Takes Nothing*, etc. See BIOGRAPHY (Baker); FICTION/NOVELS

Henry, O. *Cabbages and Kings* (1904) 🗿
O. Henry started writing the "trick" stories for which he is famous while in prison on a charge of embezzlement. His characters are simple; his plots always depend on surprise endings; but within his range he is skilled at ringing the changes. Also: *O. Henry Encore*; *The Four Million*, etc

Hoffmann, Ernst Theodor Wilhelm *The Serapion Brethren* (1819–21) ℗
The best of his supernatural stories. Urbane, Gallic Poe-try. Also: *The Devil's Elixir*

Isherwood, Christopher *Goodbye to Berlin* (1939) ★
Herr Issyvoo in his best "I am a camera" phase: decay of a civilization (Germany under the Nazis) in the form of seemingly casual sketches of Berlin life. Also: *All the Conspirators*; *Mr Norris Changes Trains*, etc. See DRAMA (Auden)

James, Henry *The Turn of the Screw* (1898) 📄
One of the finest ghost stories in English, all the better for containing no explicit ghosts. See BIOGRAPHY (Edel, James); DIARIES; FICTION/NOVELS; LITERARY CRITICISM

James, M. R. *Collected Ghost Stories* (1931) 🗿
Elegant, civilized shudders—not the melodramas of Poe (qv), but reality showing tiny, devastating cracks. Best read by candlelight, wind nibbling at the windows.

Joyce, James *Dubliners* (1914)
One story, *The Dead*, is a masterpiece. The rest would perhaps not seem so interesting now, had Joyce not gone on to write *Ulysses* and *Finnegan's Wake*. All the same, a remarkable dissection of turn-of-the-century Irish life. See BIOGRAPHY (Ellmann); DIARIES; FICTION/NOVELS

Kafka, Franz *Metamorphosis* (1916) ★
Kafka's most haunting story, in which he found a perfect image for his pervasive sense of alienation. Also: *In the Penal Colony*, etc. See DIARIES; FICTION/NOVELS

Kipling, Rudyard *Limits and Renewals* (1932)
The Kipling to value—estranged, embittered and burnt-out. This last collection of stories contains his most complex, self-gnawing work. See CHILDREN'S BOOKS; POETRY

Lardner, Ring *Collected Short Stories* (1941) ★
Edmund Wilson once said, "What bell might not Lardner ring if he set out to give us the works?" Lardner *did* give us the works. In the vernacular. There must have been something wrong with Wilson's bell. See HUMOUR

Lawrence, D. H. *Tales* (1934) ★
Lawrence at his finest. *Odour of Chrysanthemums* and *The Rocking-Horse Winner* are the most memorable; but all are interesting, surprisingly relaxed, even amusing. See DIARIES; FICTION/NOVELS; HISTORY/EUROPEAN; LITERARY CRITICISM; POETRY; TRAVEL

London, Jack *The Star Rover* (1914)
How to define London's gift? "The passing thing done in the eternal way" was his own (not bad) definition of it. Also: *The Call of the Wild*; *White Fang*. See TRAVEL

Lowry, Malcolm *Hear Us O Lord from Heaven Thy Dwelling Place* (1961)
Lowry's gift was for loading every rift with ore, or at least tequila; this posthumously published collection contains two stories— *Through the Panama* and *The Forest Path to the Spring*. See FICTION/NOVELS

Mann, Thomas *Death in Venice* (1911) 📄
Masterly novella of a civilized artist at the end of his genteel tether. Also: *Stories of a Lifetime*. See FICTION/NOVELS

Mansfield, Katherine *Collected Stories* (1945)
Mansfield's best stories, many about her childhood in New Zealand. See DIARIES

Maugham, W. Somerset *Complete Stories* (1951) ★
Maugham is the nearest thing to an English Maupassant (qv). Man-of-the-world stuff, cynical and anecdotal. Edmund Wilson compared his stories to oysters (for the ease with which they slip down). See AUTOBIOGRAPHY; DRAMA; FICTION/CRIME; FICTION/NOVELS

Maupassant, Guy de *Boule de Suif* (1880) ▧
Maupassant contributed this masterly story while still unknown to the *Soirées de Médan*, a collection of short stories by such as Zola and Huysmans. It made his reputation overnight. He is, with Chekhov (qv) and Singer (qv) one of the supreme masters in the genre. Also: *Mademoiselle Fifi*; *A Woman's Life*; *Bel-Ami*, etc

Moore, George *Celibate Lives* (1924)
Five stories, one of which, *Albert Nobbs*, a study of transvestism, was recently ranked "in the first dozen short stories of world literature". This overstates the case, but then Moore is an undervalued writer. Also: *Heloïse and Abelard*; *Evelyn Innes ; The Brook Kerith*, etc

Murasaki-Shikibu, Lady *The Tale of Genji* (c. 1004)
This collection of stories is sometimes spoken of as a novel, but is nearer to *The Arabian Nights* than to *War and Peace*. Prince Genji is the character; the country, Japan. Delicate, obliquely civilized; a masterpiece.

O'Hara, John *The Hat on the Bed* (1964)
O'Hara's stories are legion, and despite the flaws and cheapness, provide a panoramic view of East Coast American society which is proving more and more truthful as the lid comes off the USA. Ephemera, possibly; compelling, certainly. See FICTION/NOVELS

Pirandello, Luigi *Better Think Twice about It* (1933)
Pirandello was once called "the greatest short-story writer of the century". If his plays did not exist, we might value his stories more highly, for their worth is considerable. See DRAMA

Poe, Edgar Allan *Tales of the Grotesque and Macabre* (1840) 📖
Twenty-five tales include *The Fall of the House of Usher*, *William Wilson*, *Ligeia*, *Berenice* and *Manuscript Found in a Bottle*. Also: *The Narrative of Arthur Gordon Pym of Nantucket*; *Poems*; *Eureka*, etc. See FICTION/CRIME

Runyon, Damon *Guys and Dolls* (1932) 🏛
Runyon perfected the use of a certain kind of invented slang in these stories about New York hoods, their mommas and their molls. His stories seem slight and forgettable, but aren't. Also: *Take It Easy*; *My Wife Ethel*; *Runyon à la Carte*. See HUMOUR

Saki *The Best of Saki* (1976) 🏛
H. H. Munro called himself "Saki" after a South African monkey characterized by a long bushy tail, delicacy and silence. His stories send up everything in sight. Bushy tales? Also: *The Unbearable Bassington*

Saroyan, William *The Daring Young Man on the Flying Trapeze* (1934) 🏛
Saroyan's first book, an astonishing outpouring by a young man in love with life and language.

Singer, Isaac Bashevis *Gimpel the Fool* (1957) ▧
Marvellous, timeless blend of medieval and modern imagination: the human condition defined and described by a master story-teller, delighted by the teeming detail which makes up a moment. Also: *A Crown of Feathers*; *A Friend of Kafka*, etc. See FICTION/NOVELS

Stein, Gertrude *Three Lives* (1908) ○
In *Melanctha*, about a black woman, Stein showed for the first (and last?) time just how well she could write fiction. Her prose rhythms admirably follow the movements of Melanctha's mind. After this, Stein concentrated on the movement of her own mind—and turned into Old Mother Hubbard.

Stevenson, Robert Louis *The Strange Case of Dr Jekyll and Mr Hyde* (1886) 📖
Stevenson's wife Fanny read this tale in draft and complained that he had sensationalized a good allegory. Stevenson enraged, stormed out; then he returned, said she was right and set to work to produce this classic story of split personality. See CHILDREN'S BOOKS

Turgenev, Ivan Sergeyevich *A Sportsman's Sketches* (1852) ★
Sketches of 19th-century Russian peasant life characterized by what V. S. Pritchett called "their simple feeling and transparency". Also: *The House of Gentlefolk*; *On the Eve*; *Virgin Soil*, etc

Twain, Mark *The Celebrated Jumping Frog of Calaveras County and Other Sketches* (1865)
Interesting mostly for the way it foreshadows Twain's superb use of the vernacular in *The Adventures of Tom Sawyer* and *The Adventures of Huckleberry Finn*. Title piece, based on an old Californian folk tale, still has charm. See FICTION/NOVELS; HISTORY/AMERICAN; HUMOUR; TRAVEL

Wilson, Angus *Such Darling Dodos* (1950)
Splendid trifles of 1940s–1950s British life. The world of the sensitive middle class and genteel England were never the same again. Nor was Wilson, to our loss.

Zoshchenko, Mikhail *Scenes from the Bathhouse* (1961)
Zoshchenko was the (unofficial) satirist-in-chief to the court of the second most terrible utopia in history. This collection of stories is a grin full of teeth.

Film

From the start, cinema established itself as not just another medium, but as one of the great popular art forms, as wide-ranging as literature, music or painting themselves. Like those arts, it contains masterpieces and rubbish, timeless works and ephemera—and a huge range of good-quality journeyman work, popular entertainment which can, at its best, transcend its own modest aspirations. Nowadays, thanks to television showings, films (of all qualities) are accessible as never before, and there is a wide popular knowledge of film styles and techniques; television has not, however, resulted (as was predicted) in the death of creativity, but in a remarkable upsurge of new styles, new talents, new excellence. This list avoids the more arcane areas of film criticism (addicts writing in code for addicts) and also the more fleeting of fan-journalism. We have chosen good serious guides to the medium and to the industry, and biographies, studies and reminiscences of some of the most enjoyable (not to say enjoyably literate) practitioners of film.

See AUTOBIOGRAPHY (Chaplin): BIOGRAPHY (Mailer); DRAMA (McCrindle); HUMOUR (Allen)

Armes, Roy *A Critical History of the British Cinema* (1978) 📖 //
Detailed and informative, if at times rather conventional and opinionated. Avoids chauvinism; covers important ground.

Barnouw, Erik *Documentary: A History of Nonfiction Film* (1974) ♀
Standard work for students, fans and creators of documentary films. History-cum-theory-cum-criticism adds up to an extremely useful compendium.

Bawden, Liz-Anne (ed) *The Oxford Companion to Film* (1976) 📖★//
Authoritative entries, alphabetically arranged, on every aspect of film from "AA certificate" to "Zvoboda, André". Articles on national styles particularly good (Italy and Japan outstanding). Not as jolly or personal as Halliwell (qv), but far more reliable.

Bayer, William *The Great Movies* (1973) 🏛 //
Thoughtful critical assessments of sixty films which in Bayer's view represent the medium at its best and most characteristic. Covers "trash masterpieces" (eg *Gone with the Wind*; *Singin' in the Rain*) as well as films with grander pretensions (*La Grande Illusion*; *Citizen Kane*).

Brown, Karl *Adventures with D. W. Griffith* (1974) //
As a young man of immense technical ingenuity, Brown contributed much to D. W. Griffith's revolutionary discoveries. Interesting to read in conjunction with Mrs D. W. Griffith's (qv) *When the Movies were Young*.

Brownlow, Kevin *The Parade's Gone By* (1968) 🏛📖a★//
Riveting, classic collection of interview portraits of surviving Hollywood pioneers.

Burch, Noel *To a Distant Observer* (1939) ♀//
Japanese film: outstanding study of a "national cinema". Emphasis is on "formal" differences with Western cinema, but shows a strong sense of the political and cultural history that determined these differences. Also: *Theory of Film Practice*

Clarens, Carlos *Horror Movies* (1968) //
Useful survey of a uniquely fascinating genre.

Durgnat, Raymond *A Mirror for England* (1971) ✳
Eccentric, sometimes brilliant historical/sociological work on British cinema.

Eames, John D. *The MGM Story* (1975) 🏛📖//
Sumptuously produced account of every film (1,705 of them) made by this major studio.

Eisenstein, Sergei *The Film Sense* (1942) 📖//
Chiefly important for theories behind Eisenstein's own films—long section on *Alexander Nevsky*—but has profound implications for cinema as a whole. Also: *Film Form*. See Montagu; Septon.

Eisner, Lotte *The Haunted Screen* (1969) ♀//
Classic exploration of German Expressionist cinema, before and after *The Cabinet of Dr Caligari* (1919).

Fields, W. C. *W. C. Fields by Himself: His Intended Autobiography* (1973)
Letters; articles; notes towards an autobiography: beguiling chronicle of an often troubled human being, a dedicated professional and a wonderfully caustic writer, particularly on censors, studio bosses, babies, complaining wives or other health hazards. See Taylor.

Griffith, Mrs D. W. *When the Movies Were Young* (1925)
A wide-eyed, wickedly scandalous account of movie-making in the 1910s.
Rubbish? Fun. See Brown.

Halliday, Jon *Sirk on Sirk* (1972)
Important journeyman director interviewed at length. Fascinating insights into
studio production conditions in Hollywood.

Halliwell, Leslie *The Filmgoer's Companion* (1965)   🏛 **a** ★ ⫻
Cheerful reference book (regularly updated), unreliable in details but readier
with information on personalities and such questions as who was the first Tarzan
than any other source.

Kael, Pauline *I Lost It at the Movies* (1966)
Useful collection of reviews and articles by one of America's most effective, not
to say raucous, film critics. Kael is challenging, abrasive and personal—a
welcome antidote to stuffiness or picayune blandness. (But avoid *The Citizen
Kane Book*: a piece of nonsense claiming that Welles didn't create *Kane*,
subsequently discredited by Peter Bogdanovitch among others.) These pieces
show her at her perceptive/irritating best.

Knight, Arthur *The Liveliest Art* (1957)
This informal history of the movies, with emphasis on the early days in
Hollywood, is a splendid introduction to the subject. Easy reading, lots of fun.

Latham, Aaron *Crazy Sundays: F. Scott Fitzgerald in Hollywood*
(1972)
Terrible case history of Hollywood's ability to humiliate a creative artist
(compare with Tom Dardis: *Some Time in the Sun*). See BIOGRAPHY
(Milford); DIARIES (Fitzgerald); FICTION/NOVELS (Fitzgerald, West);
FICTION/SHORT STORIES (Fitzgerald)

Leyda, Jay *Kino: A History of the Russian and Soviet Film* (1960)   ⌇ ⫻
Excellent, comprehensive record of the troubled history of cinema in the Soviet
Union. Essential background reading to Eisenstein (qv); the story continues in
Liehm (qv).

Liehm, A. J. and **M.** *The Most Important Art: East European Cinema
after 1945* (1977)   ⌇ ⫻
The only account of the—often Orwellian—mechanisms of film industries in the
Sovietist east. Also: *The Milos Forman Stories* (1976)

Love, Bessie *From Hollywood with Love* (1977)
Funny, unpretentious memoirs of 65 years in movies. Love is reliable, and sharp:
she remembers, for example, how the orthodox Jews who played in *Intolerance*
found their box lunches full of ham sandwiches.

McCabe, John *Charlie Chaplin* (1978)
Writings on Chaplin are legion; this is one of the few (and first) objective, critical
biographies. Also: *Laurel and Hardy* (1975), a sumptuous picture book, with
stills from every film. See Mast; AUTOBIOGRAPHY (Chaplin)

Mast, Gerald *The Comic Mind* (1973)   🏛 ▐ ★ ⫻
Accessible, outstanding study of creativity in comic films. Fine contribution to a
neglected field. Bonus for readers is the lively, enthusiastic style: Mast blends
description with analysis, relives each scene, each routine, as he discusses it.

Mellen, Joan *Big Bad Wolves: Masculinity in the American Film*
(1977)   ▐
Serious—but hugely entertaining—study of the Hollywood myth-machine at
work on great romantic male stars, and on the sometimes limp reality behind the
macho mask. A model of how to make a movie book: it's well researched, well
written, and beautifully salts gossip with objective criticism.

Milne, Tom (ed) *Godard on Godard* (1972)   ⌇ ⫻
Collection of French director Jean Luc Godard's important reviews and articles
from the 1950s and 1960s.

Monaco, J. F. *The New Wave: Truffaut, Chabrol, Rohmer, Rivette*
(1976)
Also: *How to Read a Film*

Montagu, Ivor *With Eisenstein in Hollywood* (1963)
Montagu—film-maker, zoologist, world class table-tennis player, self-
publicizing raconteur—accompanied Eisenstein and his Soviet colleagues during
their often comically disastrous sojourn in Hollywood. A self-regarding, funny
book: *Ninotchka*, in a way, starts here. See Eisenstein; Septon.

Niven, David *The Moon's a Balloon* (1971)
By and large, Hollywood memoirs are little more than pimples on the bottom of
literature. Of late, however, the form has perked up considerably: the memoirs of
Bogarde, Bacall, Maclaine and Love (qv)—and above all those of the urbanely
scurrilous Niven—should easily counter the (directors') view that actors are a
species of cattle. Dinner-table anecdote, it's true—but served as the driest of dry
white wine. Also: *Bring on the Empty Horses*

Parrish, Robert *Growing Up in Hollywood* (1976)
Good, direct account of working in Hollywood by film editor and later director.
Excellent on John Ford, in particular. Gossip, but superior brand.

Perkins, V. F. *Film as Film: Understanding and Judging Movies* (1972) ♀

Pickard, Roy *The Hollywood Studios* (1978)
Well, here it is, folks, Hollywood with the lid off and rarin' to go. It's a large, expensive and gossipy "history", full of names, titles, apocryphal sayings and even the occasional fact. Fun for fans. Also: *The Oscar Movies*

Pudovkin, V. I. *Film Technique and Film Acting* (1958) ♀
A classic study of the aesthetics of film (by one of the great Russian directors), somewhat more accessible than Eisenstein (qv).

Pye, M. and **Myles, L.** *The Movie Generation: How the Film Generation Took Over Hollywood* (1979)
The *coup d'état* when young men with beards and passion for movies moved in on Hollywood. But for how long will Coppola (*Apocalypse Now*), Spielberg (*Jaws*), Lucas (*Star Wars*) *et al* resist becoming their own establishment? Watch for sequels: coming soon.

Ramsaye, Terry *A Million and One Nights* (1926) ⫻
Partial and overcoloured, but still the best, most readable history of early American cinema.

Reisz, K. and **Millar, G.** *The Technique of Film Editing* (1953) ♀
Standard work on this key facet of film making. Some sort of editing is important in all arts, but in none so crucial as cinema, where the editor—often the director—can make the difference between nonsense and genius. Difficult; but for the committed layman, a revelation.

Rhode, Eric *A History of the Cinema* (1976) ★

Rotha, P. and **Griffith, R.** *The Film Till Now* (1930) ▮
An early classic of film scholarship; still worth reading. Regularly updated. Also: *Documentary Film* (Rotha)

Sarris, Andrew *The American Cinema: Directors and Directions 1929–68* (1968)
In this book Sarris presents an eloquent case for the so-called "auteur" theory, holding that the director and/or screen writer are the true creators of the final product and that actors, even if stars, are decidedly secondary. (More recent studies by others have tended to seek a mean between this theory and the earlier one that the star makes the movie.)

Scheuer, Steven H. (ed) *Movies on TV* (1958) ▮ a ★
Reliable critical guide (regularly updated) to 10,000 English-language films.

Septon, Marie *Sergei M. Eisenstein* (1952) ♀
Fat, authoritative biography (revised 1978). See Eisenstein; Montagu.

Shavelson, Melville *How to Make a Jewish Movie* (1971) ▅
A very funny book: the story of the making of *Cast a Giant Shadow* on location in Israel. Biopic of General "Mickey" Marcus, who helped to win the 1948 war, starring those well-known Jewish actors Frank Sinatra, Yul Brynner and John Wayne—plus the entire population of Israel. Hollywood jokes, Jewish jokes, Israeli jokes—what a time they had.

Sklar, Robert *Movie-made America: A Cultural History of American Movies* (1975)
Engagingly written history attempts to show—what is only partly true—that just as America has shaped its movies, so movies have shaped America. An interesting thesis, and relevant by extension to other nations and cultures as well.

Taylor, Robert Lewis *W. C. Fields: His Follies and Fortunes* (1950)
Funny book about a funny man. Should be taken with a ton of salt and read in conjunction with *W. C. Fields by Himself* (qv).

Walker, Alexander *The Shattered Silents* (1978) ▅ ⫻
Blow-by-blow account of the coming of talkies, 1926–29. Exemplary use of first-hand sources; a mine of information and a lively read. Also: *Rudolph Valentino*; *Double Takes*; *Notes and Afterthoughts on the Movies*

Westmore, F. and **Davidson, M.** *The Westmores of Hollywood* (1976)
Who works quietly and unobtrusively behind every Hollywood scene, sees everything, hears everything, says nothing—till now? The makeup man. There have been seven Westmores (father and six sons), each heading the makeup department of a major studio. And what tales they have to tell! Delicious gossip—and the makeup details are fascinating too.

Wolf, W. and **L.** *Landmark Films* (1979) ★
Brilliant critical analyses of thirty-four films (from *The Birth of a Nation*, 1915, to *Seven Beauties*, 1975), placing them in historical and social context (eg *Modern Times* and the Depression; *Deep Throat* and the permissive 70s). Choice of films is excellent; critical tone is serious but not ponderous; the book is challenging on film as a programmatic 20th-century art form.

Ziebold, Norman *The Hollywood Tycoons* (1969)
Amiably tart look at the men who made the movies: Mayer, Laemmle, Goldwyn, Selznick, Cohn, and a dozen more. If this was fiction, who'd believe it?

Food and Drink

The literature of food and drink is extensive, often excellent, and notable for its relaxed, unflurried tone: the rhythms of the kitchen, the maturing pace of the cellar, blended in prose. This list includes technical manuals, historical and sociological monographs, works of philosophy and even ethics—but all of them (perhaps because their subject is of universal interest, universal experience) have an openhanded accessibility not present in the specialist literature of other subjects. Food and drink may be complex matters; but they are also, these books tell us, first and foremost fun. Censors beware! Even Plato approved of the "drinking-bout" as a social lubricant.

See HOME (Grieve)

Adams, Leon D. *The Wines of America* (1973)   📖a
Comprehensive; erudite; readable. Adams is the "dean" of American wine writers.

Amerine, M. A. and **Singleton, V. S.** *Wine: An Introduction for Americans* (1965)   ♀
Something missing from English wine literature: the academic approach. An important reference book for serious students not frightened by a drop or two of chemistry. Also: *Table Wines: The Technology of Their Production*; *Wines: Their Sensory Evaluation*, etc

Apicius *The Art of Cooking* (1st century AD)
Apicius was a millionaire gourmet at the time of the Roman Emperor Tiberius. His book is a complete guide to Roman *cuisine*, with recipes for everything from omelettes to stuffed dormice, pancakes to pine-kernel soup. Good translation (with modern quantities and equivalents, if you want to try recipes): Flower and Rosenbaum: *The Roman Cookery Book* (1958).

Ayrton, Elisabeth *The Cookery of England* (1974)
Fascinating overview of traditional English food, more scholarly than Hartley (qv), more practical than Wilson (qv). Attractive recipes. Also: *English Provincial Cooking*

Beard, James *Beard on Bread* (1973)   a
Excellent, thorough study of breadmaking, together with scores of recipes for different kinds of bread, by a famous US cook whose corpulent figure and smile-wreathed face sell many books. Also: *Beard's American Cookery*; *James Beard's Cookbook*, etc

Beeton, Isabella *The Book of Household Management* (1859–61)   📖a★📖
Probably the most influential British cookery book ever published. The huge 1906 edition is recommended above later ones, more worthy but more dull.

Better Homes and Gardens *The Heritage Cookbook* (1975)   ★
A beautiful book about the history of America's culinary melting pot, with illustrations and over 700 recipes. From the Indians who taught the early settlers how to plant and eat corn to the immigrants who brought their national foods; from how Americans "made do" in the Depression to the bountiful tables of plenty, this is a rich delicious book.

Boxer, Arabella *Garden Cookbook* (1974)
Almost every available herb and vegetable tackled in a lovely collection of recipes emphasizing the infinite possibilities of plants. Also: *First Slice Your Cookbook*; *A Second Slice*. See Conran; Lappe; Stobart; HOME (Grieve)

Bradford, Sarah *The Englishman's Wine* (1969)   📖⫽
Outstanding book on port, its history, nature and quality. Recently (1978) revised, updated and retitled *The Story of Port*.

Bramah, Edward *Tea and Coffee* (1972)   ☕✓
Thorough social history, from coffee-houses to vending machines. Where the plants are—and were—grown, harvested, shipped, distributed. How the drinks were prepared and served in the past, and how best to serve them now. An enthusiast on his passion: engaging, buttonholing style.

Brillat-Savarin, Jean-Anthelme de *The Physiology of Taste* (1826)
World-famous dissertation on gastronomy by non-practising cook. Mouth-watering entertainment. Good translation by M. F. K. Fisher (qv).

Broadbent, Michael *Wine Tasting/Enjoying/Understanding* (1979)   ☕📖
Polished but never snobbish. Common sense in a tricky area.

Carrier, Robert *Great Dishes of the World* (1963)   ⫽
Cooking as show-biz. Carrier's sensuous delight in food is the book's main charm. Also: *The Robert Carrier Cookbook*; *Cooking for You*; *Entertaining*

Chang, Kwang-Chih (ed)   *Food in Chinese Cultures: Anthropological and Historical Perspectives* (1977)   ℗
Scholarly, academic survey of one of the world's greatest cuisines. A long way from the barbecued spare ribs or the bland chop-suey of the West. See ARCHAEOLOGY

Child, Julia   *Julia Child and Company* (1978)   ★
"Company recipes", drawn largely from the famous US television series by "the French chef" (Julia Child), all in her ineffable style—if a chicken falls on the kitchen floor, pick it up, dust it off, and serve it all the same, but with great style and panache. Also: *Mastering the Art of French Cooking; The French Chef Cookbook*, etc

Conran, T. and **Krell, M.**   *The Vegetable Book* (1976)   🏠 ⫻
Sensible book on how to grow and cook all manner of vegetables. See HOME

Crewe, Quentin   *Great Chefs of France* (1978)   🏠 a ★ ⫻
Nobody remotely interested in food and cooking should miss this one. A dozen leading chefs are interviewed, and their style, experience, specialities and creations examined. Recipes and kitchen advice included for those tempted to compete. Also: *International Pocket Food Book*

David, Elizabeth   *French Provincial Cooking* (1960)   📕 a ★ ⫻
Perhaps the most influential cookery book published in Britain since World War II. Careful historical reference enlivened by anecdote and literary references and strengthened by clear personal experience. Fine clear recipes, though timings and liquid contents are sometimes idiosyncratic. Also: *Italian Food; English Bread and Yeast Cookery; Summer Cooking*, etc

Davidson, Alan   *Mediterranean Seafood* (1972)   🏠 📕 a ★ ⫻
Catalogue of all edible Mediterranean fish, illustrated and described with alternative names in up to eight languages. Splendid recipes. Also: *North Atlantic Seafood*

Duff, Gail   *The Vegetarian Cookbook* (1978)   ★
Too many vegetarian cookery books are polemical or defensive tracts. This one isn't: it's a fat, matter-of-fact fact compendium of tasty recipes. No fuss, no flab. Also: *Fresh All the Year*. See Boxer; Conran; Lappe; Stobart; HOME (Grieve)

Eekhof-Stork, Nancy   *The World Atlas of Cheese* (1976)   ✔ ⫻
Mouthwatering: not only a comprehensive introduction to a scholarly subject, but a gorgeous kitchen coffee-table book as well.

Escoffier, Auguste   *Ma Cuisine* (1934)   ★
Escoffier (1847–1935), regarded as one of greatest chefs, worked for sixty-two years in the top hotels of London. In this book he describes his dishes, creations and experience.

Evans, Len   *The Complete Book of Australian Wine* (1973)   📕 a
Every country needs its Evans; only Australia has him.

Faith, Nicholas   *The Winemasters* (1978)
A superb piece of reporting inspired by the Bordeaux scandal of 1973. It takes you further behind the scenes of the wine trade than any other book.

Farmer, Fannie   *The Boston Cooking-School Cookbook* (1896)   ℗
The most influential cookbook in American history started with directions on how to lay a fire, chop wood, bring in water—and other essentials of contemporary New England life. The book is now in its 11th edition (1965), although it has latterly assumed running water in the kitchen. The most recent reincarnation is *Fannie Farmer's New Cookbook* (1979), a complete update of all recipes and revamping of advice, which lacks the true flavour but still gives sound nourishment.

Fisher, M. F. K.   *The Art of Eating* (1954)   ★
Auden once wrote, "this is a book which Colette would have loved and wished she had written". Five of Fisher's books are collected in one volume and include an eclectic collection of recipes as well as some of the tastiest writing on food in English.

Forbes, Patrick   *Champagne* (1967)
Massive, exhaustive. Author after publication entered the trade, and became managing director of Moët Chandon, London.

Guérard, Michel   *Cuisine Minceur* (1976)   📕 ★ ⫻
Top French chef is overweight; grated carrot makes him cry; so he evolves a method of cooking which rejects fat and carbohydrates but embraces the discipline and style of *haute cuisine*. Result: a fashionable classic, neither economical nor austere. Also: *Cuisine Gourmande*

Hartley, Dorothy   *Food in England* (1954)   🏠 ★ ⫻
Social history, mainly through popular English food and recipes. Dating (of quotes and recipes), bibliography, index all hopeless; but still an indispensable book. Also: *The Countryman's England; Water in England; The Land of England*, etc

Hazan, Marcella   *The Classic Italian Cookbook* (1978)   a
Just what its title says: a thorough grounding in the arts of Italian cooking—and eating. Also: *More Classic Italian Cooking*

Hutchinson, Peggy *Old English Cookery* (1939)
Lovely, easygoing book; recipes and background preponderantly Yorkshire and the north of England. Also: *Homemade Wine Secrets*
Jackson, Michael *The World Guide to Beer* (1977)
Jeffs, Julian *Sherry* (1961)   ▮ ⫽
Meticulous; well-researched; authoritative. Also: *The Little Dictionary of Drink*; *The Wines of Europe*
Johnson, Hugh *The World Atlas of Wine* (1971)   🏛▮a★⫽
Magnificent, essential. Also: *Wine*; *Hugh Johnson's Pocket Wine Book*. See HOME
Lappe, Francis Moore *Diet for a Small Planet* (1971)   🏛a⫽
Ecological movements have inspired dozens of dull books; this one by contrast, sets out its case for high-protein, meatless food with care and well-documented argument. Recipes are good, practical and often luscious. See Boxer; Conran; Stobart; HOME (Grieve)
Leonard, Leah W. *Jewish Cookery* (1949)   a⫽
Splendid 600-page collection of (very clear) recipes, ordered by meals of day, days of week, weeks of year. Ideal for beginners; more experienced cooks will also want Florence Greenberg's *Jewish Cookery Book* (1947; 7th revised edition especially recommended).
Lichine, Alexis *Encyclopaedia of Wines and Spirits* (1967)   ▮★⫽
Formidable; essential. Latest edition, 1979. Also: *The Wines of France*
Montagné, Prosper (ed) *Larousse Gastronomique* (1938)   ▮a★⫽▯
Outstanding alphabetical encyclopaedia of world food, drink and everything to do with the kitchen, kitchen-garden or dining-room.
Murphy, B. *The World Book of Whisky* (1979)
Penning-Rowsell, Edmund *The Wines of Bordeaux* (1969)   ▮
Poupon, P. and **Forgeot, P.** *The Wines of Burgundy* (1952)   ▮
Ray, Elizabeth (ed) *The Best of Eliza Acton* (1968)   🏛★⫽
Acton's *Modern Cookery* (1845) was one of the most important early British cookery books, looted by her contemporaries and successors including Isabella Beeton (qv). This selection distils its essence.
Roden, Claudia *A Book of Middle Eastern Food* (1968)   ▮a
More than 500 recipes, with variations, from Greece, Turkey, Syria, the Lebanon, Egypt, Iran, Israel, Saudi Arabia, Morocco, Tunisia, etc. Also: *Coffee*
Rombauer, I. S. and **Becker, M. R.** *The Joy of Cooking* (1931)
One of the best-selling cookery books of all time, and deservedly so. Organized by general categories of food preparation, with basic advice followed by specific recipes—mostly good. Excellent for the beginner but also of value to experienced cooks as well, who appreciate its no-nonsense approach. If you buy only one book, this should be it.
Shand, P. Morton *A Book of French Wines* (1928)
Grand tour of French wine in scholarly company, with enough personal opinion to be lively and provoking.
Simon, André L. *The Noble Grapes and the Great Wines of France* (1960)   🏛⫽
One of the first "coffee-table" wine books, and also first to stress the importance of grape varieties. Also: *Bottlescrew Days*; *Table of Content*; *Dictionary of Gastronomy*, etc
Soyer, Alexis *The Pantropheon* (1853)   ★
Witty, well-annotated history of food and its preparation in ancient times. Not to be taken for gospel though: those who seek scholarly facts see Tannahill. Also: *The Gastronomic Regenerator*
Stobart, Tom *Herbs, Spices and Flavourings* (1970)   ▮⫽
Excellent reference book (for cooks, not botanists). Good on Indian, Far Eastern and Mediterranean ingredients. Also: *The Cook's Encyclopaedia*. See HOME (Grieve)
Tannahill, Reay *Food in History* (1973)   🏛★✓⫽
Where Soyer (qv) goes in for chatty anecdote, Tannahill prefers anthropological, sociological, historical facts—authoritative, and no less fun. She also gives recipes, and her notes and bibliography are outstanding. Also: *The Fine Art of Food*. See SEX
Veronelli, Luigi *Catalogo dei Vini d'Italia* (1972)
Veronelli is the most respected, authoritative wine writer in Italy. In Italian, but its charts and quality guides are clear and understandable.
Warner, Allen H. *A History of Wine* (1956)
Interesting glimpse into the manners and methods of the past.
Wilson, Constance Anne *Food and Drink in Britain* (1973)   ★✓⫽
Superb history of British cookery, its ingredients, the social circumstances under which it developed.

Geography and the Environment

Geography is a definitive and descriptive discipline, with procedures as precise and objective as those of any other science, and a
specialist literature to match. But it is also, in its critical and
speculative form, of crucial relevance to our whole view of the
world around us—a wide subject, shading into anthropology,
history, politics and sociology. This aspect (concern for our world
and what we make of it) is of urgent interest today—and this list,
therefore, includes books on the "new" geography as well as
those reflecting the older, more segmented scientific discipline.

See ARCHITECTURE (Clifton-Taylor, Giedion, Le Corbusier,
Gropius, Mumford, Newman, Venturi); MATHEMATICS (Moore,
R., Pough); NATURAL HISTORY (Dorst, Huth, Sears); OCCULT
(Jenkins); SOCIOLOGY (Raban, Willmott)

Abrams, C. *Man's Struggle for Shelter in an Urbanizing World* (1964)
Searching examination of housing problems in the Third World; pulls no
punches.
Arvill, R. *Man and Environment: Crisis and the Strategy of Choice*
(1967)   ℘ ⫽
Baker, J. N. L. *A History of Geographical Discovery and Exploration*
(1937)   a ✓
Essential work for anyone interested in the geographical ideas of people of other
ages. This excellent book can replace many more specialized tomes; its
bibliography points to some of them.
Barry, R. G. and **Chorley, R. J.** *Atmosphere, Weather and Climate*
(1972)
Berry, B. J. L. *The Human Consequences of Urbanization* (1973)
Global survey, highlighting the contrast in experience between Western and
Third Worlds. See ARCHITECTURE (Mumford)
Burton, I. *The Environment as Hazard* (1978)   ℘
The environment is often no kinder to man than man to the environment, and its
dangers and threats must be analysed in terms of our perception of them: that is,
they must be monitored and forecast, if we are to plan relief and reconstruction.
Difficult but important book.
Carson, Rachel *Silent Spring* (1962)   ▣ ! ▣ a ⫽
One of the first and most influential works written on the pollution of the natural
landscape by man's activities ("DDT equals RIP"); the basic thesis is still of
crucial relevance. For up-to-date assessment, see F. Graham: *Since Silent Spring*
(1970). See NATURAL HISTORY (Dorst)
Chisholm, Michael *Human Geography: Evolution or Revolution?*
(1975)   ℘ a
Concise summary: population, settlement and the use of natural resources.
Chorley, R. J. and **Haggett, P.** *Models in Geography* (1967)   ℘
Cole, J. P. *A Geography of World Affairs* (1979)   ▣ a
World "political geography" showing the distributional aspects of man's political
activity and the constraints of location and environment.
Davies, W. K. D. *The Conceptual Revolution in Geography* (1972)   a
Excellent essays on new directions in geography.
Fisher, C. A. *South East Asia* (1964)   ℘
Forde, C. Daryll *Habitat, Economy and Society* (1934)   ▣ a
Classic account of the interplay of environmental and social factors in simple
cultures—those of food gatherers and hunters, herdsmen and farmers.
Freeman, T. W. *A Hundred Years of Geography* (1961)   ✓
Readable account of the main contributions and contributors in the field.
Gottman, Jean *Megalopolis: The Urbanized Northeastern Seaboard of
the United States* (1961)   ▣
Classic study helped to popularize a new word as well as a new idea—that it was,
or shortly would be, but one city all the way from Portland, Maine, to Newport
News, Virginia. See Tunnard.
Gould, P. and **White, R.** *Mental Maps* (1974)   ℘ ⫽
Landmark study in geography-by-perception, argues that what we *think* is there
is often more significant than what actually *is*.
Haggett, Peter *Geography: A Modern Synthesis* (1972)   ℘
Comprehensive coverage of the new ideas of the 1960s.
Hall, Peter *Urban and Regional Planning* (1974)   ⫽
Systematic account, with historical introduction, of planning, particularly in
Britain and America. Also: *World Cities*
Hartshorne, Richard *Perspective on the Nature of Geography* (1959)
Concise and readable account of the classical idiographic and regional approach

(temporarily?) set aside by contemporary ideas. Highly recommended.

Harvey, David *Explanation in Geography* (1969)   ▯
One of the first and still the best account of the positivist approach to human geography. Also: *Social Justice and the City* (influential, self-conscious account of his personal swing to the academic left)

Hoskins, W. G. *The Making of the English Landscape* (1955)   ▰ a ⫽
Fascinating account of how man's activities over the centuries have created the English landscape of today. Later publication *English Landscapes* (1975) is more profusely illustrated, but this book has more meat. Thomas (qv) provides a wider view of the same subject.

Jacobs, Jane *The Death and Life of Great American Cities* (1961)
Non-statistical, common-sense approach to urban problems and planning; the author believes that living in cities should be fun—and can be again, given the right approach. See Morgan; ARCHITECTURE (Banham)

James, E. Preston *All Possible Worlds: A History of Geographical Ideas* (1972)   ℘ ⫽

Jordan, Terry *The European Culture Area* (1973)   a ⫽
Systematic approach to the human geography of Western Europe; emphasis on demographic, economic and cultural elements.

Kasperson, R. K. and **Minghi, J. V. (eds)** *The Structure of Political Geography* (1970)   ▯℘ ⫽
Storehouse of many of the most important contributions to political geography since classical times. Updated second edition needed; but indispensable.

King, L. C. *Morphology of the Earth* (1967)   ▯
It is probably an impossible task to write a concise survey of the land features of the entire earth, but King's valiant attempt makes a worthy start.

Manners, Gerald *The Geography of Energy* (1971)
Excellent, short survey of the whole field of energy and policy-making.

Morgan, Elaine *Falling Apart: The Rise and Decline of Urban Civilization* (1976)
English equivalent of Jacobs (qv); but more entertaining and of wider scope.

Nicholson, Max *The Environmental Revolution* (1969)
Important text heralded new concern with quality of environment; couched in general terms, but nevertheless acute.

Pahl, R. E. *Patterns of Urban Life* (1970)
Lively discussion of some of the basic problems of urban geography and sociology.

Paterson, J. H. *North America* (1979)

Patmore, J. A. *Land and Leisure* (1977)
Looks at the demands being made on environmental resources by increasing leisure.

Sauer, Carl O. *Agricultural Origins and Dispersals: The Domestication of Animals and Foodstuffs* (1952)   ▰
Lively, challenging book, worldwide in scope, on the overlap of geology with anthropology, history and archaeology.

Scientific American *Cities: Their Origin, Growth and Human Impact* (1973)
Succinct essays on city origins, health, transport, squatting, etc.

Simmons, I. G. *The Ecology of Natural Resources* (1974)   ℘
Comprehensive look at all the resources in the environment. Deals not only with the ecological implications of use, but also with the way in which resources are regarded by society.

Stamp, Dudley *Britain's Structure and Scenery* (1946)
The way in which the geological structure of the country has contributed to the landscape. A fascinating complement to Hoskins' (qv) account of human influence on the environment.

Thomas, W. L. (ed) *Man's Role in Changing the Face of the Earth* (1956)   ℘
Essays on the interaction of culture and environment. Book covers immense historical and regional field. See Hoskins.

Tunnard, C. and **Pushkarev, B.** *Man-Made America: Chaos or Control* (1963)   ✱
Apprehensive lest America (and then the world) becomes nothing more than one sprawling uncontrollable megalopolis, the authors suggest controlled design of the artefacts with which man shapes his environment—from suburbs, commercial and recreation areas to historic sites and the roads and freeways which link them all. See Gottman.

Ward, Barbara *The Home of Man* (1976)   ▰ ⫽
Comprehensive look at the problems of human settlements in an over-populated world. Also: *Spaceship Earth*

Watts, David *Principles of Biogeography* (1971)   ▯
This book, already a standard text, supersedes the great old (1936) *Plant and Animal Geography* of M. I. Newbigin.

History

History is an important branch of *belles lettres*, offering a writer the combined attractions of freedom of interpretation and a supposedly factual armature. When the balance between these elements is right, the results for the reader can be thrilling and compelling—for by taking in the parcelled past we take in something of ourselves as well. History cannot teach us prescriptive lessons about action, since each conjunction of character and circumstance is unique; its function is rather a moral one, offering us a mirror in which to see ourselves. To do this, we need a clear presentation of the facts combined with a critical overview which takes account of the writer's and reader's present as well as of the delineated past. The books in this list (a necessarily brief selection with no attempt at chronological completeness) have been chosen for just these qualities—and because, in many cases, they offer the pleasures of wit and style as well.

American History

There are two notable characteristics of these books—perhaps they reflect characteristics of the American nation at large. The first is an urgent, philosophical, ideological approach to the creation of a just society; the second is a powerful antithesis between town and country, with its corollary, a species of romantic nostalgia for rural innocence.

See ANTHROPOLOGY (Agee); ARCHAEOLOGY (Hume); AUTOBIOGRAPHY (Adams, Franklin, Grant, Malcolm X, Miller); BIOGRAPHY (Flexner, Freeman, Parkman, Sandburg, Van Doren, Wall); DIARIES (Lincoln); FEMINISM (Flexner); HISTORY/ASIAN (Fitzgerald); POLITICS (Acheson, Piven, Woodward, B., Woodward, C. Vann); SOCIOLOGY (Lewis, Lynd, Riesman)

Aaron, Daniel *Men of Good Hope: A Story of American Progressives* (1950)
Graceful biographical essays on assorted radicals, reformers and utopians (Henry George, Thorstein Veblen, Teddy Roosevelt, etc) by a literary historian with no discernible axe to grind. Also: *Writers on the Left: Episodes in American Literary Communism*; *The Unwritten War: American Writers and the Civil War*
Adams, Henry *History of the United States during the Administrations of Thomas Jefferson and James Madison* (4 vols, 1889–91)
Comparable in every respect to Macaulay's great Whig history of England in the later 17th century, this is possibly the best single work by an American historian. Its vast scope is too much for many people; the fascinating first six chapters of volume I are separately collected in *The United States in 1800*. Also: *The Degradation of the Democratic Dogma*. See AUTOBIOGRAPHY; HISTORY/BRITISH (Macaulay); RELIGION
Bailyn, Bernard *Ideological Origins of the American Revolution* (1967)
Stresses the role of ideas—about constitutionalism and corruptions thereof—in both Britain and pre-Revolutionary America. Also: *New England Merchants in the Seventeenth Century*; *The Origins of American Politics*, etc
Beard, C., M. and W. *The Beards' New Basic History of the United States* (1960)
Beards'-eye view of North American history, from the arrival of the Norsemen in the 11th century to the launching of the first US spy satellite in 1960. Quick-moving, sometimes glib (and a settlers' view: indigenous Americans systematically ignored); but a useful general perspective of the flow of events.
Berger, Raoul *Impeachment: The Constitutional Problems* (1973)
To many observers, the events culminating in the impeachment of Richard M. Nixon are some of the most crucial in American post-war constitutional history. This book (date of publication uncannily apt) is a judicious examination of the historical and legal issues. Also: *Executive Privilege: A Constitutional Myth*
Boorstin, Daniel J. *The Americans* (3 vols, 1958–73)
This trilogy (*The Colonial Experience*; *The National Experience*; *The Democratic Experience*) has little in common with the usual plodding textbook. Boorstin celebrates American vitality, adaptability and know-how. Lively, affectionate tribute to the American dream made flesh. Also: *The Lost World of Thomas Jefferson*; *The Image: A Guide to Pseudo-events in America*

Bridenbaugh, Carl *The Beginnings of the American People: Vexed and Troubled Englishmen, 1590–1642* (1968)
Brilliant portraits of life in late Tudor and Stuart England, with emphasis on the reasons—economic, religious, political—why emigration to North America became a powerfully attractive prospect. Also: *Mitre and Sceptre*, etc

Brown, Dee *Bury My Heart at Wounded Knee* (1971)　　　　🏛✻
The near-annihilation of the American Indian. A shaming book: white behaviour depicted as almost uniformly dark. Also: *Hear That Lonesome Whistle Blow*

Cash, W. J. *The Mind of the South* (1941)
Earnest revealing study by a Southern newspaperman of the narrow, twisted mind (as he saw it) of his beloved region. The South Cash described is now largely gone, but many still remember it—with more pain than pleasure.

Catton, Bruce *This Hallowed Ground* (1956)
American Civil War from the North (Union) side. Style sometimes purplish; interpretations sometimes superficial; but steeped in period, readable, often memorable. See Wilson for literary images from the Civil War. Also: *The Coming Fury*; *Terrible Swift Sword*; *Never Call Retreat*

Coleman, Terry *Passage to America* (1972)　　　　　　　　★
In the second half of the 19th century, over two million ordinary British people embarked on a journey as terrifying and unpredictable as any traveller's to Cathay or Arabia Deserta: from the slums and famine of Ireland and northern England they took ship for America. Swindled, robbed, plundered by diseases, insulted and terrorized, they eventually arrived. This book describes their incredible journey, mainly in the words of contemporary documents.

Commager, Henry Steele *Britain through American Eyes* (1974)　　🏛✻
Acerbic anthology of American reactions to the mother country from 1778 to 1948. What an arrogant, stuffy lot the British were! Also: *The American Mind*

Demos, John *A Little Commonwealth: Family Life in Plymouth Colony* (1970)　　　　　　　　　　　　　　　　　　　　　　🏛∥
17th-century Puritans, the history of the family.

De Voto, Bernard *Across the Wide Missouri* (1947)
De Voto was a popular historian of many facets of American life, but especially good about the West. Also: *The Course of Empire*

Dewey, John *Democracy and Education* (1916)　　　　　　　　　！
Dewey was one of America's most respected philosophers; this book was perhaps his most influential. Richly thought-provoking, it enunciates propositions that have since become dogmas. See PHILOSOPHY

Fischer, David H. *Growing Old in America* (1977)　　　　　　　✻
The young country is growing old. Ingenious, personal and polemical theories on the transition from gerontocracy, via filiocracy to senility. No solutions. Also: *The Revolution of American Conservatism*; *Historians' Fallacies*

Fredrickson, George M. *The Black Image in the White Mind* (1971)
White attitudes—callous, condescending, sometimes philanthropic, occasionally admirable—to black Americans, 1814–1917. Written in excellent clean prose. See Genovese; Jordan.

Genovese, Eugene *Roll, Jordan, Roll: The World the Slaves Made* (1975)　　　　　　　　　　　　　　　　　　　　　　　　🞋
Huge, imaginative study not of what was done for or to slaves but of their own efforts to preserve sanity and dignity, and of slaveowners who were not always monsters. Also: *The World the Slaveholders Made*. See Fredrickson; Jordan.

George, Henry *Progress and Poverty* (1879)
A fine book about the perennial conflict between rich and poor, this famous work proposed a method of resolving all economic problems—so-called "single tax"—and led to Single Tax candidates all over the country for a generation. See Aaron.

Halberstam, D. *The Best and the Brightest* (1972)　　　　　　★
Power in America: how the best and brightest brains were called to be knights in JFK's Camelot, and how their light sputtered out in the mud and slime of the Vietnam War. Halberstam's scalpel prose and clear-eyed conscience (especially on US involvement in Asia) make him one of the most readable, as well as one of the sharpest, commentators on US affairs. See MEDIA

Handlin, Oscar *The Uprooted* (1951)　　　　　　　　　　　🏛
Excellent book on the American immigrant, that maker of a civilization who has latterly come in for so much study. Handlin is a sympathetic and dependable observer; his story is compelling. See Coleman.

Hartz, Louis *The Liberal Tradition in America* (1955)
Ingenious development of an appealingly simple thesis: that the US, being a post-feudal creation, has lacked both the pain and the profundity of older, European nations. Also: *The Founding of New Societies*

Higham, John *Strangers in the Land: Patterns of American Nativism, 1860–1925* (1955)
Dispassionate analysis of the resentments and misgivings of native-born Americans in the face of large-scale immigration.

Hofstadter, Richard *The Age of Reform from Bryan to F.D.R.*
(1955)   ★
Hofstadter was one of the most gifted American historians of the
century—elegant in style, broad in scope, able to borrow from other disciplines
without going overboard. This book, an analysis of Populists and Progressives up
to New Dealers, is characteristically clear and crisp. Also: *The American Political
Tradition*; *Anti-Intellectualism in American Life*; *The Progressive Historians:
Turner, Beard, Parrington*, etc
Howe, Irving *The Immigrant Jews of New York, 1880–1922*
(1976)   ✓
Also: *The American Communist Party* (with Lewis Coser); *Steady Work*; *World
of Our Fathers*. See Handlin.
Jones, Howard Mumford *O Strange New World: American Culture, the
Formative Years* (1964)   ▮★✓
Wide-ranging, rambling, stimulating discussion of the New World's image, or
images, from Columbus to the early 19th century. Also: *The Age of Energy:
Varieties of American Experience, 1865–1915*
Jones, Maldwyn *Destination America* (1976)
Concise, expert account of "push and pull" factors that induced so many millions
to leave their own land and come to the US. Also: *American Immigration*. See
Bridenbaugh; Coleman; Handlin.
Jordan, Winthrop D. *White over Black* (1968)   ▮♀✓✓
How Americans, absorbing some of the assumptions of Europe, came to visualize
black peoples of the past as—variously—innocent and depraved, docile and
dangerous, human and subhuman, in need of civilizing yet incapable of passing
beyond savagery. An erudite, perceptive book. (Compare Fiedler: *Life and
Death in the American Novel*.) See Fredrickson; Genovese.
Josephy, Alvin M., Jr. *The Indian Heritage of America* (1968)   ★✓✓
Comprehensive survey of the Indian cultures of North and South America; brief,
savage final chapters on the arrival of the whites. Essential background to Brown
(qv). See MYTHOLOGY (Burland)
Kammen, Michael *People of Paradox: An Inquiry Concerning the
Origins of American Civilization* (1972)   *✓
Kammen, a colonial historian, argues that from the outset the Americans were
confronted with dual systems of authority and belief—those of the Old World
and the New. He carries the theme toward our own time, maintaining that
Americans have become addicted to dualisms. Witty, resourceful and
provocative. Also: *A Rope of Sand: The Colonial Agents, British Politics and the
American Revolution*; *A Season of Youth: The American Revolution and the
Historical Imagination*
Kolko, Gabriel *Main Currents in Modern American History* (1976) ♀*
Occasionally doctrinaire, but very good on class, economic structure and foreign
policy since about 1870. Also: *The Triumph of Conservatism, 1900–1916*;
Railroads and Regulation, 1877–1916
Kraditor, Aileen S. *The Ideas of the Women's Suffrage Movement,
1890–1920* (1965)   ✓
Also: *Up from the Pedestal: Selected Writings in the History of American
Feminism*. See FEMINISM (Flexner)
Lasch, Christopher *The New Radicalism in America, 1889–1963*
(1965)
Opinionated assessments of various opinionated Americans, from Jane Addams
and Randolph Bourne to Norman Mailer. Also: *The Agony of the American Left*;
Haven in a Heartless World: The Family Besieged
McNaught, K. *The History of Canada* (1970)   ▮a✓
Mencken, H. L. *The American Language* (1936)
Serious, thorough study by the *enfant terrible* of US journalism of the language
that he loved and studied all his life. Nothing escaped his quick eye and ear and all
of it is here.
Meyers, Marvin *The Jacksonian Persuasion: Politics and Belief* (1957)
Political rhetoric, economic and reformist ideas, Tocqueville, the social novels of
James Fenimore Cooper—out of such materials Meyers evokes the mood of
mid-19th-century USA.
Miller, Perry *The New England Mind: From Colony to Province*
(1953)   ▮♀★
Miller did as much as anyone to rescue Puritanism from the caricatures of
Mencken and others. A historian of ideas, he revealed the power and profundity
of Puritan theology—and in this book, the retreat of the Church (up to about
1730) in the face of New England secularism. Also: *The New England Mind: The
Seventeenth Century*; *Errand into the Wilderness: The Life of the Mind in America,
from the Revolution to the Civil War*, etc
Morgan, Edmund S. *The Puritan Dilemma: The Story of John Winthrop*
(1958)
Economical, vivid biography of the Suffolk gentleman-lawyer and Puritan

churchman who sailed for the New World in 1630 to become the first Governor of the Massachusetts Bay colony. Also: *The Stamp Act Crisis*; *The Puritan Family*

Morison, S. E. *Oxford History of the American People* (1965)
Controversial, idiosyncratic, fascinating history of America by the dean of New England historians. One of the two or three best single-volume histories—much more fun than Beard's (qv) for example. See BIOGRAPHY; TRAVEL

Parkman, Francis *The Oregon Trail* (1847)
Parkman, a frail Harvard graduate, followed the track of Lewis and Clark and in the process became a man—and a great historian. Also: *The Conspiracy of Pontiac*, etc. See BIOGRAPHY; TRAVEL (Lewis)

Peterson, Merrill *The Jefferson Image in the American Mind* (1960)
This book traces the ups and downs of the great man's reputation since his death in 1826.

Schlesinger, Arthur M., Jr. *The Imperial Presidency* (1973)   ☌★
Tends to blame Republican incumbents for creating the "runaway" presidency, and to be kinder to Democrats. Yet abundantly documented, lucid and incisive. Also: *The Age of Jackson*; *The Age of Roosevelt*; *Robert Kennedy and His Times*

Sinclair, Andrew *Prohibition: The Era of Excess* (1962)   ▦ ∥
High-spirited, boldly argued social history held together by a clear thesis: that rural and small-town America has kept on fighting last-ditch battles against the city slickers. Also: *The Better Half: The Emancipation of American Women*

Slotkin, Richard *Regeneration through Violence: The Mythology of the American Frontier, 1600–1860* (1973)
The rich and complex function of the American wilderness in the European and then the American imagination: solitude, savagery (noble and ignoble), Davy Crocketts and Daniel Boones. Eloquent, analytical follow-up to the work of Turner (qv); especially interesting to read in conjunction with Thoreau's *Walden*. See Smith.

Smith, Henry Nash *Virgin Land: The American West as Symbol and Myth* (1950)   ▦★
Still one of the best attempts to portray America, and the West in particular, as a state of mind or set of ideas (a passage to India, a desert, a land for farmers, a back-drop for dime-novel heroics). Excellent use of imaginative literature. See Slotkin; Turner.

Turner, Frederick Jackson *The Frontier in American History* (1920)   ▮★
The key essay in this collection, "The Significance of the Frontier", dates back to 1893. It brought fame to Turner and started off decades of argument as to whether—Turner's argument—American democracy was truly and wholly a product of the frontier West. See Slotkin; Smith.

Twain, Mark *Life on the Mississippi* (1883)   ★
There are those, not a few, who feel this was Twain's greatest book. Trenchant, uproarious revelations of the American character—a wise and marvellous book. See FICTION/NOVELS; FICTION/SHORT STORIES; HUMOUR; TRAVEL

Wilson, Edmund *Patriotic Gore* (1962)   ▦★
Literary history in Wilson's special vein: relaxed, ruminative; good on personality as well as on style and social context. Essays, beginning with "Uncle Tom's Cabin", on North-South antagonism, the Civil War and its aftermath. Also: *The Triple Thinkers*; *The Shock of Recognition*; *The American Earthquake*, etc. See DIARIES; LITERARY CRITICISM; POLITICS

Woodward, C. Vann *Tom Watson, Agrarian Rebel* (1938)   ☌
Watson was a Georgia demagogue, veering between sincere radicalism and the politics of resentment. Splendid introduction to the Dixie mentality. Also: *Reunion and Reaction*; *The Compromise of 1877*. See POLITICS

Ancient History

The predominance of Greek and especially Roman topics reflects, perhaps, a consistent Western preoccupation with cultural and social origins. But there are good representative books on the other principal ancient civilizations too.

See ARCHAEOLOGY (Chadwick, Clark, Cottrell, Hume, Mackendrick); ARCHITECTURE (Boethius, Lawrence, Vitruvius); AUTOBIOGRAPHY (Caesar); BIOGRAPHY (Plutarch); DIARIES (Cicero, Pliny, Seneca); FEMINISM (Pomeroy); FOOD (Apicius); HISTORY/ASIAN (Basham, Eberhard, Hall, Hambly); HISTORY/LATIN AMERICAN (Katz); LITERARY CRITICISM (Highet); MATHEMATICS (Lindsay); MYTHOLOGY (Harrison, Kirk); POLITICS (Aristotle, Plato); TRAVEL (Pausanias)

Gibbon, Edward *Decline and Fall of the Roman Empire* (1776–88)   ☌▯

Certainly the wittiest and possibly the greatest of all European historical works; should be read in its "damned thick" entirety—but for the faint-hearted there is D. M. Low's excellent one-volume abridgement.

Grant, Michael *The Ancient Mediterranean* (1969)
Grant is one of the great modern popularizers of ancient history. He takes short cuts, makes quick assessments; but he is persuasive and generally reliable. This book discusses the interplay between all the civilizations round the Mediterranean—a vast amount of disparate erudition encapsulated in 300 readable pages. Also: *A History of Rome*; *Nero*, etc

Herodotus *Histories* (5th century BC)
The "father of history" ranges far and wide to analyse and describe the confrontation between East and West with which the 5th century BC began. Discursive, anecdotal, personal: one of the most enjoyable books of the ancient world.

Heyden, A. A. M. and **Scullard, H. H.** *Atlas of the Ancient World* (1955)   a ★ ∅
Not just maps, but hundreds of splendid photographs and a well-written, informative text. Introduces classical history and culture as well as geography.

Huart, C. *Ancient Persia and Iranian Civilization* (1972)
Crisp, clear and informative on the culture, society and military achievements of the ancient Medes and Persians. See HISTORY/ASIAN (**Irving**)

Johnson, P. *The Civilization of Ancient Egypt* (1978)   ✓ ∅
For the beginner, a useful guide: enthusiastic, well-written (in attractively breathless style), reasonably accurate. Readers whose interest Johnson whets will go elsewhere for more objective, authoritative views (his bibliography points the way); but there is no better starting-point than here.

Jones, A. H. M. *The Later Roman Empire, 284–602* (1964)   ℘
"This book is not a history of the later Roman empire. It is a social, economic and administrative survey of the empire, historically treated"—and all you are ever likely to want to know about it can be found herein. Also: *The Greek City*; *The Cities of the Eastern Roman Provinces*

Josephus *A History of the Jewish War* (AD 75–79)
Jewish history, until Masada, recounted in choice vocabulary and high literary style by ex-combatant Jewish turncoat. Of particular interest to those who seek illumination on the Jewish character (or characters) at the time of Christ. Also: *Jewish Antiquities*

Lehmann, J. *The Hittites* (1977)
If you can stomach its relentlessly jolly, journalistic style, this book sheds fascinating light on a very dark corner of Old Testament history.

Lemprière, Jean *Bibliotheca Classica* (1788)   ▮ a ★
Also called *Classical Dictionary*; an absorbing alphabetical account of personalities, themes and structures of classical works, as quirky and personal as Dr Johnson's *Dictionary*. Avoid all modern editions, which soften the delights in favour of academic accuracy.

Lewis, N. and **Reinhold, M.** *Roman Civilization: A Sourcebook* (2 vols, 1955)   ▮
Anthology of translated extracts covering all aspects of Roman life: volume I the republic, volume II the empire. Authors range from the grandest of historical figures to humble soldiers writing home from barracks far overseas; translations are excellent, notes, bibliography and index are unobtrusive, helpful.

Livy *History* (1st century AD)   ▮ a ★
The remains of Livy's vast history of Rome (originally in 142 volumes, now reduced to something like 700 pages) have, more than any other works, formed later views of the Roman character. Moralistic historiography in its finest flowering.

Mellersh, H. E. L. *Chronology of the Ancient World* (1976)
Magnificently simple: chronology of events from 10,000 BC to AD 799. Covers every available area of civilization; endlessly fascinating cross-parallels.

Procopius *The History of the Wars* (c. 565)
The reign of Justinian and the achievements of Belisarius (about whom Robert Graves wrote a famous novel), recorded by a contemporary. The *Anecdota* (*Secret History*) forms an appendix not to be missed by those whose taste is (in the author's words) for "wanton crime and shameless debauchery, intrigue and scandal". Good English translation: Loeb Library. See FICTION/NOVELS (**Graves**)

Radice, Betty *Who's Who in the Ancient World* (1971)   a
Pocket reference to Greece and Rome. Mythological and historical characters presented with essential details and useful reference to their place in later art, music and literature. Good introduction on the classical tradition in the Western world, and its relevance today. See LITERARY CRITICISM (**Highet**)

Rostovtzeff, M. *The Social and Economic History of the Hellenistic World* (1941)   ℘
Planned originally as a "short survey", this monumental work is the classic

treatment of one of the most important periods of Greek history. Also: *Social and Economic History of the Roman Empire*

Saggs, H. W. F. *The Greatness That Was Babylon* (1962)
A thick book (560 pages) on a neglected subject. Comprehensive; accessible.

Sallust *The Conspiracy of Catiline* (*c.* 35 BC)
Analysis of the decline and fall of the Roman republic by a perverse, morose but not unintelligent contemporary. Vivid, stylized portrait of Catiline as a species of half-mad revolutionary mobster; much information on political and social conditions and attitudes as the republic rocked towards its end.

Selzer, M. *Caesar, Politician and Statesman* (1968)
Standard scholarly biography of the "bald-headed adulterer" (as his soldiers, marching behind his triumph, sang of him). For a cooler, less authoritative view, see Michael Grant's (qv) *Julius Caesar*; for a fictional gloss, see Rex Warner's *Young Caesar*. See AUTOBIOGRAPHY (Caesar); DIARIES (Cicero)

Suetonius *Lives of the Twelve Caesars* (*c.* 121)   🏛 a
Suetonius was the arch gossip columnist of the Roman world: his book is full of scurrilous gossip, damaging innuendo, distortion and over-emphasis. Hugely entertaining. Good English translation by Graves (who also plundered Suetonius for many of the juicier details in his *I Claudius* and *Claudius the God*). See FICTION/NOVELS (Graves)

Syme, R. *The Roman Revolution* (1939)   𝒫
The modern classic work in ancient history. The subject is the establishment of the imperial autocracy by Augustus; the style is wilful and self-pleasing, demanding several readings; the rewards are great.

Tacitus, *Annals* (*c.* 118 AD)   🏛 ▭
Tersely epigrammatic, brilliant history of early Roman Empire by pre-Republican. Coruscating prose. Best translation Grant. Also: *Histories*, etc

Thucydides *History of the Peloponnesian War* (5th century BC)   ★
Thucydides' work (perhaps the first-ever "scientific history") is idiosyncratic in its selection and treatment of material, and in style. Fascinating chiefly for intelligent discussion of some of the philosophical problems thrown up by history: the purpose of historiography itself, the sources of political power, the problems of empire, and the reasons for decline and defeat. Good translation: Crawley.

Xenophon *Anabasis* (4th century BC)   🏛
Fascinating memoir of the extrication of 10,000 Greek mercenaries from Persia by the general who led them. Xenophon's appeal is largely in his relaxed unaffected style. Without literary aspirations, he has an interesting, human tale to tell, and tells it well. Also: *Hellenica*; *Memorabilia*

Asian, African and Middle Eastern History

Many areas of the world are sparsely represented on library shelves—West Africa and Australasia, for example, offer few satisfactory comprehensive histories. Other areas, especially in the Third World, are evolving so quickly that modern histories are obsolete before they even reach the shelves. The books suggested here, therefore, are a very broad sweep: without claims to comprehensive or final coverage, they make at least a start.

See AUTOBIOGRAPHY (Gandhi); BIOGRAPHY (Howarth); DIARIES (Stanley); ECONOMICS (Myrdal); POLITICS (Cabral, Hinton); RELIGION (Guillaume); TRAVEL (Kingsley, Lawrence, T. E., Maclean, Polo, Ronay, Roy)

Ajayi, J. F. Ade *A Thousand Years of West African History* (1966)   ▮
Serious, dependable synoptic history of Africa; important and eye-opening.

Allen, Charles (ed) *Plain Tales from the Raj* (1975)   🏛 a ★ //
Book originated in a series of radio interviews with fifty surviving administrators of colonial India. Extraordinary detail of extraordinary daily lives: coping with high collars, rigid etiquette, recalcitrant natives, the Edwardian British at their dotty, pragmatic best.

Anene, J. C. and **Brown, G. (eds)** *Africa in the 19th and 20th Centuries* (1966)   ▮ //
Collection of research findings and other scholarly writings; bitty and unsystematic; but individual papers are illuminating, authoritative. See Ajayi; Thompson.

Basham, A. L. *The Wonder That Was India* (1954)   🏛 a ★ ✓ //
Catchpenny title; magnificent book. Fat (600 pages), comprehensive, badged in every sentence with the author's zest for his subject. Covers the ancient history of India from 3000 BC to the coming of Muslims in AD 1565. Particularly strong on culture and social life. Usefully read in connection with Nehru (qv).

Beasley, W. G. *The Modern History of Japan* (1963)   ▮ ✓ ◩
Excellent volume in recommended *Asia-Africa* series. Traces Japanese affairs
from its opening to the West in the mid 19th century to the amazing first fruits of
the economic boom after World War II. Annotated bibliography particularly
useful. Also: *Great Britain and the Opening of Japan*. See Bergamini.

Bergamini, David *Japan's Imperial Conspiracy* (1971)   ♀ ✓ ◩
Compendious political indictment of Hirohito and his faction; disputable
interpretations, but a readable, extraordinary book. See Beasley.

Boulnois, L. *The Silk Road* (1963)   ▦ ✓ ◩
Brilliant history of the silk trade, from Roman times to the Boxer Rebellion.

Caroe, Olaf *The Pathans, 550 BC–AD 1957* (1958)   ▮ ◩
Northwest frontiersmen withstood Greeks, Arabs, Moguls, British Raj, and
(more recently) Russian tanks. Exhaustive, illuminating study.

Eberhard, W. *A History of China* (1948)
Admirable introductory survey. Use fourth English edition and supplement (for
the 20th century) with McAleavy (qv) and especially Suyin (qv). See
ARCHAEOLOGY (Chang)

Edwardes, M. *The Last Years of British India* (1963)
Sympathetic historical study, seeking to place politics in a wider perspective.
Objectivity at times leads to opaqueness; but is otherwise admirable. See Nehru.

Elvin, Mark *The Pattern of the Chinese Past* (1973)   ▮♀ ◩
Outstanding examination of technological and social forces in pre-modern
China; essential analysis of causes and effects in Chinese imperial history.
Particularly good on agriculture and printing—and on the reasons for China's
technological stagnation after 1350.

Fitzgerald, C. P. *A Concise History of East Asia* (1966)   ✓
Divided into three sections (China; Japan and Korea; South-East Asia);
outstanding for style, precision of information, clear-sightedness of historical
judgement.

FitzGerald, Frances *Fire in the Lake* (1972)
First-hand journalistic analysis of the modern history of Vietnam, a tragi-comedy
(if you can't see the blood or smell the corpses) of East-West misunderstanding
and mismanagement. Definitive answer to those who believe "we" were right to
be in Vietnam.

Gabrielli, Francesco *The Arabs: A Compact History*
(1963)   a ✓ ◩
Also published as *A Short History of the Arabs*. Compared to Glubb (qv) a
sparrow beside an eagle; but ideal for those who want a brief, clear survey of the
facts. Particularly good on the early spread of Islam.

Glubb, John *The Course of Empire* (1965)   ▦ ★ ✓ ◩
Third volume of a monumental, recommended history of the Arabs. Offers,
among other pleasures, a unique study of the First Crusade and Moorish Spain
from the Arabian point of view.

Hall, D. G. E. *A History of South East Asia* (1965)   ▦ ▮a ★ ✓ ◩
Marvellous 1000-page survey. Modern section has been updated to 1968 (3rd
edition), but the volatility of the area outstrips even Hall's dexterous pen. For the
first 10,000 years, however, a prescriptive read.

Hambly, Gavin (ed) *Central Asia* (1969)   ▮ ✓ ◩
Historical survey from 500 BC to the Chinese invasion of Tibet in 1950. Excellent
on the Mongols, Uzbeks and Turks; a grim overview of a ruthless colonizing
process, continuously bloody, from all directions, over 2500 years. Also: *Cities of
Mughal India*

Hibbert, Christopher *The Dragon Wakes* (1970)   ▦ ✓ ◩
Excellent popular account of China's relations with the West between 1793 and
1911. The section on the Boxers is particularly good. Also: *The Great Mutiny*,
etc. See HISTORY/BRITISH

Ingham, K. *A History of East Africa* (1962)   ▮♀ ✓ ◩
Inglis, Brian *The Opium War* (1976)   ▦ ✓ ◩
Opium trade between British India and the Chinese—urbane account of one of
the most bizarre 19th-century encounters between inscrutable East and
imperious West. Also: *Roger Casement; The Forbidden Game*

Irving, Clive *Crossroads of Civilization* (1979)   a ✓ ◩
Journalistic survey of Persian history from earliest times to 1939. Continuing,
blood-soaked saga of modern Iran starts here. See HISTORY/ANCIENT (Huart)

Judd, Denis *The Boer War* (1977)   ▦a ★ ◩
Good use of first-hand documents. Popular historiography at its best. Also:
Someone Has Blundered: Calamities of the British Army in the Victorian Age

Kinross, Lord *Atatürk: The Rebirth of a Nation* (1964)   ♀ ✓
Breakup of the Ottoman Empire during World War I seen as the starting-point
for the modern Middle East and its problems.

Lockhart, J. G. and **Woodhouse, C. M.** *Rhodes* (1963)   ▮ ◩
Access to Cecil Rhodes' private papers makes this a definitive biography of the
seminal figure for 19th- and 20th-century southern Africa.

Ludowyk, E. F. C. *The Story of Ceylon* (1962)   🏛 ✓ ∥
Discursive; informative; better on events after the Portuguese arrival in the 16th
century than on earlier history. Second edition (1967) best. Usefully read in
conjunction with Silva (qv).

McAleavy, Henry *The Modern History of China* (1967)   a ✓ ∥
19th- and 20th-century China, set forth with sense and style. In conjunction with
Elvin (qv) and Suyin (qv), will supply all the necessary basic information.

McCoy, Wilfred W. *The Politics of Heroin in South-East Asia* (1972)
Fully documented account of the unsung anti-heroes of the whole Indo-Chinese
adventure between 1945 and 1972—the poppy-growers and their customers,
including the governments of South Vietnam, Laos, Cambodia, etc, who pushed
narcotics in order to finance the cause of freedom, and turned the US army in
Vietnam on to a nearly 10 per cent addiction to hard drugs. The fine print of
history, blown up.

McEwan, P. J. M. and **Sutcliffe, R. B. (eds)** *The Story of Africa*
(1965)   ▯
Comprehensive account of social, economic and political issues in modern
Africa, linked to historical causes.

Morris, Donald R. *The Washing of the Spears* (1965)   ▯ ★ ✓ ∥
Rise and fall of the Zulu nation. Unblinking, objective, devastating account of
bravery, repression and genocide.

Nehru, Jawaharlal *The Discovery of India* (1951)   🏛 ★ ∥
Passionate, partisan, personal; "history" of India written "in Ahmadnagar Fort
prison during the five months April to September 1944". History as advertising
copy: the nation pulses with life before your eyes. Those who prefer a more
objective view—and those whom Nehru excites to read further—are referred to
Basham (qv).

Phillips, Wendell *Unknown Oman* (1966)   ✓ ∥
South-eastern tip of the Arabian peninsula, explored by the first Western
historian and archaeologist to make a systematic study. Some of the book is an
account of his travels; but the second half is a valuable historical survey. Also:
Quataban and Sheba

Preble, George H. *The Opening of Japan* (1962)   🏛 ∥
Preble was a US naval lieutenant in the fleet of Commodore Perry, which first
opened Japan to Western commerce in 1853. This diary of the voyage (ed
Szczesniak) is witty, detailed, and full of delightfully wide-eyed accounts of the
wonders and customs of the fabled East. Interesting, too, for sidelights on
19th-century naval life. See TRAVEL (Dana)

Ransford, Oliver *The Great Trek* (1972)   🏛 ∥
History outstrips legend. Well told, thoroughly documented account of one of the
great epic stories of the whites in Africa. Also: *The Rulers of Rhodesia*; *The Battle
of Spion Kop*

Sadler, A. H. L. *A Short History of Japan* (1963)   a ∥
Earliest times to 1951; the flow of events is charted with brisk clarity. Usefully
read in conjunction with Beasley (qv).

Severin, Timothy *The African Adventure* (1973)   🏛 a ∥
Popular account of 400 years of African exploration. Standard names like
Stanley are given good coverage; but the book is chiefly interesting for lesser-
known Portuguese and Belgian figures. Illustrated from contemporary drawings,
many by the explorers themselves.

Silva, K. M. da (ed) *Sri Lanka: A Survey* (1977)   ⌗ a
Geography, history, politics, culture. Comprehensive; objective. See Ludowyk.

Snow, Edgar *Red Star over China* (1937)
Influential account of the Chinese Revolution based on Snow's encounters with
Mao Tse-tung, Chou En-lai and others on the 1936 Long March. See Suyin.

Stanley, R. and **Neame, A. (eds)** *The Exploration Diaries of*
H. M. Stanley (1961)   🏛 ★ ∥

Suyin, Han *The Morning Deluge* (1972); *The Wind in the Tower*
(1976)   ★
Massive two-volume biography of Mao; subtitle (*Mao Tse Tung and the Chinese
Revolution, 1893–1975*) tells all. See Snow.

Thompson, E. B. *Africa, Past and Present* (1966)   a ✓ ∥
An attempt, for the general reader, to set modern Africa in its historical context.
At its best when discussing the multifarious Western exploitation of Africa—a
sordid, riveting tale.

Vatikiotis, P. J. *The Modern History of Egypt* (1969)   ✓ ∥
Egyptian history, 1800–1969. Good on political and ideological struggles
between independence in 1922 and the establishment of the republic in 1956.

Wilson, M. and **Thompson, L. (eds)** *The Oxford History of South Africa*
(2 vols, 1969–71)   ▯ ⌗ ✓
Exhaustive account, particularly good on indigenous cultures. Donnish
objectivity is a welcome corrective to the partisan approach of many writers on
this subject.

British History

Books about breeding and taste, not least in royal circles, stud this list—and tell us, some will say, something of the British character itself. There is marked insularity too: often, it seems, the British went out into the world only to conquer, to govern or to disapprove.

See ARCHAEOLOGY (Frere); ART (Conrad); AUTOBIO-GRAPHY (Bamford, Brittain, Graves, Hervey, Macmillan); BIO-GRAPHY (Cecil, Donaldson, Longford, Nicolson, Woodham-Smith); DIARIES (Carlyle, Chesterfield, Evelyn, Greville, Montagu, Pepys); FEMINISM (Hiley, Norris); HISTORY/AMERICAN (Bridenbaugh); POLITICS (Bagehot, Clarke, Cowling); SOCIO-LOGY (Chesney, Reeves, Roberts); TRAVEL (London)

Bacon, Francis *Essays* (1597) 🪶
Pungent observations on his own changing world, on man and society, on politics, ambition, marriage, youth and age, education: all the major issues which concern Bacon as much as they do us.

Bede *The Ecclesiastical History of England* (731) ★
King Alfred thought this one of the books "most necessary for all men to know", and it's still fascinating. The history of Britain from the landing of St Augustine in 597 to the year 731, discussed in elegant, quiet prose.

Blythe, Ronald *The Age of Illusion* (1963) 🏛 ⫽
Emotive, with essays on the England of the 1920s–1930s: covers such topics as the General Strike, the Jarrow March, and Munich. Also: *The Aspirin Age*

Blythe, Ronald *Akenfield* (1969) 🏛 ▦
First-hand accounts of life in a Suffolk village at the beginning of the 20th century. Pastoral idyll in parts—but poverty, accident and illness are there as well. People talking about their own lives: the red meat of history. Also: *The View in Winter* (on old age). See Bragg; Thompson; SOCIOLOGY (Terkel)

Bragg, Melvyn *Speak for England* (1976) 🏛 ⫽
Oral history of the author's home town of Wigton, Cumbria, in the 20th century. Vivid recollections by ordinary people of their lives and experiences. Parallel to Thompson (qv). See Blythe; Briggs.

Briggs, Asa (ed) *They Saw It Happen, 1897–1940* (1960) a
Last of four volumes (all recommended) covering British history 55 BC–AD 1940. Anthology of first-hand documents, thematically arranged. The series strongly reinforces the view that history is collective memory, is people not events. Also: *Victorian People*; *Victorian Cities*, etc. See MEDIA

Brown, R. Allen *English Castles* (1954) 🏛 ⫽
Castles, the most emblematic of medieval buildings, are an essential study for anyone hoping to understand feudal society; this book (preferably use the 3rd edition) is the most comprehensive account in English. Also: *The Normans and the Norman Conquest*; *The Origins of English Feudalism*; *The Origins of Modern Europe*

Burn, W. L. *The Age of Equipoise* (1964) 🏛
Admirable general introduction to the Victorian era; covers social and artistic matters as well as historical events.

Burnet, Gilbert *A History of My Own Time* (1723)
Cocky, garrulous, unpopular Scot, who went into exile under James II, came back with William of Orange, ended up Bishop of Salisbury. Pungent style, excellent information, shrewd insights, obviously prejudiced. An invaluable eye-witness account of the Civil Wars, the Commonwealth and their turbulent aftermath.

Burton, Elizabeth *The Georgians at Home, 1714–1830* (1966) 🏛 ⫽
Daily life in Georgian England: homes and gardens, furniture and artefacts, food, medicine, diversions and amusements. Also: *The Elizabethans at Home*; *The Jacobeans at Home*

Cruickshanks, Eveline *Political Untouchables: The Tories and the '45* (1979) ⫽
The author tackles the subject of England at the time of the 1745 Jacobite rebellion with aplomb, makes full use of the French archive material without which the story makes no sense. For specialists, essential; for those interested in the politics of rebellion, fascinating.

Dillon, M. and Chadwick, N. *The Celtic Realms* (1967) ▊
Useful study of pre-Norman British society, essential for understanding the independent cultures of Ireland, Scotland and Wales, as well as the Celtic underlay of later English culture. Particularly good on religion, literature and art. *The History of Civilization* series (from which this comes) is patchy; this volume is excellent.

Elton, G. R. *Studies in Tudor and Stuart Politics and Government* (2 vols, 1974)   ♀
Important collection of articles, mainly on the government of Tudor England, by an influential British historian. Also: *The Tudor Constitution,* etc

Ensor, R. C. K. *England, 1870–1914* (1936)   ▮
By far the best of the volumes on modern history in the *Oxford History of England* series. Detailed, accurate, sensible.

Feiling, Keith *A History of England* (1966)   ▟ a ✓
Basic one-volume history from pre-Roman times to World War II. Clear, readable text gives a swift but not unreliable view of the flow of events. Superb index; helpful bibliography; useful maps and charts. A model, in short, of what such a book should be. Also: *The Life of Neville Chamberlain; The Second Tory Party, 1714–1832*

Fitzgibbon, Constantine *Red Hand: The Ulster Colony* (1971)
Good historical survey of the relations between Ireland and (particularly) England from the time of Elizabeth I to the troubled end of the 1960s. Clear-eyed, dismaying read. Also: *Out of the Lion's Paw: Ireland Wins Her Freedom.* See Woodham-Smith.

George, M. Dorothy *English Political Caricature* (2 vols, 1959)   ▟ ▮ ∥
Historians ignore political caricature at their peril; the general reader will be amused as well as informed by this excellent two-volume survey of the great age of caricature, 1700–1832. No subject is sacred: ministers, taxation, the loss of the American colonies, the French Revolution, Napoleon—all are here.

Glover, Janet R. *The Story of Scotland* (1960)   a ✓
Revised 2nd edition best. Series, *The Story of . . . ,* generally recommended: crisp, authoritative, concise.

Harrisson, Tom *Living through the Blitz* (1975)
The London Blitz, recorded through the war-time reports of Mass Observation. Fascinating record of civilian morale, the hardships of the home front, and hopes for a better future. (Compare C. Perry: *Boy in the Blitz.*)

Hibbert, Christopher *George IV* (2 vols, 1972–73)
Fascinating; satisfying. Plumb's dictum on George IV, "never, never a dull moment", is fully justified. Also: *The Court at Windsor; The Grand Tour; London: The Biography of a City.* See Plumb; HISTORY/ASIAN

Hill, Christopher *The World Turned Upside Down* (1972)   ▟ ★
Study of radical groups (scientific, religious, political, sexual) during the English Revolution. Essential reading for anyone who believes that England during the 1640s and 1650s was "Puritan". Also: *The Century of Revolution, 1603–1714; Milton and the English Revolution; The Intellectual Origins of the English Revolution*

Laslett, Peter *The World We Have Lost* (1965)   ▟
A grass roots—or rather parish register—enquiry in depth into the lives of the ordinary people of 16th- and 17th-century England. Does for Britain what Demos did for 17th-century America. See HISTORY/AMERICAN (Demos)

Longford, Elizabeth *Victoria R. I.* (1964)   ▟ ∥
Easy to read, well researched biography, in a different class to Lytton Strachey's *Queen Victoria,* which is for those who are looking for imaginative literature, not history. See BIOGRAPHY

Macaulay, T. B. *The History of England* (4 vols, 1848–55)   ▟ ▣
Old hat, of course; the quintessential Whig historian. Make allowance for his prejudices, and—*pace* T. S. Eliot—enjoy the superb narrative style. Famous, long Chapter 3 still gives an unrivalled picture of 17th-century English society. Also: *The Lays of Ancient Rome.* See LITERARY CRITICISM

Magnus, Philip *King Edward the Seventh* (1964)   ▟ ∥
Workmanlike combination of essential facts with a reasonable ration of titbits. Biographies of Edward VII are a crowded field; this is one of the very best. Also: *Kitchener; William Ewart Gladstone,* etc

Mathew, Gervase *The Court of Richard II* (1968)   ▟ ★ ✓ ∥
Mathew's study of the literature, art and way of life of Richard and his courtiers uncovers the origins of Renaissance court culture and of the cult of sensibility. Also: *Byzantine Aesthetics*

Mattingly, Garrett *The Defeat of the Spanish Armada* (1959)   a ∥
Absorbing account based entirely on contemporary record; more exciting than any fiction. Also: *Catherine of Aragon; Renaissance Diplomacy*

More, Thomas *Utopia* (1516)   ★ ▣
Ironic commentary on early Tudor England; the wit and wisdom of the "man for all seasons" and his vision of a new society won him admirers as diverse as High Tory Anglicans and Russian Leninists.

Neale, J. E. *Queen Elizabeth* (1934)   ▟ ∥
Brilliant mingling of scholarship with humane and compassionate understanding of a woman in high politics. Its only weakness is the somewhat pervasive view that the queen could do no wrong. Also: *The Elizabethan House of Commons; Elizabeth I and Her Parliaments.* See Read; Rowse.

Orwell, George *The Road to Wigan Pier* (1937)　　　　　📖 ★
Perceptive, harrowing account of "life on the dole" in the 1930s; helped
influence a generation's attitude to the spectre of mass unemployment. See
FICTION/NOVELS; LITERARY CRITICISM; POLITICS

Plumb, J. H. *The First Four Georges* (1956)　　　　　★ 📗
Plumb was the first scholar to stress the complexity of George I; here he surveys
the following three Georges with a similarly unjaundiced eye. Compulsive. Also:
Sir Robert Walpole; *The Growth of Political Stability, 1675–1725*; *Chatham*, etc.
See Hibbert.

Power, Eileen *The Wool Trade in English Medieval History* (1941)　📖 📙
Unlikely-sounding subject; but fascinating and of far more than parochial
interest. Economic history at its elegant best.

Priestley, J. B. *English Journey* (1934)
Sensitive evocation of England during the early 1930s by famous author and
broadcaster.

Read, Conyers *Mr Secretary Walsingham and the Policy of Queen*
Elizabeth (1925)　　　　　📙
Major study of Elizabethan foreign policy and elucidation of the intelligence
system built up and operated by the spiritual ancestor of MI5 and the CIA. Also:
Mr Secretary Cecil and Queen Elizabeth; *Lord Burghley and Queen Elizabeth*. See
Neale; Rowse.

Rowse, A. L. *The England of Elizabeth* (1950)　　　　　📖 ✳
First and best of a series of studies of the Elizabethan age. Better on aristocrats
than on what he calls "the idiot people", especially the Puritans. Furious fun. See
Neale; Read.

Rudé, George *Hanoverian London, 1714–1808* (1971)　　　　📗
Marvellous evocation of Georgian London; when and why the churches were
built and the squares laid out; shows how the 1715 rebellion affected the capital
with its Jacobite versus Hanoverian protagonists. Also: *Wilkes and Liberty*; *A
Social Study of 1763–1774*

Scarisbrick, J. J. *Henry VIII* (1968)
Scarisbrick sees Henry's reign as fractured by the break with the papacy, and
portrays the king as a complex, Renaissance ruler, cruel and cultivated, foolishly
intent on war with France, against all reason. Authoritative, accessible.

Stenton, F. M. *Anglo-Saxon England* (1943)　　　　　📙
Master-work on the subject; another outstanding volume from the *Oxford
History of England* series. Also: *The First Century of English Feudalism*

Strong, Roy *Splendour at Court: Renaissance Spectacle and Illusion*
(1973)　　　　　📖 📗
The politics of spectacle. Fascinating illustrations.

Tawney, R. H. *Religion and the Rise of Capitalism* (1926)　　　📙
Classic which finally destroyed the concept of "the Puritan Revolution" by
showing the connections between Puritanism and the needs of developing
capitalism. Also: *History and Society*; *Equality*, etc

Taylor, A. J. P. *English History, 1914–1945* (1965)　　　　📖 ★
Invigorating survey of 20th-century Britain. Taylor's occasionally idiosyncratic
evaluations of people and events only add to the liveliness of the narrative. Also:
*The Origins of the Second World War; The Struggle for Mastery in Europe,
1848–1918; The Habsburg Monarchy, 1815–1918*, etc. See BIOGRAPHY

Thomas, Keith *Religion and the Decline of Magic* (1971)　　　📙 ℗
Anthropological and sociological techniques uncover the life and thought of
ordinary people in 17th-century England. Book that transformed its subject:
essential reading.

Thompson, E. P. *The Making of the English Working Class* (1963)
Superb book by one of this century's leading British historians. Also: *Protest and
Survive* (crucial polemic on need for disarmament). See BIOGRAPHY

Thompson, Paul *The Edwardians: The Remaking of British Society*
(1975)　　　　　℗ ✔
Based largely on interview material; vividly conveys the texture of grass-roots
Edwardian society.

Trevelyan, G. M. *England under Queen Anne* (1930–34)　　　📖 📙
Charts the rise, through war and peace, of England as mistress of the seas, an
equal of France on land and the cradle of the Golden Age. Fluent, authoritative
style. Also: *England under the Stuarts*; *English Social History*; *British History in
the Nineteenth Century*, etc

Willson, David Harris *King James VI and I* (1956)
Fascinating account of the baffling character who united the crowns of England
and Scotland and who was a combination of wit and pedantry, learning and folly.

Woodham-Smith, Cecil *The Great Hunger: Ireland, 1845–49*
(1962)　　　　　📙 📗
One of the best books on Irish history. If you are English it should make you blush
with shame. Also: *The Reason Why*; *Queen Victoria*, etc. See Fitzgibbon;
BIOGRAPHY

European History

This list concentrates, in the main, on the most useful and accessible surveys of this vast subject (the history, in part, of the whole modern civilization of the West). A few books on specific topics are included (usually where the subject is neglected or the treatment unique); but for the multitude of specific topics we recommend browsing in the bibliographies of Cantor (qv), Fisher (qv) and Lichtheim (qv).

See ARCHAEOLOGY (Piggott, Sandars); ARCHITECTURE (Clark, Conant, Harvey, Murray); AUTOBIOGRAPHY (Kropotkin, Saint Simon, Speer); BIOGRAPHY (Bainton, Bullock, Huizinga, Lachouque, Taylor); DIARIES (Frank); FEMINISM (Porter, Thomas); MATHEMATICS (Irving, Mendelssohn); MEDICINE (McNeill); POLITICS (Carr, Orwell, Stern, Trotsky); RELIGION (Deanesly); SOCIOLOGY (Blok, Elias); TRAVEL (Ley, Michener, Polo)

Barraclough, Geoffrey *The Medieval Papacy* (1968)
Fine study of what many regard as the single most important institution in the history of Western Europe. Brisk; short; complete. See HISTORY/WORLD
Boussard, Jacques *The Civilization of Charlemagne* (1968) 🏛 ✒
Good account of the first unifier of Europe—salutary reading for those *illiterati* who try to use history as an argument against European solidarity. If it worked for Charlemagne . . .
Braudel, Fernand *The Mediterranean and the Mediterranean World in the Age of Philip II* (1973) ★
Dextrously interweaves public with private affairs; makes more sense out of the tangled events of this turbulent time than might have been thought possible.
Calmette, Joseph *The Golden Age of Burgundy* (1949) 🏛 ✒
Cantor, Norman F. *Medieval History* (1963) a ✓
Accessible, authoritative study of Europe in the 2nd–15th centuries. Particularly good on Church and State; Carolingian section outstanding.
Chandler, David *The Campaigns of Napoleon* (1967) 📖 a ★ ✒
Outstanding; essential companion to the biography by Lachouque. Also: *The Art of Warfare in the Age of Marlborough*, etc. See Geyl; BIOGRAPHY (Lachouque)
Cohn, Norman *Europe's Inner Demons* (1975) 🏛 📖
Scathing, scholarly attack on supposed Devil-worship leading to the witch hunts of the Middle Ages and later. Also: *Warrant for Genocide; The Pursuit of the Millennium*
Derry, T. K. *A History of Scandinavia* (1979) 📖 ✓
Fawtier, Robert *The Capetian Kings of France* (1960) ★
Fisher, H. A. L. *A History of Europe* (1936) a ✓
If European history can be covered at all in 1200 pages this book does so.
Geyl, Pieter *Napoleon, For and Against* (1965) ★
Exactly what the title says: the arguments lucidly and elegantly marshalled.
Gilmore, Myron P. *The World of Humanism, 1453–1517* (1952) a ✓ ✒
Characteristic volume from (recommended) *The Rise of Modern Europe* series.
Grey, Ian *Catherine the Great* (1961) 🏛 a ✒
Grierson, Edward *The Fatal Inheritance* (1969) ✓
Urbane account of bloodthirsty, terrible events: Philip II and the revolt of the Spanish Netherlands. Slips down as easily as milk—but what an aftertaste! See Braudel.
Hale, J., Highfield, R. and **Smalley, B. (eds)** *Europe in the Late Middle Ages* (1970) 🔍 ✒
Hart, Basil Liddell *History of the First World War* (1935) 🏛 📖 a
Authoritative one-volume history of the "war to end wars". Also: *History of the Second World War; The Other Side of the Hill*. See AUTOBIOGRAPHY
Haskins, Charles H. *The Normans in European History* (1915) 📖
There were few more formative influences on Europe than the Normans. This unpretentious, well-written survey of their manifold achievements is the best introduction. Also: *Norman Institutions; The Twelfth-century Renaissance*
Hole, Edwyn *Andalus: Spain under the Muslims* (1958) 🏛 a ✒
Readable, popular treatment of an important subject. Fascinating to compare with the Arabian view in Glubb (HISTORY/ASIAN).
Huizinga, Johan *Men and Ideas* (1969) ★
Luminous essays by a leading 20th-century scholar and humanist. "The Task of Cultural History"; "Patriotism and Nationalism"; "Chivalric Ideals"; biographical studies of John of Salisbury, Abelard, St Joan, Erasmus and Grotius. Contains famous, influential pieces on "The Problem of the Renaissance" and "Renaissance and Realism". See BIOGRAPHY

Jones, Gwyn *A History of the Vikings* (1969) 🏛📖a ♪

Keegan, John *The Face of Battle* (1976) ★ ♪
The uncharted (perhaps unpalatable) face of much history: an anatomy of the soldiers who stood in line, who did the *work*. Their conditions, feelings, reactions. Disturbing, unforgettable book, despite weak conclusions. See Middlebrook.

Ladurie, E. le Roy *Montaillou* (1975) ℗★
Pyrenean village, 1294–1324, caught between Albigensian heretics and the Inquisition, brilliantly reconstructed from contemporary documents. Ordinary community is laid bare as authentically as in a novel. Also: *Carnival*, etc

Larkin, Maurice *Gathering Pace* (1969) a ✓ ♪
Excellent textbook on continental Europe, 1870–1945. Readable, objective.

Lawrence, D. H. *Movements in European History* (1921) ✱
Conceived as a school textbook, for money, this "series of vivid sketches of movements and people" encapsulates some of Lawrence's most idiosyncratic views of the historical process, leadership, political morality. 1971 edition (recommended) includes later Epilogue on fascism, Russian communism and British democracy post-1918. Rare, fascinating oddity. See DIARIES; FICTION/NOVELS; FICTION/SHORT STORIES; LITERARY CRITICISM; POETRY; TRAVEL

Lewis, Peter *Later Medieval France* (1968) 📖

Lichtheim, George *Europe in the 20th Century* (1972) ℗ ✓ ♪
Cultural survey, seeking to place political, social and artistic movements in philosophical/historical context. Good on the decline of bourgeois liberalism, and on the effect of supra-national organizations on the nation state.

Macartney, C. A. and **Palmer, A. W.** *Independent Eastern Europe* (1962) ℗ ✓
Authors believe that Eastern Europe between 1919 and 1939 presented a unity, posing an identity of problems and playing a single crucial role in the development of subsequent political attitudes. This view, persuasively argued, underlies a good general survey of the area and the period.

Massie, Robert K. *Nicholas and Alexandra* (1968) 🏛a ★ ✓ ♪
Dispassionate account of moving, tragic events, often more like Dostoyevsky than real life. Good use of diaries, letters and other first-hand evidence.

Maurois, André *A History of France* (1949) 🏛📖a ★
Personal, discursive, engrossing—a great polymath in full control. Third edition (1960) revised (and extended to cover the rise of de Gaulle).

Middlebrook, Martin *The First Day on the Somme* (1971) a ★
Compilation based on hundreds of first-hand accounts. Like Keegan (qv) essential reading for anyone who believes in the glory and nobility of war. Fine maps and appendices. Also: *The Kaiser's Battle*; *Battleship*, etc

Moss, H. L. B. *The Birth of the Middle Ages, 395–814* (1935) 📖 ♪
Finely written account of the decline of the Roman empire, barbarian settlements in the West, Byzantium, Muslim conquests, the history of the Franks to Charlemagne, and the early history of the papacy. No Dark Ages here: a luminous, exciting book.

Mundy, J. H. *Europe in the High Middle Ages, 1150–1309* (1973) 📖℗

Nelson, W. H. *The Soldier Kings* (1970) 🏛 ✓ ♪
The house of Hohenzollern, from its shabby 15th-century origins to the abdication of Kaiser Wilhelm II after World War I. Best read with the pinch of salt provided by E. J. Feuchtwangler in *Prussia, Myth and Reality* (1970).

Origo, Iris *The Merchant of Prato* (1957) ★
Evocative study of the archives of the Datini family, makes it possible to revive an individual 14th-century merchant in all facets of his commercial and social life.

Pares, Bernard *A History of Russia* (1926)
Marvellous account to the Revolution, and good on the politics of the succeeding Bolshevik years. Second edition (1947) extends the story to include Russia under Stalin, by an old man out of sympathy with communism. This dying fall should not obscure the book's general objectivity and excellence.

Pernoud, G. and **Flaissier, S.** *The French Revolution* (1959) ★
Story of aristocrats and ordinary people, told entirely in eye-witness accounts.

Psellus, Michael *Fourteen Byzantine Rulers* (1063–75) 🏛★
Contemporary statesman on emperors and empresses of the Byzantine golden age. Extravagant lives; extravagant, splendid telling.

Runciman, Steven *A History of the Crusades* (3 vols, 1951–54) ★ ♪
One of the best, most thrilling historical books of the 20th century, engrossing for specialists, accessible for all. Also: *The Sicilian Vespers*; *The Fall of Constantinople*; *The Last Byzantine Renaissance*

Ryder, A. J. *Twentieth-century Germany: From Bismarck to Brandt* (1973) a ✓ ♪
Solzhenitsyn, A. I. *The Gulag Archipelago* (1973) ★
Extraordinary, heart-rending report on the lives—and deaths—of the victims of Stalin's repression. The Gulag was the system of prison camps through which millions of Russians passed in the years before and after World War II.

Solzhenitsyn's account is fervently biased—but how could it be otherwise? As a writer, he has here found his great theme; beside this book his fiction (worthy enough but grossly overpraised— political rawness is no guarantee of literary quality) pales into its proper subordinate place.

Southern, R. W. *The Making of the Middle Ages* (1953)   a ★ ⫻
Begins more or less where Moss (qv) leaves off, and ends in 1200. This is the period of the founding of our civilization, and the author, steeped in every aspect of it, writes quite beyond the range of most historians. Simply outstanding. Also: *Western Society and the Church in the Middle Ages*

Thompson, David *Europe since Napoleon* (1957)   ▮ ♀ ✓
Fat (800 pages), comprehensive, smoothly written. Weaker on culture than on politics and military history; notably good on 19th-century colonialism.

Tuchman, Barbara *The Guns of August* (1962)   ★
To be compared with Middlebrook (qv), Tuchman's book reminds us again that never in human history was so much folly manifested by so many as in World War I—the "Great War", as we ironically call it. Also: *A Distant Mirror: The Calamitous 14th Century*; *The Proud Tower*

Tyler, Royall *The Emperor Charles the Fifth* (1956)   ▮ ✓ ⫻
Wilmot, Chester *The Struggle for Europe* (1952)   ▲ ▮ a
Outstanding first-hand account of World War II.

Latin American History

These books catalogue the (continuing) collisions between the Old World and the New, and, less obviously, the progress of one of the last and bloodiest confrontations between Christianity and ordered pagan civilization. The ideological conflicts of the wider world are galvanized by technological overkill; but they yield nothing in violent dogma, dogmatic violence, to the death-throes of the old.

See ARCHAEOLOGY (Deuel); BIOGRAPHY (Madariaga, Morison); MEDICINE (McNeill): MYTHOLOGY (Burland); SOCIOLOGY (Lewis); TRAVEL (Chadwick)

Boxer, C. R. *The Portuguese Seaborne Empire, 1415–1825* (1969)   ▮ a ⫻
Portuguese expansion in Asia and in the Americas; stylish general history of colonial Brazil. Useful background to Freyre (qv) and Hemming (qv). Also: *The Golden Age of Brazil, 1695–1750*; *The Dutch Seaborne Empire, 1600–1800*

Collier, Simon *From Cortes to Castro* (1974)   a
General history of Latin America to 1973, combined with chapters of social, economic and political analysis. Also: *Ideas and Politics of Chilean Independence, 1808–33*

Freyre, Gilberto *The Masters and the Slaves* (1933)   ♀ ✳ ★
According to one critic (Tannenbaum), the creation of national identity and pride, which in Mexico required "a bloody revolution, untold suffering and the loss of a million lives", was achieved in Brazil "by this one man and this one book". Also: *The Mansions and the Shanties; Order and Progress*

Gerbi, Antonello *The Dispute of the New World: The History of a Polemic, 1750–1900* (1973)   ♀
Masterpiece of intellectual history traces in witty, learned style the origins and development of the great debate on the alleged inferiority of both man and environment in the Americas.

Gibson, Charles *The Aztecs under Spanish Rule* (1964)   ▮ ♀ ⫻
History of Mexico from the Spanish conquest to 19th-century independence, reconstructed with scholarly care and told with sympathy and objectivity. Also: *The Inca Concept of Sovereignty and the Spanish Administration in Peru; Spain in America*

Hemming, J. *Red Gold: The Conquest of the Brazilian Indians, 1500–1800* (1976)
Well-researched, readable corrective to Freyre's (qv) somewhat roseate view of Brazilian racial integration; powerful case study of this central, if grim, theme in Latin American history. Also: *The Conquest of the Incas*

Hennessy, Alistair *The Frontier in Latin American History* (1978)   ♀
Something of a misnomer. Sees the frontier (political, military, economic, racial) as a central theme of Latin American history from the Conquest to the present; this allows coverage of a wealth of topics (some neglected in conventional narrative histories). Difficult, but worthwhile.

Katz, Friederich *The Ancient American Civilizations* (1972)   ▲ a ✓ ⫻
Stimulating analysis of pre-Columbian civilizations, particularly good on social and economic structures (less so on art and literature); usefully points the way to

further reading. Also: a major study of Pancho Villa and the Mexican Revolution, in preparation and should be worth waiting for.

Lynch, John *The Spanish American Revolutions, 1808–26* (1973)
Good general study of the independence movements which liberated Latin America from Spanish colonial rule, concentrates on Argentina, Venezuela, Colombia and Mexico. Also: *Spain under the Habsburgs*

Meyer, Jean A. *The Cristero Rebellion: The Mexican People between Church and State, 1926–29* (1976)   ♀ **a** ⁄⁄
A brilliant account by French historian of the "alternative" Mexican Revolution, focusing on the Catholic peasant revolt of the 1920s but illuminating wider aspects of religion and politics in modern Mexico. Also: *The American Revolution, 1910–40*

Parry, J. H. *The Spanish Seaborne Empire* (1966)   🏛 **a** ⁄⁄
Probably the best general account in English of the Spanish empire in the New World. Also: *The Age of Reconnaissance*; *Europe and a Wider World*

Prescott, William H. *History of the Conquest of Mexico* (1843)   ▮ ♀
One of those monumental narrative histories which (rightly or wrongly) historians seldom now attempt; describes Cortés's conquest of the Aztec empire in grandiloquent style and with immense local detail—even though Prescott never once set foot in Mexico. Also: *History of the Conquest of Peru*

Thomas, Hugh *Cuba: The Pursuit of Freedom* (1971)   ♀ **a** ⁄⁄
Comprehensive history of Cuba from the Spanish conquest to Castro (concentrating attention on the modern period). Prolix, chaotic. Also: *The Spanish Civil War*

Wachtel, Nathan *The Vision of the Vanquished: The Spanish Conquest of Peru through Indian Eyes, 1530–1570* (1976)
Poignant contrast to Prescott's (qv) account; draws on Indian sources to give Indian perspective.

Womack, John *Zapata and the Mexican Revolution* (1968)
Pedants cavil at the book's colloquial style, and the social scientists at its dearth of sociological analysis; it remains the best work in English on the Mexican Revolution.

World History

A convincing, definitive synthesis of world history remains to be written. For future master-masons, these books may offer guidelines; for the rest of us, interested visitors to the quarry, they are intriguing, rough-hewn blocks announcing a potential they cannot yet fulfil.

Barraclough, Geoffrey *The Times Atlas of World History* (1978)   ▮ ★ ⁄⁄
Geographical, historical, cultural and military information clearly and concisely displayed. Essential reference book, and a model of its kind. See
HISTORY/EUROPEAN

Bowra, M. et al *Golden Ages of the Great Cities* (1952)   🏛 ✓ ⁄⁄
Athens, Rome, Constantinople, Paris, Venice, Vienna, London, New York—each described at a moment of cultural or historical supremacy by one of a galaxy of respected historians.

Cambridge Modern History (1957)   ▮
Fourteen-volume standard history of the world since the Renaissance. Essential work of reference, flawed only by excessive concentration on Europe.

Durant, Will *The Story of Civilization* (1935)   🏛 ▮
Multi-volume one-man's view of human history and achievement. Durant's style is lucid and elegant. His judgements can seem selective and glib; but this remains a monumental work, at once stimulating and unique.

Grenville, J. A. S. *A World History, 1900–1945* (1979)   ▮ ♀
Wide-ranging, authoritative study by a leading scholar. Also: *Lord Salisbury and Foreign Policy*; *Europe Reshaped, 1848–1878*

Grun, B. *The Timetables of History: A Chronology of World Events* (1975)   ▮
Fascinating compendium of dates and events.

Roberts, J. M. *The Hutchinson History of the World* (1976)   **a** ★ ⁄⁄
Ambitious attempt at a full history of the world from earliest times to the present day. Compression; judgement—an impressive achievement. Also: *Europe, 1880–1945*; *The Mythology of the Secret Societies*

Toynbee, A. J. *Cities of Destiny* (1967)   ⁄⁄
Magnificent history of the city—its origins, development and ultimate domination of the civilized world.

Wells, H. G. *A Short History of the World* (1922)
Still the most accessible brief world history. Displays many of Wells' prejudices, but is coherent and perceptive. See FICTION/NOVELS; FICTION/SF

Home and Garden

Many animals, many insects, make beautiful homes; but there is no evidence that any man derive aesthetic pleasure as well as practical benefit from home-making, however fine. Despite Bacon's remark "Homes are built to be lived in, not to be looked at" man is a voracious observer—we smile or shudder at other people's homes as well as at our own; we envy, we aspire, we imitate. The books on this list, therefore, as well as giving practical advice, offer basking pleasure too: whether they prescribe or reflect, their subject is comfort, and their tone (almost unique in the lists in this book) is uniformly relaxed and positive.

See ARCHITECTURE (Clifton-Taylor, Lancaster); FOOD (Beeton, Conran, Tannahill)

Berral, Julia J. *An Illustrated Guide to the Garden* (1966)
Authoritative accessible study of gardens through the ages, from that known as "Eden" to those being designed today for garden lovers of tomorrow. Also: *History of Flower Arrangement.* See Crowe.

Bowles, E. A. *My Garden in Spring* (1914)
Winning combination of light, often funny, writing and botanical scholarship. Also: *My Garden in Summer,* etc

Bray, Lys de *The Wild Garden* (1978)   a ★ ∥
Illustrated guide to weeds, of immense interest. After all, a weed is only a plant in the wrong place at the wrong time—acceptability has as much to do with fashion as anything else.

Brittain, J. (ed) *Good Housekeeping's Step-by-step Encyclopaedia of Needlecraft* (1979)   a ★ ∥
Sepia line drawings of stitches and techniques for embroidery, needlepoint, patchwork, crochet, macramé, weaving, sewing and knitting. The "makes" are lively, colourful, well designed and up-to-date.

Bryd-Gnaf, Alfred *Exotic Plant Manual* (1974)   ∎ ∥
Straightforward reference book of greenhouse and indoor plants.

Coats, Alice M. *The Quest for Plants* (1969)
Beguiling account of the lives of explorer-botanists of all ages and classes. Also: *The Book of Flowers*

Conran, Terence *The House Book* (1974)   ∎ a ∥
Lavishly illustrated tome explains and displays Conran's own particular style of interior design as applied to every room in the house. British orientation, but will enthuse and stimulate US readers too. Full of ideas to suit every type of budget. Also: *The Bed and Bathroom Book; The Kitchen Book.* See FOOD

Crowe, Sylvia *Garden Design* (1958)   ★ ∥
Concise, thoughtful and beautifully written summary of the whole range and history of garden design. See Berral.

Dixon, Margaret *The Wool Book* (1979)   ∥
Guide to spinning, dyeing and knitting. Readable text; attractive illustrations.

Editors of *Apartment Life Magazine* *The Apartment Book* (1979)
Useful, helpful information about creating a living space to suit your lifestyle and your purse, presented with hundreds of photographs, illustrations and step-by-step instructions.

Encyclopaedia of Organic Gardening (1978)   a ∥
Weighty, dependable, ingenious reference book compiled by the editors of *Organic Gardening* magazine. Everything is here, presented in clear pictures and text. Valuable.

Free, Montague *All about House Plants* (1946)   ∎ ▚
Frewing, Nicholas J. (ed) *The Reader's Digest Repair Manual* (1972)   ∎ ∥
Step-by-step diagrams for house repairs, decorating, restoring and renovating around the house and garden.

Grieve, Maude *A Modern Herbal* (1931)   ▙ ∎
Medicinal, culinary, cosmetic and economic properties, cultivation and folklore of grasses, herbs, fungi, shrubs and trees.

Hay, R. and Beckett, K. A. (eds) *Reader's Digest Encyclopedia of Garden Plants and Flowers* (1964)   ∎ ∥
Hay, R., McQuown, F. R. and Beckett, G. and K. *The Dictionary of Indoor Plants in Colour* (1974)   ∎ ∥
Hellyer, Arthur *The Shell Guide to Gardens* (1977)   ▤
Concise historical account and guide to the gardens of Britain and Ireland.

Hessayon, D. G. and J. P. *The Garden Book of Europe* (1973)   ▙ ∥
Comparative facts and figures about European gardens, gardening styles.

Hillier, Harold *Hillier's Manual of Trees and Shrubs* (1971)
Innes, Jocasta *The Pauper's Homemaking Book* (1976) **a**
Good drawings; hundreds of lively ideas for making the most of what you have.
Jeffs, Angela (ed) *Creative Crafts* (1977) ◗ ⫽
Compendium of over 40 crafts ranging from embroidery to pottery, origami to
metalwork and glass blowing. Stimulating; full of sound advice. Also: *Rugs from
Rags*; *Wild Knitting*
Jekyll, Gertrude *Wood and Garden* (1899)
The first and best of Jekyll's revolutionary books. She looked at plants with a
painter's eye, recognized beauty in many new forms and moulded the thinking of
many of the best gardeners of the 20th century.
Johnson, Hugh *The Principles of Gardening* (1979) **a** ★ ⫽
Described as "the science, practice and history of the gardener's art", a superb
book in every way. Also: *The International Book of Trees*, etc. See FOOD
Kron, J. and **Slezin, S.** *High-Tech: The Industrial Style and Sourcebook
for the Home* (1978)
American best seller introduces the concept of high-tech interior design, using
industrial products to domestic ends, tells where to get materials and how to use
them to the required effect—visual as well as practical.
Martensson, Alf *The Book of Furniture Making* (1979)
The author being of Swedish extraction, all the projects in this basically
"practical" book show a distinct Scandinavian influence—clean lines, plain wood
or bright clear colours. Designs for every room in the house; emphasis on storage;
sturdy toys; complete guide to tools and how to use them. Also: *Making Plywood
Furniture*; *The Woodworker's Bible*
Page, Russell *The Education of a Gardener* (1962)
Fine book on the philosophy of gardening by one of the best garden designers of
our time.
Phillips, C. E. Lucas *The Small Garden* (1952)
Wide learning and experience worn with ease and delivered with wit.
Phillips, Derek *Planning Your Lighting* (1976) ▨
One of a range of publications (all Design Centre, UK; all recommended) about
interior design and how to plan your home. Also in series: *Planning Your
Kitchen*; *Rooms for Living*; *Children about the Home*, etc
Reader's Digest Book of Sewing (1978) ◗ ★ ⫽
528 pages of advice, information and guidance on all aspects of home sewing and
dressmaking.
Reader's Digest Practical Guide to Home Landscaping (1972) ★ ⫽ ▨
Beautiful, useful, topically organized volume on every kind of landscaping in
every kind of climate and circumstance—from narrow city backyards to
expansive suburban acres, from the bleak north-east (US) to the desert south-
west. An essential source.
Robinson, Julian *The Penguin Book of Sewing* (1973) **a**
Good basic reference book for the not-too-creative. Subjects range from toys and
tailoring to upholstery; anyone with the least practical bent will find it invaluable.
Royal Horticultural Society *The Vegetable Garden Displayed*
(1941) ◗ **a** ▨
Useful and popular easy guide to growing vegetables in Britain; regularly
updated. Also: *The Fruit Garden Displayed*; *Dictionary of Gardening*
Salisbury, E. J. *The Living Garden* (1935)
The background biology of gardening humanely examined by a Director of Kew
Gardens, London.
Seymour, John *The Complete Book of Self Sufficiency* (1976) ◗ **a** ⫽
Seymour and his wife have proved that self-sufficiency can and does work,
writing with authority and sensitivity about their experiences and how their
example can be followed. Beautifully illustrated. If you are interested in the
countryside, rural life, growing things and craft skills, an engrossing book. Also:
The Gardener's Delight, etc
Sunset Magazine *New Western Garden Book* (1979) **a** ⫽ ▨
Although intended for Californian gardeners, this is such a good reference book
with so much useful background information that it is well worth using, with due
allowance for the different climate, anywhere farther east.
Thomas, Graham Stuart *Perennial Garden Plants* (1976) ◗
A model of observation, conciseness and practical helpfulness.
Wilson, Erica *Erica Wilson's Embroidery Book* (1973) **a** ★ ⫽
Also: *The Craft of Crewel Embroidery*; *Erica Wilson's Quilts of America*; *More
Needleplay*, etc
Wright, Michael (ed) *The Complete Indoor Gardener* (1974) **a** ⫽
If you are an aspiring urban gardener with no garden but potentially green
fingers, this will guide you to success of jungle-like proportions. Cacti, window
boxes, house plants all excellently covered; good section on growing your own
food without access to the usual basic plot.

Humour

These are all funny books: classics whose funniness has weathered time, more recent books whose excellence seems set to override topicality. Not a long list; but a merry one.

See ART (Adburgham); ARCHITECTURE (Lancaster); DRAMA (Aristophanes, Coward, Travers, Wilde); FICTION/NOVELS (Amis, Beerbohm, Firbank, Gogol, Hašek, Heller, Jarrell, Peacock, Rabelais, Waugh); FICTION/SHORT STORIES (Runyon, Saki); FILM (Fields, Mast); HISTORY/BRITISH (George); MEDIA (Fisher); MUSIC (Hoffnung); SEX (Southern); SOCIOLOGY (Rourke); TRAVEL (Wilson)

Allen, Woody *Without Feathers* (1972) ★
Allen's saturnine wit works marvellously on the page, uncluttered by the physical slapstick which weakens some of his early films. Many of these pieces are from the *New Yorker*; the book also contains two plays (*Death* and *God*), characteristically neat and sharp. Also: *Getting Even*

Benchley, Robert *The Benchley Roundup* (1956)
Benchley was a favourite 1940s actor and after-dinner speaker, a dry, bumbling wit in a long American line (Mark Twain, Will Rogers, even Thurber). He writes with dry urbanity, and has a wonderful line in domestic fantasy.

Bissell, Richard *Say, Darling* (1957)
Bissell, secretary and stylist for a Chicago clothes company, wrote *The Pajama Game*. This book is an account of how it became a hit Broadway musical. Backstage showbusiness, urbanely sliced.

Bruce, Lenny *The Essential Lenny Bruce* (1975)
Collection from Bruce's scabrous solo stage performances. Horrid, bilious humour, picking the scabs of Western decadence.

Chevalier, Gabriel *Clochemerle* (1936)
Saga of village *pissoir* in the Beaujolais avoids archness by precise characterization (especially of French officialdom), and fast-moving plot. Subsequent volumes far less good: this one has staying power.

Daudet, Alphonse *Lettres de Mon Moulin* (1866) ★
Delightful stories of rural cunning and innocence, in barbed, poetic style. Resists translation; for full flavour, best read in French. Also: *Tartarin of Tarascon*; *Contes du Lundi*, etc

Dennis, Patrick *Auntie Mame* (1955)
Interesting example of a splendid creation engulfed by its own success. Forget film, stage musical, turgid sequels: this novel of an unprincipled, elegant *dame d'affaires* sends up WASP society brilliantly, affectionately.

De Vries, Peter *Reuben, Reuben* (1956)
De Vries has written wittily and well for the *New Yorker* (collection *No, But I Saw the Movie*, 1952); but his enduring fame will rest on a series of fine novels outlining the comic desperation of Long Island Commuter Man. Elegant stories of the ordinary aches of life, often (eg on crackerbarrel philosophy, picayune journalism and small-town politics) rising to Juvenalian, galvanic wit. Also: *The Mackerel Plaza*; *Comfort Me with Apples*, etc

Frayn, Michael *Towards the End of the Morning* (1967)   📖
Newspaper Man, Northwest London Man, Almost Middle-aged Man, deftly, sharply characterized. Frayn is a kind of intellectual's Wodehouse (qv). In his best novel, *The Russian Interpreter*, he finds depth by writing about real people in a real love affair. Also: *The Tin Men*; *A Very Private Life*

Green, Michael *The Art of Coarse Acting* (1964) 🎭 ♫
Documentary study of the problems and triumphs of Thespian life, subtitled *How to Wreck an Amateur Dramatic Society*. The book causes strong men to break up on public transport: a painful read. Also: *The Art of Coarse Rugby*, etc

Grossmith, G. and W. *The Diary of a Nobody* (1892) ★ ♫
Fictional diary of humourless, aspiring Pooter, clerk in would-be-genteel Victorian London. The disasters and humiliations of everyday life (bootscraper; red bath; son Lupin's romance with Daisy Mutlar) all risen above with sublime unsinkable dignity.

Hollowood, Bernard *Pont* (1969)
In 1930s *Punch* Pont captured the Britishness of the British in a set of drawings called "The British Character". Heavy-going text should be ignored; selection of drawings is excellent.

Jerome, Jerome K. *Three Men in a Boat* (1889) ★
Three young men (to say nothing of the dog) take a boating-trip up the Victorian Thames. Quintessentially English humour? Only if Leacock (qv) is parochially Canadian, Runyon (qv) parochially American. A marvellous, universal book. Also: *Three Men on the Bümmel*

Langley, Noel *There's a Porpoise Close Behind Us* (1936)
Gently whimsical story of two innocents on 1930s London stage. Will they lose their dewy eyes, their fresh faces, their ideals? They will, they will. Also: *Cage Me a Peacock* (urbane mythological satire); *Land of Green Ginger* (acerbic fantasy)

Lardner, Ring *Roundup* (1920) ★
Lardner's bitter-sweet comedy—finally more bitter than sweet—verges on pungent social satire—a fact largely hidden by his linguistic jokes. A great comic writer; a useful collection. See FICTION/SHORT STORIES

Larry *Larry's Art Collection* (1977) ◢
Larry (Terence Parks) was one of the funniest British cartoonists of the 1970s. This tour of the art world is a superbly drawn, side-splitting collection on a single theme.

Leacock, Stephen *Nonsense Novels* (1911)
Collection of pieces on dystopian Canadian life, when everything was raw, new and terrifying. Leacock's little men are the ancestors of Thurber's (qv): a special, delightful view of life.

Loos, Anita *Gentlemen Prefer Blondes* (1925)
Memoirs of a wide-eyed flapper, the Girl Like I who knows just one thing for sure, that Diaminds are a Goil's Best Friend.

Milligan, Spike *Rommel? Gunner Who?* (1974)
Sendup war memoirs. Ur-goon Milligan was one of the seminal British humorists of the 1950s and 60s: surreal, slapstick, self-deflating. These memoirs are a kind of British *Catch 22*. See CHILDREN'S BOOKS

Morton, J. B. *The Best of Beachcomber* (1974) ★
Morton was one of the best-ever British parodists, one of the few daily journalists whose pieces look better between hard covers. The naming of names, Mr Justice Cocklecarrot and red-bearded dwarves start here.

New Yorker Album of Drawings (1975) ★ ◢
Superb. Sample: two men in a bar (stock pose); one says, "Look, Nixon's no dope. If people really *wanted* moral leadership, he'd give them moral leadership." Put in whatever name you like, it's funny.

O'Brien, Flann *The Best of Myles Na Gopaleen* (1968) ★
Irish whimsy, retailed with flint-eyed, diamond wit.

Perelman, S. J. *The Most of S. J. Perelman* (1979) ★
Perelman wrote some of Marx Brothers' funniest lines, went on to become the world's most complete humorist, a seminal influence on every comic writer since. He is his own anti-hero; his subject is the Hostility of Things, and none have done it better. Also: *Vinegar Puss*; *Eastward Ha!*, etc

Petronius *The Satyricon* (1st century AD) ★
Marvellous sendup of Homer's *Odyssey*: Petronius' heroes search hard and unavailingly for sexual utopias in the tumbling, raucous underworld of Nero's Rome. Good translation: Arrowsmith.

Potter, Stephen *Oneupmanship* (1952)
Trouble starts in Yeovil, England, when Potter sets up a school for people who want to win life's race without actually cheating. Also: *Lifemanship*; *Gamesmanship*, etc

Queneau, Raymond *Zazie dans le Métro* (1959)
Coruscating "experimental" novel, about a wise-cracking, self-willed little girl and the luscious and ludicrous adults who look after her. Monsieur Hulot stirred with the Dead End Kids. Best read in French (as puns and wordplay resist translation); but Bray's translation (*Zazie*, 1960) very nearly comes off.

Rosten, Leo *The Education of Hyman Kaplan* (1937)
New York night-school teacher copes with unusual student. Fractured English is the joke; knowing Middle-European wisdom the staying quality. Also: *The Return of Hyman Kaplan*; *The Joys of Yiddish*

Runyon, Damon *The Best of Damon Runyon* (1938) ★
Hoods, marks, punks, guys and dolls swagger and fret in a fantasy New York. Like Chandler's, Runyon's invented world seems to create, not reflect, reality. Don't the British think that *all* New Yorkers behave and talk like this? See FICTION/SHORT STORIES

Schulz, Charles *Snoopy and It Was a Dark and Stormy Night* (1971)
One of the many cartoon collections about the lovable beagle Snoopy, Charlie Brown and other friends.

Searle, Ronald *The Penguin Ronald Searle* (1960)
Searle is world-famous for one of his lesser works: *St Trinians*. This collection of drawings shows his true standing—satiric stance, elegant draughtsmanship. "The Rake's Progress" (in this book) is an outstanding updating of Hogarth.

Sellar, W. C. and **Yeatman, R. J.** *1066 and All That* (1930)
Wonderful, English-schoolboy, *Punch* view of British history. The combination of Mrs Malaprop and Mr Chips works well. One joke, endlessly varied; but a funny read, not to say a Good Thing.

Smith, Thorne *The Bishop's Jaegers* (1934)
The novel as Marx Brothers film. Surreal, priapic adventures in a fantasy New

York filled with wandering underpants, bishops, nudists, ferries and fog: *Hellzapoppin'* captured on the page. Also: *Topper Takes a Trip*; *The Night Life of the Gods*, etc

Steadman, Ralph *America* (1974)

Steadman is regarded by some as a modern Gillray: dyspeptic, spattered anatomies of modern life, writhing figures tortured with satiric, emblematic force. Grosz, too, comes to mind: but he's not so funny. Also: *Alice in Wonderland*, etc

Steinberg, Saul *Passport* (1954)   ★ ∥

Endless originality of theme and style, perfect draughtsmanship, humour that is both warm and acerbic. Few cartoonists under 45 are uninfluenced by Steinberg. This early collection shows his work at its most fertile and energetic. Also: *All in a Line*, etc

Thurber, James *My World and Welcome to It* (1942)   ★ ∥

In *The Secret Life of Walter Mitty*, Thurber's typical henpecked hero daydreams as he dances attendance on his wife, finally refusing a blindfold to face a firing squad. "Erect and motionless, proud and disdainful, Walter Mitty, the undefeated, inscrutable to the last." Thurber is timeless, uniquely lateral—prose poems of the indignity of man. Also: *My Life and Hard Times*; *Men, Women and Dogs*, etc

Tinniswood, Peter *A Touch of Daniel* (1969)   ▨

At first glance, parochial and opaque: glum working-class household in the north of England, flat caps, pork pies and mushy peas, racing pigeons, temperance bar and trams. But Tinniswood is up to something else: the human condition, no less. It works. Also: *I Didn't Know You Cared*; *Except You're a Bird*, etc

Trudeau, Gary *Call Me When You Find America* (1973)

Perpetual 60s student attempts to deal with the establishment, and fails. All human life (US) is here.

Twain, Mark *Extract from Captain Stormfield's Visit to Heaven* (1903)   ★

Relatively little known but one of Mark Twain's funniest books. Takeoff of religious pretensions and, in fact, all pretensions—Captain Stormfield discovers a heaven that makes so much sense it could never be sold to the faithful. Also: *Innocents Abroad*, etc. See FICTION/NOVELS; FICTION/SHORT STORIES; HISTORY/AMERICAN; TRAVEL

Westlake, Donald *A New York Dance* (1978)

Caper comedies: bungling, endearing crooks (often lower-echelon Mafia) outfaced by traffic, supermarkets, unopenable biscuits, the whole never-never-land of daily life. Slick as movie scripts, as pleasurable as ice cream. Also: *Up Your Banners*; *The Busy Body*, etc

White, E. B. and **K. S. (eds)** *A Subtreasury of American Humor* (1941)   ▣ a

Still the best collection of American humour, and a book it is almost impossible to put down. See CHILDREN'S BOOKS; DIARIES (Garnett, White); REFERENCE (Strunk)

Wodehouse, P. G. *The Inimitable Jeeves* (1924)   ★

Whether you enter his world with Jeeves, Psmith, Mulliner or the Earl of Blandings, the self-styled Performing Flea of English letters will charm and delight. Also: *Leave It to Psmith*; *Summer Lightning*, etc

Literary Criticism

Literary critics fulfil two main offices: those of commentator and guide. In the first place, they tell us what we have just read, and what it meant; in the second, they tell us what we ought to read, and why. At his best (and it is for their excellence that books are listed here) the literary critic has a brave, prescriptive and dynamic role to play, both in our reading of literature and (often) in its writing. By explaining the recipe, he may just enhance our enjoyment of the dish.

See ANTHROPOLOGY (Dodds, Street); BIOGRAPHY (Bate, Coleridge, Edel, Green, Johnson, Nabokov, Starkie, Troyat); DRAMA (Artaud, Braun, Brook, Esslin, Grotowski, Masefield, Roberts, Van Doren, Williams); FEMINISM (Millet); FILM (Mast); HISTORY/AMERICAN (Wilson)

Aristotle *Poetics* (4th century BC)   📖 ♀ a ★
One of the most influential of all works of criticism, especially for its unique eliciting of principles from particular instances (for example, the principles of tragedy from Sophocles' *King Oedipus*). All thinking about *mimesis* (imitation) and about *catharsis* (the purging effect of tragedy) starts from here; yet essentially a modest and undogmatic set of notes. See PHILOSOPHY; POLITICS

Arnold, Matthew *On Translating Homer* (1861)   📕 ♀
Penetratingly lucid about the principles of translation, with deft examples and comparisons. Written in "a prose such as we would all gladly use if only we knew how" (Arnold elsewhere on Dryden). Not just for translators; of importance to all interested in verbal nuance and resonance, in any literature. Also: *Culture and Anarchy.* See POETRY (Arnold, Homer)

Auden, W. H. *The Dyer's Hand* (1963)   📕
Auden always had, in strict and sententious eyes, a reputation for technical genius and dubious seriousness; his literary essays bring his expertise intelligently and practically to bear on other poets, from Shakespeare to Cavafy, and allow his unschematic wit to play ingeniously and informatively among the great and the fugitive. Also: *Forewords and Afterwords.* See DRAMA; POETRY

Auerbach, Erich *Mimesis* (1953)   ♀
Subtitled *The Representation of Reality in Western Literature* (no less), of massive range (from Homer and the Old Testament to Virginia Woolf), and masterly presentation. Moves with assured ease from close stylistic analysis to generalizations on literary and cultural history.

Barthes, Roland *Writing Degree Zero* (1953)   ♀ ✳ ★
With Gallic urbanity—and to the outrage of some Anglo-American critics—Barthes offers a brusque dismissal of traditional concepts of criticism: of discovering "the truth" or "meaning" of a work, of the evaluative function of the critic. He was an influential and eloquent defender of experimental modern literature. Also: *S/Z*; *Mythologies*

Beckett, Samuel *Proust* (1931)
Indispensable to the study not of Proust, but of Beckett himself. 24-year-old Beckett is haughty, affected, unignorable. See BIOGRAPHY (Painter, Pickering); DRAMA (Beckett, Johnson); FICTION/NOVELS (Beckett, Proust); FICTION/SHORT STORIES (Beckett)

Benjamin, Walter *Illuminations* (1970)   ♀ ★
Perceptive, enigmatic thoughts on literature (Proust, Baudelaire, Kafka), philosophy and the social context of art from one of the greatest, most humane writers of the century. Also: *One-Way Street*; *Charles Baudelaire*; *The Origin of German Tragic Drama*

Bradley, A. C. *Shakespearian Tragedy* (1904)   📕 📘 a ★
Best single book on Shakespeare's tragedies; written with clarity and passion and by no means limited to its central belief: that Shakespeare's characters are a supreme aspect of his genius. Also: *Oxford Lectures on Poetry.* See Johnson; Knight; Stendhal; DRAMA (Granville-Barker, Masefield, Shakespeare, Van Doren); POETRY (Shakespeare)

Brooks, Cleanth *The Well-Wrought Urn* (1947)
One of the best of the American New Critics, Brooks in this book gathered his finest pieces, several of which are small classics that will endure as long as metaphysical poetry is read.

Burke, Kenneth *A Grammar of Motives* (1945)   ♀
Complex, ingenious "new" critic, Marxist maverick whose capacity to see what is going on in a work of literature is enthralling and revealing; his manner is mannered, but the realization of the interplay between character and "scene" is valuable and stimulating.

Carlyle, Thomas *English and Other Critical Essays* (1915) ★
Acerbic essays (1830–50) by the great Scots critic who seems so far from our life nowadays—to our loss? See BIOGRAPHY (Froude); DIARIES

Crane, R. S. *The Languages of Criticism and the Structure of Poetry* (1953) ♀
The dean of the so-called "Chicago school" in his best known work. The odour of the study is always present, but the book is accessible to perseverance—and the views are stimulating.

Dryden, John *Of Dramatic Poesy and Other Critical Essays* (*c.* 1668) ◧♀
"The father of English criticism" (according to Johnson) offers here the first sustained critical writing in English, continually illuminated by Dryden's own humane and fluent art. See POETRY

Eliot, T. S. *Selected Essays, 1917–32* (1932) ◧♀a★
Most of the best criticism by a great poet-critic. Radical in its sense of the value of a living tradition; varied (Hamlet, Baudelaire, Marvell, Dante) and with "the intellect at the tips of the senses". Also: *After Strange Gods*; *The Sacred Wood*; *The Use of Poetry and the Use of Criticism*. See Gardner; DRAMA; POETRY

Empson, William *Seven Types of Ambiguity* (1930) ♪◧♀
Work of genius by student in his mid-20s; brilliant for choice of instances and wealth of speculation, all held together by a fervour for the way in which words can valuably mean many things at once. It changed the course of 20th-century criticism in English; and profoundly affected the teaching of literature. See POETRY

Fadiman, Clifton *Any Number Can Play* (1960) ♜
Collection of graceful, highly readable essays by one of the most urbane of modern critics. Towards the end he verges on despair at our civilization's future—as well he might.

Gardner, Helen *The Composition of the Four Quartets* (1978) ♀
Unique treatment of the wealth and detail of Eliot's manuscript revisions; a fully documented study of the growth of a great poem. See Eliot; POETRY (Eliot, Gardner)

Hazlitt, William *The Spirit of the Age* (1825) ♜
Twenty essays about the great influencers of the early 19th century; from philosophers (Bentham), politicians (Canning) and economists (Malthus) to writers (Coleridge, Scott, Byron, Wordsworth, Cobbett, Crabbe, Lamb, etc). Also: *Lectures Chiefly on the Dramatic Literature of the Age of Elizabeth*; *Lectures on English Poets*

Highet, Gilbert *The Classical Tradition* (1949) ♀★
Magnificent study of Greek and Roman influence on Western literature. Exhaustive, erudite, endlessly fascinating: a previously neglected topic, definitively done. Also: *Poets in a Landscape*

Horace *The Art of Poetry* (1st century BC) ♜♀
Storehouse of admonitions to writers and readers, vastly influential, especially in the Renaissance. You'll never follow his precepts yourself, but they'll illuminate the many great poets who did. See POETRY

James, Henry *Selected Literary Criticism* (1865–1914) ♀
Superb on words and novelists; weighty and witty; reviews from Dickens (1865) to Conrad and Lawrence (1914); central sanity about Balzac, Flaubert, Hawthorne and Zola. Significant for its influence upon thinking about fiction and the narrative. Also: *The Art of the Novel*; *The House of Fiction*, etc. See BIOGRAPHY (Edel, James); DIARIES; FICTION/NOVELS; FICTION/SHORT STORIES

Jarrell, Randall *Poetry and the Age* (1953) ♜★
Fine book on American poetry. Lucid, intelligently unpretentious, and quite without envy. A model, in manner and manners, of humane criticism. See FICTION/NOVELS; POETRY

Johnson, Samuel *Johnson on Shakespeare* (1795) ★
The scholarship in this monumental edition is less than one might have expected but the preface and the notes to the various plays are masterly. These were collected soon after their original publication and have appeared in numerous editions down the years. See Bradley; Knight; Stendhal; BIOGRAPHY (Bate, Boswell, Johnson, Krutch); DRAMA (Granville-Barker, Masefield, Shakespeare, Van Doren); POETRY (Shakespeare); REFERENCE; TRAVEL

Kazin, Alfred *On Native Grounds* (1942) a
An American critic writing of American writers with an intensity few bring to the task. Also: *Bright Book of Life*; *New York Jew*, etc

Keats, John *Letters of John Keats* (1816–20) ♜◧a★
Teems with creative critical excitement; ranges from specific to speculative; has a magnanimity which can engage with Shakespeare, Milton and Wordsworth, and a comedy of perception shot through with the tragedy of Keats's life. One of the greatest letter-writers in English. Best edition by Robert Gittings (1970). See BIOGRAPHY (Bate, Gittings); POETRY

Knight, G. Wilson *The Wheel of Fire* (1930)   🏛📕
One of the seminal books on Shakespeare, and the truest in scale since Bradley
(qv). Has had huge influence on criticism—and on production—through its
imaginative sense of Shakespearian imagery and of how plays are also poems.
Also: *The Imperial Theme*; *The Shakespearian Tempest*; *Lord Byron's Marriage*,
etc. See Bradley; Johnson; Stendhal; DRAMA (Granville-Barker, Masefield,
Shakespeare, Van Doren); POETRY (Shakespeare)

Lawrence, D. H. *Selected Literary Criticism* (1955)   🏛♀
Raised crucial questions, particularly about great American writers and the state
of the novel. Least cloistered, most directly engaged, of critics, particularly in his
principled hostility to academia, to philosophizing, to professionalizing. Also:
Studies in Classic American Literature. See DIARIES; FICTION/NOVELS;
FICTION/SHORT STORIES; HISTORY/EUROPEAN; POETRY; TRAVEL

Leavis, F. R. *Revaluation* (1936)   ♀✳★
Sub-titled *Tradition and Development in English Poetry*, a magnificent piece of
cartography, indebted to Eliot's (qv) pioneering work but not slavish to him—or
to anyone. Argues with lucidity and passion for a particular view of the clarities
and strengths of English poetry. Also: *The Common Pursuit*; *The Great Tradition*

Macaulay, T. B. *Critical and Historical Essays* (1843)
Often reprinted—although not so often now as formerly—essays by the great
critic-historian who reviewed some of the great books when they first came out
(eg Boswell's *Life of Johnson*). See HISTORY/BRITISH

Orwell, George *The Collected Essays, Journalism and Letters of George
Orwell, 1920–50* (1968)   🏛★
Orwell never separates literature from life; responds to everything, from comic
postcards to Tolstoy, from Swift to Dickens. Empson called him, with
affectionate gruffness, "the eagle-eye with the flat feet". See FICTION/NOVELS;
HISTORY/BRITISH; POLITICS

Pope, Alexander *An Essay on Criticism* (1711)   🏛📕a★
The great English poem on criticism and the art of poetry; sympathetic yet
divergent re-creation of Horace (qv). Sly, funny, endlessly quotable and
memorable; a monument of Neo-classicism in England. See POETRY

Pound, Ezra *ABC of Reading* (1934)   🏛
Spoof text-book, in deadly witty earnest; creative anthology with trenchant,
poignant comments. Lives up to its own dictum: "literature is news that stays
news". See POETRY

Ruskin, John *Ruskin as Literary Critic* (1928)   📕♀
Art, social, economic and literary criticism—all seen as independent but
interdependent. Ruskin was one of the great Victorian sages imbued with moral
fervour, deep interest (even in things which horrified him), and an extraordinary
range of knowledge. See ARCHITECTURE

Shelley, Percy Bysshe *The Defence of Poetry* (1821)   ♀
Quivers with indignation at the slights done to poetry; speculative about
imagination in general as well as about poetry; grand but not grandiose paean to
the whole poetic enterprise. See BIOGRAPHY (Holmes); POETRY

Steiner, George *After Babel* (1975)   ♀
Masterly, sometimes maddening study of translation in all its aspects. "The
'elements' of language are not elementary in the mathematical sense. We do not
come to them new, from outside, or by postulate. Behind the very concept of the
elementary in language lie pragmatic manoeuvres of problematic and changing
authority. I shall return to this point." He does, too—a superb, obsessed,
heterodox critic, serious in a vital and rare way. See Arnold.

Stendhal *Racine et Shakespeare* (1823)   📕♀
Intelligent comparison of French literature with English. No cramping or
warping, and all in Stendhal's incomparable transparency of style (the French,
that is: we know of no translation). See Bradley; Johnson; Knight; DRAMA
(Granville-Barker, Masefield, Racine, Shakespeare, Van Doren);
FICTION/NOVELS; POETRY (Shakespeare)

Tolstoy, Leo *What is Art?* (1898)
Breaks taboos, not only about discussion of whether certain kinds of "high art"
are truly valuable but also about particular great artists: Baudelaire, Monet,
Beethoven. Nothing is sacred except the search for the deepest truth, and that
means the truth accessible to millions, not the refinements that coddle the chosen
few. See BIOGRAPHY (Troyat); FICTION/NOVELS

Trilling, Lionel *The Liberal Imagination* (1950)
Intense, thought-provoking essays mostly on English novels—and the English
novel—by one of America's finest critics. Though Trilling sometimes stumbles,
at his (frequent) best he soars. Also: *Beyond Culture*, etc. See FICTION/NOVELS

Wilson, Edmund *Classics and Commercials* (1950)   🏛!📕★
Hugely entertaining, informative bumper bundle of articles on contemporary
(1920s onwards) literature; puffs and polemics, always lively and well-argued, in
quick succession. Also: *Red Black Blond and Olive*; etc. See DIARIES;
HISTORY/AMERICAN; POLITICS

Mathematics, Science and Technology

This list gathers together books on a vast area of human experience normally splintered into a dozen exclusive, specialist disciplines. Specialist volumes, in technical language, have been excluded (as they have from music, say, or from literary criticism). The books chosen introduce and discuss their subjects, often at considerable depth, in terms accessible to everyone—it is, after all, possible to appreciate and benefit from the study of radio astronomy (or fugues, or Russian literature) without needing expertise in physics (or counterpoint, or Russian grammar). Above all, they offer a synthesis, they link the various aspects of man's study of his world to each other, and to his whole perception of himself. They are passionate and absorbed, exactly because science is a species of empirical philosophy. The subject is man the measurer, and the messenger himself is a central part of the report he brings.

See AUTOBIOGRAPHY (Hahn); BIOGRAPHY (Rolt); MEDIA (Berry, Steinberg); MEDICINE (Gray, Thomas); PSYCHOLOGY (Luria); RELIGION (Barbour)

American Chemical Society *Chemistry in the Economy* (1973) ✓
600 pages, covering all aspects of the use of chemicals. As well as dealing with what everyone thinks of as "chemicals", it also goes into areas such as food processing. Important "fact" book, for reference as much as reading.

Asimov, Isaac *The Collapsing Universe* (1977) a★
Clear discussion of particles and forces, stellar evolution, neutron stars, black holes, cosmology in general. Asimov, a noted writer of science fiction, also writes readably, reliably, about every kind of science fact. Also: *Asimov on Chemistry*; *The New Intelligent Man's Guide to Science*, etc. See FICTION/SF

Barnett, Lincoln *The Universe and Dr Einstein* (1947) a
This book was a response to the enormous curiosity about modern physical theory evoked by the atomic bomb. Barnett was a science writer for *Life* magazine but this is far more than a Time-Life book; in fact it immediately became a classic of its kind and is still regarded (although events have overtaken many of its facts) as a model of popular science writing.

Bell, E. T. *The Development of Mathematics* (1945) ▮
Standard history of mathematics by a distinguished scholar and president of Cal Tech. Can be read with pleasure by laymen but if you know any mathematics, so much the better.

Bernal, J. D. *The Extension of Man* (1972) ▦a
Compact, anecdotal history of pre-modern physics. Gives a splendid feeling of the great scientists (Archimedes, Galileo, Franklin) as people with human foibles as well as superhuman abilities. Also: *Science in History*; *Marx and Science*

Bernard, Claude *Introduction to the Study of Experimental Medicine* (1865) ℘
Bernard's thesis (that life consists in the maintaining of an interior milieu) helped to revolutionize not only the teaching of medicine but medicine itself; he was a great theoretician in a field largely dominated by practitioners. An essential work for anyone interested in the history of the subject.

Bronowski, Jacob *The Ascent of Man* (1973) ▦a★✓⫽
Popular history of man's inventive and conceptual genius from early times to the present day. Bronowski has never heard of the two cultures; his easy synthesis of all human knowledge and experience irritates some, enthuses others. The book brilliantly analyses the problems faced by human ingenuity; the answers are explained in occasionally glib terms. But the zest for experiment and discovery, the sense of the oneness of human endeavour, have seldom been better communicated. Also: *The Western Intellectual Tradition*; *Nature and Knowledge*

Brown, Hanbury *Man and the Stars* (1978) ▦a
Effects of celestial bodies on mankind: calendar, navigation, time—and the views we take about the stars.

Bunn, Charles *Crystals* (1964)
Readable introduction to crystallography. Technical matters successfully explained in non-technical language; admirable mixture of history, geology and chemistry.

Calvin, Melvin *Chemical Evolution* (1969) ℘✓⫽
How life may have arisen on earth through ordinary chemical processes. Able summary of key research to time of publication.

Chapman, J. M. *Basic Electricity* (1959) a ⫽
Ideal for older-than-school person seeking to educate himself. Illustrations say more than thousands of words.

Clark, Ronald W. *The Scientific Breakthrough* (1974) ℗
The "breakthrough" is not simply $E = mc^2$ (or any particular topic), so much as the breakthrough along the entire frontier of knowledge. For readers with at least some scientific background, though not aimed at specialists. Also: *Einstein: The Life and Times*

Clarke, A. C. *Profiles of the Future* (1963) ★
One of the best books of prophecy ever published. Clarke is the dean of living SF writers, and something of a scientist in his own right. In this work he forecasts events and discoveries of the next 200 or 300 years. Many have already come true; the rest are now seen to be likely. Also: *Interplanetary Flight; The Exploration of Space*. See Rosen; FICTION/SF

Cottrell, T. L. *Chemistry* (1963) a ✓ ⫽
Covers "difficult" ground in a relatively easy way. Eschews mathematics, but explains the essentials of chemistry as a science. Interesting chapter on the methodology of scientific research.

Courant, R. H. *What Is Mathematics?* (1941) ℗ ★
This book has withstood the test of time: one of the really great popular expositions of mathematics.

Dainseth, John (ed) *A Dictionary of Physical Science* (1976)

Davis, Nuel Pharr *Lawrence and Oppenheimer* (1968) 🏛 a ✓
Fascinating account of the meeting (and eventual clash) of representative American and European scientific traditions (that is, inventor-extraordinary and theoretician), sparked and fuelled by World War II and the development of the atomic bomb. Provokes a sombre question: what is in charge, man's will, or the progress of events? Well-written, stimulating biography; case study for the apocalypse?

Dunn, P. D. *Technology with a Human Face* (1978) 🏛 ⫽
Assumes no prior technical knowledge; full of informed opinion and of facts concerning the state of the world, natural resources, health, education, economics, etc; eschews the panic writing of the popular press.

Faraday, Michael *The Chemical History of a Candle* (1860) 🏛 a
As director of the Royal Institution in London, Faraday gave popular lectures each year at Christmas, the most famous of which is the above. The chemical history of a candle took Faraday and his audience—and still takes the modern reader—through the entire gamut of the chemical and physical sciences of his day; most of what he said then is still true. A delightful book.

Fishlock, David *The New Scientists* (1978)
The author is a science journalist of wide experience; the book describes the lives and achievements of many great 20th-century scientists. Excitingly readable and stimulating.

Gardner, Martin *The Ambidextrous Universe* (1964) a ★ ⫽
Physics with the lid off. Appraises the work of modern physics with sideswipes where needed and an approach fresh as new-baked bread. Even better than his *Mathematical Puzzles and Diversions* (herewith recommended). Attractive style; profound matters clearly explained in simple, non-technical language. Also: *The Annotated Alice*

Gordon, J. E. *Structures, or Why Things Don't Fall Down* (1978) a ⫽
Written in plain language, takes the mystery out of an aspect of technology which affects the lives of everyone. Subjects range from buildings to balloons, even into physiology.

Heisenberg, Werner *Physics and Beyond* (1971) ℗
Remarkable "scientific autobiography" by Nobel Prize-winning physicist who remained in Germany during Hitler's regime and fought to keep German science sane during the war years. Thoughtful, penetrating, revealing of the man, also important for its insights into the history of physics in the 20th century. Also: *Physics and Philosophy*

Hey, J. S. *The Evolution of Radio Astronomy* (1973) ℗
Historical survey of the subject, from its beginnings just before World War II to the present day. Written by one of the great pioneers.

Hofstadter, Douglas *Goedel, Escher, Bach: An Eternal Golden Braid* (1979) ★
Exciting book by a computer scientist, tying together mathematics with the creative work of painter M. C. Escher and composer J. S. Bach and the theorems of logician Kurt Goedel. An intellectual gallop—requires concentration, and some mathematics (no matter how far in the dim past) will help.

Hogben, Lancelot *Mathematics for the Million* (1936) ℗ a ★
What mathematics is, and how to do it, explained in clear, masterly prose. Follow the calculations if you can; even if you can't, the explanations and historical survey offer a good general introduction. Revised and updated edition (1967) essential. Also: *Science for the Citizen*

Hoyle, Fred *Ten Faces of the Universe* (1977)   ♀
The *enfant terrible* of British astrophysics and the leading light of the "Cambridge school" has published many books including several excellent SF novels. This book is an interesting attempt to reveal the image of the universe as it appears to physicists, chemists, biochemists, and other scientific specialists. Also: *From Stonehenge to Modern Cosmology*

Irving, David *The Virus House* (1967)
Fully documented account of Germany's atomic research just prior to and during World War II, and of Allied intelligence operations and counter-measures. Both scientific and political aspects are complicated, but clearly explained. See Davis; AUTOBIOGRAPHY (Hahn)

Jeans, James *The Universe around Us* (1944)   a
Jeans was a distinguished scientist who hoped to acquaint the general reading public with some idea of how contemporary astronomers viewed the universe. He succeeded. See Hoyle.

Kaner, P. and **Langdon, N.** *It Figures* (1979)   a
Takes the mystery out of mathematics and all related concepts; approximation, fractions, decimals, percentages, statistics—test questions (and answers) supplied. For the uninitiated, for the bewildered, an essential and useful book.

Kasner, E. and **Newman, J.** *Mathematics and the Imagination* (1940)
What is a googolplex? What is a klein bottle? These and hundreds of other aspects of mathematics are described in over 300 pages of easy text and clear diagrams. Puzzles; some history; optical illusions; speculation and fantasy. Education without tears.

Kaufmann, William *Exploration of the Solar System* (1977)
First-class survey of all aspects of the solar system. For reading and for reference. Also: *Astronomy: The Structure of the Universe*; *Black Holes and Warped Space Time*

Koestler, Arthur *The Sleepwalkers* (1959)   🏛 a
From earliest times, scientific speculation (particularly about the heavens) has embraced both observation of natural events and a kind of conceptualizing "philosophy". We are defined by what we think about what we see. Koestler examines the interplay between empirical and theoretical work, relating the achievements of many great past scientists to the response of their contemporaries. Usefully read in conjunction with McGlashan (qv) and Stableford (qv), who bring the discussion into the modern age, and with Ziman (qv), whose approach is more rigorously science-oriented. See FICTION/NOVELS; NATURAL HISTORY; OCCULT

Kuhn, Thomas *The Structure of Scientific Revolutions* (1962)   ♀ ✱
Revolutionary study of the character of scientific revolutions in thought and theory, suggesting that science generally is not entirely inductive and that waves of opinion deeply affect its development.

Laithwaite, E. R. *Exciting Electrical Machines* (1973)
Guide for undergraduate students; including special electricity and magnetism projects, but simply written and requiring no higher mathematics. Describes and explains the action of all types of electric motors from electric clocks to rolling mill motors. Also: *Propulsion with Wheels*; *Engineer in Wonderland*; *Why Does a Glow-worm Glow?*

Larkin, S. and **Bernbaum, L. (eds)** *The Penguin Book of the Physical World* (1976)
Good short encyclopaedia covers natural phenomena and also landmarks of man's technological and scientific progress. Notably clear style: for children (and adults) who want to know what heat is, how atoms are split, why an engine works as it does, etc. Also: *The Penguin Book of the Natural World*

Lewis, John E. (ed) *Teaching School Physics* (1972)   a ∥
Despite the narrowing title, this is one of the best books on elementary physics for non-scientists, non-pupils and non-teachers alike. The start of Chapter 5 is essential reading, for anyone.

Lietzmann, W. *Visual Topology* (1965)   🏛
Mazes, ancient wall-drawings, mysticism, knots, string games, etc, all treated with strict logic but without the awesome formulae found in more formal maths books.

Lindsay, Jack *Blast Power and Ballistics* (1974)   🏛 ✓
Notably lucid account of ancient applied physics: describes how observation of lightning and earthquakes led to ballistics, catapults, and other war machines. Lindsay is a marvellous exponent of the ancient world, particularly its more arcane areas; this book is one of his best. Also: *The Origins of Alchemy in Graeco-Roman Egypt* (splendid study, despite title, of ancient scientific theories and methods); *The Origins of Astrology.* See BIOGRAPHY

Lovell, Bernard *In the Centre of Immensities* (1979)   🏛 a
Survey of the development of man's knowledge of the universe and of the earth's status in it. Discusses the origin of the universe, and includes a thoughtful section on the potentially destructive activities of mankind. Also: *Out of the Zenith*; *The Story of Jodrell Bank*; *Emerging Cosmology*

McGlashan, Alan *Gravity and Levity* (1976)   ✱
Unique, witty polemic: the discoveries of modern physics treated as a kind of liberating mythology, a conceptual platform for man's new understanding of himself and the forces which play upon his world. Logic and causality are dead: unconscious processes are at work, and we lock into them to unlock ourselves. Science? Debatable. Worth reading? Certainly.

Mendelssohn, Kurt *Science and Western Domination* (1976)   ✱
Why, in the Middle Ages and subsequently, did Western civilization expand so fast? Mendelssohn's answer is that it had unique keys: scientific thought and technological ingenuity. Stimulating personal view of science and of history, in witty, non-technical prose. Also: *The Riddle of the Pyramids.* For an interesting parallel view of China's technological stagnation at same time, see HISTORY/ASIAN (Elvin).

Mitton, J. and **S.** *Discovering Astronomy* (1979)
Ideal introduction. Also: (for more advanced readers) *Astronomy: An Introduction*

Moore, Patrick *Concise Atlas of the Universe* (1970)   ★ ⫽
Lavishly produced introduction to all branches of astronomical science. Non-mathematical. Also: *The Atlas of Mercury*; *The Astronomy of Birr Castle*, etc

Moore, Ruth *The Earth We Live On* (1956)
Distinguished history of man's study of the earth: rocks, seas, volcanoes, mountains and deserts. Well-documented, readable. Avoids scientific jargon: for that see Robson. Also: *Man, Time and Fossils*; *Charles Darwin*

Moszkowski, Alexander *Conversations with Einstein* (1970)
Einstein tends to slip out of biographers' grasp: this book comes nearer than most to his essential self. His views (aged 40) on education, literature, scientific creativity, physics, his great predecessors, even the occult, are here shared with a notably wise, cosmopolitan and cultured man (a Berlin journalist and music critic, 30 years his senior). Among other things, Einstein clearly explains the Special Theory of Relativity in a single page; it is worth buying the book for that alone.

Murphy, Patrick *Applied Mathematics Made Simple* (1971)

Nicholson, Iain *The Road to the Stars* (1978)
Survey of all the possibilities for interstellar travel. Various ideas are scientifically examined; a hand-book for the now voyager. Also: *Simple Astronomy*; *Astronomy*; *Black Holes in Space*

Norton, A. P. *Star Atlas and Reference Handbook* (1910)   ★
Standard, essential reference work, regularly updated.

Pannell, J. P. M. *An Illustrated History of Engineering* (1964)   🏛 a ✓
Brief, brisk text; well-chosen pictures. Roads; rivers and canals; railways; docks and harbours; water supply and public health; bridges—all in 250 pages. You may want to go deeper and further, but this is an excellent start.

Partington, J. R. *A Short History of Chemistry* (1937)   a
Not "history" as a historian might recognize it, more a compilation of facts, "what happened in chemistry", from prehistoric times to the present day. Regularly updated.

Pauling, L. and **P.** *Chemistry* (1975)   📖 ♀
Basic text for first-year college students for more than a generation; an excellent basic book for those with some scientific background. 1975 edition supersedes all others.

Poincaré, Henri *The Foundations of Science* (1913)
Collection of fundamental essays by the great French mathematician/scientist on mathematics and its relation to the physical world.

Pough, Frederick H. *A Field Guide to Rocks and Minerals* (1953)   ♀ ⫽
Excellent handbook, regularly updated, ideal for the professional and amateur geologist alike. The technical descriptions and illustrations are a model of their kind.

Pyke, Magnus *About Chemistry* (1959)   a
Each brand of the subject is clearly and enthusiastically explained, for absolute beginners. Ideal for the teenager who wants to know what chemistry is—and many adults will be grateful for Pyke's unassuming, unpatronizing style.

Reid, Robert *Marie Curie* (1974)   🏛 ⫽
Biography of one of world's best-known chemists, gives a clear picture of how chemical research used to be carried out. Curie's personal life is included as well as her scientific life; but the book avoids the hero-worship of most other biographies.

Ridley, B. K. *Time, Space and Things* (1976)   a ★
Book begins: "There are some splendidly bizarre ideas in physics, and it seems a pity to keep them locked up in narrow boxes, available only to a small esoteric crowd of keyholders"—and lives up to this opening. Non-mathematical.

Robson, D. A. *The Science of Geology* (1968)
Good introduction to the scientific aspects of geology. Necessary balance to Moore's (qv) more general, historical account.

Rosen, Steven *Future Facts* (1976)   🏛
Lively piece of futurology, discussing where present trends will lead in the next generation. Not fantasy: these speculations are rooted in present facts. Imagine the scepticism with which such a book would have been read in 1880s—then read on. For a comparable view, see Clarke.

Rossotti, Hazel *Introducing Chemistry* (1975)
More advanced than Pyke (qv), less difficult than Pauling (qv). Some scientific background required to make full use of it.

Schrödinger, Erwin *Nature and the Greeks* (1954)   *
Fascinating short book by Nobel physics laureate: its thesis, that science is nothing more nor less than the habit of "looking at the world in the Greek way." Provocative; not difficult. Also: *What Is Life?* See Koestler

Sherwood, Martin *New Worlds in Chemistry* (1974)   ♀ ✓ ⊘
Developments in chemistry since World War II. Leans heavily towards the applications of chemistry in "glamorous" research areas (such as studies of the origin of life and molecular biology). Non-technical, but requires concentration.

Sperling, A. and **Stuart, M.** *Mathematics Made Simple* (1967)
What can be said about most books in this *Made Simple* series is that they *do* live up to their titles. For adult education, for reference, for pleasure. See Murphy.

Stableford, Brian M. *The Mysteries of Modern Science* (1977)   🏛 a
Sensible survey of the history, content and philosophy of science. How scientists mould, and are moulded by, their world; the need for "conceptual leaps" akin to the leap of religious faith. For the baffled layman, useful and stimulating; for the scientist, an essential re-establishment of parameters.

Taylor, Dennis *Introduction to Radar* (1966)
From World War II to radio astronomy. Some mathematics are included, but can be skipped.

Taylor, Stuart Ross *Lunar Science: A Post-Apollo View* (1975)   ♀ ⊘
Concise summary of the present state of our knowledge about the moon. For reading and for reference.

Thompson, D'Arcy Wentworth *On Growth and Form* (1917)   ★
Cuts across all disciplines, deals with the growth of living and nonliving things (for example, bank accounts under compound interest), and the forms of plants and animals, mountains, anthills, galaxies—all affected by the bell curve of normal distribution. Unique, stimulating. Revised edition (1961) recommended.

Waddams, A. L. *Chemicals from Petroleum* (1962)
Thorough, regularly-updated introduction to the way in which chemical products are made from crude oil. Fairly technical, but accessible to the perseverant layman. Because the industry is still changing, avoid any but the latest edition.

Watson, James D. *The Double Helix* (1968)   🏛 a ⊘
Subtitled "A personal account of the discovery of the structure of DNA", this book upset some scientists because its highly personal account implied that, even when doing research, they behave like human beings, occasionally even losing their tempers or thinking about sex.

Whitehead, A. N. *An Introduction to Mathematics* (1920)   ♀ ★
Whitehead is one of the great mathematician/philosophers of the 20th century; his most famous (although it's almost unreadable) book being *Principia Mathematica*, written with his young Cambridge colleague, Bertrand Russell. Whitehead came to America before World War I and wrote more popular books, notably this one which is exactly what its title says. Also: *Science and the Modern World*

Wright, Lawrence *Clockwork Man* (1968)   🏛
Comprehensive account of man's attempts to tell the time and to order the hours, days and months. Calendars, clocks, sextants, compasses, from primitive times to the digital present day. Also: *Warm and Snug: The History of the Bed*, etc

Ziman, John *The Force of Knowledge* (1976)   🏛 a ⊘
The author is a professor of physics, but his book is more philosophical than physical. He paints the history of physics delightfully, and shows how indebted we are to the great thinkers. Same subject as Koestler (qv), but usefully viewed here from the scientist's "side".

Media

The products of the media, apparently ephemeral, in fact lodge themselves in the mind. They *are*, in part, what everybody knows: they help significantly to form popular consciousness, popular knowledge and belief. Even ten, twenty years later we can clearly remember, in detail, radio sequences, television images, newspaper cartoons and commentaries. Books, too, are talismans, though of a slightly different kind. As our punchdrunk century staggers on, they seem to promise reliable solidity; they are a doorway to the certainties and apparently clearer visions of the past and a guarantee, in the present, that someone else is with us (an expert, an authoritative voice), that we are not alone. The books on this list discuss the ethics of media communication, its methods and its power. They concern us all—for we are all listeners, viewers, readers, the validating figures in the communicative act.

See DIARIES (Fitzgerald); POLITICS (Woodward, B.)

Appelbaum, J. and **Evans, N.** *How to Get Happily Published* (1978) ★✓
Delightfully fresh American approach to the publishing jungle: author's-eye view makes an intriguing contrast with that of Unwin (qv). Everything from how to write a book proposal, to how to cope with success. A splendid, and very helpful, read.

Bailey, Herbert Smith *The Art and Science of Book Publishing* (1971) 🏛
Excellent American book on the *why* and *how* of publishing.

Berg, A. Scott *Max Perkins: Editor of Genius* (1978) 🏛
Breathless biography of the great editor who discovered and nursed such authors as Wolfe, Fitzgerald and Hemingway. Perkins was himself a better writer than Berg, for evidence of which see *Editor to Author: The Letters of Maxwell E. Perkins*. See DIARIES (Fitzgerald)

Berry, W. T. and **Poole, H. E. (eds)** *Annals of Printing* (1966) 📘a ✄
Chronological encyclopaedia of printing and publishing, from Gutenberg to 1966. Exhaustive, competent, engrossing.

Briggs, Asa *A History of Broadcasting in the United Kingdom* (3 vols, 1961–70) 📘♀📺
Authoritative survey. Essential background to the more personal accounts of Curran (qv) and Goldie (qv). Also: *Essays in the History of Publishing*; *Communications and Culture, 1823–1973*. See HISTORY/BRITISH

Curran, Charles *A Seamless Robe* (1979) ♀📺
Ex-director of the BBC examines what he calls its "competent integrity". How philosophy (liberal, utopian, sometimes paternalistic) is translated into practice. Urbane antidote to the sharpness and concision of H. Greene: *The Third Floor Front* (herewith recommended).

Dessauer, John P. *Book Publishing: What It Is, What It Does* (1974) 📕📚
Authoritative study of the publishing business in America. No sentiment: the text concentrates on real problems of real publishers—royalty-rates, production schedules, fulfilment mix-ups, the problems and the joys. Regularly updated.

Evans, Harold *Pictures on a Page* (1978) 🏛📘★✄
One of a remarkable series of manuals on newspaper production and design, but of general relevance because of its discussion of the effect of design on meaning. Presentation of news—or manipulation? The argument begins here. Fascinating commentary on some of the most famous news photographs of the century.

Fisher, John *Funny Way to be a Hero* (1973) ★📺
Marvellous evocations of British radio comedians of the last 50 years, the last great flowering of the music-hall tradition. Routines and gags lovingly reconstructed, but criticism is sharp as well. Also: *Call Them Irreplaceable* (on international stars of the century)

Goldie, Grace W. *Facing the Nation* (1977) 📺
The author was a founder-member of the team that made BBC television the best in the world. This book is an account of its development from 1936 to the present, and particularly of its handling of politics and current affairs (the author's own special field).

Hackett, A. P. and **Burke, H. J.** *80 Years of Best Sellers* (1977)
A book of records, a chronicle of American times and tastes and a fascinating account of book sales and reading habits. For literary criticism along similar lines see Claud Cockburn: *Best Sellers*.

Halberstam, David *The Powers That Be* (1979)   🔲🔳
In-depth journalism about journalists— *Washington Post, Los Angeles Times,
Time* magazine and CBS television—recreates newsroom tensions, anxieties,
with all the verve of moves like *The Front Page* or *All the President's Men.* Packed
with incident, thin on comment and analysis. A riveting, but finally tabloid book.
(Compare with Talese: *The Kingdom and the Power,* on the *New York Times.*)
See HISTORY/AMERICAN; POLITICS (Woodward, B.)

Higham, David *Literary Gent* (1978)   🔲🔳
Witty autobiography of a leading London literary agent from the 1920s–1970s.
Good on publishers, music, jacks-in-office of all kinds; sensitive account of
service in the two World Wars.

Hoggart, Richard *The Uses of Literacy* (1957)   *
Seminal study of 1950s British working-class culture, as expressed in and
influenced by publications and entertainments. We may think our attitudes have
changed since 1957, just as our entertainments have moved on: re-reading
Hoggart may make us revise that view. (See also Hall and Whannell: *The Popular
Arts*; J. D. Halloran: *The Effects of Mass Communication.*) Also: *Speaking to
Each Other* (vol I, *About Society*; vol II, *About Literature*)

King, Cecil *The Cecil King Diary, 1965–1974* (2 vols, 1972–75)   ✳🔳
British press baron (he controlled four of the major national tabloids) walks like a
cat amid contemporary great affairs, reflects cattily on personalities and issues.
Endearing as the memoirs of an influential crank; enduring as a picture of the
interrelation between politics and the popular press. Should be read with the
memoirs of his (equally forthright) editor-in-chief, Hugh Cudlipp: *Publish and
Be Damned,* and with Richard Boston: *The Press We Deserve.*

Knopf, Alfred A. *Publishing Then and Now, 1912–64* (1964)
Reminiscences by the dean of American publishers.

McLean, Ruari *Magazine Design* (1969)   𝄢
Massive volume; contains reproductions of covers of famous magazines of
America, Britain and many European countries. A feast for the eyes, but also full
of useful information.

McLuhan, Marshall *The Medium and the Massage* (1967)   *
In the 1960s, guru McLuhan's terrifying vision of an existential, all-engulfing
trash culture (electronic media replacing books) seemed as self-fulfilling a
prophecy as Orwell's Newspeak. It remains (just) an unfulfilled prediction, but
no less scary for all that. Useful critical analysis by Rebecca West in *McLuhan
and the Future of Literature* (1969). Also: *The Gutenberg Galaxy*; *Understanding
Media,* etc

Merrill, J. C., Bryan, C. R. and **Alisky, M.** *Foreign Press: A Survey of the
World's Journalism* (1970)   𝄠
Excellent concise survey of the newspaper publishing industry all over the world.
Some knowledge of the American press is assumed, but the book is so valuable
that this should not deter serious students.

Nowell-Smith, Simon (ed) *Letters to Macmillan* (1967)   ★
Who wrote to Macmillan (the famous British publisher)? Tennyson, Gladstone,
Lewis Carroll, Churchill, Yeats, all the Sitwells, Shaw, Joyce, Housman—to say
nothing of Hugh Walpole and Ethel M. Dell. The Macmillan replies are splendid,
too. See AUTOBIOGRAPHY (Macmillan)

Packard, Vance *The Hidden Persuaders* (1957)   *
Twenty-five years ago, in an age of innocence, this book on the processes and
ethics of mass advertising was greeted with shock, horror and (on the advertisers'
part) self-righteous disengagement. Nowadays advertising uses exactly the same
methods, we have all digested Packard's words—and still we allow ourselves to
be persuaded. Failure of communication? Or of moral standards? The conman's
mark often willingly cooperates in being conned. Compare with Inglis: *The
Imagery of Power* (1972)

Peterson, Theodore *Magazines in the Twentieth Century* (1964)   ▮
Scholarly survey not only of many noted magazines *per se* but also of the social
scene that saw their birth. Sober, but important and useful.

Steinberg, S. H. *Five Hundred Years of Printing* (1955)   ▮
Standard history of printing methods and achievements. Dry, concise narrative
(no analysis or comment), dull illustrations, but the ground is ably covered.

Wilk, Max *The Golden Age of Television* (1976)   ★🔳
Affectionate survey of the first 30 years of American TV. Do you find today's
programmes junk, look back with longing to *Studio One, Mr Peepers,* Jack Benny,
Art Carney, Dave Garroway *et al* ? *Should* you?

Williams, Raymond *Communications* (1962)   ▮
Founding-father textbook, laid the basis for systematic British study of the
subject. Analysis, criticism and proposals for the future of all forms of mass
communication. Details and examples are dated and entirely UK-oriented, but
the general conclusions are still stimulating and essential. 1969 edition
recommended. Also: *Culture and Society, 1780–1950*; *The Long Revolution*;
Television, Technology and Cultural Form. See DRAMA

Medicine and Psychiatry

Owners' manuals for laymen on body and mind vary in tone from arcane to simplistic, from the mysterious to the plumber's guide. The prime qualities of the books on this list are authority, accessibility, and a feeling (elusive to some medical writers, and to some surgeons and doctors too) that humanity is common to the owner of the body and to the mechanic who maintains it.

See BIOGRAPHY (Jones, Pickering, Woodham-Smith); DIARIES (Hall); MATHEMATICS (Bernard); PSYCHOLOGY (Burton); SEX (Breecher, Kinsey, Masters, Peel); SOCIOLOGY (Goffman, Jacoby)

Belleveau, F. and **Richter, L.** *Understanding Human Sexual Inadequacy* (1971)
Shorter, more readable version of Masters and Johnson. Recommended reading, *before* visiting a sex or marriage counsellor, for those convinced that they—or their partners—will never make it sexually again. See Kaplan; SEX (Masters)

Boston Women's Health Collective *Our Bodies, Ourselves* (1972)　　★
Clever, helpful health-guide. Describes symptoms and treatments in straightforward style; aimed principally at women, but helpful to men. Particularly lucid on childbirth and on sexuality. Unfrightening: a good book to have in a household with young teenagers.

Copeland, James *For the Love of Ann* (1973)
The story of an autistic child and of how she and her family coped, taken from her father's diaries. Moving and readable.

Dubos, René *Mirage of Health: Utopias, Progress and Biological Change* (1959)　　✳
Discusses the social, cultural and environmental factors that have guided humanity's search for health. Lively, sometimes shocking, look at past and future, makes the point that perfect health and happiness are an unhealthy illusion; unhappily, they are outside the realm of possibility.

Freud, Sigmund *New Introductory Lectures on Psychoanalysis* (1963)　　📖★📖
Like other profound thinkers, Freud writes with enviable clarity and simplicity. He is also often extremely funny. Many of his ideas have fallen into disrepute or into the wrong hands, but he is still the single most influential figure in this field. These lectures are an ideal key for newcomers to his work. But see Timpanaro, *The Freudian Slip*, for a Marxist critique. Also: *The Psychopathology of Everyday Life*; *The Interpretation of Dreams*; *Civilization and Its Discontents*, etc

Fuchs, V. R. *Who Shall Live? Health, Economics and Social Choice* (1975)　　✳★
Economist's view of the overwhelming problems facing the American system of health services. Equal access to medical care does not exist; heredity, environment, money and personal lifestyles influence the quality of care citizens receive. Challenging; readable; ends with specific recommendations for change.

Gray, Henry *Gray's Anatomy* (1901)　　📖⫽
Detail, structure and anatomy of the human body in all its gory glory: a must for doctors, students, artists and the medically curious. Naming of parts starts here.

Isted, Charles R. *Learning to Speak Again . . . After a Stroke* (1979)
Author suffered a stroke; the book details his experiences, and the exercises and therapies which helped him recover. Of particular value for stroke victims and their families.

Kaplan, Helen Singer *The New Sex Therapy* (1974)　　℘
Though clinical in language, a fairly rousing study of male/female dysfunction. Concentrates, helpfully and sympathetically, on methods of treatment. See Belleveau; SEX (Masters)

Kovel, J. *A Complete Guide to Therapy* (1976)
Reliable account and evaluation of most forms of psychotherapy on offer in Britain and the USA.

Laing, R. D. *The Divided Self* (1960)
Laing has a guru status which annoys and repels many, but does not totally invalidate what he has to say (the classic double bind!). His work is programmatic as well as analytical: what we can do about what we are, the creative use of self. Also: *The Politics of Experience*; *Sanity, Madness and the Family* (with Esterson)

Lehrer, Steven *Explorers of the Body* (1979)　　a
Fascinating anecdotes about some of the dramatic events that shaped modern medicine; many important discoveries, it seems, were flukes. Stories about glamorous heroes—Pasteur, Jenner, Curie, Salk—as well as about backroom researchers who never made it to the front.

McNeill, William H. *Plagues and Peoples* (1977) ★
Eye-opening account of the importance of disease in explaining many puzzling events in human history—the conquest of the Aztecs by smallpox not Spaniards, the decline of the Roman Empire explained by measles.

Miller, Jonathan *The Body in Question* (1978) ▣ ★ ✓ ⫽
The body, Miller says, sends us signals about itself, and our response to them, our view about pain, location of organs, ease and dis-ease, largely governs whether we feel well or ill. The book also includes a useful account of the history of medicine. Tough style in parts, but generally a vivid study of a neglected subject.

Parish, Peter *Medicines: A Guide for Everybody* (1976)
Useful if prosaic reference book giving details of commonly-used prescriptions and over-the-counter drugs, their side effects and their selection.

Potts, M., Diggory, P. and **Peel, J.** *Abortion* (1977)
Comprehensive account of the history of abortion, its sociological, biological and legal aspects. Stuffed with statistics, a welcome counterblast to opinionated tracts.

Sacks, Oliver *Awakenings* (1973) ★
Sacks was in charge of a colony of elderly patients totally incapacitated as children by the 1920s world epidemic of *encephalitis lethargica*. In the late 1960s treatment became possible for these people; their awakening is the subject of this tremendous book.

Selye, Hans *The Stress of Life* (1976) ▮
Classic study: how the human body responds to a huge variety of nonspecific stresses, and how many diseases are totally or partially the result of life's pressures. Don't worry though: it also outlines programmes for minimizing stress.

Singer, C. and **Underwood, E. A.** *A Short History of Medicine* (1928) a ★ ✓ ⫽
Still in print 50 years after its first appearance; regularly updated; outstanding.
Also: *A Short History of Anatomy from the Greeks to Harvey*

Smith, Anthony *The Body* (1968) ★
Clear, comprehensive: "your body made easy". Smith makes statistics come to life. Also: *The Human Pedigree; Blind White Fish in Persia*

Sontag, Susan *Illness as a Metaphor* (1978)
How tuberculosis and cancer have been "encumbered by the trappings of metaphor" to the detriment of the patient. Many of Sontag's elegant examples are from literature, including Kafka, Dickens, Joyce, Auden. Illuminating reading. See Miller.

Stodard, Sandol *The Hospice Movement* (1979)
The hospice movement is revolutionizing—some say civilizing—the care of the dying, particularly those dying of cancer. This attractive, if emotionally written, account will bring solace and comfort to many.

Sutherland, S. *Breakdown* (1976)
Experimental psychologist's account of his own mental breakdown, in which he evaluates the alternative forms of treatment available, from a scientific point of view but with his own experience in mind. An honest, disturbing book.

Szasz, Thomas *The Second Sin* (1973) ♀
Szasz is the leader of the anti-psychiatrists, who believe that mental illness is a convenient label applied by society to non-conformist elements; his polemically argued view that mental illness is a myth has been widely adopted by critics of orthodox psychiatry. Also: *The Myth of Mental Illness; Psychiatric Slavery; Law, Liberty and Psychiatry*. See Wing.

Thomas, Lewis *The Lives of a Cell* (1975)
Thomas was puffed by the *New Yorker* as one of the "few scientists who can make his work intelligible to a non-scientific reader". Here he looks at the workings of cells and the way that our knowledge of them is used in the conquest of disease.
Also: *The Medusa and the Snail: More Notes of a Biology Watcher*

Trevor-Roper, Patrick *The World through Blunted Sight* (1970)
This "inquiry into the influence of defective vision on art and character", by a leading London opthalmologist, is beautifully written and handsomely illustrated. The author's selection of great artists is discriminating and his language is non-technical.

Veut, Ilza (trans) *Huang Ti Nei Ching Suwen* (*c*. 2600 BC)
The Yellow Emperor's Classic of Internal Medicine is the origin of both the concepts of yin and yang and of the science of acupuncture. Its elegance and imagery make reading it a pleasure: no risk of pins and needles here. Veut's translation is clear and readable.

Wing, J. K. *Reasoning about Madness* (1978) ♀
So much nonsense has been written about mental illness that Wing's account of orthodox psychiatry is especially valuable because he destroys the arguments of the anti-psychiatrists with impeccable logic. He also gives a clear account of the difference between Western and Russian psychiatry. Also: *Institutionalism and Schizophrenia: A Comparative Study of Three Mental Hospitals*. See Laing; Szasz.

Music

Of all the arts, music is one of the most elusive of description. Its "product" is intangible; our response is personal and sensuous; objectivity (for example, analysis) can hinder as much as enhance our pleasure. All this makes music a challenge for writers: to express the inexpressible, define the indefinable, distil an essence, is to make the blueprint for a butterfly. Prose-poetic ramblings have been excluded from this list: the few "aesthetics" books left are outstanding for objective sense, and for the insight they offer into the creative process. Other, easier areas (history, memoirs, analysis) offer wider choice, and our selection is based on the interest of a subject, the excellence of its treatment, or usually (and happily) on both.

See AUTOBIOGRAPHY (Shostakovich); DIARIES (Anderson, Wagner); MATHEMATICS (Hofstadter)

Austin, William *Music in the 20th Century* (1966) 🗎♀✓
Excellent survey of music many listeners find inaccessible. Copious musical examples; consistently illuminating. See Whittall.

Balanchine, G. and **M. F.** *Balanchine's Festival of Ballet* (1977) 🏛 a ⫽
History of ballet; scene-by-scene guides to over 400 ballets; commentaries by leading choreographers, composers and critics. Does the same service for ballet as Kobbé (qv) does for opera.

Barzun, Jacques *Berlioz and the Romantic Century* (1950)
An important critic of 19th-century art in all its forms here concentrates on one of the great enigmatic composers of the last century. Also: *Darwin, Marx, Wagner; The House of Intellect*

Berlioz, Hector *Memoirs* (1870) ★
Berlioz, one of the great showmen of 19th-century musical life, was a wit and a fine writer. For amateurs of the 1840s artistic scene, a book not to be missed. Good translation: Cairns (1969).

Bernstein, Leonard *The Joy of Music* (1960) 🏛 a
Conductors shouldn't be allowed to write this well. A book explaining music for the layman: simple, clear language—and the same energy and sense of enjoyment as Bernstein provides when conducting or composing.

Blesh, Rudi *Shining Trumpets: The History of Jazz* (1948) a ⫽
Comprehensive introduction to the history and aesthetics of jazz. Controversial, as no two musicians agree about what jazz was, or is. Written in breathless Hollywoodese, but sound.

Collier, James L. *The Making of Jazz* (1978) 🗎 a
Refreshingly non-partisan, affectionate history of jazz up to and including the 1970s. Its innovative and accurate explanations of what actually happens musically in a jazz performance are perhaps its greatest value.

Cooke, Deryck *The Language of Music* (1959) 🗎♀
A book on the ability of music to express emotional, non-musical ideas. Fine treatment of a neglected area of aesthetic philosophy. You'll need to read music to get the most from it.

Cross, M. and **Ewen, D.** *The Milton Cross Encyclopedia of the Great Composers and their Music* (1969)
Programme notes on most of the greatest works of classical music. Handy; readable; stimulating. See Tovey.

David, H. and **Mendel, A.** *The Bach Reader* (1945)
Delightful collation of documents, letters, etc, germane to Bach and his life.

Einstein, Alfred *Mozart* (1946) 🗎 a ★
Affection and scholarship combined; deals with both life and works; has never yet been bettered. See DIARIES (Anderson)

Fischer-Dieskau, Dietrich *The Fischer-Dieskau Book of Lieder* (1976)
Enjoyment of *lieder* partly depends on appreciation of the subtle marriage of words and music. This book, with German texts and English translations (by Bird and Stokes), provides a basis—and is also a splendid anthology of German lyric poetry.

Frith, Simon *The Sociology of Rock* (1978)
Full of information on how the music business operates and why it plays such a large part in the lives of young people. Dense, sociological style makes the book a tough but rewarding read.

Green, Benny *The Reluctant Art* (1962)
Subtitled "Five Studies in the Growth of Jazz": penetrating critical essays on Bix Beiderbecke, Benny Goodman, Lester Young, Billie Holiday and Charlie Parker. Move on to this after Lee (qv) and in conjunction with Collier (qv) and Wilmer (qv).

Green, Stanley *The World of Musical Comedy* (1968)　　　　🏛 ⫽
Backstage showbiz glitter-chat on some of the greatest shows of the century.
Irresistible.

Greenfield, Edward (ed) *The Penguin Stereo Record Guide* (annual)
Reviews, alphabetically by composer, of available stereo recordings. Rosettes
indicate quality. Invaluable for record collectors—and engrossing for other
music-lovers too.

Hadley, Benjamin (ed) *Britannica Book of Music* (1980)　　　　📖 a
Excellent encyclopaedia, in one volume rather than Grove's (Sadie, qv) twenty.
See Hindley.

Harman, A., Mellers, W. and **Milner, A.** *Man and His Music* (1969)
Good, standard history of music, accessible to the layman but with sound
scholarly pretensions. See Mellers; Robertson.

Hindley, Geoffrey (ed) *Larousse Encyclopaedia of Music* (1971) ★ ✓ ⫽
Superb. Magnificent pictures; well-researched, readable, thorough text (one
volume, too). Steak meal where many encyclopaedias offer only soup.

Hoffnung, Gerard *The Hoffnung Symphony Orchestra* (1955)
Inspired, zany cartoons. If music was never like this, it's music's loss. Also: *The
Maestro*; *The Hoffnung Companion to Music*

Hopkins, Antony *Understanding Music* (1979)　　　　🏛 ⫽
Informative survey of the processes and "meaning" of music, with a fresh,
stimulating approach to the pleasures of listening. You'll need to read music to
get the utmost benefit from it, alas. Also: *Talking about Music*; *The Nine
Symphonies of Beethoven*, etc

Hutchings, Arthur *The Invention and Composition of Music* (1958)　　ϙ
Textbook of harmony, counterpoint and other compositional techniques. For
beginners, one of the clearest and best.

Jacobs, A. and **Sadie, S. (eds)** *The Pan Book of Opera* (1969)
Shorter than Kobbé (qv) but covers similar ground. Short articles about opera
composers, synopses of principal works. If Kobbé is for dedicated opera-lovers,
this is for the rest of us. See Sadie.

Kirkpatrick, John (ed) *Charles E. Ives: Memos* (1972)
Ives the man was as quirky and mind-stretching as his music. A pleasure—and
not just for fans.

Knapp, J. Merrill *The Magic of Opera* (1972)　　　　a ★ ✓
Excellent layman's introduction to this most sumptuous of forms. Sections on the
function of each of the basic components (libretto, aria, chorus, singers, staging)
are followed by chapters on conventions, aesthetics and outstanding
achievements in the medium. A thoughtful book, by an enthusiast who is never
besotted. Not technical.

Kobbé, Gustav *The Complete Opera Book* (1918)　　　　★ ⫽
Summaries of great operas, listed alphabetically by composer. Especially
recommended to those who find plots of most operas arcane, simplistic or
ridiculous—here are the facts to support this opinion. Updated edition (ed
Hallwood) recommended. See Jacobs.

Lee, Edward *Jazz: An Introduction* (1972)　　　　a
Logan, N. and **Woffinden, B. (eds)** *The Illustrated New Musical Express
Encyclopaedia of Rock* (1976)　　　　📖 a ⫽
Useful collection of rock data. Thoroughly researched information on rock
artists; subjective assessment of their work; informative and entertaining.
Updated annually.

Mellers, Wilfrid *Music in a New Found Land* (1964)　　　　📖
Important study of American music, from its European and folk roots in the 19th
century onwards. Very good on jazz; for concert music, supplement with Austin
(qv). See Harman.

Morgenstern, Samuel (ed) *Composers on Music* (1956)　　　　ϙ
Selection of composers' writings, from 1500 to the present day. Serious in tone;
contains many fascinating, important documents.

Munrow, David *Instruments of the Middle Ages and Renaissance*
(1976)　　　　a ⫽
Dry title conceals scholarly work of delightful freshness and zest. A passionate
man discussing his passion. Superb.

Newman, Ernest *Wagner Nights* (1949)
Definitive work on the Wagner operas; detailed analyses of the plot and music of
each opera. See Wagner; DIARIES (Wagner)

Nichols, Roger *Ravel* (1977)　　　　a ✓ ⫽
Example of the *Master Musicians* series at its best. Each book clearly, briefly
discusses a composer's life and works. For the layman in search of fairly deep
biographical detail, excellent value.

Nolan, Frederick *The Sound of Their Music* (1978)　　　　⫽
Gloriously glossy showbiz biography of Rodgers and Hammerstein, cunningly
blended with a cool critical appreciation. A book for fans—and also for those
intrigued by why, as well as how, the musical evolved the way it did.

Osborne, Charles (ed) *The Dictionary of Composers* (1977)
Short critical biographies, alphabetically arranged, of 200 great composers.
Entries reliable, often detailed; critical judgements fresh and lively.
Rauchhaupt, Ursula von (ed) *The Symphony* (1972) ★
Coffee-table book (size and weight of the average coffee-table). Pictures superb;
text precise and meaty.
Robertson, A. and **Stevens, D. (eds)** *The Pelican History of Music*
(3 vols, 1962–68) a
Short books with necessarily compressed judgements, and the usual
shortcomings of an over-general approach. Covers earliest times to 1920 in 600
pages.
Rosen, Charles *The Classical Style* (1973) ◧♀★
Study of (mainly) Haydn, Mozart and Beethoven: how they wrote, how their
style developed, their aesthetic ideals and technical means. Magnificent. You
need to be able to read music—and it's worth learning, if this is the reward. Also:
Schoenberg
Sadie, Stanley (ed) *New Grove Dictionary of Music and Musicians*
(1980) ◧a★✓∥
Musicians' and musicologists' bible; necessitates long shelves and a limitless
purse. Musical equivalent of the *Encyclopaedia Britannica*. This, 6th, edition is
completely revised and recast—but earlier editions make fascinating browsing,
the cobwebby attics of the past. See Hadley; Hindley.
Simon, George *The Big Bands* (1967) ◨∥
The great days of swing recalled in breathless prose with interminable, fascinating
detail. Who played third trombone with Tommy Dorsey in 1938, and what did he
think of the caviar? This book will tell you, for sure.
Simpson, Robert *The Symphony* (1966) ◧a★
Analyses of many great symphonies, historically by composer, from Haydn to the
present day. You get most from it if you can read music, but nevertheless an
essential book.
Slonimsky, Nicolas *Lexicon of Musical Invective* (1969) ◨
Great critics of the past and how wrong they were: the worst reviews ever written.
Read it to confirm your prejudices—about music you hate, or the art of criticism.
Stravinsky, I. and **Craft, R.** *Conversations with Igor Stravinsky*
(1959) ★∥
One of the 20th century's leading composers, Stravinsky was also wit, raconteur,
caustic and irreverent commentator on everything around him. This selection
concentrates mainly on matters musical. Also: *An Autobiography*; *The Poetics of
Music*. See White.
Tovey, D. F. *Essays in Musical Analysis* (1936) ◧a
Stimulating analyses of standard classics; originally programme notes, but
enduringly valuable for perception and indeed wit. Also: *Essays and Lectures on
Music*; *Beethoven*; *Musical Textures*. See Cross.
Varèse, Louise *Varèse: A Looking-glass Diary* (1972)
What is the quest for new sounds all about—and why is it so hard for the modern
creator to reach an audience? These chatty memoirs of a thorny,
uncompromising creator (perhaps even a genius) suggest some answers.
Wagner, Richard *Stories and Essays* (c. 1880)
Wagner's stories inhabit the same world as his operas; his essays are often
outrageous, always stimulating. See Newman.
White, Eric W. *Stravinsky: The Composer and His Works* (1966) ◧★✓
Admirable clarity; exhaustive thoroughness; elegant, clear style. Superb. Also:
Benjamin Britten: His Life and Operas. See Stravinsky.
Whittall, Arnold *Music since the First World War* (1977) ♀
Study of 20th-century music, shorter and less comprehensive than Austin (qv),
but outstanding for aesthetic criticism—a rare quality in books on this subject.
Wilder, Alec *American Popular Song* (1972) ◧★
Huge critical survey of Kern, Berlin, Gershwin, Rodgers, Porter, Arlen and a
dozen other equally distinguished men. Technical (musical examples crucial);
useful glossaries and lists. For anybody interested in the popular music of this
century, essential.
Wilmer, Valerie *As Serious as Your Life* (1977) ✓
What has jazz been doing since 1960? This survey covers some of the trends
(musical and sociological) and provides a critical introduction to the work of John
Coltrane, Ornette Coleman, Cecil Taylor and over 100 other luminaries. An
enthusiast's book, ideal for reference—but its eager tone could breed
enthusiasm, too. Also: *Jazz People*; *The Face of Black Music*; *The Jazz Scene*
(with Charles Fox)

Mythology

A major step in the evolution of rational from instinctive man is the development of myth, a "story" which enables him to give formal shape to his experience of the inexplicable and thus, if not to control it, at least to contain it within a framework of experience, of rationality, of precedent. Indeed, by altering and delimiting its myths, a society develops its relationship with the world beyond its reasoning. For the modern reader, myth thus offers a series of parables for his own experience, case studies as it were of the human mind grappling with religious, moral and ethical dilemmas. The study of myths is, at the objective level, a kind of philosophical anthropology; at a subjective level, it shades into philosophy itself. Thus the stories (often engrossing and delightful in themselves, not the least of their attractions) are charged with self-renewing relevance (compare Freud's use of Oedipus), with an urgency of meaning which both informs and universalizes their local particularity. The books on this list gather (and sometimes interpret) myths from many areas of the world; taken together, they give a picture of the developing consciousness of man at large.

See ANTHROPOLOGY (Dodds, Malinowski); CHILDREN'S BOOKS (Anderson, Kingsley, Lang, Lines, Perrault); DRAMA (Aeschylus, Euripides); FICTION/SHORT STORIES (Grimm); HISTORY/AMERICAN (Slotkin); POETRY (Homer); REFERENCE (Opie); RELIGION (Bible); SEX (Duffy)

Branston, Brian *The Lost Gods of England* (1957)
Examines the religious and moral beliefs of the unconverted pre-Norman British. Readable account of ancient myths associated (among others) with Wayland the Smith. See Raffel.
Burland, C. *The Gods of Mexico* (1967)
Imposing but accessible study of ancient Mexican religion—an ethical system as self-contained and programmatic as Judaism. Excellent, clear interpretations of the myths, and of the symbolism of wall-paintings, stone carvings and temple decorations: the convincing answer (if one is needed) to von Däniken and all that nonsense. See HISTORY/LATIN AMERICAN (Katz)
Burland, C., Nicholson, L. and **Osborne, H.** *Mythology of the Americas* (1968)   █ a ★ ✓ ♫
Comprehensive survey of Indian mythologies from North, Central and South America. Copious quotations; sensible interpretations; superb illustrations. See HISTORY/AMERICAN (Josephy); HISTORY/LATIN AMERICAN (Katz, Wachtel)
Clark, Anne *Beast and Bawdy* (1975)   ▒ ✓ ♫
A lovely witty book on mythological beasts from the Middle Ages: dragons, hippogriffs, unicorns, hairy hippopotami, and "men whose heads do grow beneath their shoulders". What a Rabelaisian crew they were!
Dasent, G. W. (trans) *The Story of Burnt Njal* (1861)
Probably the greatest of the Icelandic sagas; Dasent's version—the first in English—is compelling.
Davidson, H. R. E. *Gods and Myths of Northern Europe* (1964)   ▒
Full account of the gods of Teutonic and Norse Europe who eventually gave way to Christianity. Some scholars dispute Davidson's conclusions; but these need not disturb those mainly interested in the narrative.
Dowson, J. *A Classical Dictionary of Hindu Mythology and Religion* (1878)
Easy to read, if prosaic; basic information about the principal characters of Hindu mythology. 11th edition (1968) recommended. See Dutt.
Dutt, R. C. *The Ramayana and Mahabharata* (1920)   ★
Poetic, rather Victorian version but conveys much of the flavour of these two famous epics of the Indian world. See Dowson.
Eliade, Mircea *Myths, Dreams and Mysteries* (1968)   ♀
Eliade is an authority on the concepts and ideas underlying religions of the world. Here he expands the contention that "myths reveal the structure of reality, and the multiple modalities of being in the world." Also: *From Primitives to Zen: An Anthology from the World's Religious Texts*
Fahs, S. L. and **Spoerl, D. T.** *Beginnings* (1958)   ▒
The authors communicate the fabulous richness and beauty of myth in a book likely to fascinate younger readers. Far-ranging anthology; sensitive style.

114

Feldman, Susan (ed) *African Myths and Tales* (1963)　　　　🐚 a
Very little introductory or "academic" material in this book. Its fascinating stories will come as a surprise to readers brought up exclusively on Greece and Rome.

Frazer, James *The Golden Bough* (1890–1915)　　　　🐚 !◨ a ★ ▣
Frazer's 12-volume study (also available in a one-volume condensation) of comparative myth, magic, religion, and belief was the foundation of modern, "Cambridge school" anthropology. Starting with the sacred kingship of the grove of Nemi near Rome, Frazer covers the world of myth and magic from China to Peru. Much detail out of date or plain wrong; but still a magic book. Also: *Totemism and Exogamy*; *Aftermath*

Gantz, Jeffrey (trans) *The Mabinogion* (1976)
Fairy tales of a world magically, recognizably Welsh, a Celtic world unadulterated by medieval chivalry. Gantz's modern translation supersedes all others. See Branston; Rees.

Gardner, John (trans) *The Complete Works of the Gawain Poet* (1965)
"Sir Gawain and the Green Knight," "The Pearl" and other minor works of the poet known only as "the Gawain poet," in a fine modern translation.

Geoffrey of Monmouth *History of the Kings of Britain* (c. 1130)
Geoffrey purports to give an account of "the kings who dwelt in Britain before the incarnation of Christ" and especially of "Arthur and the many others who succeeded him after the incarnation". He was an unscrupulous liar and forger, but his accounts of the early myths of England, from its colonization by Brutus through Lear to Arthur, are charming and seminal. See Gardner; Malory; CHILDREN'S BOOKS (White)

Graves, Robert *The Greek Myths* (1955)　　　　◨ ✳ ★
Graves' two volumes recounting the stories of Greek gods and heroes include conclusions of modern archaeology and other branches of scholarship as well as his own hobbyhorses (notably that of the Moon Goddess). Immensely readable, though subject to academic sniffs: usefully read in conjunction with Kerenyi (qv). Also: *The White Goddess*. See AUTOBIOGRAPHY; FICTION/NOVELS; POETRY

Gray, John *Near Eastern Mythology* (1969)　　　　◨
Useful illustrated survey. Avoids interpretation and is thin on quotation, but the facts are excellently covered. See Hooke.

Harrison, Jane *Prolegomena to the Study of Greek Religion* (1903)　　Ϙ ✳
Now something of a curiosity, a great Cambridge scholar's imaginative reading of neglected data of pre-Olympian Greek religion and myth gave rise to a new approach, less pious and more generous, to the whole field of ancient studies. Also: *Themis*. See Kerenyi; Kirk; ANTHROPOLOGY (Dodds)

Hatto, A. T. (trans) *The Nibelungenlied* (c. 1260)
13th-century epic develops from a chivalric fairy tale to the grim realities of treachery, revenge and desperate human courage in the face of inevitable doom. As well as for the *Ring* operas of Wagner, this saga was an important source for Tolkien's *Lord of the Rings* (see CHILDREN'S BOOKS).

Hooke, S. H. *Middle Eastern Mythology* (1963)　　　　◨ ✳ ★
One of the few books to examine Bible myths, quite properly, in the context of Mesopotamian and Egyptian mythology. Includes narratives of the birth and resurrection of Jesus. See Gray; RELIGION (Bible)

Huxley, Francis *The Invisibles* (1966)
Thorough, and thoroughly scary, study of the myths and rituals of the voodoo cult. Huxley is an anthropologist and this book combines scholarly detachment with personal enthusiasm for the island of Haiti and its people, if not for every one of their weird practices. Also: *Affable Savages* (praised anthropological study of Brazilian Indians)

Ions, Veronica *The World's Mythology in Colour* (1974)
Sumptuously illustrated survey. Necessarily brief text (heavy on wonder, light on interpretation) will whet the appetite, and the bibliography points the way to more substantial diets.

Kerenyi, C. *The Gods of the Greeks* (1951)　　　　✳
Somewhat flowery Jungian reading of Greek mythology, but lively with *recherché* variants; to be sipped, with a long spoon, for devilish pleasure. Also: *The Heroes of the Greeks*. See Graves; Harrison.

Kirk, G. S. *Myth: Its Meaning and Functions in Ancient and Other Cultures* (1970)　　　　◨ Ϙ
Critical examination of the theories of Lévi-Strauss (qv) in particular; though coloured by his views, an important and useful book for readers wishing to understand the anthropological sources of the myths of the ancient Near East and Greece. Also: *The Nature of Greek Myths*. See Harrison; Hooke; Slater; ANTHROPOLOGY (Dodds); PHILOSOPHY

Larousse (publisher) *New Larousse Encyclopaedia of Mythology* (1959)　　　　🐚 ◨ a ★
Abundantly illustrated, full of clearly presented information, with quotations from literature and reference to modern archaeological discoveries. Outstanding.

Lévi-Strauss, Claude *The Raw and the Cooked* (1969) ▮♀★
Lévi-Strauss founded the "structural" method of analysing cultures. His
explanation of the "reality" behind the mythology of primitive cultures,
especially those of South America, created a revolution in the study of myths.
Also: *Totemism*; *Tristes Tropiques*. See ANTHROPOLOGY (Leach, Lévi-Strauss)

Lewis, Lloyd *Myths after Lincoln* (1929)
Lewis was a poet and scholar who became fascinated by the body of myth that
built up about President Lincoln after his death, and that still endured in Lewis's
time. (For example, most visitors to the Lincoln Memorial in Washington, DC,
think that Lincoln is buried there; he is not—he is actually buried in Springfield,
Illinois—and this gives him multiple sepulchres, one of the essential
characteristics of the mythical heroes of old.) Absolutely fascinating: proof that
mythologizing is by no means dead in our "scientific" world. See Raglan; Rank.

Malory, Sir Thomas *Le Morte d'Arthur* (1485) ★▯
Arthur and Guinevere, the Knights of the Round Table, the quest for the Holy
Grail and the rest are the most potent of British myths, known in the Middle Ages
as "the Matter of Britain". See Gardner; Geoffrey of Monmouth; CHILDREN'S
BOOKS (White, T. H.)

Mitchison, Naomi *The Corn King and the Spring Queen* (1931) ▦
An extraordinary novel about a ritual king and queen from the outer reaches of
the Black Sea area who journey to Rome in the era of the Gracchi and become
caught up in the "real" (as opposed to "mythical") events of Roman history.

Narayan, R. K. *Gods, Demons and Others* (1964) ▦a★
Essential primer for those wishing to enter the world of Hindu culture. Also:
Waiting for the Mahatma; *The Guide*; *The Man Eater of Malgudi*. See Dowson;
Dutt; O'Flaherty.

O'Flaherty, W. D. *Hindu Myths* (1975) ★
This does for Hinduism what Graves (qv) did for the Greeks, but is more
accessible for the general reader.

Ovid *Metamorphoses* (1st century AD) a★▯
Not only a treasure-house of mythological stories, but also a source-book for all
Western writers from the 12th century on—Chaucer, Dante, Shakespeare,
Milton, etc—and for painters, sculptors and musicians. Good translation: Innes.

Raffel, Burton (trans) *Beowulf* (1963) ★
Good modern translation of "the oldest English epic". Still a great story and a
fine, scary one to while away a winter's night. See Branston.

Raglan, Lord *The Hero* (1952)
A remarkable study, by an amateur anthropologist and mythologist, of the
characteristics of mythical heroes, showing how they are common to many
cultures and eras—even shared by such a modern "hero" as Lincoln. Also:
Jocasta's Crime. See Lewis; Rank.

Rank, Otto *The Myth of the Birth of the Hero* (1952) ♀
Fine discussion, by a noted psychoanalyst, of the unconscious elements in
mythopoeic thought—with emphasis on the psychic backgrounds of the birth-
stories of heroes.

Rees, A. and **B.** *Celtic Heritage* (1961) ▮♀
Scholarly, detailed study of the myths of Ireland and Wales. First part considers
the various cycles of tradition and their characteristics; second examines the
cosmological framework; third discusses themes. Myths are narrated in each
section. See Gantz.

Sandars, Nancy *The Epic of Gilgamesh* (1960)
Famous, most important non-Biblical myth of the ancient Near East, deserves to
be as well known as stories of ancient Greece. This book gives the full version,
with useful introduction. See Gray; ARCHAEOLOGY

Slater, Philip *The Glory of Hera* (1971) ♀
Psychoanalytic account, never glib or ideological, of the roots (and branches) of
Greek myths, especially of the tangled "life" of Herakles, but ranging through
Oedipus, etc. See Kirk.

Thomas, P. *Epics, Myths and Legends of India* (1942) ▦▮a★⫽
Comprehensive reference book and anthology; exhaustively factual but
readable. Essential background for Dutt (qv), Narayan (qv), O'Flaherty (qv);
usefully read in conjunction with Dowson (qv). 13th edition (1973)
recommended. Also: *Hindu Religion, Customs and Manners*; *Festivals and
Holidays of India*; *Christians and Christianity in India and Pakistan*

Weston, Jessie *From Ritual to Romance* (1920)
Study (by cultural historian) of the roots of medieval romances in earlier ritual
religions. Fascinating; one of the sources of Eliot's *The Waste Land* (see
POETRY, Eliot and LITERARY CRITICISM, Gardner).

Natural History

The science of life has always had wide general appeal. On the one hand it offers the observer examples of miraculous engineering, self-generating and evolving mechanisms of the rarest ingenuity and beauty. On the other, because it concerns the mysterious life-force itself, it leads to elaborate and intriguing philosophical speculation: far more than rocks or stars, the existence of animate nature raises questions about creation, evolution and the meaning of consciousness which each new theory or discovery, from the evolution of species to genetics, seems to open up to wider speculation rather than to answer. Observation and speculation are kept in balance in the books on this list—and they also offer passion, a sense of wonder, and not least the satisfying beauty of the subject matter: nowadays photography is as much a medium for the natural scientist as the written word.

See ARCHAEOLOGY (Ucko); AUTOBIOGRAPHY (Gosse); GEOGRAPHY (Carson); HOME (Bray, Grieve); MATHEMATICS (Bronowski, Calvin, Thompson, Watson); MEDICINE (Thomas); RELIGION (Teilhard de Chardin); TRAVEL (Muir)

Adams, Alexander B. *The Eternal Quest* (1969) 🏛 a ✓ ∥
Lives and discoveries of sixteen great naturalists (including Linnaeus, Lamarck, Darwin, Mendel), in readable, enthusiastic prose. Also: *John James Audubon*

Aitchison, Jean *The Articulate Mammal* (1976)
"Are babies born with a blueprint for language in their brains? Do children all over the world acquire language in the same way? Can chimpanzees be taught to speak?" These and other equally intriguing questions on the phenomenon of speech lucidly and amusingly discussed.

Ardrey, Robert *The Territorial Imperative* (1967)
The territorial behaviour of animals analysed and applied to the human race. Caused controversy in its conclusion that the common cause for war lies in man's ignorance of his animal nature and that family loyalty lies in the joint attachment to territory. Also: *African Genesis; Social Contract.* See Lorenz.

Attenborough, David *Life on Earth* (1979) a ★ ✓
Outstanding illustrations; lively, lucid text expounds the origins and development of all forms of life. Author's zest for and love of creation is informative, infectious. A beautiful book. Also: *Zoo Quest in Paradise*, etc

Audubon, J. J. *The Birds of America* (1827–38) 📖
Unsurpassed illustrations; a model of how to deal with a specific group of animals.

Banks, Sir Joseph *Sir Joseph Banks in Newfoundland and South America* (1766) ★
Personal diaries of Captain Cook's companion on one of his voyages. Banks, a founder of modern botany, was instrumental in stocking London's botanical gardens at Kew with exotics and making it a place for scientific study.

Bewick, Thomas *A Memoir of Thomas Bewick Written by Himself* (1862) ∥ 📖
Autobiography of one of the great Victorian wild life engravers. Bewick revived the ancient art of wood engraving; he illustrated the first edition of White's (qv) *Natural History of Selbourne.* Also: *General History of Quadrupeds; History of British Birds*

Blunt, Wilfred *The Complete Naturalist* (1971) 🏛 ∥
Biography of Linnaeus, the father of modern botanical classification. Lavish quotations from his diaries and letters; contemporary illustrations add to the 18th-century flavour. Useful appendix on scientific classification.

Buchsbaum, Ralph *Animals without Backbones* (1948) 📖 a ∥
Step-by-step biology of all animals more lowly than fish; simply explains their anatomy and how they work.

Burton, Sir Richard *Wanderings in West Africa* (1863)
Travel tales of one of the great 19th-century explorers, the discoverer of Lake Tanganyika. Not entirely devoted to natural history but excellent foundation material. See SEX (Boccaccio, Nefzawi, Vatsyayana); TRAVEL

Corner, E. J. H. *The Life of Plants* (1964)
Popular guide to the life and evolution of plants.

Cousteau, Jacques *The Silent World* (1953)
The first in a series of best sellers by an extraordinary scientist-publicist who developed the method of skin-diving with the aqua-lung. Cousteau is a popularizer, but a brave and thoughtful man as well, and a capable writer.

Darwin, Charles *The Origin of Species* (1859)   🏳
Created a huge outcry on first publication for its conclusion that man and apes have a common ancestor. Written twenty-one years after Darwin's epic voyage to the Galapagos Islands and South America (on which, see Moorehead). Lucid, readable prose, full of personality and enthusiasm. Also: *The Expression of the Emotions in Man and Animals*; *Autobiography*, etc. See Huxley; Lack; Smith; RELIGION (Barbour, Teilhard de Chardin)

Desmond, Adrian J. *The Hot-blooded Dinosaurs* (1975)   🏛 a ✓ ∥
Were the dinosaurs cold-blooded, pea-brained lizards—or hot-blooded proto-mammals? Revolutionary, influential and enjoyable study of a major new turn in palaeontology.

De Wit, H. C. D. *Plants of the World* (3 vols, 1963)   ∥
One of the few surveys of the world's plants largely free of technical terms; interesting sidelights on their evolution and uses to man.

Dorst, Jean *Before Nature Dies* (1965)
Useful European adjunct to Carson's *Silent Spring*: emphasis is on pollution and over-exploitation of the natural resources of land and sea; contains proposals for a radical revision of our attitudes. Also: *Field Guide to the Larger Mammals of Africa*. See GEOGRAPHY (Carson, Ward)

Douglas-Hamilton, I. and **O.** *Among the Elephants* (1975)
Diary of five years spent among the elephants of Tanzania, remarkable for the pioneering of radio-tracking animals and the discovery of "the elephants' graveyard".

Durrell, Gerald *The Bafut Beagles* (1947)   🏛
Tales of animal collecting in the Cameroons, by the founder of the conservation-based Jersey Zoological Park. Delightful, humorous portraits of both animals and men. Also: *The Overloaded Ark*; *A Zoo in My Luggage*, etc. See CHILDREN'S BOOKS

Elton, Charles *Animal Ecology* (1927)   🏳 ρ
On first appearance a pioneering work for zoology, then dominated by the study of anatomy. Explains why animals live where they do and describes their strategies for survival. Also: *The Pattern of Animal Communities*; *The Ecology of Invasions by Animals and Plants*

Fabre, J. H. *The Sacred Beetle and Others* (1887)   ★
Fabre did not accept the theory of evolution and therefore was (is) out of the main stream of naturalists of our time. But nobody was ever a better observer, as is evident from this small book. The title piece, on the dung beetle, is delightful.

Frisch, Karl von *The Dancing Bees* (1954)   ★
Greeted with amazement when first published: it seemed impossible that insects could devise such a sophisticated and complex means of communicating and finding food. Also: *Bees: Their Vision, Chemical Senses and Language*.

Fry, C. H. and **Flegg, J. (eds)** *World Atlas of Birds* (1974)   🏳 a
Continent by continent catalogue of the world's natural aviary; excellently illustrated.

Good, Ronald *The Geography of the Flowering Plants* (1947)
World atlas of plants not only catalogues what grows where but explains the reasons why. Not a book for complete beginners, because it gives only botanical names for plants; but it is invaluable once this hurdle has been passed.

Goodall, Jane *In the Shadow of Man* (1971)
Fascinating first-hand account of life with the chimpanzees; lively text; excellent photographs (by Hugo van Lawick). Also: *Innocent Killers*

Gray, Sir James *Animal Locomotion* (1968)   🏳 ∥
Enlarged version of author's earlier *How Animals Move*; an elegant combination of physics and biology, in lucid, non-specialist terms.

Grzimek, B. and **M.** *Serengeti Shall Not Die* (1960)
Pioneering study that led to the establishing of Crater in the Serengeti as a conservation area. Also: *Among the Animals of Africa*

Hardy, Sir Alister *The Open Sea* (2 vols, 1956–59)
Biographies of who eats whom in the food-chains of the oceans. First volume devoted mainly to the eaten (plankton), second to the eaters (fish). Also: *Great Waters*

Holden, Edith *The Country Diary of an Edwardian Lady* (1977)   🏛 ∥
Remarkable illustrated diary of Edith Holden, written in 1906 but not published until the 1970s. Like her 18th-century predecessor White (qv), she records the natural history of the seasons with eyes and ears alert to every change.

Hubbard, C. E. *Grasses* (1968)
Beautifully illustrated catalogue; limited in scope to Europe, but a model of its kind.

Hudson, W. H. *Birds in Town and Village* (1919)   ρ ∥
South-American-born poet-naturalist arrived in England in 1860 and revelled in all he saw around him. Book contains a bitter-sweet essay berating fashionable women for wearing bird feathers. Sensitive; unsentimental; fascinating. Also: *Birds and Man*; *The Naturalist in La Plata*. See AUTOBIOGRAPHY

Huth, Hans *Nature and the American: Three Centuries of Changing Attitudes* (1957)
Pioneer history of the conservation movement in America, highlighting the link between natural history and natural resources.

Huxley, Thomas H. *Evolution and Ethics* (1893)   *★*
Application of Darwinian evolution to man's morality by one of Darwin's great champions. Knotty prose, but worth persevering—the arguments are still vital today. Also: *The Crayfish*; *Manual of the Comparative Anatomy of Vertebrated Animals*; *Man's Place in Nature and Other Essays*. See Darwin.

Imms, A. D. *Insect Natural History* (1947)   🏛📘a ⫽
Types of insects and the way they live, as recorded by one of the great entomologists. Excellent, regularly updated introduction to entomology.

Jefferies, Richard *Nature near London* (1885)
Observations of natural history in the days when the suburbs really were at the fringes of the countryside. Also: *Wild Life in a Southern County*; *The Game-Keeper at Home*; *Hodge and His Master*

Koestler, Arthur *The Case of the Midwife Toad* (1971)   ★
Riveting story of how the German scientist Paul Kammerer set out to prove Lamarck right by showing that toads could inherit acquired characteristics. Splendidly clear on the motivation and method of scientific research, and on the morality of science. See FICTION/NOVELS; MATHEMATICS; OCCULT

Krutch, J. W. *The Desert Year* (1952)
Superb evocation of the life of the south-western American desert by a New Englander who moved there because he loved it more than anywhere else in the world. Krutch, a professor of literature turned naturalist, always wrote extraordinarily well. Also: *The Twelve Seasons*; *Grand Canyon: Today and All Its Yesterdays*, etc. See BIOGRAPHY

Lack, D. *Darwin's Finches* (1947)
Accessible modern study of Darwin's famous finches. Fascinating detail on how each bird is suited to one particular life style. Also: *Life of the Robin*; *Natural Regulation of Animal Numbers*. See Darwin.

Lorenz, Konrad *On Aggression* (1963)   *✳★
"Nature red in tooth and claw", or why aggression is a good thing (because the fighting instinct is the essence of survival, not destruction). Interesting parallels between behaviour of men and animals; hopeful conclusions. Also: *King Solomon's Ring*; *Studies in Animal and Human Behaviour*. See Ardrey.

Maxwell, Gavin *Ring of Bright Water* (1960)
Life of the author and his otters Mijbil and Edal in the Highlands of Scotland. Good on local wildlife; Maxwell manfully resists the temptations of anthropomorphism. Also: *The Rocks Remain*; *Raven Seek Thy Brother*

Medawar, P. B. and **J. S.** *The Life Science* (1977)   ℘
Useful summary of biological ideas and research since 1950. Technical language, but accessible with perseverance. Also: *The Uniqueness of the Individual*; *The Art of the Soluble*; *The Hope of Progress*, etc

Moorehead, Alan *Darwin and the Beagle* (1969)   a ⫽
Travelogue of Darwin's famous voyage round the world. Illustrations include drawings and paintings by Darwin's fellow passengers. See Darwin; TRAVEL

Mountfort, S. *Wild Paradise: The Story of the Coto Donana Expeditions* (1958)
Portrait of the unspoilt wilderness of southern Spain and its varied wildlife. Vivid descriptions of migratory wildfowl.

Peterson, Roger Tory *Field Guide to the Birds* (1934)   📘a ⫽🪶
This is the first in an extraordinary series of field guides that are the most dependable such works for the student of North American flora and fauna. Wonderful text (with wry comments) and illustrations; convenient pocket size; indispensable companions of walkers and watchers everywhere in America. Revised edition (1942) recommended.

Rhodes, F. H. T. *Evolution of Life* (1962)   ℘
Excellent guide to the history of life on earth, without an excess of technical language. Not the first book to read on the subject (see Attenborough); but invaluable follow-up material.

Romer, Alfred Sherwood *The Vertebrate Story* (1959)   ℘ ⫽
Authoritative account of the life and evolution of vertebrates, by one of America's foremost zoologists.

Savory, T. H. *The Spider's Web* (1952)   🏛 ⫽
A hundred and one ways in which spiders say "come into my parlour". Details of spinning techniques and capture methods make creepy, fascinating reading.

Scheffer, Victory B. *The Year of the Whale* (1870)
Chronicle of a 12-month period in a whale's life; delightful details of birth and suckling. Unpretentious charm; joyful style. Also: *The Year of the Seal*

Sears, P. B. *Deserts on the March* (1935)   ℘
The science of the dust-bowl, and man's devastating effects on desert animals and plants. In the 1980s, rather a case of "I told you so." Also: *The Ecology of Man*

Simpson, George Gaylord *Horses* (1951)
History of horse evolution over many millennia; guide to the biology of the
modern horse. Splendid illustrations include T. H. Huxley's famous "Eohippus
and Eohomo" cartoon.

Smith, John Maynard *The Theory of Evolution* (1958)
Confirms Darwin's conclusions on evolution and expands them in the light of
modern knowledge. Hard going in parts, for the beginner, but worth the effort.
See Darwin.

Spinar, Z. V. *Life before Man* (1972)   🏛 a ∥
Glossy guide to the world of prehistory with detailed reconstructions of our
planet as it once was. Sound introduction to dinosaurs.

Tansley, Sir Arthur G. *Britain's Green Mantle* (1949)
Scientific study of plant communities, written with a rambler's enthusiasm. One
of the first books to stress the importance of conservation.

Tinbergen, Nikolaas *The Herring-gull's World* (1960)
Study of instinct in the life history of the herring-gull. Outstanding for its
demarcation between "inherited" and "learned" behaviour; good introduction
to the author's more advanced works. Also: *The Study of Instinct; Social
Behaviour in Animals; Animal Behaviour*

Tomkins, P. and **Bird, C.** *The Secret Life of Plants* (1973)
The supposed powers of plants to memorize, mindread and even commit murder
propounded in highly entertaining style by two serious botanists. Also records
how plants communicate, how they select classical music in preference to pop.
Sceptically received by many; not to be missed.

Walker, E. P. *Mammals of the World* (1968)

Walton, Izaak *The Compleat Angler* (1653)   📖
A catch for any lucky reader.

Ward, Ritchie, R. *The Living Clocks* (1972)
Biorhythms, hibernation, celestial navigation—fascinating areas of biological
research enthusiastically, accessibly discussed.

Waterton, Charles *Wanderings in South America, the North-West of the
United States and the Antilles* (1825)   ★
Vivacious, unconventional account of wildlife and adventures in the Americas.
On his return Waterton turned his Yorkshire park into a miniature zoo. Highly
entertaining.

White, Gilbert *The Natural History and Antiquities of Selbourne*
(1789)   📖 a ★ 📖
Diary of a naturalist, records year-by-year changes in the author's curacy at
Selbourne, Hampshire, in minute detail down to the first snowdrops of spring and
the departure of summer's last swallow.

Young, J. Z. *The Life of Vertebrates* (1950)   🏛 ∥
A textbook, in technical language, but an outstanding one. Author's enthusiasm
for his subject shines through the matter-of-fact presentation. Carries the student
from prehistory to the present with lucidity and ease. Also: *The Life of Mammals*.

Occult and Paranormal

Are we alone? Whatever we may think of the underlying premises of this study, these books offer serious and intellectually responsible examinations of the "evidence". Treading delicately on the borderline between objective and subjective, fact and fiction, rarely letting "I wish it were" shade into "It must be so", they may not give definitive answers; but certainly (whether you regard the subject as an examination of actual phenomena or as a bypath of the human mind at its most darkly and fantastically ingenious) they leave the right questions posed, and poised.

See HISTORY/EUROPEAN (Cohn); MATHEMATICS (Lindsay); RELIGION (Hick)

Bennett, Ernest *Apparitions and Haunted Houses* (1939) 📕
Classic study of the evidence for all kinds of ghosts and hauntings, plausibly authenticated.

Bennett, J. B. *Witness* (1974)
Autobiography of one of Gurdjieff's leading followers, and a remarkable man in his own right; fascinating, detailed account of Bennett's "search for the miraculous". See Reyner.

Conway, David *Magic: An Occult Primer* (1972)
Most sensible people take it for granted that magic is basically nonsense. Yet there is now a widespread minority belief that it is not quite as absurd as we think. Sensible, balanced book by a man who claims actually to practise magic—a good introduction to a bewildering subject.

Coxhead, Nona *Mindpower* (1976)
Balanced, readable account of "parascience and the study of consciousness"—telepathy, psychic healing, mystical experience, etc.

Gauquelin, Michael *Cosmic Influences on Human Behaviour* (1973)
Persuasive arguments for treating astrology as a science. Attempts objectivity, and assumes an open mind in the reader: win or lose, an interesting, well-argued book.

Grant, Kenneth *The Magical Revival* (1972)
An underrated writer, Grant was an Aleister Crowley disciple, so writes with insight and authority of this century's revival of interest in magic and occultism. Also: *Aleister Crowley and the Hidden God*; *Cults of Shadow*; *Nightside of Eden*

Gris, H. and **Dick, W.** *The New Psychic Soviet Discoveries* (1979)
A crisis of scientific conscience exists in Russia about psychic phenomena, but nevertheless they are doing much more research than we in the West. This book is a thorough, intelligent account of recent work.

Hansel, C. E. M. *ESP: A Scientific Evaluation* (1966) ✶
Highly critical review of the experimental literature of the field. Interesting comparison with Rao (qv).

Head, J. and **Cranston, S. L.** *Reincarnation* (1967)

Jenkins, Stephen *The Undiscovered Country* (1977)
Good introduction to the mysterious subject of "ley lines", the lines of magnetic force around the earth, which may have had sacred significance for ancient man.

Koestler, Arthur *The Roots of Coincidence* (1972)
Investigates the Rosenheim case in fascinating detail. See FICTION/NOVELS; MATHEMATICS; NATURAL HISTORY

LeShan, Lawrence *The Medium, the Mystic and the Physicist* (1966) 📖★
LeShan is a scientist who began as a sceptic, but slowly became convinced of the reality of "paranormal phenomena"—and that they are related to the "underlying reality" glimpsed by mystics. Outstanding, especially if approached with scepticism.

Lethbridge, T. C. *The Essential T. C. Lethbridge* (1979) 📖a★
Lethbridge, a retired archaeologist, was one of the most remarkable "psychical researchers" of the 20th century, fascinated by dowsing, ghosts, extra-sensory perception and the mystery of time. His books are readable, eccentric, full of personal anecdote and experience.

Myers, F. W. H. *Human Personality and Its Survival of Bodily Death* (1903) 📕

Prince, Walter Franklin (ed) *Noted Witnesses for Psychic Occurrences* (1928) 📖★
Absorbing anthology of strange occurrences: ghosts, out-of-the-body experiences, premonitory dreams, telepathy and so on. The point of the title is that all the "witnesses" were "respected figures"—writers, politicians, lawyers, etc—a fact assumed to lend weight to what they claimed.

Rao, K. R. *Experimental Parapsychology* (1966)
Sympathetic account by a scientist of the literature of the field of parapsychology.
Gives most experiments described the benefit of the doubt, at least where there is
doubt. Should be balanced by a reading of Hansel (qv).

Reyner, J. H. *The Diary of a Modern Alchemist* (1974)   a
The "alchemy" Reyner writes about is more closely related to the ideas of
Gurdjieff than to the alchemy of the Middle Ages. See Bennett, J. B.

Rhine, J. B. and **Pratt, J. G.** *Parapsychology: Frontier Science of the
Mind* (1957)
Rhine was one of the best known American experimenters in the field; he
undertook studies with Zener cards at Duke University for many years. As with
so much in parapsychology, the final verdict on his work is inconclusive. See Rao.

Roll, William G. *Poltergeists* (1977)   🔖♀
Up-to-the-minute scientific study by an acknowledged expert. See Sitwell.

Sakoian, F. and **Acker, S.** *The Astrologer's Handbook* (1973)   a
Best single-volume introduction to astrology; comprehensive treatment, sensible
and well written.

Siggwick, D. *et al* *Phantoms of the Living* (1918)   ♀
Vast, diligent work on the subject of people who have been seen in one place
while they were actually in another.

Sitwell, Sacheverell *Poltergeists* (1940)   🔖 a
Stylish account of the knockabout comedians of the spirit world, which we now
believe to originate in our own unconscious minds. See Roll; AUTOBIOGRAPHY
(Sitwell, O.)

Smith, Adam *Powers of Mind* (1975)
Written in gratingly "with-it" journalese; but a useful survey of modern research
into the mysteries of the mind, bio-feedback, etc.

Stevenson, Ian *The Evidence for Survival from Claimed Memories of
Former Incarnations* (1961)   ♀
Valuable study, treated as scientific inquiry rather than speculation and theory.

Steiger, Brad (ed) *Project Blue Book: The Top Secret UFO Findings
Revealed* (1976)
Project Blue Book—the official reports assembled by the US Air Force up to
1969, when the project was discontinued. Steiger's book is a good account;
repeats many of the "best" stories.

Summers, Montague *The History of Witchcraft and Demonology* (1926)
The "Reverend" Summers writes as a totally convinced believer in the reality of
witches and powers of evil—demons, etc. Also: *The Vampire; The Werewolf; The
Geography of Witchcraft*

Targ, R. and **Puthoff, H.** *Mind-Reach* (1977)   ♀
Two scientists, both of whom worked with Uri Geller at the Stanford Research
Institute, examine psychic ability with particular reference to "remote viewing".

Tart, Charles (ed) *Altered States of Consciousness* (1969)   🔖♀
Collection of papers on strange and hidden aspects of consciousness; necessary
foundation for any study of the "paranormal".

Thouless, R. H. *From Anecdote to Experiment in Psychical Research*
(1972)   ♀
Thouless' detailed and comprehensive approach is essential for those who wish to
attain real understanding of parapsychology as opposed to psychic anecdote.

Tyrell, G. N. M. *Science and Psychical Phenomena* (1939)   a
This, together with Tyrell's *Apparitions*, is an excellent book on ghosts, extra-
sensory perception and telepathy.

Vaughan, Alan *Patterns of Prophecy* (1973)
Vaughan, fascinated by the possibility of precognition, conducted exhaustive
research of which this book is a readable, scientific account.

Vyvyan, John *A Case against Jones* (1966)
Sensible, balanced study of the whole field of psychical research. Ernest Jones,
Freudian biographer, said that anyone who believes in the paranormal needs his
head examined: hence this book.

Watson, Lyall *Lifetide* (1979)   🔖
Watson achieved an overnight reputation with *Supernature*, an attempt to
demonstrate that there is a sound scientific basis for many so called "supernatural
phenomena". This book, his most important so far, bases its theories of the
paranormal on Jung's idea of the collective unconscious. Also: *The Romeo Error,
Gifts of Unknown Things*

Webb, James *The Flight from Reason* (1971)   🔖 a
Webb writes about "occultism" as a sceptic; his knowledge is immense, his
approach entertaining. Also: *The Occult Establishment*

Wilson, Colin *The Occult* (1971)   📕 a ★
Comprehensive summary of the whole field, from extra-sensory perception and
second-sight to vampires and the Kabbalah. Also: *Mysteries*

Philosophy

What other subject ever aroused such passion in its devotees or such impatience among outsiders? "Why do you only *talk* of virtue?" someone asked Socrates (who proceeded, philosophically, to explain). Certain philosophers have themselves become so impatient with philosophical pretentiousness that they have advocated closing down the talking shop. But the philosophical standard—the attempt to argue honourably and reasonably—affects nearly all intellectual and aesthetic disciplines. It proposes an ideal for the conduct of all kinds of disputes; it asks us to be honest with ourselves; it refuses to go away. Mere words? "Words are loaded pistols," said Brice–Parrain. The picker and chooser of philosophical texts intrudes in a field where every corner claims that every other is swarming with impostors and trespassers. No single point of view has been allowed to prevail in this list: there are no definitive answers, but at least the questioning can be begun.

See DIARIES (Kierkegaard, Seneca, Teilhard de Chardin); ECONOMICS (Heilbroner, Robinson); MATHEMATICS (Koestler, Ziman); POLITICS (Mannheim, Niebuhr, Rowls); RELIGION (Buber, Pascal, Teilhard de Chardin, Tillich); SOCIOLOGY (Bottomore, Marcuse)

Adler, M. J. *The Conditions of Philosophy* (1965)   *
History of philosophy by a renowned—and controversial—philosopher who holds (hence the controversy) that most "modern" philosophy (ie post-Cartesian) is of little worth. Fascinating to see history through the wrong end of his telescope; it redresses the bias towards relentless modernity in other authors and critics. Also: *The Common Sense of Politics*; *How to Think about God*. See REFERENCE

Aquinas, Thomas *Summa Theologica* (1267–73)   ▯
Written, Saint Thomas said, to "instruct beginners," this extraordinary work—its numerous volumes dictated to a team of scribes because one alone could not keep up with the Master—is one of the unbending monuments of the human intellect. See Gilson.

Aristotle *Nicomachean Ethics* (4th century BC)   ▮★
Aristotle ("the Master of those that know") treats human behaviour as natural history, not as a subject for dogmatic metaphysics. A far more open-minded and humane thinker than his stiff predecessor, Plato, he accepted the diversity of man, creation's paragon, the "reasonable animal". Also: *Metaphysics*; *The Organon* (collected logical treatises), etc. See LITERARY CRITICISM; POLITICS

Austin, J. L. *Sense and Sensibilia* (1964)
Posthumously published dry-as-sneezing powder lectures assailing the hallowed traditions of the philosophy of perception, in particular as represented by Ayer's (qv) *The Foundations of Empirical Knowledge*. For Austin's own explanation of the methodological principles involved, see "A Plea for Excuses", in *Philosophical Papers*. Also: *How to Do Things with Words*

Ayer, A. J. *Language, Truth and Logic* (1936)   ▮▯
Concise, superb British restatement of the doctrines of the Vienna Circle of Logical Positivists. Ayer later said of it: "Being in every sense a young man's book, it was written with more passion than most philosophers allow themselves to show, at any rate in their published work." Also: *The Foundations of Empirical Knowledge*

Berkeley, George *Treatise Concerning the Principles of Human Knowledge* (1710)   *
A favourite target for professional philosophers, Berkeley's arguments are popularly associated with the view that "everything exists in the mind". Dr Johnson famously refuted him (or did he?) by kicking a stone, thus anticipating the commonsense prejudice of British philosophy. Crucial specialist text; for the layman, delightfully fresh, lucid, fun. Also: *Three Dialogues between Hylas and Philonous*; *Alciphron, or The Minute Philosopher*; *Essay towards a New Theory of Vision*

Chomsky, Noam *Language and Mind* (1968)   *▮▯
Clear statement of Chomsky's influential philosophy of language, in the form of three lectures on linguistic contributions to the study of mind—past, present and future. Chomsky's official pigeon-hole is linguistics—but the implications of his thought have wider philosophical significance, eg on the *tabula rasa* idea of the mind. Also: *Syntactic Structures*; *Cartesian Linguistics*; *Problems of Knowledge and Freedom*

Descartes, René *Meditations on First Philosophy* (1641)   ❗♀★▣
Classic whose influence has been profound and prolonged. In questioning
scepticism Descartes shows a talent for lateral thinking: instead of direct
confrontation, he chooses to allow the process of doubt to run its course until it
arrives at an (allegedly) indubitable truth: "I think, therefore I am." Therefore,
he concludes with more faith than reason, God undoubtedly exists and all's well
with the world. Also: *Discourse on the Method of Rightly Conducting the Reason*;
Principles of Philosophy; *Passions of the Soul*

Dewey, John *Experience and Education* (1938)   🏛
Deriving from the American "pragmatist" school, Dewey has been particularly
influential as a philosopher of education. This little volume gives a concise
summary of his theories; it was written twenty years after (and modifies) his
Democracy and Education, in the light of experience with progressive schools.
Also: *Experience and Nature*; *Logic: The Science of Inquiry*. See
HISTORY/AMERICAN

Frege, Gottlob *Logical Investigations* (1977)   ♀
A "philosopher's philosopher", Frege had enormous influence on the philosophy
of mathematics, logic and language—crucially on Russell (qv) and Wittgenstein
(qv). *Logical Investigations* is the title of an unfinished book for which the three
articles in this volume (written in 1918 and 1923) were intended. Also: *The
Foundations of Arithmetic*; *The Basic Laws of Arithmetic*; *Philosophical Writings*

Gilson, Étienne *The Christian Philosophy of St Thomas Aquinas* (1924)
Sympathetic critique by a leading Thomist. No modern philosopher writes with
more grace than Gilson. But compare Henri-Georges Égouttier: *Cuisses
Blanches, Idées Noires* (1980). See Aquinas; ART

Hegel, Georg Wilhelm Friedrich *The Phenomenology of Mind*
(1807)   ❗▣♀
Massive; magnificent; metaphysical. Seminal influence (alas) on Marx, Sartre
and many more. Also: *The Philosophy of Mind*; *Science of Logic*; *The Philosophy
of History*, etc

Heidegger, Martin *Being and Time* (1927)   ▣♀
Classic of German existentialism; heavy on meaning (correction:
meaninglessness) of life, authentic choice, conscience, freedom, nothingness, etc.
Almost unreadable without assistance: Gelven's *Commentary* and Steiner's
Heidegger are recommended introductions. Also: *An Introduction to
Metaphysics*; *The End of Philosophy*; *The Question Concerning Technology*, etc

Hobbes, Thomas *Leviathan* (1651)   ❗▣▣
Mainly read nowadays for Chapters 13–30, developing his political ideas; other
chapters give the gist of the remainder of Hobbesian philosophy. (See, for
instance, Chapter 46 for mischievous, mordantly deflationary comments on the
Roman Catholic doctrine of transubstantiation.) Also: *De Cive, de Corpore
Politico*; *Questions Concerning Liberty, Necessity and Chance*

Hume, David *An Enquiry Concerning Human Understanding*
(1748)   ❗▣★
Easier-going than his earlier *Treatise*, the *Enquiry* encapsulates the central
doctrines and themes of Hume's radically empiricist philosophy. Dr Johnson
accused Hume of "writing French", but his language remains vintage Scotch.
Also: *A Treatise of Human Nature*; *An Enquiry into the Principles of Morals*;
Dialogues Concerning the Natural History of Religion, etc

Husserl, Edmund *The Paris Lectures* (1950)   ❗♀
These lectures by the founder of "phenomenology" (the correlation of subject
and object in the act of perception) provide a concise introduction to his mature
thought. Husserl was perhaps the most prominent of modern "continental"
philosophers and his influence (not least as a progenitor of existentialism) is
extensive. Also: *Ideas*; *Cartesian Meditations*; *The Crisis of European Sciences*

James, William *Pragmatism* (1907)   ♀
James' dedication reads: "To the memory of John Stuart Mill from whom I first
learned the pragmatic openness of mind and whom my fancy likes to picture as
our leader were he alive today". These lectures seek to "unify the picture" of the
pragmatic movement. See RELIGION

Jaspers, Karl *Philosophy of Existence* (1937)   ♀✳
Together with Heidegger, Jaspers is the leading luminary of German
existentialism. Although focusing on the "concrete human situation" he is a
self-proclaimed apostle of reason—a poignant perspective in view of the fact that
he delivered these lectures in Germany in 1937, soon after he had been dismissed
from his university professorship by the Nazis. Also: *Reason and Existence*;
Reason and Anti-Reason in Our Times; *The Great Philosophers*

Kant, Immanuel *Prolegomena to Any Future Metaphysics* (1783)   ❗▣★
In *Prolegomena* Kant sketches the cool outlines of his magnificent vision—a
reconciliation of rationalism and empiricism—as an introduction to his *Critique
of Pure Reason* (which is much longer, even more influential and—for the
layman—almost inaccessibly hard). Also: *Groundwork of the Metaphysics of
Morals*; *Critique of Practical Reason*, etc

Kierkegaard, Søren *The Concept of Dread* (1844)   ♀
In this early study, published under the pseudonym of Vigilius Haufniensis (the Watchman of Copenhagen), Kierkegaard composes the theme (freedom, nothingness, anguish) on which existentialism has played so many variations.
 Also: *Either/Or*; *Fear and Trembling*; *Concluding Unscientific Postscript*, etc. See DIARIES

Kirk, G. S. and **Raven, J. E.** *The Pre-Socratic Philosophers* (1957)   ▮♀
In the beginning were Parmenides, Heraclitus and a host of other honourable names who appear on the roll-call of the First Philosophers—names already venerated (or vilified) by the time of Socrates and Plato. Invaluable collection of the earliest Greek philosophical fragments, with full commentary. See MYTHOLOGY

Leibniz, Gottfried Wilhelm von *The Monadology* (1714)   ▮♀★
If you've never thought of yourself as a monad, now's your chance. Each of us has a place in the marvellous metaphysical system of the mathematical genius of 17th-century rationalism, who exercised powerful influence—in philosophy, in mathematics, and in the world at large. Also: *Discourse on Metaphysics*; *Theodicy*; *New Essays Concerning Human Understanding*, etc

Locke, John *An Essay Concerning Human Understanding* (1690)   ▮♀★
Locke's forthright *Essay* pioneered the tradition of exploring, by empirical observation and analysis, the supposed limits of our understanding. Opens with the famous attack on the Cartesian doctrine of innate ideas. Also: *Essays on the Law of Nature*; *Thoughts Concerning Education*. See POLITICS

Marcel, Gabriel *Philosophy of Existence* (1949)   ▮♀
Marcel was articulating (Christian) existentialism in France at about the same time as Heidegger and Jaspers in Germany. This volume contains three papers, written in 1933 and 1946, plus an autobiographical essay. Of special interest is the second paper which is a critical survey of Sartre's (qv) philosophy. Also: *Metaphysical Journal*; *Being and Having*; *Creative Fidelity*, etc

Merleau-Ponty, Maurice *The Phenomenology of Perception* (1945)   ♀
Here is a philosopher who talks about "body image". Very French and very sensuous. For the layman his preface gives a valuable short account of what he understands by "phenomenology". Also: *Signs*; *Sense and Nonsense*; *The Structure of Behaviour*, etc.

Mill, John Stuart *Utilitarianism* (1861)
Valiant, stylish defence of Bentham's celebrated "greatest happiness" principle. Also: *System of Logic*. See ECONOMICS; FEMINISM; POLITICS

Montaigne, Michel de *Essays* (1580)   ▲!▮★▯
Sceptical, humane and urbane, Montaigne wrote, in an age tormented by savage ideological conflict, essays not so much in technical philosophy as in a tolerant and civilized philosophy of life.

Moore, G. E. *Principia Ethica* (1903)   !▮♀
One of the major works of British philosophical ethics, written by the man who, together with Russell (qv), was a prominent mover in the contemporary British reaction against idealism. Source-book for the pretensions of the Bloomsbury Group. In Chapter 1 the phrase "naturalistic fallacy" begins its long and continuing career. Also: *Philosophical Studies*; *Some Main Problems of Philosophy*; *Philosophical Papers*

Nietzsche, Friedrich *Beyond Good and Evil* (1886)   ▲▮★
Representative, thunderous work by the fallen angel of Western philosophy, about whom it is impossible to have a placid opinion. It is hard to doubt Nietzsche's statement, "I have at all times written my work with my whole body and my whole life". Also: *Thus Spake Zarathustra*; *The Gay Science*; *Twilight of the Idols*; *The Origins of Tragedy*, etc

Ortega y Gasset, José *The Revolt of the Masses* (1929)
Powerful critique of modern man and modern democracy by a leading Spanish philosopher. Ortega, though not against democracy, is franker than most in assessing the consequences of runaway egalitarianism. Also: *Towards a Universal History*; *The Idea of a University*, etc

Passmore, John *A Hundred Years of Philosophy* (1957)   a
Compressed account of main trends and major thinkers in philosophy— especially epistemology, logic and metaphysics—from the mid 19th century to the mid 20th. Second edition (1966) revised and updated. Readable style: accurate summaries—a difficult job well done. Also: *Man's Responsibility for Nature*; *Philosophical Reasoning*; *The Perfectibility of Man*

Plato *Phaedo* (4th century BC)   ▲!▮a★▯
Excellent introduction to Socrates' character, and to the thought and style of Plato. Centred on the question of the immortality of the soul, the dialogue includes a myth of the after-life, and ends with a touching account of Socrates' death. Plato's limpid style and firm (if to philosophers debatable) personal views make him especially attractive to the general reader. Also: *The Symposium*, etc. See POLITICS

Popper, Karl *Conjectures and Refutations* (1963) *! ♀*
A bigger, better introduction to Popper's important and influential philosophy of science than *The Logic of Scientific Discovery*. Bryan Magee's *Popper* (1973) and Popper's own *Unended Quest* (1974) are also good sources of guidance. Also: *Objective Knowledge*. See POLITICS (Plato)

Quine, Willard van Orman *From a Logical Point of View* (1953) ♀ *
Quine's name constantly recurs in current mainstream analytic philosophy. His controversial tenets are summed up in this selection of essays. Also: *Word and Object*; *Methods of Logic*; *The Ways of Paradox and Other Essays*, etc

Russell, Bertrand *The Problems of Philosophy* (1912) ♟ a
One of the first books commissioned for *Home University Library*, in which Russell outlines proposed solutions as well as problems. Platonism and empiricism are both anatomized. Lucid, honest, thoroughly engaging: excellent introduction to academic philosophy. Also: *A History of Western Philosophy*; *Mysticism and Logic*, etc. See MATHEMATICS (Whitehead)

Ryle, Gilbert *The Concept of Mind* (1949) ▮ ♀
Ryle attacks the Cartesian view of man as an incorporeal soul in the machine of the body. Acute, amusing analysis of mental concepts, the plausible upshot seeming to be a totally implausible behaviourism. Also: *Dilemmas*; *Collected Papers*; *Plato's Progress*

Sartre, Jean-Paul *Being and Nothingness* (1943) *! ♀ * ★*
Unofficial gospel of the Paris café, whose tidings are not exactly glad: "Man is a useless passion". Dense terminological thickets alternate with vivid insights and penetrating descriptions of human folly and foibles. Impassioned, atheistic existentialism. Also: *Existentialism and Humanism*; *Critique of Dialectical Reason*; *Sketch for a Theory of the Emotions*, etc. See BIOGRAPHY; DRAMA; FICTION/NOVELS

Schopenhauer, Arthur *The World as Will and Idea* (1819) ▮
Rare combination of Kant and Buddha underlies Schopenhauer's thought. Lively, lucid style, replete with entertaining and mordant chatter, especially about his hated Hegel. Discussion of human character and the unconscious anticipates Freud and psychoanalysis. Strong influence on Nietzsche (qv), also on Wittgenstein (qv). Also: *The Fourfold Root*; *Parerga and Paralipomena*; *Essay on the Freedom of the Will*

Sextus Empiricus *Outlines of Pyrrhonism* (c. 200) *! ♀*
Classic statement of philosophical scepticism. With Sextus's rediscovery in the 16th century, and his influence on such writers as Montaigne (qv), scepticism flourished in Europe. Thus indirectly, Sextus triggered Descartes (qv) in his crucial search for true knowledge by means of systematic doubt. Good translation: Loeb Library. Also: *Against the Dogmatists*; *Against the Professors*

Spinoza, Benedict *Ethics* (1677) ♟ *! ★▮*
Arguably the most perfect, most sublime metaphysical system of them all. Spinoza proceeds in a "geometrical" manner, commencing with definitions and axioms, from which he derives his propositions. Excommunicated by the Dutch Jewish community as an atheist, his entire system is a kind of intellectual panegyric to "God or Nature". Also: *The Treatise on the Correction of the Understanding*; *A Theologico-Political Treatise*, etc

Wittgenstein, Ludwig *Philosophical Investigations* (1953) *! ▮ ★▮*
A series of observations, loosely collected into numbered paragraphs and short sections, in which the older Wittgenstein wrestles with his younger self of the *Tractatus*—and with the philosophical proclivities of generations of thinkers. Not so much a work, more a working out; less a handbook of thought than a model of how to think. Also: *Tractatus Logico-Philosophicus*; *The Blue and Brown Books*; *On Certainty*, etc

Poetry

Making lists of recommended poets is a subjective exercise. Poetry is of the senses before it is of the mind; to state a preference for this poem or that is to utter autobiography, not criticism. We have included poets of many ages and languages (though all are available in good English translations)—though this feature of the list is perhaps more real than apparent. A good poem often stands outside its locality and time, and speaks directly, now, at the moment of reading, of shared perception of human experience. This quality of timelessness was our main criterion, whether of individual poets or of the many "one-poem" writers listed in anthologies.

See LITERARY CRITICISM (Arnold, Brooks, Crane, Gardner, Horace, Jarrell, Pope, Shelley); MUSIC (Fischer-Dieskau); MYTHOLOGY (Ovid); SEX (Ovid)

Akhmatova, Anna *Selected Poems* (1959)
Style aims at sense rather than sound, clarity rather than vagueness— and is particularly susceptible to translation. Love poems, against vividly conjured Russian backgrounds, in the tradition of Pushkin (qv), and excellent. Good translation: McKane.

Apollinaire, Guillaume *Alcoöls* (1913) ★
Experimental, lyric poet of the early 20th century, in style somewhat akin to Owen (qv), though without the toughening process of the trenches. Short story writer, art critic (friend of Picasso and Cubists). Good translation: Bernard. Also: *Le Poète Assassiné* (a novel); *Calligrammes*, etc

Arnold, Matthew *Collected Poems* (1869)
Arnold's poems are at once more sensuous and more intellectual than Tennyson's (qv) and a few of them (*The Scholar Gipsy, Dover Beach, Sohrab and Rustum*) are unforgettable. See LITERARY CRITICISM

Auden, W. H. *Collected Shorter Poems, 1927–1957* (1966) ★
Early brilliance; exaggerated coolness and cleverness; emotional doldrums and quirky middle-aged philosophy—these things comprise but do not encompass the full attractiveness and the sheer size of Auden. A major figure. Also: *Another Time; For the Time Being.* See DRAMA; LITERARY CRITICISM

Baudelaire, Charles *The Flowers of Evil* (1857) 🗐
Classical in form, personal in outlook, Baudelaire's poetry has a weight and dignity in keeping with his themes of human suffering and the limits of love: and he evokes brilliantly the bustle and sleaziness of urban life. See Sartre's "psycho-biography" of Baudelaire. See ART; BIOGRAPHY (Starkie); DIARIES

Berryman, John *Selected Poems, 1938–68* (1972) ★
Berryman is one of the giants of modern American poetry and—since his poetry is so personal—of the American soul.

Blake, William *Songs of Innocence* (1789) 🗐
In his lyric poems and visionary drawings, and in his epigrams, Blake is the unlikeliest of all the products of late-18th-century London; infinitely complex, and intellectually more powerful, than at first he appears; from several points of view the greatest English poet after Shakespeare. Also: *Songs of Experience*

Browning, Robert *Men and Women* (1855) 🏛
A few poems (like *The Grammarian's Funeral*) put Browning high among 19th-century poets; although much of his work is mid-Victorian rubbish, startling, regular outbursts of genuine poetry make it worthwhile. Also: *Dramatic Lyrics; Dramatic Romances.* See DIARIES

Burns, Robert *Poems, Chiefly in the Scottish Dialect* (1786)
Those who know only Burns's often whimsical, sentimental popular poems will be surprised at the grandeur and reflectiveness of his other work: his is an individual, grainy and neglected voice.

Byron, Lord *Don Juan* (1819) 🏛
Byron, the most brilliant figure of his age, was sometimes a very good poet too. *Don Juan* is his wittiest, most sustained poem, surprisingly beautiful; Auden used to cite it as a book that most of the time one just can't read, at certain times one can read nothing else. Also: *Childe Harold's Pilgrimage.* See BIOGRAPHY (Marchand, Trelawny); DIARIES

Campion, Thomas *Bookes of Ayres* (1610–12)
The best Elizabethan words are given a seductive, syncopated overtone by the best Elizabethan music.

Catullus *Poems* (1st century BC) 🗐
Erotic, tender, witty and sentimental, Catullus is personal, intense, a poet of his own time and quintessentially for now. Good translation: Raphael and McLeish.

Cavafy, Constantinos *Complete Poems* (1963)　　　　　　　　📖

Greek-born but resident in Alexandria, Cavafy was a subtle poet of luxuriant decline, of poignant moments of love, dramatic and haunting. Good translation: Keeley and Sherrard. (Useful biography by R. Liddell.)

Césaire, Aimé *Return to My Native Land* (1947)

Revolutionary Negro poetry of marvellous fineness and precision. Good translation: Berger.

Chaucer, Geoffrey *Canterbury Tales* (*c.* 1388)　　　　　　　📖

Chaucer writes with a vigour, a vividness and a humanity which add up to a bracing reminder that the best work escapes the sanctions of time. Avoid "translations": the original transcends them all. Also: *Troilus and Criseyde*, etc

Clare, John *The Shepherd's Calendar* (1827)

Best "peasant" poet in English, the last to remember the English countryside unenclosed, Clare lived, mostly in madhouses, in the 19th century; his formal strength and his "eye" are outstanding; the life he speaks of makes him unique. Also: *Poems of Rural Life*; *The Village Minstrel*

Coleridge, Samuel Taylor *The Ancient Mariner* (1797)　　　　★

Coleridge made a permanent contribution in a very few sharply moving, resonant poems, notably *Kubla Khan* and *The Ancient Mariner*. He has a quality of mystery attained by no other of his romantic contemporaries. (See John Livingston Lowes' *The Road to Xanadu* for brilliant exegesis.) See BIOGRAPHY (Lefebure, Coleridge)

Dante *The Divine Comedy* (*c.* 1300)　　　　　　　　　　　　📖

Dante was one of the greatest medieval poets: worth learning Italian for. Best translation (alas): Sayers. See POLITICS

Dickinson, Emily *Poems* (1890)

The poems of this reclusive New England lady have the same kind of purity as those of Hopkins (qv); she is one of the most elegant, most honest American poets of the last century. Also: *The Single Hound*; *Further Poems*; *Bolts of Melody*

Donne, John *Collected Poems* (1633)　　　　　　　　　　　📖

Pure distillation of early-17th-century intelligence—troubled, multiple, leaping and swooping, raising self-love to the height of compassion.

Dryden, John *Miscellany Poems* (1684)　　　　　　　　　　📖

Between the organ-roar of Milton and the Mozartian subtlety of Pope, Dryden's verse at its best can hardly be bettered in English: it has the qualities of perfect prose, and so does his prose. Some of his translations, particularly of Virgil's *Eclogues* and *Georgics* and of Lucretius, are almost finer than his own work, but his serious public poems are passionate and magnificently dramatic. Also: *MacFlecknoe*. See LITERARY CRITICISM

Durrell, Lawrence *Private Country* (1943)

Dazzling and delightful. Durrell's poetry is among his best work, with a freshness, seriousness and discipline his longer writings sometimes lack. Also: *Cities, Plains and People*; *On Seeming to Presume*. See CHILDREN'S BOOKS (Durrell, G.); DIARIES; FICTION/NOVELS; TRAVEL

Eliot, T. S. *Collected Poems and Plays* (1969)　　　　　　　📖

Eliot is one of the greatest English-speaking poets of the modern age, a formidable intellect chastely exploring the sensuous dark. See DRAMA; LITERARY CRITICISM (Eliot, Gardner)

Empson, William *Poems* (1935)　　　　　　　　　　　　　　📖

Witty, difficult poems, full of dead-pan jokes and intellectual fireworks. See LITERARY CRITICISM

Frost, Robert *The Poetry* (1969)　　　　　　　　　　　　　📖

Frost's work has the sweetness, sharpness and freshness of an apple; he is the most accessible and readable great poet of this century. (See Alfred Kazin's *New York Jew* for testy portrait.)

Gardner, Helen (ed) *Book of Religious Verse* (1972)

Much of the best poetry in English is religious poetry by obscure poets; this is a perfect collection of a vital tradition. Also: *New Oxford Book of English Verse, 1250–1950*. See LITERARY CRITICISM

Gascoyne, David *Collected Poems* (1965)

Gascoyne's is a lonely voice, grave and with long-drawn-out harmonies. He is a sound, admirable poet, whose effect comes more from his work as a whole than from a few show-pieces.

Goethe, Johann Wolfgang von *Poems* (1812)　　　　　　　　📖

One of Goethe's major achievements, sometimes taken for granted because he was such a polymath, is his love and nature poetry of the Strasburg and Sesenheim periods. His intensity and his limpid use of a language sometimes thought by foreigners to be too harsh for lyricism represent a still prominent landmark. Resists translation, even so; best read in the original. See DRAMA

Graves, Robert *Collected Poems* (1975)　　　　　　　　　　★

Graves is a strong, spare, almost classical poet; sometimes over-brisk, always invigorating. His epigrams about love are marvellous. See AUTOBIOGRAPHY; FICTION/NOVELS; MYTHOLOGY

Gray, Thomas *Poems* (1747)
Gray's lyric gift makes him seem always fresh and crisp (though his *Elegy* has
been compared to a Victorian glass dome). Early-18th-century urbanity at its
most characteristic—and unhappiest?
Gunn, Thom *Fighting Terms* (1953)
Intelligent, striking poetry: smooth and readable, intellectually elegant, morally
sophisticated. 1962 revision spoils the line. Also: *The Sense of Movement*; *Moly*
Hamburger, Michael (ed) *German Poetry, 1910–1975* (1977)
Bilingual anthology, with good introduction and notes, gives a first-class
impression of the period it covers, fairly reflects the diversity of 20th-century
German writing.
Hardy, Thomas *Complete Poems* (1976)
In his rhythms, his truthfulness and honesty, his subtlety of tone and experience
of life, Hardy is one of the most rewarding of English poets. See
FICTION/NOVELS
Heaney, Seamus *North* (1975)
Fine poet from Northern Ireland talks about realities in a serious tone: his talent
has strong roots; his poems will outlast their grim inspiration.
Hecht, Anthony *Millions of Strange Shadows* (1977)   ▟
Urbane, discursive, elegant, Hecht's poems show a sense of ease and security rare
in contemporary literature. He brings to American writing an essentially
European temperament; his fluent celebration of life is a source of real pleasure.
Heine, Heinrich *Book of Song* (1827)   ★
A Jew among Germans, a seeker after a God his reason told him to dismiss, Heine
is a poet of contradictions with an outstanding lyrical gift. Particularly good are
his nature poems, the marvellous North Sea cycles (translated by Watkins, 1955)
and the later Lazarus poems (translated by Elliot, 1979). Also: *New Poems*, etc
Herbert, George *The Temple* (1633)   ★
Whatever was best in the English temperament and in the Church of England
between the times of Elizabeth I and Cromwell is present in these strong and
lovable poems.
Herrick, Robert *Hesperides* (1648)   ▟
Herrick celebrates the fragility of life and love, and with the lightest of touches.
His poems are notable for their rhythmic beauty and for their skilfully-worked
grace. Also: *Noble Numbers or Pious Pieces*
Homer *Iliad*; *Odyssey* (12th–9th century BC)   ▯
Homer is easy and enthralling for readers, but a towering Everest for translators.
Rieu's graceful prose *Odyssey* is readable, but misses the vigour and pounce of
the verse; Graves' *Iliad* (*The Anger of Achilles*—see also his novel *Homer's
Daughter*, about the writing of the *Odyssey*) is tight and sharp; Fitzgerald and
Lattimore offer modern sprung verse, alternately excellent and dreadful. Perhaps
Chapman and Pope are still the best; though Logue's *Patrocleia* gives a tantalizing
glimpse of how it might be done, if he could sustain it over the remaining books.
For a fascinating modern "sequel" to the *Odyssey* (by no means dwarfed
by it) see Kazantzakis' *The Odyssey* (1938). See LITERARY CRITICISM
(Arnold)
Hopkins, Gerard Manley *Poems* (1918)   ★
Hopkins was a Jesuit with a mind as intricate as unfolding leaves, a mystic in love
with Christ in nature and in mankind. His poetry gives a marvellous sense of the
world we hunger for but can never have again. This collection (edited by Robert
Bridges) first published 30 years after Hopkins' death.
Horace *Odes* (1st century BC)   ▯
A poet's poet, Horace has been endlessly translated. To follow through the
translations of a single ode in English is to learn much not only about the original
but also about the history of our own verse. For the full flavour of Horace himself
(elusive of translation, as it happens) the best translation is that of Michie. Also:
Satires; *Epistles*. See LITERARY CRITICISM
Hughes, Ted *Selected Poems, 1957–67* (1972)
A confident, craggy voice. It may be morally and philosophically depressing and it
misses genuine rusticity; but the dark, Jacobean imagination of these poems
does reflect our sombre age. See CHILDREN'S BOOKS
Jarrell, Randall *The Complete Poems* (1969)   ★
Jarrell was an exceptionally warm-hearted poet, who occupies by temperament
the ground between Whitman (qv) and Dickinson (qv)—more like Whitman in
form, but with Dickinson's sure touch in writing the perfectly natural line. See
FICTION/NOVELS; LITERARY CRITICISM
Jay, Peter (ed) *The Greek Anthology* (1973)   ★
Translations by divers excellent hands of the great age—between the 7th century
BC and the 6th century AD—of Greek Mediterranean culture; short, witty,
touching and erotic; a scintillating world.
Jennings, Elizabeth (ed) *Anthology of Modern Verse, 1940–60* (1961)
Jennings is herself a good though uneven poet. Her anthology is marvellous; her
taste sharp but generous.

John of the Cross *Poems* (16th century)
Spanish poet of the soul's dark adventures into God, John of the Cross carries the reader high on unexpected wings. Good translation: Campbell.

Jones, David *The Anathemata* (1952)   ♀ ★
Jones is difficult, but immensely rewarding and moving; his gravity and beauty impressed Auden and Eliot, and will haunt the mind.

Juvenal *Satires* (1st century AD)   🗎
These powerful poems are filled with the anger and bitterness of their author, who saw through everything and liked not what he saw. Like Horace, Juvenal has been translated by many noted English poets; dip here and dip there to feel the savage intensity of the man. Good translations: Johnson (*Satires*, 3 and 10); Peter Green (complete work).

Keats, John *Poems* (1817)   🗎
Uneven and at times too obvious in his appeal to adolescence, Keats is one of the stereotypes, almost, of a Romantic poet. But the best of his poems, as well as many individual lines, are marvellous and memorable. See BIOGRAPHY (Bate, Gittings); LITERARY CRITICISM

Kipling, Rudyard *Collected Poems* (1886)
Product, bard and victim of the British Empire, Kipling has a robustness that outweighs his occasional vulgarity or silliness. See CHILDREN'S BOOKS; FICTION/SHORT STORIES

Larkin, Philip *Poems* (1945)
Larkin's poetry is alive with convincing rhythms that take hold of you at once and never let go. He is the voice of the post-Auden generation, in the provincial register.

Lawrence, D. H. *Collected Poems* (1922)
His animal poems are wonderful and liberating, and many others are convincing in their rhythms. To be read for his sense of beauty and his delight in creation. See DIARIES; FICTION/NOVELS; FICTION/SHORT STORIES; HISTORY/EUROPEAN; LITERARY CRITICISM; TRAVEL

Leopardi, Giacomo *Selected Prose and Poetry* (1966)
Leopardi is the poet of despair—his own and that (by assumption) of the human race, which he considered to have no reason for hope in this world or the next. All of his poems are imbued with these feelings, but their grace and line make them irresistible. Worth struggling with the Italian; translations hardly capture him.

Levine, Philip *Ashes* (1979)
Levine is one of the best of the younger American poets. His short line and lapidary descriptions mask verse of deep seriousness and power.

Lowell, Robert *Poems, 1938–1949* (1950)   🗎
Finely-wrought, haunting and graceful poems of love and loss. His translations are important, variable: *Imitations* is magnificent, *Prometheus Bound* and *The Oresteia* dreadful. Also : *Life Studies*; *Notebook*

MacLeish, Archibald *Collected Poems* (1952)   ★
One of America's most eminent 20th-century men of letters, MacLeish was first and foremost a poet, and a fine one. Much influenced in the 20s by his life in Paris among the famous *emigrés*, he later became an eloquent patriot and served in important governmental posts. Also a playwright—*J.B.* is his best known play—he wrote one of the finest lyrics in the language, "You Andrew Marvell."

MacNeice, Louis *Collected Poems* (1966)
His finest poems were early and late; his work had honesty and sober intelligence; his reputation goes on increasing, and rightly. Fine translation of Aeschylus' *Agamemnon*.

Marlowe, Christopher *Poems* (*c.* 1590)   ★
His Ovid, sometimes better than Ovid, had to circulate in private manuscript copies, since it gleefully and effectively introduced to the English a pagan view of sex. With him the technique of English verse begins to have a continuous history; his influence is immense, even on Shakespeare. See DRAMA

Marvell, Andrew *Poems* (1681)   🗎
The *Horatian Ode upon Cromwell's Return from Ireland* is a thrilling, serious attempt at political poetry. Otherwise his poetry resembles a 17th-century formal garden, and is often about one. Marvell's verbal fireworks have perfect phrasing, intense visual resonance; he freshens and sharpens the senses.

Masters. E. L. *Spoon River Anthology* (1915)   ★
Short, beautifully right inscriptions, modelled on the Greek Anthology—how did these exquisite little poems come out of the Illinois prairie where Masters was born and brought up? This book is one of the high points in the history of American verse, and not to be missed.

Milton, John *Paradise Lost* (1667)   ♀🗎
Early, shorter poems are enough to put him among the greatest English poets; long epics have many passages of penetrating harmony and beauty. Also: *Paradise Regained*; *Comus*; *Samson Agonistes*, etc

Moore, G. and **Beier, U. (eds)** *Modern Poetry from Africa* (1970)
Fascinating guide to one of the growth areas of literature in European languages.

Neruda, Pablo *Selected Poems* (1975)   ★
Neruda, the foremost modern poet of Latin America, acknowledged the influence of Whitman—like him, he combines enormous range with a wonderful eye for the particular. This selection by Tarn recommended.
Owen, Wilfred *Poems* (1920)   🏛
Stupendous sadness and despair, lightened by compassion. (See John Stalworthy's biography.)
Palgrave, F. T. (ed) *The Golden Treasury* (1861)   ★
Anthology chosen with the help of Tennyson; the best Victorian taste. Well worth considering: still marvellous. (Latest edition, 1973.)
Pope, Alexander *Eloise to Abelard and Other Poems* (1717)   📖
Balanced on a razor's edge between sunlit rationalism and the emerging modern world, Pope is at once light and grave, supple and stinging. Also: *The Rape of the Lock*; *The Dunciad*, etc. See LITERARY CRITICISM
Pound, Ezra *The Cantos, 1–84* (1948)   ★
He requires patience; start with his translations and the earliest *Cantos*, then move to the *Pisan Cantos*. Pound was a tragic (rather vile) figure and his best poetry is tragic. See DRAMA (Sophocles); LITERARY CRITICISM
Pushkin, Alexander *Eugene Onegin* (1833)   📖
Pushkin is magnificent, moving; makes Byron look common and Tolstoy clodhopping. Good translation: Johnstone. (See Nabokov's critical edition and translation for a literary mausoleum contrived by a doting genius.)
Rilke, Rainer Maria *Sonnets to Orpheus* (1923)   🏛
Outstanding lyric poet, whose work has a difficult surface but a rewarding interior. Good translation: Leishman. Also: *Duino Elegies* (translated by Leishman and Spender). See DIARIES
Robinson, E. A. *Collected Poems* (1928)
Perhaps the best known American poet half a century ago, Robinson is now too much ignored, not to say forgotten. In fact, he was and is first rate, from his careful, jocular descriptions of the people of his birthplace in Maine (he called it Tilbury town) to the grand pessimistic dramas of his later years.
Roethke, Theodore *Collected Poems* (1968)   🏛
A loose, serious, late modern American style. His early poems are charming and interesting; his last rough and fine.
Rosenberg, Isaac *Complete Works* (1979)
Rosenberg, a painter as well as a poet, was killed in the World War I at the age of 27: and the loss was a great one. His work is remarkable for its exciting use of language and its imaginative intensity.
Seferis, George *Collected Poems, 1932–55* (1969)   ★
The moral authority of the poems and the moral courage of Seferis as a man made him a towering national figure. He was also amusing and amused; his work is sensuous, eclectic (influenced by Eliot, qv) and intellectually curious.
Shakespeare, William *Sonnets* (late 16th century)   📖
This giant dominates our literature and our language; with Montaigne, he dominates the soul of Europe in his century. The universal poet, yet no one speaks with more crushing personal force. See DRAMA (Granville-Barker, Masefield, Shakespeare, Van Doren); LITERARY CRITICISM (Bradley, Johnson, Knight, Stendhal)
Shelley, Percy Bysshe *Adonais* (1821)   📖
Shelley's delicate Muse is best seen, perhaps, in his short lyrics: *To a Skylark*, *Ode to the West Wind*, *The Cloud*, and the opium-scented *Ozymandias*. *Adonais*, an elegy for Keats, shows a robuster and darker side, characteristic of his longer works. A brooding, private voice, shot through with a melancholic perception of the "tears of things". Also: *Queen Mab*; *Prometheus Unbound*, etc. See BIOGRAPHY (Holmes); LITERARY CRITICISM
Sisson, Charles *In the Trojan Ditch* (1974)
Haunted and haunting, Sisson's very English, very Church of England poetry takes a bleak but honest view of the world as it is.
Sitwell, Edith (ed) *The Atlantic Book of British and American Poetry* (1959)
Magnificent anthology of the whole of English poetry. Sitwell had a sharp ear and a fine critical sense; her selection is full, generous, exciting. See AUTOBIOGRAPHY (Sitwell, O.)
Snyder, Gary *Collected Poems* (1966)
The poems are daring and solid, and as Thom Gunn remarked, "preserve experience in the process of formation". His version of *Cold Mountain* by Han-Shan is a thrilling version of one of the most thrilling Chinese poets (7th century AD). His own poems have some of the same spirit and atmosphere.
Spender, Stephen *Poems* (1939)
Underestimated poet of the 1930s generation, he has gone on writing for 50 years and fits no category. He expresses liberal, intelligent sensibility and is its faithful witness, but he can also be a startling and liberating individual poet.

Spenser, Edmund *The Shephearde's Calendar* (1579)   ★
The odes of Spenser are the most successfully inventive metrical system in
English. Indispensable. Also: *The Faerie Queene*, etc
Stevens, Wallace *Selected Poems* (1953)   ★
Stevens' poems are a splendid combination of the meditative and the sensual. His
careful concern with style and vocabulary, together with a sense of rhythm and
refrain reminiscent of Apollinaire (qv), make him one of the most satisfying
writers of the "modern" movement.
Swinburne, Algernon *Poems and Ballads* (1866)
Late Victorian who thrilled the Edwardians with poetic wildness and
intoxication. Reading Swinburne is like bathing in scented ass's milk: cheering,
but a little goes a long way.
Tennyson, Alfred *Poems* (1842)   ★
Tennyson can be moralizing, morbid, extravagantly decorative, sentimental: but
his poems still give pleasure in a very different age. Victorian certainties offer
comfort in our own, torn times. See BIOGRAPHY (Ricks)
Thomas, Dylan *Collected Poems* (1952)   🏛
Intense visions (especially of provincial Wales) and exuberant language make
him easy to like or denounce; but he is serious, and, in about a dozen poems, a
great poet. See DIARIES
Thomas, Edward *Collected Poems* (1920)
Sympathetic and private: an English Robert Frost (they were friends).
Villon, François *Le Grand Testament* (1461)   📖
A connoisseur of the dramatic incongruities of life, Villon displays an astonishing
zest for it. He is one of the wittiest, most reflective poets of any age. Good
translation: Dale.
Virgil *Georgics* (1st century AD)   📖
Dryden thought *Georgics* "the best poem of the best poet"; his own version shows
why he thought so, and he makes a persuasive case. Good modern translations:
Bovie; Day Lewis. Also: *Eclogues*; *Aeneid*
Watson-Taylor, S. and **Lucie-Smith, E. (eds)** *French Poetry Today*
(1971)
Excellent bilingual anthology of poems written and published since 1955.
Whitman, Walt *Leaves of Grass* (1855)   📖
There is no better poet of 19th-century war or of democracy. The full height of his
achievement is hardly recognized in Britain. His liberation and Yankee tone
make Tennyson look provincial. His power and precision are amazing.
Wilbur, Richard *Poems, 1943–1956* (1956)   🏛
Like Hecht (qv), Wilbur writes with grace and confidence. Attractive, intelligent
and accessible, his poetry is perfectly at ease—and at its best, it is something
more.
Wordsworth, William *Poems* (1807)   📖
Born and brought up in the English Lake District, Wordsworth found in its
landscapes the perfect raw material for his verse, even though it is often, as he
said, "emotion recollected in tranquillity". As articulate as a diarist, he retains a
sense of innocence which makes him inimitable and unforgettable. See DIARIES;
LITERARY CRITICISM (Coleridge)
Yeats, W. B. *Collected Poems* (1933)   📖
Yeats is one of our finest poets; his greatest poems were written late in life, but
the development (from the 1890s onwards) is continuous and the quality
extraordinary, despite its sometimes dotty rationale. See DRAMA

Politics

Books on "the art of the possible" are prospective or retrospective: programmatically confident about the future, scathing (or, less often, apologetic) about the past. Meanwhile, the present remains the meeting-point, the inhabited no-man's-land between philosophy and history, an enclave of contingent circumstance and compromise in which the layman, unfortified by the professional politician's theory or casuistry, actually has to live. Once or twice in human history (Periclean Athens? Medician Florence? Founding-fathers' America?) everything seemed (to some, at least) to come momentarily and thrillingly right: theory fitted circumstance and mood, no-man's land flowered into utopia, and the citizen was served, not ruled, by politics. Why that happened, and whether it could happen again is in part the subject of this list.

See ANTHROPOLOGY (Epstein); ART (Morison); AUTOBIOGRAPHY (Franklin, Kropotkin, Macmillan, Malcom X); DIARIES (Crossman, Lincoln, Wilson); ECONOMICS (Friedman, Galbraith, Gamble, Glynn, Harrison, Kidron, Marx); FEMINISM (Evans, Rowbotham, Norris); GEOGRAPHY (Cole); HISTORY/ AMERICAN (Bailyn, Berger, George, Halberstam, Schlesinger); HISTORY/ANCIENT (Sallust, Thucydides); HISTORY/BRITISH (More, Tawney); HISTORY/LATIN AMERICAN (Freyre); MEDIA (King); PHILOSOPHY (Hobbes, Mill, Ortega y Gasset); RELIGION (Hebblethwaite, Struve); SEX (Reich); SOCIOLOGY (Anderson, Bottomore, Marcuse, Wallerstein, Weber)

Acheson, Dean *Present at the Creation* (1967)
US foreign policy in the post-1945 golden age; perceptive account of the way Washington works, or worked.
Arendt, Hannah *Eichmann in Jerusalem* (1963)   ♀ ★
Perhaps her most accessible and penetrating book: notions of the "banality of evil" and Eichmann as bureaucrat caused a furore at time of publication. Also: *The Origins of Totalitarianism*; *The Human Condition*; *On Violence*. See Stern; AUTOBIOGRAPHY (Speer); BIOGRAPHY (Bullock)
Aristotle *Politics* (4th century BC)   ✦ ▣
Beginning of the practical study of politics as distinct from speculation. See LITERARY CRITICISM; PHILOSOPHY
Bagehot, Walter *The English Constitution* (1867)   ▦ ★ ▣
No other book on the British constitution begins to approach this in scope and elegance. Edition by Crossman (1963) recommended. Also: *Physics and Politics*
Burke, Edmund *Reflections on the Revolution in France* (1791)   ▣
Burke was *the* great English conservative politician. This book was a response to a liberal defence of the 1789 French Revolution. Burke's rhetoric is devastating and his style unforgettable. His speeches and letters make equally good reading: especially *Letter to a Noble Lord*; *Letter to the Sheriffs of Bristol*; *On American Taxation*, etc
Cabral, Amilcar *Revolution in Guinea* (1969)   ♀
Selection from writings, speeches and interviews of one of Africa's most powerful revolutionary thinkers. Also: *Return to the Source*
Carr, E. H. *The Russian Revolution from Lenin to Stalin, 1917–29* (1979)
One-volume distillation of a 14-volume history of Soviet Russia. Like the total work, masterly. Also: *The New Society*; *The Twenty Years' Crisis, 1919–39*; *What is History?*; *The Romantic Exiles*, etc
Clarke, Peter *Liberals and Social Democrats* (1979)   ★ ▦
Evolution, from 1880 onwards, of the politics of the middle way in Britain, from Whigs to Welfare State. The New Liberals emerge, convincingly if surprisingly, as the natural party of the working class. Also: *Lancashire and the New Liberalism*
Claude, I. L. *Power and International Relations* (1962)   ♀
Tough-minded, clear study of the relationship between sovereign states.
Cowling, Maurice *The Impact of Hitler* (1977)   ♀
Starchy but stimulating analysis of the domestic British effects of the Hitlerian challenge.
Dante *Of Monarchy* (c. 1305)
Careful argument by a great poet in favour of world government— approximately 650 years before anybody else thought of it. An extraordinarily little-known book. Dante's arguments still seem unanswerable. See POETRY

133

Eldersveld, S. J. *Political Parties: A Behavioral Analysis* (1964)   📖📑
The US constitution is a curious document in that it leaves out any mention of how (by what agency) government is to be organized. This task should in fact be left—said the Founding Fathers—to political parties, who have been at it ever since. Of many books on the history and workings of US political parties, this is one of the best. Compare Arnold Thurman: *The Symbols of Government*

Fanon, Frantz *The Wretched of the Earth* (1961)   ✳
Fanon holds that imperialism injected violence into the fabric of the Third World. Does it follow that the resort to violence by Third World nations is neither surprising nor reprehensible? Dated, brilliant. Also: *Black Skins, White Masks*

Hamilton, A., Jay, J. and **Madison, J.** *The Federalist* (1787–88)   ★
The birth of a nation; the Federalist papers are the best of all testimonies to the relationship between political theory and practice in the USA.

Hinton, William *Fanshen* (1966)   ★
A book of great humanity and intellectual vigour which, in dealing with the impact of China's revolution on the peasants of one village in 1948, takes us to the heart of what may have been the major world political event of our times. Fanshen means "to turn over".

Laqueur, Walter *Terrorism* (1977)
The politics of despair and paranoia coolly analysed. Also: *A History of Zionism*

Lenin, Ivan Ilyich *State and Revolution* (1917)   ❗
Written on the eve of the October Revolution, a utopian prospectus at odds with Lenin's other books, it failed as prophecy but remains influential. Also: *Imperialism*; *What is to be Done?*

Locke, John *Second Essay of Civil Government* (1690)
This book, published two years after the "Glorious Revolution" of 1688, validated and justified it to English Whigs. The last section on the "right of revolution" was influential on Jefferson when he wrote the Declaration of Independence. See PHILOSOPHY

Machiavelli, Niccolò *The Prince* (1514)   ❗📖
Handbook for enlightening despots stands as a classic analysis of the relationship between means and ends.

Mackenzie, W. J. M. *Politics and Social Science* (1967)   ℗
What the academic study of politics is about. Also: *Biological Ideas in Politics*; *Political Identity*; *Power, Violence, Decision*

Mannheim, Karl *Ideology and Utopia* (1929)   ℗
Flawed but noble attempt not only to comprehend the nature of ideology but also to analyse how far there could be an intellectual resolution of the schisms in European society. Also: *Freedom, Power and Democratic Planning*; *Man and Society in an Age of Reconstruction*; *Essays on the Sociology of Knowledge*

Marx, K. and **Engels, F.** *The Communist Manifesto* (1848)   ❗✳
12,000 words, the liveliest and most influential in all their voluminous writings, though Marx's witty *18th Brumaire of Louis Napoleon* runs it close. Also: *German Ideology*; *The Condition of the Working Class in England*, etc. See ECONOMICS; SOCIOLOGY (Bottomore, Marx)

Michels, Robert *Political Parties* (1913)   ✳
The "iron law of oligarchy" book. Michels argued that all organizations, but particularly political parties and pressure groups, however democratic in origin and intent, succumb to oligarchic tendencies. See DIARIES (Crossman)

Mill, John Stuart *On Liberty* (1859)   ❗
Mill's attempt to define the limits of individual behaviour and state interference is liberal thought at its rounded peak. See ECONOMICS; FEMINISM; PHILOSOPHY

Montesquieu, Baron de *The Spirit of Laws* (1734–48)
Classic treatise by great political observer and thinker on the relationship between the spirit of a people and their laws. Analyses such apparently irrelevant matters as economic system, climate, history, morals and habits, sports and diversions.

Moore, Barrington *The Social Origins of Dictatorship and Democracy* (1906)
Were the relationships between lords and peasants fundamental in shaping modern parliamentary democracy, communism and fascism? Excellent combination of social science and history. Also: *Injustice*; *Political Power and Social Theory*; *Soviet Politics and the Dilemma of Power*, etc

Niebuhr, Reinhold *Moral and Immoral Society* (1932)   ❗℗
Seminal work of political philosophy, influential on many present-day European politicians and political movements. Niebuhr (a religious philosopher) analyses moral stances of individuals and groups, and holds that ethical standards appropriate to individuals are not necessarily appropriate to groups. Also: *The Nature and Destiny of Man*; *Children of Light and Children of Darkness*; *An Interpretation of Christian Ethics*

Oakeshott, Michael *Rationalism in Politics and Other Essays* (1962)
Subtle, elegant essays by one of the outstanding British conservative political thinkers of the century. Also: *Experience and Its Modes*; *On Human Conduct*

Orwell, George *Homage to Catalonia* (1938)
Orwell's personal, devastating account of the Spanish Civil War, with an excellent chapter on trench warfare. Forerunner of *1984*; Orwell encounters both the Soviet Union and rats. See FICTION/NOVELS; HISTORY/BRITISH; LITERARY CRITICISM

Owen, Robert *A New View of Society and Other Writings* (1813–21) 🏛
Owen was one of the greatest English utopian socialists—his kibbutz-like programme still merits consideration. His son went to America and established a socialist community at New Harmony, but discord soon set in.

Piven, F. F. and **Cloward, R. A.** *Poor People's Movements: Why They Succeed, How They Fail* (1977) ✱
A study of four movements in the US to delimit the possibilities of power for the poor in representative democracy. Challenging conclusion is that success comes through mass defiance rather than formal organization. Also: *Regulating the Poor*

Plato *The Republic* (c. 380 BC) ★ 🗐
Masterpiece of political philosophy argues for a hierarchical society in which everyone performs only the function for which he is fitted by nature and education. Very special pleading in the guise of a dispassionate intellectual exercise. (For provocative critique see Karl Popper: *The Open Society and Its Enemies*). Good translation: Cornford. See PHILOSOPHY

Rawls, John *A Theory of Justice* (1971) ✱ ★
Key book in the argument among contemporary political theorists and moral philosophers concerning distributive justice.

Rousseau, Jean-Jacques *The Social Contract* (1762) 🏛 🗐
More attractive, challenging and puzzling than the other social contract theorists, Hobbes and Locke. Participatory democracy, socialism and modern despotism start here. Also: *Émile*. See AUTOBIOGRAPHY

Sartori, Giovanni *Parties and Party Systems* (1976) ♀
Schattschneider, E. E. *The Semisovereign People* (1960) ♀
Major contribution to the debate about the pluralist nature of Western democracy. "The flaw in the pluralist heaven is that the heavenly chorus sings with a strong upperclass accent." Also: *Politics, Pressures and the Tariff*

Schumpeter, Joseph *Capitalism, Socialism and Democracy* (1943) ♀
Critique of classical democracy. Schumpeter reluctantly recognizes that if capitalism is to survive it must transform itself into a version of social democracy. He is best known, however, for his "minimal concept of democracy": that it provides at periodic elections, a choice between competing élites. Also: *Business Cycles*; *Imperialism and Social Classes*; *History of Economic Analysis*

Sorel, Georges *Reflections on Violence* (1912) ✱
"Violence is the only practical political method." Sorel had no way of knowing how right—and wrong—he would be proved in the succeeding 60 years. See T. E. Hulme: *Speculations* (1924)

Stern, J. P. *Hitler: The Führer and the People* (1975)
Concise, brilliant book focuses on Hitler's use of language as a method of domination. Far more searching and penetrating than most "weightier" books about the Hitler phenomenon. Also: *Thomas Mann*; *On Realism*. See AUTOBIOGRAPHY (Speer); BIOGRAPHY (Bullock); HISTORY/EUROPEAN (Ryder)

Tocqueville, Alexis de *Democracy in America* (1835–40) ★
Excellent as history and social science; but its enduring value is as political theory. Tocqueville's notion of the "tyranny of the majority" highlighted the dominance of beliefs and codes of behaviour that ensured conformity and stifled dissent. Also: *L'Ancien Régime*

Trotsky, Leon *The History of the Russian Revolution* (1932–33)
The revolution described and interpreted by one of its major participants. Partisan but never bigoted; patchy but compulsive.

White, Theodore H. *The Making of the President, 1960* (1961)
A famous election brilliantly described and analysed. Exemplary political journalism. Also: *The View from the Fortieth Floor*; *The Making of the President, 1968*, etc

Wilson, Edmund *To the Finland Station* (1940)
Delightful, moving and literate study of the development of Western socialist thought. Also: *Axel's Castle*; *The Wound and the Bow*; *The Shores of Light*. See DIARIES; HISTORY/AMERICAN; LITERARY CRITICISM

Woodward, B. and **Bernstein, C.** *All the President's Men* (1974)
Two reporters on the *Washington Post* uncover Watergate and win a Pulitzer Prize. A study of political corruption which will live as one of the greatest and most hyped scandals in politics. Also: *The Final Days*

Woodward, C. Vann *The Strange Career of Jim Crow* (1955) 🏴
Best short account of the politics and history of segregation in the USA. Also: *The Origins of the New South, 1877–1913*. See HISTORY/AMERICAN

Psychology

Psychology, like sociology, has been a characteristic 20th-century study, with political, social and artistic implications beyond the horizons of formal science. At one extreme, it is a physical science, the study of the mechanisms of the brain, emotion and instinct. (The comparative study of animal behaviour is a branch held by many "human" psychologists to be irrelevant.) At the other extreme, it concerns the analytical observation of behaviour, particularly that of the individual in his relationships with himself and his environment. In the work of many psychologists (including some of the most controversial) science is inextricably blended with philosophy: observation of behaviour and response leads to programmatic theories. The books here collected reflect but can never comprise the whole spectrum from scientific detachment to prescriptive dogmatism; their style is accessible; their subject is nothing less than the wellsprings of man himself.

See BIOGRAPHY (Jones); MEDICINE (Freud, Laing, Kovel, Sutherland, Szasz, Wing); NATURAL HISTORY (Aitchison, Ardrey, Lorenz); PHILOSOPHY (Ryle, Schopenhauer); SOCIOLOGY (Jacoby, Mead, G. H.); RELIGION (James)

Argyle, M. *Bodily Communication* (1975) ♀
Soberly written, effective demonstration that social psychologists can help us to understand the unspoken messages our bodies send out whenever we are with other people. Also: *Person to Person; Social Skills and Mental Health*. See ANTHROPOLOGY (Hall)

Aronson, Elliott *The Social Animal* (1976)
Social psychology is one of the fastest-growing (and most obviously practical) areas of psychology today. "Fun" text; delicious pictures (by Saul Steinberg). Serious science presented in a winning way.

Baddeley, A. D. *The Psychology of Memory* (1976) ♀
Comprehensive review of what experimental psychologists can tell us about the way our memories work. Not an easy read, but the practical nature of the subject makes it an important book. See also Francis A. Yates: *The Art of Memory* (1966)

Berne, Eric *Games People Play* (1964) 🏛
This popular book by a prominent Californian psychiatrist is readable at two levels: for its amusing accounts of the games people really do play with one another (sometimes without being aware of it), and for its insights into typical human behaviour patterns. You'll certainly recognize your friends (if not yourself) in these pages.

Birren, J. E. *The Psychology of Ageing* (1964)
Despite its own increasing age, still one of the best single sources of information about an area in which psychologists have made a vital contribution.

Brown, Roger *Social Psychology* (1965) 🏛 a
Lucid treatment of some key topics in social psychology. Choice of themes is idiosyncratic, but the discussion is elegant and entertaining.

Burton, Robert *Anatomy of Melancholy* (1621) 📖
In this, one of the great and curious books of the English literary past, Burton undertook to analyse the symptoms, causes, and cure of "this *atra bilis*, this melancholy," which was one of the favourite medical concerns of his time. His book is filled with digressions and quirky asides on every subject, but its ideas are surprisingly up-to-date. Endorsed by Johnson, Sterne and Lamb.

Clarke, A. M. and **A. D. B.** *Early Experience: Myth and Evidence* (1976) ♀
Devastating attack on the idea that what happens to you in the first few years of life has a disproportionate influence on what sort of person you turn out to be. Difficult, challenging. Also: *Mental Deficiency: The Changing Outlook*

Donaldson, Margaret *Children's Minds* (1978)
Clear account of how children's minds develop. Essential reading for all interested in education; style tempered to non-specialists (parents?). Also: *A Study of Children's Thinking*

Erikson, Erik *Childhood and Society* (1950) 📖
An influential work: Erikson's calm common sense comes as a relief after some of the extravagances of the psychoanalysts.

Eysenck, H. J. *Psychology Is About People* (1972) 🏛 a
Psychological angle on a number of controversial issues: pornography, politics, sex, the effectiveness of psychotherapy, etc. Excellent advertisement for the usefulness of the social scientific approach. Like all popularizers, Eysenck seems

frivolous to some specialists, heterodox and simplistically propagandist to others. But he has a gift for clear exposition: a useful start. Also: *Uses and Abuses of Psychology*; *Fact and Fiction in Psychology*; *Know Your Own IQ*, etc

Groddeck, Georg *The Book of the It* (1923)   *
Extraordinary book about the unconscious—what Groddeck calls the It—that was written independently, so the story goes, of Freud's work (Freud called It the Id). Funny, touching, undeniable.

Hilgard, E. R. and **Atkinson, R. C.** *Introduction to Psychology* (1953)   ▮♀a
Comprehensive introductory textbook, used by a generation of first-year students. Regularly updated (7th edition, 1979, recommended); clearly written.

Jung, Carl *Psychology and Religion: East and West* (1958)   ♀★
Jung is the psychotherapist of our century who was most open to religion and to other subjective (non-scientific?) considerations. This volume shows the immense range of his sympathies, and includes such classics as his "Answer to Job" and "Aron". Also: *Modern Man in Search of a Soul*; *Archetypes and the Collective Unconscious*; *Man and His Symbols*, etc

Kamin, L. J. *The Science and Politics of IQ* (1974)   ♀
Savage, influential attack on the idea that IQ is largely inherited. The subject is a major one for specialists: laymen will find this glimpse into the professional jungle riveting; they may find Eysenck (qv) a helpful guide.

Lindsay, P. H. and **Norman, D. A.** *Human Information Processing* (1977)   ▮a
Standard textbook both on how we perceive and what we do with what we perceive. Scientific basis for psychology usefully, clearly explored. Should be read with Oatley (qv).

Luria, A. *The Working Brain* (1973)   ♀
The physiology of the brain: essential background to all psychological study, clearly laid out. Neuropsychology is a vital area today; Luria is one of the leading and most lucid practitioners.

McLeish, John *Soviet Psychology* (1975)
Straightforward account of some notably neglected and even vilified figures in the 20th-century history of psychology. Undogmatic, unpolitical and clear accounts of theories. Also: *The Science of Behaviour*

Mandler, G. *Mind and Emotion* (1975)   ♀
Emotion is not precisely "sited" in the brain—so where or what is it? Mandler, a well known cognitive psychologist, sets out the necessary clues, including the view that interpretation of emotion may be the essential key to the understanding of the balance between heart and mind.

Miller, G. A. and **Buckhout, R.** *Psychology: the Science of Mental Life* (1970)   ♀a★
Excellent general introduction; technical, but accessible with perseverance.

Murphy, Gardner *Historical Introduction to Modern Psychology* (1972)   ▮
Psychology is one of the oldest studies of mankind although modern researchers often ignore or despise earlier discoveries, insights and concepts. This worthy account of the history of the subject is a good balance to other volumes on this list.

Oatley, Keith *Perceptions and Representations* (1978)   ♀
Accessible, if demanding adjunct to Lindsay (qv).

Rutter, Michael *Maternal Deprivation Reassessed* (1972)
Effective debunking of the idea that young children will inevitably suffer unless brought up exclusively by their own mothers. Describes the quality of mothering a child requires to develop normally. Aggressive; dogmatic; stimulating. See ANTHROPOLOGY (Kitzinger).

Skinner, B. F. *Beyond Freedom and Dignity* (1971)   ♀★
Skinner is the controversial exponent of behaviourism (the doctrine which rejects assessment of subjective or introspective accounts of individual response in favour of exclusive concentration on the objectively measurable). He treads ably and thrillingly the borderline between psychology and philosophy: a stimulating, heterodox figure. Also: *Science and Human Behaviour*; *Walden Two* (novel)

Walker, S. *Learning and Reinforcement* (1975)   a
Representative title from the *Essential Psychology* series (herewith recommended): short, crisp summary introductions to all aspects of the subject.

Warr, P. and **Wall, T.** *Work and Well-being* (1975)
Sober, sensible discussion of research findings in an area of enormous significance as we consider the post-industrial age.

Watson, R. I. *The Great Psychologists: From Aristotle to Freud* (1971)   a
Zimbardo, P. G. and **Ruch, F. L.** *Psychology and Life* (1975)   ▮♀
Mammoth review of the subject; not only describes what psychologists have discovered about human behaviour but also demonstrates the relevance of laboratory work to everyday life. Also: *Shyness: What It Is, What to Do About It*

Reference

We have elsewhere suggested lists of useful reference books for the British and American home. The books recommended here offer access to a larger body of knowledge—indeed, in a more or less compact form, they offer all knowledge. But this is by no means a comprehensive list; it is, rather, a personal choice. We have tried to offer a selection of available titles rather than settling for definitive works in each area; each of the books listed has specific attractions, which mark it out from the competent run of information books. Encyclopaedias and dictionaries of specific areas of knowledge (eg economics or music) will be found in the appropriate lists.

See ARCHAEOLOGY (Bray); ARCHITECTURE (Colvin, Fleming); ART (McGraw-Hill, Murray, Osborne); CHILDREN'S BOOKS (Uden); FILM (Bawden, Halliwell); FOOD (Johnson, Lichine, Montagné); HISTORY/ANCIENT (Heyden, Lempriere, Radice); HISTORY/WORLD (Barraclough, Grun); HOME (Brittain, *Encyclopaedia*, Frewing, Hay); MATHEMATICS (Larkin, Moore, Norton); MEDIA (Berry); MEDICINE (Gray, Parish); MUSIC (Cross, Greenfield, Hadley, Hindley, Logan, Osborne, Sadie); MYTHOLOGY (Dowson, Larousse); NATURAL HISTORY (Fry); RELIGION (Crosse); SOCIOLOGY (*International*)

Adler, M. J. and **Van Doren, C.** *Great Treasury of Western Thought* ★
Massive collection of classic quotations from leading authors and thinkers of the Western tradition. See BIOGRAPHY (Van Doren); PHILOSOPHY (Adler)

Atlante Internazionale del Touring Club Italiano (1968)
One of the finest single-volume atlases, though this edition is dating fast.

Bartlett's Familiar Quotations (1855)
Soon after its first publication this book became the standard American collection of quotations, chosen on the basis of familiarity. Useful; dependable. 13th edition (1955) recommended.

Brewer's Dictionary of Phrase and Fable (1870)
Literally fabulous; an indispensable mine of information; even its cross-references entertain ("*scrambled egg*: see *brass hat*"). But be warned: there is no such thing as a quick dip into this book. Its pool has only a deep end. Also: *The Reader's Handbook of Allusion*; *Dictionary of Miracles*

Britannica Atlas (1979)
A superb one-volume atlas, perhaps the most recommendable of them all.

Bullock, A. and **Stallybrass, O.** *The Fontana Dictionary of Modern Thought* (1977)
This book handily sets out to define, in as few clear words as possible, over 4,000 of the key terms in 20th-century thought (eg cybernetics, OECD, retro-rocket, turnpike theorem). It is, in part, a guide to jargon, immensely useful for the layman; but it is also wide enough and detailed enough in scope to act as a brief encyclopaedia of how our century thinks.

Chambers Twentieth Century Dictionary (1901)
It is meant as a compliment to call this a straightforward, no-nonsense dictionary ("hello. Same as hallo"). Its main indulgence in the current edition is the inclusion of words normally only to be found in the vocabulary of crossword-puzzle compilers and other lexical antiquarians.

Craigie, W. A. and **Hulbert, J. R.** *A Dictionary of American English on Historical Principles* (1938–1944)
Thorough, scholarly treatment of the history of English in America up to the end of the 19th century, extending and supplementing *The Oxford English Dictionary*.

Crowley, E. T. *Acronyms, Initials and Abbreviations Dictionary* (1960)
Not a beautiful book, but a serviceable one, containing thousands of stunted word-forms. American, but includes British, European and other entries. Can never be completely up-to-date, but regular supplements (latest 1978) ensure that it is never too far behind.

Ekwall, E. *The Concise Oxford Dictionary of English Place-Names* (1936)
Scholar's handbook of English place-names, with no rivals in its class. 15,000 place-names painstakingly traced through early records back to their original meanings. Magisterial. Also: *English River Names*

Encyclopedia Americana
30 volumes, 27,000 pages, 53,500 articles, 353,000 entries, 31,141,000 words, 21,500 illustrations including 1,194 maps. Although, as its name implies, it is

American in origin and written in American English, it is no more parochial in its coverage than *Britannica*. Lack of colour makes it look dull; but the articles on the whole are well researched and well written. More adult and comprehensive than *World Book* (qv), less specialized and easier to read than *Britannica* (qv). Alphabetically arranged; good index.

Encyclopaedia Britannica
33,000 pages, 106,500 articles, 25,200 illustrations including 1,100 maps. Authoritative work for educated adults; in two main parts, 19-volume *Macropaedia* containing long articles and 10-volume *Micropaedia* with short, quick reference articles; all volumes have A to Z arrangement of subjects. So-called index (the *Micropaedia*) is deficient and cumbersome. Latest edition (15th) essential.

Fowler, H. W. *A Dictionary of Modern English Usage* (1926)
A model of persuasive prescriptivism notorious for its capacity to delight one reader and infuriate the next, yet universally acclaimed for its enlightening scholarship. Fowler's outspoken adherence to the rule of law in written English is tempered by the benign, firm authority of Sir Ernest Gowers in the 1965 revision. M. H. Nicholson produced its analogue, *A Dictionary of Modern American Usage*. Also: *The King's English* (Fowler); *The Complete Plain Words* (Gowers)

Fowler, H. W. and F. G. *The Concise Oxford Dictionary of Current English* (1911)
Precision and reliability of a Swiss watch; more information per page than in any comparable dictionary. 1976 facelift has added a great deal of new vocabulary without greatly disturbing the important Fowlerian imprint on which the greatness of the book still (ultimately) depends.

Gran Atlas Aguilar (3 vols, 1969)
This magnificent Spanish work, the third volume of which is an incredibly thorough index, first appeared in 1969. A new edition has been announced for an undetermined date but the original is still enormously useful and beautiful. If your funds are unlimited, buy this and the *Times* (qv); if not, nag the local library—it's a gorgeous book.

Johnson, Dr Samuel *Dictionary of the English Language* (1755)
Not the first English dictionary, far less the first dictionary of a European language. Dr Johnson's definitions are often insular ("oats"), idiosyncratic ("lexicographer") and prejudiced ("patron"). But a work to be preserved and perused forever as the only English dictionary compiled by a writer of the first rank. See BIOGRAPHY (Bate, Boswell, Krutch, Johnson); LITERARY CRITICISM; TRAVEL

Jones, Daniel *English Pronouncing Dictionary* (1917)
Guide to "Received Pronunciation", covering not only "dictionary" words but personal and place-names too. Foreign words are given both anglicized and "correct" pronunciation; alternative, rare, and old-fashioned pronunciations are shown. Quite technical: the reader must be prepared to learn the international phonetic alphabet.

Kaye and Ward (publishers) *Official Rules of Sports and Games* (1980)
Immensely useful, and fascinating for the amateur sportsman: clearly stated rules of everything from archery and athletics to volleyball and water polo. Regularly updated.

McWhirter, R. and N. (eds) *The Guinness Book of Records* (1963)
Treasury of fascinating information on the largest, smallest, longest, fattest, most prodigious phenomena in nature. Records of every kind, from running the marathon to holding one's breath. Some of the information is bizarre, much of it useless—all of it riveting. Annually updated.

Mathews, M. M. *A Dictionary of Americanisms on Historical Principles* (1951)
"Those words and meanings which came first into the English language in the United States" in 2 volumes: *Adultery to Lincolnism* and *Lincolnite to Zwieback*. "Americanisms" is more restrictively defined than in Craigie (qv), but 20th-century items and earlier illustrative examples are included.

Merit Students Encyclopedia (1980)
20 volumes, 12,000 pages, 22,000 articles, 20,700 illustrations including 1,500 maps. Written for the American school system; suitable for home use, though expensive.

Mitchell Beazley Encyclopaedia (Random House Encyclopaedia) (1977)
Subtitled *The Joy of Knowledge*: 10 volumes, 3,350 pages, 26,000 articles, 15,000 illustrations including 300 maps. A unique concept in encyclopaedias, this work successfully combines the thematic approach with an A to Z arrangement for quick reference. Eight volumes of *Colourpaedia*, arranged mainly as 2-page spreads devoted to one topic; 8th volume has countries of the world (A to Z) and an atlas. Two volumes of *Fact Index* have mainly short A to Z articles, illustrated and cross-referenced to each other and to the *Colourpaedia*. General volumes can be too diffuse, index volumes too brief in their entries.

Mitchell Beazley New Concise Atlas of the Earth (1973)
105 pages of maps, preceded by a preliminary "world encyclopaedia". Lavish, large and lovely, though cumbersome to use.

New Arthur Mee's Children's Encyclopaedia
20 slimmish volumes, 4,000 pages, 1,000 articles, 5,500 colour illustrations. Large type for easy reading. Aimed at 7- to 11-year-olds; more ambitious (though less bulky) than many such works. Although it carries Arthur Mee's name and pedigree, it is a far cry from the original famous work. Subjects are handled thematically (with an adequate index), and an attempt is made to capture some of the Mee nostalgia by including nursery rhymes and fairy stories (well illustrated). But gone are the prejudices and blatant racism of its original creator.

New Columbia Encyclopedia
1 volume, 3,000 pages, 650 illustrations including 250 maps. Written in American English, *Columbia* has hardly any illustrations and is pitched at an adult level, although it is still the best single-volume straight reference encyclopaedia; not for browsers. Suffers from lack of an index, in spite of A to Z arrangement, because cross-references are not as profuse as they might be. New edition badly needed, as last edition (1975) is rapidly becoming dated.

Onions, C. T. *The Oxford Dictionary of English Etymology* (1966)
Advances the claims of etymology to be a science rather than a lexical sub-art or a branch of folklore. Anyone interested in the origins of words should not be put off by its austere scholarly presentation; these definitions are often fun. Also: *The Oxford Shakespeare Glossary*

Opie, I. and **P.** *The Oxford Dictionary of Nursery Rhymes* (1951)
The nursery rhyme accorded full scholarly treatment—"detailed without being tedious", as the authors claim. Standard, authoritative work, delightfully and relevantly illustrated. Also: *The Lore and Language of Schoolchildren*; *Children's Games in Street and Playground*; *Classic Fairy Tales*, etc

***Oxford Advanced Learner's Dictionary of Current English* (1948)**
A byword for lucidity and clarity of explanation, this book has served learners and foreign users of English everywhere from Calais to Krakatoa; even native speakers will occasionally admit to using it in preference to a conventional dictionary. Also: *A Guide to Patterns and Usage in English*

Oxford Dictionary of Quotations (1941)
Some of the most interesting quotations are, as you'd expect, anonymous, and these have a section that steals the day. Shakespeare as usual gets nearly half the book but he does deserve it; Shaw is, if anything, under-represented. A serviceable book: both this edition and the unsatisfactory 1979 updating are required.

Oxford English Dictionary on Historical Principles (1884–1928)
With Webster's (qv), a monument both to scholarship and to the richness, strangeness and sheer magnificence of our language. The history and meanings of each word are documented and fully illustrated by precisely dated quotations for literary and other works down the centuries. New supplements in progress. For home use, *The Concise Oxford Dictionary* is recommended.

Oxford Home Atlas of the World (1960)
Excellent short atlas, of mainly physical and political maps.

Partridge, E. *A Dictionary of Slang and Unconventional English* (1937)
All-inclusive collection of English slang through the ages. Jargon, cant and obscenity dated and documented where possible, often in idiosyncratic ways: quotations from printed sources rarely have page references and dating can be based on a letter, a reminiscence, or the author's recollections of 50 years ago. Delightful, personal authority, a browser's joy. Also: *Usage and Abuvase*; *A Dictionary of Clichés*; *A Dictionary of Catch Phrases*, etc

Pascoe, L. C. (ed) *Encyclopaedia of Dates and Events* (1968)
Each double-spread is divided into four columns covering respectively History, Literature, the Arts and Science. The key events of each important year (5000 BC–AD 1970) are covered, with brief cross-references and a full index. Did you know when the Treaty of Aix was signed? When wallpaper was invented? What Thierry did? At one level, a quiz-addict's delight; at another, a serious and useful reference tool. Regularly updated: seek latest edition.

Procter, P. *Longman Dictionary of Contemporary English* (1978)
Stimulating, enterprising dictionary that lives up to its title and goes a step further than exemplification by including comments on usage of a kind that you will need if you don't know the difference between *already* and *all ready*.

Random House Dictionary of the English Language (1966)
Massive dictionary, the result of new lexical principles. A fine work which hardly ever fails the diligent searcher. Good small atlas included in unabridged edition.

Roget's Thesaurus of English Words and Phrases (1952)
"A commodious succour to dissertators searching their pockets for the well-pitched locution" is how Roget could lead you to express it, but most of us would say that it is a useful aid to writers seeking the exact word in a forest of apparent synonyms. See Webster.

Smith, W. G. and **Heseltine, J. E.** *The Oxford Dictionary of English Proverbs* (1935)
Thorough documentation of the history rather than the significance of everything in written English that can be regarded as proverbial. Weak points are inadequate standards of bibliographical citation, a poor grasp of the classical sources, and a shortage of quotations after about 1800.

Stewart, G. R. *American Place-names* (1970)
Selective: only well-known, repeated, or unusual names are included. Explanations, each with a cameo of American history, are untechnical—look elsewhere for (eg) exact Indian etymologies. But names like *Enough, Enola* ("alone" backwards) and *Cape Nome* (a misreading of a query on a map) are of its essence.

Strunk, William, Jr. and **White, E. B.** *The Elements of Style* (1935)
In 1919 Strunk was White's English professor at Cornell and his *The Elements of Style* was a required text known only to his students. Sixteen years later, White introduced to the general public Strunk's attempts to cut the vast tangle of English rhetoric down to size and write its rules and principles on the head of a pin. A must for students, the good professor's advice includes everything from "Words and Expressions Commonly Misused" to "Write with verbs and nouns not adjectives and adverbs." See CHILDREN'S BOOKS (White); DIARIES (Garnett, White); HUMOUR (White)

Tilley, M. P. *A Dictionary of the Proverbs in England in the Sixteenth and Seventeenth Centuries* (1950)
Full of wise saws and modern instances, with painstaking scholarship expended alike on the homely, the humorous, the bawdy, and the consoling ("there is a difference between staring and stark mad", etc). Concludes with detailed bibliography and index to proverbial uses in Shakespeare, some previously unsuspected.

Times Comprehensive Atlas of the World (1980)
Huge (240 maps); hugely expensive; worth every penny. For those with slim purses, its little brother *The Times Concise Atlas of the World* (143 maps) is an excellent alternative.

Van Der Meer, Frederic *Atlas of Western Civilization* (1960)
Maps, profuse and spectacular photographs, informative text, superb index—the superlatives pile up. For ancient world equivalent, see HISTORY/ANCIENT (Heyden)

Wallechinsky, D., Wallace I. and **W. (eds)** *The Book of Lists* (1977)
This is one of those serendipitous ideas that, once thought of, seem so obvious and so obviously right. The editors have commissioned and compiled lists of every kind: 20 largest lakes in the world, 12 writers who ran unsuccessfully for public office, 8 cases of spontaneous combustion, Orson Welles' 12 best movies of all time . . . Not a serious reference work—a delight. Should be on everyone's shelf—but keep a few spare copies if you have light-fingered visitors. It's irresistible.

Webster's New Collegiate Thesaurus (1976)
The first entirely new thesaurus since Roget. This one, based on a different principle, is in many situations simpler and more effective to use. There should be room for both this and Roget on any reasonable shelf of reference books.

Webster's New Dictionary of Synonyms (1942)
Aimed at those who daren't admit they use Roget. Arranged alphabetically under key-words, with elaborate cross-referencing; scores by giving examples in use of many of the synonyms listed. Most quoted authors are American.

Webster's Third New International Dictionary of the English Language (1961)
One of the greatest of all reference works in (and on) English: only the *Oxford English Dictionary* (qv) has anything like the same authority. 1961 updating covers many 20th-century additions to the language, makes this an indispensable book for every library. For home use, *Webster's New Collegiate Dictionary* is recommended.

World Book Encyclopedia
26 volumes, 16,000 pages, 22,500 articles, 30,000 illustrations including 2,500 maps. Well-established American encyclopaedia with 2 British Isles volumes added on, this work uses A to Z arrangement but with copious cross-references. Level of the text is aimed at high school students; design and pictorial layout are old-fashioned by modern European standards. The only major encyclopaedia that is thoroughly revised each year.

Yule, H. and **Burnell, A. C.** *Hobson-Jobson: A Glossary of Colloquial Anglo-Indian Words and Phrases* (1886)
Sprawling and undisciplined repository of the priceless vocabulary (*bundobast, gymkhana, shikaree*, etc) that sprang from the association of English and Indian peoples down to the end of the 19th century. The curious title, for example, is an anglicization of *Ya Hasan! Ya Husayn!* ("O Husan! O Husain!") chanted by Muslims as they beat their breasts in the Muharram procession.

Religion

The Introduction to Occult and Paranormal could stand, unaltered, here. The fact that it does not—and that making it do so would seem both frivolous and provocative—is perhaps an indication of the abiding authority and strength of religious studies, if not of the claims of religion itself. Certainly, whatever follies and barbarities have been inherent in religious *practice*, its *principle* has often synthesized the best moral, ethical and philosophical thought (to say nothing of poetry and other arts) of which the human mind is capable. Hence, the bias of the books on this list is less towards the detail of specific religions (though some outstanding works of Christian apologetics are included) than towards discussion of those spiritual and philosophical dilemmas to which religious thinkers have notably and regularly addressed themselves. There are, in fact, very few recommendable books on the validity and transcendental potentiality of "paganism," or on systems of moral, philosophical and artistic life which exclude the religious initiative—and this lack focuses attention on two fundamental questions. Is religious belief an essential prerequisite of such matters, and are those who think they can manage without it therefore deluded? Or does the flaw in objectivity—crucial at least philosophically—tell us something about the exclusive nature of religious belief itself?

See ANTHROPOLOGY (Dodds, Lewis, Lienhardt, Radin); AUTOBIOGRAPHY (Augustine, Fox, Gosse); BIOGRAPHY (Bainton, Renan); DIARIES (Kierkegaard, Kilvert, Pope John, Teilhard de Chardin, Woodforde); DRAMA (Sayers); HISTORY/BRITISH (Bede, Tawney, Thomas); HISTORY/EUROPEAN (Barraclough, Cohn, Ladurie); MYTHOLOGY (Branston, Burland, Dowson, Eliade, Frazer, Harrison, Huxley, Weston); PHILOSOPHY (Aquinas, Gilson, Marcel, Spinoza); POETRY (Gardner); PSYCHOLOGY (Jung); SOCIOLOGY (Berger)

Adams, Henry *Mont St Michel and Chartres* (1904) ★
Extraordinary study of 13th-century Catholicism in France, its cathedrals and its Mariolatry. The book could also be recommended under Architecture; either way Adams is delicious (and malicious) on the Virgin and her worship. See Warner; AUTOBIOGRAPHY; HISTORY/AMERICAN

Aletrino, N. *Six World Religions* (1968)
Brief sketch of the origin, growth and meaning of each of six great non-Christian religions of the world. Unpolemical; thorough; readable.

Barbour, Ian G. *Issues in Science and Religion* (1968) ♀
Masterly contribution to the debate between science and religion; issues discussed with exemplary clarity and fairness. Also: *Science and Religion*. See MATHEMATICS (Koestler)

Bernstein, Marcelle *Nuns* (1976) 🏺
What are nuns? Why? How? Where? This book is jolly and journalistic in places, but also manages to document the need for solitude, celibacy and a life of worship in the contemporary West. No history; concentrates mainly on modern British and US convent life.

Bettenson, Henry *Documents of the Christian Church* (1963) 📖
Selection runs from the Neronian persecution (AD 64) to the revised constitution of the World Council of Churches (1961). Useful if you want to know exactly what Luther nailed to the door of Wittenberg Cathedral or what the Council of Trent said about original sin.

Bible ✦ ♀ ★ 📖
Those approaching the Bible as a central plank in their Christian faith and practice will probably use a modern translation; those approaching it as one of the seminal books of the Western literary tradition will be more familiar with the words of the Authorized Version (1611). There are no really good recensions for children, preserving both the poetry and the mystery: Edwards and Steen: *A Child's Bible* (1973) comes nearest. See Bultmann; MYTHOLOGY (Hooke)

Bonhoeffer, Dietrich *Letters and Papers from Prison* (1953) ★
Bonhoeffer, a martyr to the cause of Christian resistance to Hitler, propounded the idea of "religionless Christianity"; *Letters and Papers* is one of the most-quoted Christian documents from World War II. Also: *Ethics*; *The Cost of Discipleship*; *Life Together*, etc

142

Buber, Martin *I and Thou* (1923)
The core of Buber's philosophy of religion, education, society and politics;
concise and sensitive. Also: *Between Man and Men*; *Good and Evil*; *Paths in
Utopia*
Bultmann, Rudolph *Jesus Christ and Mythology* (1960)   ♀
Bultmann is concerned to "demythologize" the Christian faith, to make it
intelligible and relevant to those who can no longer take literally statements
about a supernatural world. Also: *Jesus and the Word*; *Primitive Christianity*;
Theology of the New Testament
Butterfield, Herbert *Christianity and History* (1949)
Influential views on the meaning of history, and the relation of historical
processes to Christian thinking; light in touch; graphic; provocative. Also: *The
Origins of Modern Science*, etc
Castaneda, Carlos *The Don Juan Trilogy* (1969–1972)
These three volumes— *The Teachings of Don Juan*; *A Separate Reality*; *Journey
to Ixtlan*—by a young anthropologist who met a wise old Yaqui Indian in the New
Mexico desert, created a sensation in the early 1970s and also some controversy:
was the whole affair a complicated hoax? Anyway, the books are excellent and
thought provoking—the religion of peyote, out of time out of place.
Chadwick, Henry *The Early Church* (1967)   ▌
A good account of the way in which the Christian church, having taken root in the
cracks of the Roman Empire, came to tower over every aspect of life and culture.
Also: *Early Christian Thought and the Classical Tradition*
Conze, Edward (trans) *Buddhist Scriptures* (1959)
Comprehensive selection, including many of the best-known Buddhist texts.
Also: *Buddhism*. See Humphreys.
Crosse, F. L. *The Oxford Dictionary of the Christian Church* (1957)   ▌
Everything from Original Sin to Last Judgement, lucidly and alphabetically
explained.
Davies, Horton *Christian Deviations* (1954)   *
Compassionate but hard look (from a position of inexorable orthodoxy) at such
"fringe" movements as Spiritualism, Christian Science and Moral Rearmament.
Also: *Puritan Worship*. See ANTHROPOLOGY (Lewis)
Deanesly, Margaret *The History of the Mediaeval Church, 590–1500*
(1925)   ▌
Splendid guide to the medieval Christian church; particularly good on the more
human (and less political) subjects like friars, hospitals and heretics. Also: *The
Lollard Bible*
Dodd, C. H. *The Founder of Christianity* (1971)   ▌
Award-winning book by British New Testament scholar who directed the
translation of *The New English Bible*; result of a life-time's meditation on the text
of the New Testament. Also: *The Apostolic Preaching and Its Development*; *The
Parables of the Kingdom*; *The Authority of the Bible*
Dunham, Barrows *The Heretics* (1961)   ▌✓
Fascinating study of heresy in the last 2000 years, concentrating on specific
figures but addressing itself to the general proposition that heresy and
persecutions are dynamic elements in the evolution of thought. Challenging and
authoritative on what orthodoxy is and how it is made and remade. Dunham
knows what he's talking about: he conceived this book when he was arraigned by
Senator McCarthy. See HISTORY/EUROPEAN (Ladurie)
Epstein, Isidore *Judaism* (1970)
This book does not deal exclusively with religion, but also covers political, social
and economic issues. Provocative; authoritative.
Ferraby, John *All Things Made New* (1957)   a
Comprehensive introduction to the history and teachings of the Baha'i faith,
usefully incorporating many quotations from Baha'i holy writings.
Guillaume, Alfred *Islam* (1954)
The resurgence of Islam as a world force makes a book for Westerners on the
subject of great importance. This one is excellent: clear, thorough, unprejudiced.
Happold, F. C. *Mysticism* (1963)
Good introduction to, and anthology of, the writers and seers (of all spiritual
traditions) who have sought to penetrate the heart of being, if it has one. Also:
Religious Faith of Twentieth-century Man
Hebblethwaite, Peter *The Christian-Marxist Dialogue and Beyond*
(1976)   ♀
A book of capital importance for those who want to understand some of the
apparently odd ecclesiastico-political alignments in the Third World. Knotty
contents; easy style. Also: *Runaway Church*
Hick, John *Death and Eternal Life* (1976)   ♀
Comprehensive examination of contemporary attitudes to death in literature,
empirical "evidence" of survival, parapsychology, the doctrines and attitudes of
religion. Christian bias does not unbalance a generally fascinating, eclectic book.
Also: *Evil and the God of Love*; *Faith and Knowledge*

Humphreys, Christmas *Buddhism* (1962)   a
James, William *The Varieties of Religious Experience* (1902)   ☿
There has been much new thought since this study of religious conversion first
appeared; but it remains a classic in its field. Also: *Psychology*; *The Will to Believe*
Kapleau, Philip *The Three Pillars of Zen* (1966)
The cult of Zen among the rootless young of the 1960s has tended to leave in our
minds a barely understood, misguided and partial view of a serious and coherent
religious philosophy. Zen is a mystic system (derived in Japan from the Ch'an
Buddhist sect of China): its aim is personal tranquillity, and its methods are
austerity and the encouragement of the fine arts and education. This book ignores
Western hippy accretions and concentrates on the central pillars of the original
philosophy.
Marcus Aurelius *Meditations* (2nd century)   ▣
If there are any spiritually mature books on "paganism" (see introduction to this
list), these calm, rigorous Stoic reflections head the list. This was the seedbed of
Christian morality, too.
Newman, John Henry *Apologia pro Vita Sua* (1864)   ☿▣
Charles Kingsley had said that truth had never been a virtue of the Roman
Catholic clergy. Newman replied by defending his own intellectual integrity and
commenting, in splendid prose, on his spiritual history. Also: *An Essay on the
Development of Christian Doctrine*, etc. See BIOGRAPHY (Strachey)
Oman, John *Grace and Personality* (1917)   ☿
Classic exploration of one of the most important of all theological problems, the
relationship of divine grace and human free will. Also: *Vision and Authority*
Pascal, Blaise *Pensées* (1669)   ★▣
Pascal's luminous notes for an unfinished apology for Christianity which would
confound the followers of Descartes. Also: *Provincial Letters*
Phillips, Margaret Mann *Erasmus on His Times* (1967)   ♟
Shortened version of *The Adages of Erasmus*. The original bedside book, full of
urbane wit and charm. See BIOGRAPHY (Huizinga)
Smart, Ninian *The Phenomenon of Christianity* (1979)
Fresh approach to Christianity as a religious phenomenon. The author slaps a
"phenomenological grid" over it, and describes the many facets into which it is
then broken up. Also: *The Religious Experience of Mankind*; *Philosophers and
Religious Truth*
Struve, Nikita *Christians in Contemporary Russia* (1963)   ✲
Teilhard de Chardin, Pierre *The Phenomenon of Man* (1959)   ☿★▣
Published exactly 100 years after Darwin's *The Origin of Species*, this book
Christianized evolution. Despite some theological and philosophical cavils,
Teilhard's great and humane vision has attracted a multitude of followers, and
some critical disdain. Also: *The Future of Man*, etc. See DIARIES: NATURAL
HISTORY (Darwin, Huxley, Lack, Medawar, Smith)
Tillich, Paul *The Boundaries of Our Being* (1966)   ☿
Collection of addresses together with autobiographical sketch; theme is how the
human predicament, seen against "divine reality", challenges man to become a
new being. Also: *The Courage to Be*; *The Shaking of the Foundations*
Vidler, A. R. *The Church in an Age of Revolution* (1961)   ☿
Pithy, wide-ranging study of the Christian church as it faces the political, social
and theological revolutions of our time. Also: *A Variety of Catholic Modernists*;
20th-Century Defenders of the Faith; *Soundings*
Ward, Keith *The Concept of God* (1974)   ☿
Fresh, readable account of the philosophy of religion, holding that it is an integral
part of human experience, the true focus of which must be some concept of God.
Also: *Ethics and Christianity*
Warner, Marina *Alone of All Her Sex* (1978)   ♟
Unshrill feminist history of Mariolatry—the Catholic Church's anti-female
creation of the mother of God into a kind of unattainable and unsexing model for
women.
Wat, W. Montgomery *Muhammad, Prophet and Statesman* (1974)   ▮
Well-researched biography; especially good on the sociological perspectives of
the man and his ministry.
Weil, Simone *Waiting on God* (1951)   ☿
Collection of letters and essays marking some of the stages in Weil's ascetic
pilgrimage from revolutionary Marxism to the threshold of the Catholic Church,
but no further. Also: *Gateway to God*; *Gravity and Grace*; *The Need for Roots*
Wendel, Françoise *Calvin* (1963)   a
Good introduction to the life and thought of a man who, apart from Augustine
and Luther, had more influence than any other religious thinker on Western
secular society.
Zaehner, R. C. *Hinduism* (1966)
Straightforward guide to the various epochs and styles of Hindu thought. Also:
Hindu Scriptures; *The Bhagavad-gita*; *The Koran*. See MYTHOLOGY (Narayan,
O'Flaherty)

Sex and Love

The attempt to apply a criterion of literary merit has kept this list short. But if reading turns you on . . .

See BIOGRAPHY (Masters); MEDICINE (Belleveau, Boston Women's Collective, Kaplan)

Boccaccio *The Decameron* (1471)
Rumbustious, thigh-slapping medieval sexuality, like Brueghel with dirty bits. Exhausting to swallow whole; sampling makes for appetite. Good translation: Burton.

Brecher, R. and **E.** *An Analysis of Human Sexual Response* (1967)
If more people read this book there would be more happy— and successful—lovers around. A layperson's guide to Masters and Johnson's (qv) *Human Sexual Response*. Also: *The Sex Researchers*

Cleland, John *Fanny Hill: Memoirs of a Woman of Pleasure* (1749)
Has Westminster School ever recovered from producing the author of what the British Dictionary of National Biography once described as a "scandalously indecent book"? A "novel" but marvellously instructive in its lubricious vitality.

Comfort, Alex (ed) *The Joy of Sex* (1974)
Sub-title *A Gourmet Guide to Lovemaking* might put off those who resist the "I-could-eat-you" school of modern practice; but this refreshingly shameless and practical manual can only increase the pleasures of sex. Also: *More Joy of Sex*

Duffy, Maureen *The Erotic World of Faery* (1978)
So that's the appeal of all those folk tales about elves, goblins, toadstools and (if you'll pardon the expression) fairy rings! Serious, delightful book; human sexuality at its most unexpected.

Foucault, Michel *The History of Sexuality* (1979)   ♀
Polemic by a French philosopher against the idea that sexuality has been repressed and is now being liberated. He argues that our obsession with analysing, investigating and discussing sex constitutes yet another form of guilt.

Genet, Jean *Our Lady of the Flowers* (1943)
In Genet's super-masculine world a "male who fucks a male is a double male". This "novel", composed while Genet was in prison awaiting trial, describes an implacable society of homosexuality, crime, betrayal and oppression. See DRAMA (Esslin); BIOGRAPHY (Sartre); TRAVEL

Haddon, Celia (ed) *Venus Reveal'd* (1977)
Too much pornography lacks wit, style, and an interest in anything but the sexual act. This book, a parody of *Fanny Hill*, supplies them all, and is sexy too.

Hite, Shere *The Hite Report* (1977)   ♀
Based on a fairly wide, though allegedly unscientific, survey of American women, the results contribute to an understanding of female sexuality. Compulsory reading for all males of the "Wham, bam, thankyou ma'am" school—though (like other readers) they may find the rancorous, self-satisfied tone monotonous.

Kinsey, Alfred C. *et al* *Sexual Behaviour in the Human Male* (1949); *Sexual Behaviour in the Human Female* (1953)   ▌♀
Although now a little outdated and attacked for his research methods, the peeking Dr Kinsey produced what was in its time a classic catalogue of the rich variations of human behaviour and a form of liberation through statistics from the secrecy and falsehood which prejudices morality.

Laclos, Choderlos de *Les Liaisons Dangereuses* (1782)   ★
For anyone who wants reassuring that sex is (a) pointless and (b) inevitable. A fine book on the corruption of innocence by unmotivated evil. The hero, Valmont, spends a large part of his life writing finely drafted but tedious letters to his girlfriend, Merteuil, about planning an expedition to climb yet another *mons veneris* just because it's there. Good translation: Baldick.

Masters, W. H. and **Johnson, V. E.** *Human Sexual Response* (1966)   ▌♀
Detailed physiological and psychological facts, disproving fantasies, fallacies, myths and taboos which surround the subject of orgasmic response. Zero for style, full marks for content. Also: *Human Sexual Inadequacy*

Miller, Henry *Tropic of Cancer* (1931)
Miller was once described as "the first writer outside the Orient who has succeeded in writing naturally about sex on as large a scale as novelists ordinarily write about the dinner table or the battlefield." Could be that he was also a whoremongering, narcissistic bore. For excellent corrective to his scandalously chauvinistic hedonism, see Millet (FEMINISM). Also: *Sexus*; *Plexus*; *Nexus*. See DIARIES (Durrell)

Nefzawi, Sheikh *The Perfumed Garden* (16th century)   🏛▌a★
What sheikhs used to get up to before they discovered oil. Thorough, if over-poetic. Good translation: Burton.

Nin, Anaïs *Delta of Venus* (1978)
When Anaïs Nin started to write erotica for a dollar a page in the 1940s she was instructed "concentrate on sex. Leave out the poetry". Luckily, she was incapable of doing so. Also: *The Diary of Anaïs Nin; Little Birds*

Ovid *The Art of Love* (1st century BC)   ▲
One of the oldest and funniest handbooks of amorous siege tactics. Deals with sexual one-upmanship with cynical, timeless stylishness.

Partridge, Burgo *A History of Orgies* (1964)
Serious study of an extraordinary, rather repellent phenomenon.

Peel, J. and **Potts, M.** *A Textbook of Contraceptive Practice* (1969)   ▯♀

Reage, Pauline *The Story of O* (1970)
Much speculation has been whipped up about who actually wrote *The Story of O*. The way in which a woman, O, achieves sexual gratification by voluntarily subjecting herself to male sadism convinces many people that a male imagination lurks behind the words. Highly erotic; highly literary; Graham Greene called it "a rare thing, a pornographic book well written and without a trace of obscenity".

Rechy, John *City of Night* (1963)
A meaty book in every sense, about male hustlers in New York City. Just the book for people with strong stomachs who cannot imagine what drives homosexuals. Also: *The Sexual Outlaw*

Reich, Wilhelm *The Sexual Revolution* (1930)   ♀
When a Marxist, Reich analysed the family as the key institution within capitalist society responsible for economic repression and sexual perversion. For his insistence on the political significance of sex he was expelled from the Freudian Psycho-Analytical Association. He later became a committed anti-communist, finally dying in prison after being prosecuted by the American Food and Drug Administration for fraud. Thorny style; influential book. Also: *The Imposition of Sexual Morality*

Sade, Marquis de *Justine* (1797)   ♀✳
Libertine, philosopher and pornographer extraordinary, the Marquis de Sade wrote books he expected to be banned. More read about than read; a curiously enervating author, for all his disturbing zest. Compare Angela Carter: *The Sadeian Woman*. Also: *The Hundred and Twenty Days of Sodom; Philosophy in the Bedroom*, etc

Silverstein, C. and **White, E.** *The Joy of Gay Sex* (1977)
Intimate alphabetical guide to the pleasures of gaiety, ranging from "androgyny" to "wrestling". Less serious (and less helpful and supportive) than the companion volume, *The Joy of Lesbian Sex* (1977) by Sisley and Harris. But is solemnity obligatory?

Southern, Terry *Blue Movie* (1973)
Scintillating, Hollywood satire: frivolity laced with splendid, poker-faced sex. They'll film this—and completely miss the point. A funny, and a splendidly erotic, read. Also: *Candy*

Tannahill, Reay *Sex in History* (1980)   ★
Gorgeous scholarly survey of the place of sex (as opposed to love, family life, patriotism, honour, etc) in societies from ancient China and India (oh, those temple-carvings! What were they *for*? For fun, of course, says Tannahill) almost right up (but not, thank goodness, all the way) to the Home Life of Dear Queen Victoria. This really is everything you never dared to ask, about such matters as Greek homosexuality, those medieval girls and their unicorns, Victorian flagellation, even the rationale and methods of castration in the Middle East. Thorough scholarship; deadpan wit; a lovely book. See FOOD

Vatsyayana *The Kama Sutra* (4th-6th century)   ▲▯★
Classic Indian sex manual on the "art of love"; remarkable mixture of sophistication and urbanity. It might give you a headache trying to work out what goes where in some of the sex positions described, just as putting them into practice will almost certainly result in backache. Good translation: Burton.

Wolff, Charlotte *Love between Women* (1971)
Using a case history approach, Charlotte Wolff, a psychoanalyst, gives a good, lucid account of the nature of lesbian relationships. Also: *An Older Love* (fiction)

Sociology

From its 19th-century beginnings, sociology has been an analytical rather than a dogmatic study: its role is to examine the beliefs, principles and processes which control social behaviour, to codify them where possible, and to draw conclusions. Increasingly, however, as the study develops, those conclusions are tending towards dogma, theories of social change becoming recipes, blueprints for vast upheavals of human behaviour and organization. Many of the books on this list show a proselytizing zeal for this or that political way; others, perhaps purer in sociological terms, take the detached stance of the observer, preserving that coolness of analysis of ideas in action which, at its best, makes sociology a true counterpart of philosophy.

See ANTHROPOLOGY (Dumont, Lloyd, Thrasher, Tiger); ARCHITECTURE (Newman); FILM (Durgnat); GEOGRAPHY (Pahl); HISTORY/BRITISH (Blythe, Bragg, Thomas, Thompson); MEDIA (Hoggart, McLuhan, Packard, Williams); MUSIC (Frith); POLITICS (Mackenzie, Mannheim, Mill, Moore, Niebuhr, Piven, Rousseau, Schumpeter); PSYCHOLOGY (Aronson, Erikson)

Anderson, Perry *Considerations on Western Marxism* (1976)   ℗
Lucid survey of "Western Marxist" theorists, including Lukács, Gramsci, Althusser, Sartre, and the Frankfurt School (Horsheimer, Adorno, Marcuse, Benjamin, etc). Their main common feature for the uninitiated is their relative inaccessibility; Anderson's book eases initiation. Also: *Lineages of the Absolutist State*

Andreski, Stanislav *The Social Sciences as Sorcery* (1972)   *
Are modern sociologists actually no more than ju-ju men? Andreski cuts wittily to the heart of the subject, and finds it not so much a religion, more a passionate superstition.

Banton, M. P. *Rôles* (1965)   ℗
One of the founders of the group of sociologists known as "rôle theorists", Banton here presents a clear case for the theory. For reference, essential. See North.

Barnes, Barry *Interests and the Growth of Knowledge* (1977)   ℗
Sound introduction to the sociology of knowledge. See PHILOSOPHY (Mannheim)

Becker, Howard S. *Outsiders* (1963)
The book which launched "labelling theory". Sensitive application of the interactionist viewpoint to such topics as marijuana use and the culture of dance-band musicians.

Berger, Peter L. *The Social Reality of Religion* (1967)
The author looks at Western secularization and asks how theology is possible in an age without religious assumptions. Neglected aspect of contemporary life; challenging treatment. Also: *The Social Construction of Reality*; *A Rumour of Angels*

Blauner, Robert *Alienation and Freedom* (1964)
Influential study of the way in which industrial experience influences the worker's sense of control and his feelings of purpose, isolation and discontent.

Blok, Anton *The Mafia of a Sicilian Village, 1860–1960* (1974)   ★ ♫
Stimulating blend of sociology/history/anthropology, on an endlessly fascinating subject. Compare L. Barzini: *The Italians*; G. Maxwell: *God Protect Me from My Friends.*

Bottomore, T. B. and **Rubel, M.** *Karl Marx: Selected Writings in Sociology and Social Philosophy* (1963)   ℗
Marx would have been amused by present attempts to allocate his work to such narrow disciplinary categories as "sociology", "economics", and "philosophy". However here is a useful "sociological" set of extracts from his work grouped under such headings as "class", "alienation" and "ideology". See Marx; ECONOMICS (Marx); POLITICS (Marx)

Chesney, Kellow *The Victorian Underworld* (1970)   🏛 a ★ ✓ ♫
Horrifying, riveting account of lurks, lays, rookeries, rampsmen and muck snipes. Makes Dickens' fictionalized Hell seem like Sunnybrook Farm. Even the magnificent Doré illustrations are dwarfed by the scabrous, squalid detail of the text. The underside of Empire, brilliantly laid bare.

Durkheim, Emile *Suicide* (1897)   ℗ ★
Perhaps the greatest work of one of the founders of sociology. Central argument, based on statistics available at the time, is that the suicide rate can only be understood by reference to the structure of the society in which it prevails. The

innovating origins of a modern truism. Also: *The Division of Labour in Society*; *The Rules of the Sociological Method*; *Elementary Forms of the Religious Life*

Elias, Norbert   *The Civilizing Process* (1939)   a★
How the development of manners in Europe since the Middle Ages is related to the growth of the State—in other words, how the growth of social control leads to the growth of *self*-control, *con*straint to *re*straint. Neglected, stimulating classic. Also: *What Is Sociology?*

Garfinkel, H.   *Studies in Ethnomethodology* (1967)   ♀✱
Despite its forbidding title (and even more forbidding prose), an important account of a new school of thought which insists that the "organized activities of everyday life" provide the most appropriate focus for sociologists' attention.

Goffman, Erving   *Asylums* (1961)   ★
Although this study of the social world of the inmates of a mental hospital has been widely employed as an attack upon closed institutions, it is also a fine example of Goffman's pessimistic "world vision". Also: *The Presentation of Self in Everyday Life*; *Stigma*; *Behaviour in Public Places*

Gouldner, Alvin W.   *The Coming Crisis of Western Sociology* (1971)   ✱
Interesting, somewhat self-serving attempt to describe the proper task of radical sociologists in the coming years. Perhaps more a symptom of the "crisis" than a recipe for its solution. Also: *Enter Plato*

International Encyclopaedia of the Social Sciences (17 vols, 1968)
One of the very best of the special-subject encyclopaedias. Contains some classic articles, making it unnecessary to wade through less brief specialist tomes.

Jacoby, R.   *Social Amnesia* (1975)   ♀✱
Stylish, polemical account of the various attempts by psychoanalysts, ego-psychologists and others to suppress the sociological import of Freud's writings. Controversial discussion of Reich, Fromm, Marcuse, and Laing. Also: *Critical Interruptions: New Left Perspectives on Herbert Marcuse*

Lewis, Oscar   *La Vida* (1965)
La Vida—"the life" in the *barrios* of Puerto Rico and in their continental offshoots, the dim streets and alleys of New York's East Harlem.

Lipset, S. M.   *Class, Status and Power in Comparative Perspective* (1966)
Lipset is a leading analyst of class structure, recommended for coolness, balance and readability. Also: *Sociology*; *Revolution and Counterrevolution*, etc

Lynd, R. S. and **H. M.**   *Middletown: A Study in American Culture* (1929)
Exhaustive sociological study of the inhabitants of a middle-sized Indiana town (Muncie, it is said) that reveals the best and worst in them (and us?). Attacked for its methods as well as for the secrets it gave away, the work became a foundation stone of American sociology.

Marcuse, Herbert   *One Dimensional Man* (1964)   ！★
How does capitalist society manage to survive? What are the forces which may even yet break it apart? Marcuse's dramatic attempts to update Marx informed and propelled the American student movement in the late 1960s: cf the sorcerer and his apprentices. Also: *Eros and Civilization*; *Reason and Revolution*; *Soviet Marxism*

Marx, Karl   *Economic and Philosophical Manuscripts of 1844* (1959)   ！♀
Written when Marx was 26, these essays attempt to clarify the relationship between philosophy, economics and socialism—a union of ideas which did much to fuel those humanistic revolutionary movements, which reached their peak in capitalist societies in the late 1960s. See ECONOMICS; POLITICS

Matza, David   *Becoming Deviant* (1969)
Sparkling historical review of criminological theory; subtle demonstration of the inadequacies of causal determinism in the understanding of human behaviour. Also: *Delinquency and Drift*

Mead, G. H.   *Mind, Self and Society* (1934)   ▮
Collection of pieces by one of the founders of American social psychology. Superb essay on the creation of the human "self", and an important introduction to "role"—the concept which was later so much used (and abused) by "role theorists".

Mead, Margaret   *Male and Female* (1949)   ▮
Anthropologist's view of male and female roles in different societies, including 20th-century USA. Describes the inexorable cultural pressure on both males and females to conform to specific gender rules of their societies. See ANTHROPOLOGY; AUTOBIOGRAPHY

Mills, C. Wright   *The Sociological Imagination* (1959)   a
Spirited essays about the purpose of sociology—Mills' effective, perhaps overrated response to those who were beginning to make sociology a servant not a critic of the state. Also: *The Power Elite*

North, C. C.   *Social Differentiation* (1926)   ▮
Founding document of the rôle theorist school of thought. Important; interesting.

Raban, Jonathan *Soft City* (1974)　　　　　　　　　　　　　　🏛
Hustling study of city life, the nature of citizenship, the "feel" of a city man, especially in London and New York. Mixed-bag of autobiography, anthropology and literary criticism (the city being a major character in fiction).
Reeves, Magdalen Pember *Round about a Pound a Week* (1913)　　🏛📷
British working-class life before World War I, seen through the eyes of the wives of London workmen. An almost incredible story of cramped, confined life on a meagre budget.
Riesman, D., Denny, R. and Glazer, N. *The Lonely Crowd: A Study of the Changing American Character* (1962)　　　　　　　　　　　　　　⦚
This book created a great controversy and its title passed instantly into the language. Its analysis of inner- and outer-directedness may be finally somewhat superficial but was important for explaining how we felt (and feel?) about ourselves.
Roberts, Robert *The Classic Slum: Salford Life in the First Quarter of the Century* (1971)　　　　　　　　　　　　　　　　🏛 ⫽ 📷
Wonderfully detailed picture of life in a slum district of northern England. Particularly impressive account of the effects of the Great War in bringing new attitudes and experiences into the lives of ordinary people.
Rourke, Constance *American Humor: A Study of National Character* (1931)　　　　　　　　　　　　　　　　　　　　　　　　　📕
The first serious book to connect the tall tale with the national character.
Schutz, Alfred *Collected Papers* (3 vols, 1962)　　　　　　　📕
Although Schutz's version of phenomenology has recently come under attack, his work still forms the best introduction to the modern sociologist's obsession with the nature of "everyday life".
Simmel, Georg *The Sociology of Georg Simmel, 1890–1918* (1964)　　　　　　　　　　　　　　　　　　　　　　　　📕★
Stylish essays (ed Kurt Wolff). Simmel's unwillingness to provide the type of systematic analysis favoured by some of his contemporaries has led to quite unreasonable neglect.
Sumner, W. G. *Folkways* (1907)　　　　　　　　　　　　　🏛
Now classic compilation of social behaviour by a noted 19th-century American sociologist; still fascinating; still relevant.
Suttles, G. D. *The Social Order of the Slum* (1968)　　　　　🏛📷
Fascinating accounts of the variety of groups who live on the West Side of Chicago, with analyses of the relations between them. See Whyte.
Terkel, Studs *Working* (1977)　　　　　　　　　　　　🏛 a ★
Taped interviews of ordinary Americans talking about their daily work: white-collar, blue-collar, executive, professional, breadline. This is where sociology begins—and it makes often unexpected, hopeful reading. Also: *Division Street*. See HISTORY/BRITISH (Blythe, Bragg)
Veblen, Thorstein *The Theory of the Leisure Class* (1899)　　🏛✳
Deliriously ironic study of the lifestyle and "conspicuous consumption" of the American upper classes, and of how such a pecuniary culture became a model for all other groups in society. Also: *The Instinct of Workmanship*
Wallerstein, Immanuel *The Modern World System* (1974)　　　📕
Outstanding example of the world of "dependency theorists" who in the last decade have shown that the situation of underdeveloped countries is not to be understood by faults or weaknesses within their own social structure, but rather in terms of their dependency—increasing and developing over several centuries—on the "developed" parts of a single "world-system". See POLITICS (Fanon)
Weber, Max *The Theory of Social and Economic Organization* (1921)　　　　　　　　　　　　　　　　　　　　　　　　　⦚
Weber, with Marx, has exerted a dominant influence over contemporary sociology and political studies. This book includes his discussion of charismatic authority which has been as widely influential as it has been misunderstood. Also: *The Protestant Ethic and the Spirit of Capitalism*; *From Max Weber: Essays in Sociology*; *On the Methodology of the Social Sciences*, etc. Good selection edited by Runciman (1978).
Whyte, W. F. *Street Corner Society* (1955)　　　　　　　　📕
Whyte spent three and a half years living in an Italian slum area of Chicago before writing this sensitive, readable account of perhaps the most famous small group in sociological literature—"Doc and the Nortons". See Suttles.
Willis, P. *Learning to Labour* (1977)　　　　　　　　　　　✳
Why is it that working-class children end up not just taking dead-end jobs but actually appearing to want them? Unfashionable subject; good treatment.
Willmott, P. and Young, M. *Family and Kinship in East London* (1957)　　　　　　　　　　　　　　　　　　　　　　　　📕
Examination of how modern housing developments affect the freedom of one generation to live near another; the starting point of all contemporary studies of the British family. Also: *Family and Class in a London Suburb*

Travel and Exploration

The catlike curiosity of the human race guarantees vivid interest in the people across the valley; the traveller, who turns that interest into action, is a kind of outsider, a privileged scapegoat who breaks through the barriers of the local, the familiar, and reports on what he sees. The more extraordinary his tales, the more matter-of-fact his narration—for *he* is not amazed, he is at home with himself wherever he goes—and the more wide-eyed our listening amazement. For those who wish to sample the new global village for themselves, a handful of standard guidebook series are recommended here (not Michelin, not Baedeker, for they go without saying, everywhere—and who *reads* them in any case?); from the other books on the list, armchair excitement is guaranteed.

See ANTHROPOLOGY (Greenway); AUTOBIOGRAPHY (Hudson); BIOGRAPHY (Morison, Parkman); HISTORY/AMERICAN (Coleman, Parkman); HISTORY/ASIAN (Severin, Stanley); NATURAL HISTORY (Banks, Burton, Cousteau, Moorehead, Waterton)

Bartram, William *Travels* (1791)
The author travelled through territory that is now Georgia and northern Florida and described the fabulous—real but almost unbelievable—animals and plants that he saw. Deservedly a classic.

Botting, Douglas *One Chilly Siberian Morning* (1965)
To most people Siberia is a vast, cold wilderness peopled by inscrutable peasants and dissident intellectuals. Botting sees it also as the seedbed for huge, dynamic change.

Burton, Sir Richard *A Personal Narrative of a Pilgrimage to Al-Madinah and Mecca* (1855)
Victorian traveller uses his knowledge of the languages and cultures of the Middle East to travel in disguise to Muslim holy cities in Arabia, forbidden to non-Muslims under pain of death. See NATURAL HISTORY; SEX (Boccaccio, Nefzawi, Vatsyayana)

Chadwick, Lee *A Cuban Journey* (1975)
Cuba since Castro: well-written, objective account of how it seemed to one British traveller.

Cherry-Garrard, Apsley *The Worst Journey in the World* (1922)
Captain Scott's polar expeditions have, for the British, the perennial fascination of heroic failure. This classic account uses letters, diaries and personal reminiscence to build an amazing picture of doggedness and heroism in appalling conditions. Should be read in conjunction with two modern books, Elspeth Huxley: *Scott of the Antarctic* (1977) and R. Huntford: *Scott and Amundsen* (1979).

Chitty, S. and **Hinde, T.** *The Great Donkey Walk* (1977)
The authors, with two small children, travelled from Spain to Greece by pilgrim roads and mule tracks. Lively, witty narrative, escapist reading *par excellence*.

Cook, Captain James *The Journals of Captain Cook in His Voyages of Discovery* (4 vols, 1955)
Great accounts of the sea voyage *par excellence*. All these marvels really happened, Captain Cook really did discover Hawaii (the Sandwich Islands) and so forth. Engrossing armchair read.

Dana, Richard H. *Two Years before the Mast* (1840)
Dana worked his way from Boston round Cape Horn to California and back on a wooden sailing-ship in 1834; this classic account of sailors' life compares interestingly with Newby's (qv) *The Last Grain Race*, on a modern sailing ship, and with Preble's *The Opening of Japan* (HISTORY/ASIAN), on US navy life in 1853.

David-Neel, Alexandra *Tibetan Journey* (1936)
Undauntable Frenchwoman's adventures in eastern Tibet. Reminiscent, for style and liveliness, of Kingsley (qv). Fascinating, too, to compare with Harrer's (qv) view of Tibet, at once more mystical and more pragmatic. Also: *My Journey to Lhasa*; *Magic and Mystery in Tibet*

Durrell, Lawrence *Reflections on a Marine Venus* (1953)
Durrell's travel books (of which this is the best) are informed with a poet's stylish intensity and a quirky eye for idiosyncrasies of landscape or character. This book is a palimpsest of the history and manners of Rhodes. *Prospero's Cell* (about Corfu) and *Bitter Lemons* (about Cyprus, and notably good on the 1950s "troubles" there) are equally enjoyable: Durrell writing with rare power,

discipline, clarity. See CHILDREN'S BOOKS (Durrell, G.); DIARIES;
FICTION/NOVELS; POETRY

Farre, Rowena *The Beckoning Land* (1969) 🏛
Oriental journey from Hong Kong to the Himalayas, in search of spiritual
enlightenment. Unique combination of autobiography and travel diary, in light-
hearted, entertaining style. Also: *Seal Morning*

Fawcett, P. H. *Exploration Fawcett* (1953) ★ ◢
Great classic of jungle exploration in the Mato Grosso, Brazil. Fawcett is at once
the epitome of British Grit and a true exemplar of explorer-as-mystic. Leeches,
spiders and piranha fish play featured, lively roles—not a book to read in the
Great Outdoors.

Fermor, Patrick Leigh *A Time of Gifts* (1977)
18-year-old rebel in 1933 sets out to walk from the Hook of Holland to
Constantinople—a modern Grand Tour crucial to his development, as
unpredictable and as fascinating as any young sprig's of the 18th century. Also:
Roumeli (travels in northern Greece); *The Traveller's Tree* (journey through the
Caribbean islands), etc

Fodor, E. and Curtis, W. (eds) *Fodor's Guide to Islamic Asia*
(1973) 🏛 📖 a ✓ ◢
Representative title (revised annually) from magnificent guidebook series; long
on history and topography, clear thematic arrangement, helpful attention to the
needs of the unfamiliar visitor.

Gale, John *Travels with a Son* (1972)
Travels by jeep in Morocco, Mauritania, Senegal, Mali, Sierra Leone, Ivory
Coast, Ghana. For those who like travel-as-autobiography, a treat. Also: *Clean
Young Englishman* (fine autobiography); *The Family Man* (novel)

Genet, Jean *The Thief's Journal* (1949)
Fascinating account of Genet's life in the 1930s underworlds of several European
countries, as beggar and thief. Wonderful incident when some French tourists
discuss whether the beggars in Spain or Morocco are more picturesque, assuming
that Genet can't understand what they're saying. See BIOGRAPHY (Sartre);
DRAMA (Esslin); SEX

Greene, Graham *Journey without Maps* (1936)
Colourful, unusually genial account of an expedition journey upcountry in
Liberia. See FICTION/NOVELS

Harrer, Heinrich *Seven Years in Tibet* (1953)
Austrian mountain-climber trapped in India by the outbreak of World War II
escapes across the Himalayas into Tibet, lives in Lhasa, gives a vivid picture of
pre-Chinese Tibetan life. See David-Neel.

Heyerdahl, Thor *The Kon-Tiki Expedition* (1948) ★ 📖
Six men sail across the Pacific from Peru on a raft of balsa wood, to prove it can
be—and could have been—done. Also: *Aku-Aku*; *The Ra Expeditions*, etc.

Hillaby, John *Journey through Britain* (1968)
Author walked from Land's End to John O'Groats, taking footpaths wherever
possible. Also: *Journey through Europe*; *Journey to the Jade Sea*

Johnson, Dr Samuel *Journey to the Western Islands of Scotland*
(1775) ★
The fascinating encounter of a disciplined 18th-century mind with the alien,
half-barbarian civilization of the Hebrides. See BIOGRAPHY (Bate, Boswell,
Krutch, Johnson); LITERARY CRITICISM; REFERENCE

Kinglake, A. W. *Eothen* (1844)
Light-hearted account of one Englishman's middle Eastern travels in the 1830s,
in the course of which, among other adventures, he deliberately stayed in Cairo
during an epidemic of plague.

Kingsley, Mary *Travels in West Africa* (1897) ★ 📖
Intrepid Victorian lady travels extensively in West Africa, discovers vocation,
writes engrossing, Jane Austenish account, a monument to unflappable
competence and confidence. " 'Señora, you see more bare skin here than on a
regiment of grenadiers!' I worried for a *week* at the awfulness of the pun." A
perceptive, funny book.

Lawrence, D. H. *Sea and Sardinia* (1921)
Another of Lawrence's potboilers—but this one a magical evocation of a
beautiful place. Any reader will desire somehow, some time, to visit Sardinia,
preferably (if they read Lawrence) during February, when the almond trees are in
bloom. See DIARIES; FICTION/NOVELS; FICTION/SHORT STORIES;
HISTORY/EUROPEAN; LITERARY CRITICISM; POETRY

Lawrence, T. E. *Seven Pillars of Wisdom* (1926) ★ ◢
Ostensibly a military chronicle, by an Englishman who took part in a revolt in
Arabia against the Turks. In fact a tapestry of memoirs, philosophy, travel
writing, anthropology and fiction. The opening of Chapter 121 tells all, about the
style and about the Man: "Quiveringly a citizen awoke me, with word that Abd el
Kadir was making rebellion. I sent over to Nuri Said, glad the Algerian fool was
digging his own pit . . ." Also: *The Mint*. See BIOGRAPHY (Aldington)

Lewis, M. and **Clark, W.** *The Journals of Lewis and Clark* (1964)
The quintessential American journey, across the continent, seeking the Pacific.
Lewis and Clark were a remarkable pair, and their companions—Indians and
white men—are no less interesting. These journals, read continuously, will take
many winter evenings; a one-volume selection (ed De Voto) appeared in 1953.
Ley, Charles David (ed) *Portuguese Voyages, 1498–1663* (1947)
Contemporary accounts of the great age of Portuguese discoveries in South
America, Africa and Asia. See Morison; BIOGRAPHY (Morison)
Lindbergh, Charles *The Spirit of St Louis* (1953)
Rewrite—more thoughtful, more detailed, more dramatic—of bestselling *We*
which Lindbergh published shortly after his 1927 flight. This later book is
absolutely unputdownable—until the end, when the plane, too, puts down, to a
great sigh of relief.
London, Jack *The People of the Abyss* (1903)
Horrifying picture of the poverty of most East End Londoners at the time;
interesting comparisons between conditions in London and those in American
cities. See AUTOBIOGRAPHY (Chaplin); FICTION/SHORT STORIES;
SOCIOLOGY (Chesney, Roberts)
Maclean, Fitzroy *A Person from England* (1958)
English visitors to Turkestan, Central Asia, in the heyday of the British Empire.
Travellers, spies, merchants, adventurers—the factual stuff of every ripping yarn.
For armchair travellers, a one-sitting book. Also: *Eastern Approaches*
McPhee, John *Coming into the Country* (1977)
Extraordinary account of travels in Alaska since 1950 (ie since Statehood).
McPhee is one of the great travel-writing stylists of our time, always interesting;
his love for far Alaska irradiates this book. Also: *The Crofter and the Laird*; *The
Pine Barrens*; *The Survival of the Bark Canoe*
Magnusson, M. and **Palsson, H. (trans)** *The Vinland Sagas: The Norse
Discovery of America* (1965) ◗
Two medieval Icelandic accounts of the discovery by Norse seamen of Greenland
and the land beyond.
Matthiessen, Peter *Snow Leopard* (1979)
Impressive account of a search for the legendary inhabitants of the Himalayas.
Grand landscapes and honourable self-analysis in the light of hardships and
splendour. Rather a lot of Zen.
Meyer, Gordon *The River and the People* (1965)
An Etonian in Paraguay. Clear, dispassionate, fascinating; superb footnotes.
Also: *Summer at a High Altitude*
Michener, James A. *Iberia* (1968) ★ ◿
In part an account of the author's many Spanish journeys, since he first visited the
country in 1932. But stuffed with history, topography, descriptions of literature
and art—an aficionado's book, fat (800 pages) and enticing. Also: *Tales of the
South Pacific*
Moorehead, Alan *Cooper's Creek* (1963) ★ ◿
Burke and Wills expedition of 1860: first south-north crossing of Australia by
white men, recounted in fine style, with excellent use of original documents.
Also: *The White Nile*; *The Blue Nile*; *The Fatal Impact* (modern man and the
South Sea islands). See NATURAL HISTORY
Moorhouse, Geoffrey *The Fearful Void* (1974)
Moorhouse crossed the Sahara from west to east, partly by camel and partly on
foot. This book brings to life the hunger and thirst, depression and fear that the
author went through in the hostile desert universe. See Lawrence; Thesiger (for
alternative views of desert life); Cherry-Garrard (for life in an implacable desert
of a different kind)
Morison, Samuel E. *The Great Explorers* (1978) 🏚 🏳 a ★ ◿
Selected from two massive tomes, *The European Discovery of America: The
Northern Voyages, AD 500–1600* and *The Southern Voyages, 1492–1616*.
Monumental record of voyages to the Americas; enthralling to read, scholarship
at its effervescent best. See BIOGRAPHY; HISTORY/AMERICAN
Morris, James *The Great Port* (1970) ★
One of Morris's lesser-known books, but filled with the same sharp perception
and lucid style as all the others. Subtitled *A Passage through New York*, it offers
an unrivalled world-traveller's view of the horrors and charms of megalopolis.
Also: *Venice*; *Oxford*; *Spain*, etc. See AUTOBIOGRAPHY (Morris, Jan)
Morton, H. V. *A Traveller in Italy* (1964) ★
A book preserved in its own amber; dated, personal, inaccurate and wholly
pleasurable. Cosy 1930s style, but Italy springs to warm, enticing life. Also:
Ghosts of London, etc
Muir, John *The Mountains of California* (1894)
Imagine being the first white man to see the Valley of the Yosemite! Muir was a
great walker and a fine writer; the combination is an exciting one, in a series of
books of which this is the best. Excellent collection: *The Wilderness of John Muir*
by Edwin Way Teale (whose works are also herewith recommended).

Murphy, Dervla *Full Tilt: Ireland to India with a Bicycle* (1965)
Author pleasantly describes how she cycled across Europe and Asia, meeting mishaps and dangers with unassailable verve and courage. A touch of the blarney—and none the worse for that.

Naipaul, V. S. *An Area of Darkness* (1964)
Author, West Indian of Indian origin, lived for a year in India; this book vividly, caustically, describes his experiences, his conclusions. Also: *The Middle Passage*; *India: A Wounded Civilization*, etc

Neatby, Leslie H. *The Search for Franklin* (1970)　　　　🏛 √ 〃
Franklin found the Northwest Passage and then got lost; the search for Franklin took another 11 years (1848–59). This book is a well-told narrative of outstanding bravery, large personalities, beautiful and hostile landscape. Also: *In Quest of the Northwest Passage*

Newby, Eric *A Short Walk in the Hindu Kush* (1958)
Newby is a contemporary traveller in the splendid British eccentric tradition. Absorbing narrative in excellent Boy's-Own-Paper style. What's it about? Exactly what the title says. Also: *The Last Grain Race* (account of six months before the mast on one of the last commercial square-rigged sailing ships)

O'Sullivan, Firmin *The Egnatian Way* (1972)　　　　🏛 √ 〃
The Egnatian Way was the first Roman road built outside Italy, a vital highway across the Balkans which has been in continuous use for over 2,000 years. Author sketches its history, offers guidance for those who wish to travel it now. Unusual, even for travel books; absorbing.

Patterson, J. H. *The Man-Eaters of Tsavo and Other East African Adventures* (1907)
From the days of the British Empire, a gripping account of the hunt for man-eating lions preventing work on a railway in East Africa.

Pausanias *Guide to Greece* (2nd century)　　　　♀ ★
Untiring antiquarian's tour of the ruins of classical civilization. Makes Baedeker seem casual; but full of delectable nuggets for the occasional hellenophile. Good translation: Levi.

Polo, Marco *The Travels* (1298)　　　　★
Vivid description of the marvels of Asia, by Venetian merchant who travelled overland to China, lived there for years, and came home via India. Fascinating to read in tandem with Ronay (qv).

Powell, Dilys *An Affair of the Heart* (1957)　　　　🏛
Books on Greece are something of an industry: this is one of the most stylish, most evocative, a memoir of visits spread over several years to a small Peloponnesian village, and reflections on the changes brought about by politics, archaeology and the shifting patterns of a peasant community evolving into the 20th century.

Ronay, Gabriel *The Tartar Khan's Englishman* (1978)　　　　🏛 √ 〃
By the mid 13th century Tartar armies occupied half Europe, stood at the gates of Vienna. Their leader, Batu Khan (grandson of Genghis) depended on an English envoy, diplomat, adventurer, spy. This book is the story of his life, his incredible travels, and his role in the convulsive conflict between Christendom and the Mongol hordes.

Roy, Jules *Journey through China* (1965)
Sensitive, detailed account of a journey across China meeting ordinary people, official and unofficial. Style *belle-lettriste*, full of aphorisms and general philosophical asides. At its worst, irritating; at its best, of the standard of Voltaire or Johnson (qv) themselves.

Schultz, J. W. *My Life as an Indian* (1907)　　　　🖎
Vivid autobiography of a 19th-century American trader in Montana who came to prefer the Blackfoot Indian way of life to that of the whites. Fascinating detail of a vanished everyday life; no movie Indians here.

Slocum, Joshua *The Voyages of Joshua Slocum* (1958)
Slocum was the first man to sail, from Boston, alone around the world, in a small sailing vessel during the 1890s. At the time it seemed an impossible journey, Slocum a madman to his friends. His books were immediately and deservedly popular.

Stark, Freya *Riding to the Tigris* (1959)　　　　★
Valiant British lady traveller, of our time, has journeyed everywhere in Africa, Asia and the Middle East, and written wonderful books about her journeys. This one is especially good; *The Journey's Echo* (1964) is a useful collection of her writings, with an introduction by Lawrence Durrell. Also: *Southern Gates of Arabia*; *Valleys of the Assassins*; *Dust in the Lion's Paw*, etc

Steinbeck, John *Travels with Charley* (1962)　　　　★ ▣
Classic journey through the USA by distinguished author and undistinguished mutt. As vivid and personal (and as well written) as Stevenson's *Travels with a Donkey* (herewith recommended). Steinbeck's love of his country never rose-tints his dry, satirical vision of what is there, and why. See DIARIES; FICTION/NOVELS

Sterne, Laurence *A Sentimental Journey through France and Italy* (1768)
18th-century tourist uses the incidents of his travels, as travellers will, to display sly, sardonic humour about the way of the world. See FICTION/NOVELS

Theroux, Paul *The Great Railway Bazaar* (1975)
Theroux set out to travel on as many trains in Asia as possible. The trains themselves are interesting (they include the trans-Siberian Express, and the dismal Hue-Danang Express, across war-devastated Vietnam): but what makes the book is Theroux's quizzical, captious eye for fellow-passengers and the people he meets when the trains stop, and his own WASPish Massachusetts supercool. Also: *The Grand Patagonia Express*, etc

Thesiger, Wilfred *Arabian Sands* (1959)   ★ ▣
Thesiger crossed the Arabian deserts with Bedouin companions, and his book makes the reader feel both the hardships of the journey and the tension that builds up when there is nobody else around who shares one's background and ways of thought. Also: *The Marsh Arabs* (and see Gavin Maxwell: *A Reed Shaken by the Wind* for another version of the same events). See Lawrence, T. E.

Tomlinson, H. M. *The Sea and the Jungle* (1912)
Tomlinson's first book is an account of a 2,000-mile journey up the Amazon in a small boat captained by his brother-in-law. He gives a sensitive account of the flora, fauna and people he saw; although he wrote many later books, none surpass this perennial favourite.

Turnbull, Colin M. *The Forest People* (1961)   ★ ✍ ▣
Elegant memoir of author's encounters with the pygmies of central Africa. Turnbull shares with Van Der Post (qv) an ability to enter the mind and spirit of the people he visits; but he avoids Van Der Post's arachnoid philosophizing.
Also: *The Mountain People*; *Man in Africa*

Twain, Mark *Roughing It* (1873)
Mark Twain's life as a young man, vagabonding around the American West in the middle of the 19th century. Wise, sly prose, a one-sitting read. See Steinbeck (for modern equivalent); FICTION/NOVELS; FICTION/SHORT STORIES; HISTORY/AMERICAN; HUMOUR

Van Der Post, Laurens *Journey into Russia* (1964)
Author best known for books on the Bushmen of southern Africa: an eclectic mixture of travel-writing, anthropology and mysticism. This book is a robust account of several months in Russia, seeking the essence of its people in their daily lives. Its claims to open-mindedness are decidedly suspect (the style is a magnificent example of unvoiced bias); but the descriptions and indeed the scope of his journey are remarkable. Also: *Venture into the Interior*, *Lost World of the Kalahari*, etc

Victory, Paul-Émile *Man and the Conquest of the Poles* (1962)
History of polar expeditions, from that of Pytheas the Greek (4th century BC) to the current voyages of American nuclear submarines.

Wilson, Sloan *Away from It All* (1969)
Best-selling American novelist takes off for the new life-style cruising through the Bahamas in his own boat. Fast, funny account of his trials and successes; he is a sort of wisecracking 20th-century Pooter. Splendid escapist fun.

Winks, Robin W. *An American's Guide to Britain* (1977)
Despite what may seem a patronizing title, this is an outstandingly helpful and detailed guide, full of necessary information and unfussy advice. Concentrates on picturesque, "tourist" Britain (few satanic mills or stale canals in sight); ideal for first visit or brief, basic stay.

Author index

In the case of books with several authors, only the first named author has been included in the index.

Aaron, D. 79
Abrams, C. 77
Achebe, C. 54
Acheson, D. 133
Adams, A. B. 117
Adams, H. 22, 79, 142
Adams, L. D. 74
Adams, R. 31
Adburgham, A. 18
Adler, M. J. 123, 138
Aeschylus 41
Aesop 67
Agee, J. 10
Agnon, S. Y. 68
Aiken, J. 31
Aitchison, J. 117
Ajayi, J. F. A. 84
Akhmatova, A. 127
Alain-Fournier 54
Albee, E. 41
Alcott, L. M. 31
Aldington, R. 25
Aldiss, B. 66
Aletrino, N. 142
Algren, N. 54
Allen, C. 84
Allen, W. 96
Allingham, M. 51
Almedingen, E. M. 31
Amado, J. 54
Ambler, E. 51
Amerine, M. A. 74
Amis, K. 54
Anderson, E. 36
Anderson, H. C. 31
Anderson, P. 147
Anderson, S. 68
Andreski, S. 147
Anene, J. C. 84
Anouilh, J. 41
Apicius 74
Apollinaire, G. 127
Appelbaum, J. 107
Aquinas, T. 123
Arden, J. 41
Ardrey, R. 117
Arendt, H. 133
Argyle, M. 136
Aristophanes 41
Aristotle 99, 123, 133
Armes, R. 71
Arnold, M. 99, 127
Arnott, P. 41
Aronson, E. 136
Artaud, A. 41
Arvill, R. 77
Asad, T. 10
Asimov, I. 66, 102
Attenborough, D. 117
Atwater, F. 31
Auden, W. H. 41, 99, 127
Audubon, J. J. 117
Auerbach, E. 99
Augustine, 22
Austen, J. 54
Austin, J. L. 123
Austin, W. 111
Ayer, A. J. 123
Ayrton, E. 74
Ayrton, M. 54

Babel, I. 68
Bacon, F. 87
Baddeley, A. D. 136
Bagehot, W. 133
Bailey, F. G. 10
Bailey, H. S. 107
Bailyn, B. 79
Bainton, R. H. 25
Baker, C. 25
Baker, J. N. L. 77
Balanchine, G. 111
Baldwin, J. 54
Ballard, J. G. 66
Balzac, H. de 54
Bamford, F. 22
Banham, R. 15
Banks, J. 117
Banton, M. P. 147
Barber, W. J. 47
Barbour, I. G. 142
Bardin, J. F. 51
Barnes, B. 147
Barnett, L. 102
Barnouw, E. 71
Barraclough, G. 90, 93
Barrett, E. 36
Barry, R. G. 77
Barth, J. 54
Barthes, R. 99
Bartram, W. 150

Barzun, J. 111
Basham, A. L. 84
Bate, W. J. 25
Battock, G. 18
Baudelaire, C. 18, 36, 127
Baum, F. L. 31
Bawden, L.-A. 71
Bawden, N. 31
Bayer, W. 71
Beard, C. 79
Beard, J. 74
Beasley, W. G. 85
Becker, H. S. 147
Beckerman, W. 47
Beckett, S. 41, 54, 68, 99
Bede, 87
Beerbohm, M. 54
Beeton, I. 74
Behrman, S. N. 18
Bell, C. 18
Bell, E. T. 102
Bell, Q. 25
Bellow, S. 54
Belleveau, F. 109
Bellwood, P. 13
Benchley, R. 96
Benjamin, W. 99
Bennett, A. 36, 54
Bennett, E. 121
Bennett, J. B. 121
Berg, A. S. 107
Bergamini, D. 85
Berger, J. 18
Berger, P. L. 147
Berger, R. 79
Berkeley, G. 123
Berlioz, H. 111
Bernal, J. D. 102
Bernard, C. 102
Berne, E. 136
Bernstein, L. 111
Bernstein, M. 142
Berral, J. J. 94
Berry, B. J. L. 77
Berry, W. T. 107
Berryman, J. 127
Bester, A. 66
Betjeman, J. 22
Bettenson, H. 142
Bewick, T. 117
Bierce, A. 68
Bird, C. 49
Birren, J. E. 136
Bishop, W. 13
Bissell, R. 96
Black, J. A. 18
Blake, W. 127
Blauner, R. 147
Blesh, R. 111
Blish, J. 66
Blok, A. 147
Blunt, W. 117
Blythe, R. 87
Boas, F. 10
Boccaccio 145
Boethius, A. 15
Bonhoeffer, D. 142
Boorstin, D. J. 79
Borges, J. L. 68
Boston, L. M. 31
Boswell, J. 25, 36
Botting, D. 150
Bottomore, T. B. 147
Boulnois, L. 85
Boussard, J. 90
Bowen, E. S. 10
Bowles, E. A. 94
Bowles, J. 68
Bowra, M. 93
Boxer, A. 94
Boxer, C. R. 92
Bradbury, R. 66
Bradford, S. 74
Bradley, A. C. 99
Bragg, M. 87
Bramah, E. 74
Branston, B. 114
Braudel, F. 90
Braun, E. 41
Bray, L. de 94
Bray, W. 13
Brecher, L. 145
Brecht, B. 42
Bridenbaugh, C. 80
Briggs, A. 87, 107
Brillat-Savarin, J. A. de 74
Brittain, J. 94
Brittain, V. 22
Broadbent, M. 74
Bronowski, J. 102

Bronte, C. 55
Bronte, E. 55
Brook, P. 42
Brooks, C. 99
Brothwell, D. R. 13, 31
Brown, D. 80
Brown, H. 102
Brown, K. 71
Brown, R. 136
Brown, R. A. 87
Browning, R. 127
Brownlow, K. 71
Brownmiller, S. 49
Bruce, L. 96
Brunhoff, J. de 31
Bryd-Gnaf, A. 94
Buber, M. 143
Buchan, J. 31
Buchsbaum, R. 117
Bullock, A. 25, 138
Bultmann, R. 143
Bunn, C. 102
Burch, N. 71
Burgess, A. 55
Burke, E. 133
Burke, K. 99
Burland, C. 114
Burn, W. L. 87
Burns, R. 127
Burnet, G. 87
Burnett, F. H. 31
Burney, F. 36
Burnham, D. H. 15
Burton, E. 87
Burton, I. 77
Burton, R. 136
Burton, Sir R. 117, 150
Butler, S. 55
Butor, M. 55
Butterfield, H. 143
Byron 36, 127

Cabral, A. 133
Caesar, J. 22
Calmette, J. 90
Calvin, M. 102
Campion, T. 127
Camus, A. 55
Canning, V. 51
Cantor, N. F. 90
Capote, T. 25
Cardigan, Countess of 22
Carlyle, T. 36, 100
Caroe, O. 85
Carr, E. H. 133
Carrier, R. 74
Carroll, L. 32
Carson, R. 77
Cash, W. J. 80
Castaneda, C. 143
Cather, W. 55
Catton, B. 80
Catullus, 127
Cavafy, C. 128
Cecil, D. 26
Cellini, B. 22
Ceram, C. W. 13
Cervantes, M. de 55
Cesaire, A. 128
Chadwick, H. 143
Chadwick, J. 13
Chadwick, L. 150
Chagnon, A. A. 10
Chandler, D. 90
Chandler, R. 51
Chang, K. C. 13, 75
Chaplin, C. 22
Chapman, J. M. 103
Charters, A. 26
Chaucer, G. 128
Cheever, J. 55, 68
Chekhov, A. 42, 68
Cherry-Garrard, A. 150
Chesney, K. 147
Chesterfield 36
Chesterton, G. K. 68
Chevalier, G. 96
Child, J. 75
Chisholm, M. 77
Chitty, S. 150
Chomsky, N. 123
Chorley, R. J. 77
Christie, A. 51
Christopher J. 32
Clurman, H. 42
Cibber, C. 42
Cicero, M. T. 37
Clare, J. 128
Clarens, C. 71
Clark, A. 114
Clark, G. 13

Author index

Clark, K. 15, 22, 19
Clark, R. W. 103
Clarke, A. C. 66, 103
Clarke, A. M. 136
Clarke, P. 133
Clarke, R. 10
Claude, I. L. 133
Clavell, J. 55
Cleland, J. 145
Clifton-Taylor, A. 15
Coats, A. M. 94
Cohen, A. 10
Cohn, N. 90
Cole, J. P. 77
Cole, W. 32
Coleman, T. 80
Coleridge, S. T. 26, 128
Coles, J. 13
Colette 55
Collier, J. L. 111
Collier, S. 92
Collins, P. 15
Collins, W, 51
Colvin, H. 15
Comfort, A. 145
Commager, H. S. 80
Compton-Burnett, I. 55
Conant, K. 16
Congreve, W. 42
Conrad, J. 55, 68
Conrad, P. 19
Conway, D. 121
Conze, E. 143
Cook, J. 150
Cooke, D. 111
Coon, C. S. 10
Cooper, S. 32
Cooper, W. 55
Copeland, J. 109
Corner, E. J. H. 117
Cottrell, L. 14
Cottrell, T. L. 103
Courant, R. H. 103
Cousteau, J. 117
Coward, N. 42
Cowling, M. 133
Cowper, W. 37
Coxhead, N. 121
Craigie, W. A. 138
Crane, R. S. 100
Crevecoeur, H. St J. de 37
Crewe, Q. 75
Crispin, E. 51
Cross, M. 111
Crosse, F. L. 143
Crossman, R. 37
Crowe, S. 94
Crowley, E. T. 138
Cruickshanks, E. 87
Cunliffe, B. 14
Curran, C. 107

Dahl, R. 32
Dainseth, J. 103
Dali, S. 37
Dalton, G. 10
Dana, R. H. 150
Daniel, G. 14
Dante 128, 133
Darwin, C. 118
Dasent, G. W. 114
Daudet, A. 96
David, E. 75
David, H. 111
David-Neel, A. 150
Davidson, A. 75
Davidson, H. R. E. 114
Davidson, L. 51
Davies, H. 143
Davies, W. K. D. 77
Davis, N. P. 103
Deanesly, M. 143
Defoe, D. 56
Deighton, L. 52
Delacroix, E. 19
De La Mare, W. 32
Demos, J. 80
Dennis, P. 96
De Quincey, T. 26
Derry, T. K. 90
Descartes, R. 124
Desmond, A. J. 118
Dessauer, J. P. 107
Deuel, L. 14
De Voto, B. 80
De Vries, P. 96
Dewey, J. 80, 124
De Wit, H. C. D. 118
Dick, P. K. 66
Dickens, C. 56
Dickinson, E. 128
Dickinson, P. 32, 52
Dillon, M. 87
Dinesen, I. 68
Dixon, E. 32
Dixon, M. 94
Dodd, C. H. 143

Dodds, E. H. 10
Donaldson, F. 26
Donaldson, M. 136
Donaldson, P. 47
Donne, J. 128
Dorst, J. 118
Dos Passos, J. 56
Dostoyevsky, F. 56
Douglas, M. 10
Douglas-Hamilton, I. 118
Downing, A. J. 16
Dowson, J. 114
Doyle, A. C. 52
Drabble, M. 56
Dreiser, T. 56
Drucker, P. F. 47
Dryden, J. 100, 128
Dubos, R. 109
Duff, G. 75
Duffy, M. 145
Dumont, L. 11
Dunham, B. 143
Dunn, P. D. 103
Durgnat, R. 71
Durkheim, E. 147
Durnant, W. 93
Durrell, G. 32, 118
Durrell, L. 37, 56, 128, 150
Dutt, R. C. 114

Eames, J. D. 71
Eberhard, W. 85
Edel, L. 26
Edgeworth, M. 37
Edwardes, M. 85
Eekhof-Stork, N. 75
Einstein, A. 111
Eiseley, L. 11.
Eisner, L. 71
Ekwall, E. 138
Eldersveld, S. J. 134
Eliade, M. 114
Elias, N. 148
Eliot, G. 56
Eliot, T. S. 42, 100, 128
Ellin, S. 52
Ellison, R. 56
Ellman, R. 26
Elton, C. 118
Elton, G. R. 88
Elvin, M. 85
Empson, W. 100, 128
Ensor, R. C. K. 88
Epstein, A. L. 11
Epstein, I. 143
Erikson, E. 136
Escoffier, A. 75
Esslin, M. 42
Euripides 42
Evans, H. 107
Evans, L. 75
Evans, S. 49
Evans-Pritchard, F. E. 11
Evelyn, J. 37
Eysenck, H. J. 136

Fabre, J. H. 118
Fadiman, C. 100
Fahs, S. L. 114
Faith, N. 75
Fanon, F. 134
Faraday, M. 103
Farmer, F. 75
Farquhar, G. 42
Farre, R. 151
Farrel, R. 151
Faulkner, W. 56, 68
Fawcett, P. H. 151
Fawtier, R. 90
Feiling, K. 88
Feldman, S. 115
Fermor, P. L. 151
Ferraby, J. 143
Fielding, H. 56
Fields, W. C. 71
Figes, E. 49
Firbank, R. 56
Fischer, D. H. 80
Fischer-Dieskau, D. 111
Fisher, C. A. 77
Fisher, H. A. L. 90
Fisher, J. 107
Fisher, M. F. K. 75
Fishlock, D. 103
Fitzgerald, C. P. 85
FitzGerald, F. 85
Fitzgerald, F. S. 37, 57, 68
Fitzgibbon, C. 88
Fitzsimons, R. 42
Flaubert, G. 37, 57, 68
Fleischman, S. 32
Fleming, J. 16
Flexner, E. 49
Flexner, J. 26
Fodor, E. 151
Forbes, E. 32
Forbes, P. 75
Ford, F. M. 57

Forde, C. D. 77
Forster, E. M. 57
Forsyth, F. 52
Fowler, H. W. 139
Fowles, J. 57
Foucault, M. 145
Fox, G. 23
Francis, D. 52
Frank, A. 37
Frankenberg, R. 11
Frankfort, H. 19
Frankl, P. 16
Franklin, B. 23
Frayn, M. 96
Frazer, J. 115
Fredrickson, G. M. 80
Free, M. 94
Freeling, N. 52
Freeman, D. S. 26
Freeman, T. W. 77
Frege, G. 124
Frere, S. 14
Freud, S. 26, 109
Frewing, N. J. 94
Freyre, G. 92
Friedan, B. 49
Friedman, M. 47
Frisch, K. von 118
Frisch, M. 43
Frith, S. 111
Frost, R. 128
Froude, J. 26
Fry, C. H. 118
Fry, R. 19
Fuchs, V. R. 109
Furer-Haimendorff, C. von 11

Gabrielli, F. 85
Gag, W. 32
Galbraith, J. K. 47
Gale, J. 151
Galsworthy, J. 57
Gamble, A. 47
Gandhi, M. 23
Gantz, J. 115
Gardner, H. 100, 128
Gardner, J. 115
Gardner, M. 103
Garfield, L. 32
Garfinkel, H. 148
Garner, A. 32
Garnett, D. 37
Gascoigne, B. 43
Gascoyne, D. 128
Gaskell, E. 26, 57
Gaunt, W. 19
Gauquelin, M. 121
Gelpel, J. 11
Genet, J. 145, 151
Gennep, A. van 11
Genovese, E. 80
Geoffrey of Monmouth 115
George, H. 80
George, M. D. 88
Gerbi, A. 92
Gerin, W. 26
Geyl, P. 90
Gibbon, E. 82
Gibson, C. 92
Gide, A. 57
Giedion, S. 16, 19
Gilbert, M. 52
Gilmore, M. P. 90
Gilson, E. 19, 124
Ginsberg, A. 38
Giraudoux, J. 43
Gittings, R. 27
Glanville, B. 57
Glover, J. R. 88
Glubb, J. 85
Glynn, A. 47
Goethe, J. W. von 43, 128
Goffman, E. 148
Gogol, N. 57
Goldie, G. W. 107
Golding, W. 57
Goldoni, C. 43
Goldsmith, O. 43
Gombrich, E. 19
Goncourt, E. de 38
Good, R. 118
Goodall, J. 118
Gordimer, N. 57
Gordon, J. E. 103
Gorki, M. 38
Gosse, E. 23
Gottman, J. 77
Gould, P. 77
Gouldner, A. W. 148
Grahame, K. 32
Grant, K. 121
Grant, M. 83
Grant, U. S. 23
Granville-Barker, H. 43
Grass, G. 57
Graves, R. 23, 57, 115, 128
Gray, H. 109
Gray, J. 118

Gray, John 115
Gray, T. 129
Green, B. 111
Green, H. 58
Green, J. 38
Green, M. 96
Green, P. 27
Green, S. 112
Greene, G. 58, 151
Greenfield, E. 112
Greenway, J. 11
Greer, G. 49
Gregory, K. 38
Grenville, J. A. S. 93
Grey, I. 90
Grieve, M. 94
Griffiths, Mrs D. W. 72
Grierson, E. 90
Grigson, G. 27
Grimm, J. 68
Gris, H. 121
Groddeck, G. 137
Gropius, W. 16
Grossmith, G. 96
Grotowski, J. 43
Grun, B. 93
Grzimek, B. 118
Guerard, M. 75
Guillaume, A. 143
Gulliver, P. H. 11
Gunn, T. 129

Hackett, A. P. 107
Haddon, C. 145
Hadley, B. 112
Haggard, H. R. 32
Haggard, W. 52
Haggett, P. 77
Hahn, O. 23
Halberstam, D. 80, 108
Hale, J. 90
Hall, D. G. E. 85
Hall, E. T. 11
Hall, P. 77
Hall, R. 38
Halliday, J. 72
Halliwell, L. 72
Hambly, G. 85
Hamburger, M. 129
Hamilton, A. 134
Hammett, D. 52
Hampton, C. 43
Hansel, C. E. M. 121
Handlin, O. 80
Happold, F. C. 143
Hardy, A. 118
Hardy, T. 58, 129
Harman, A. 112
Harrer, H. 151
Harrison, H. 66
Harrison, J. 47
Harrison, Jane 115
Harrisson. T. 88
Harrod, R. 47
Hart, B. L. 23, 90
Hartley, D. 75
Hartley, L. P. 58
Hartnoll, P. 43
Hartshorne, R. 77
Hartz, L. 80
Harvey, D. 78
Harvey, J. 16
Hasek, J. 58
Haskins, C. H. 90
Hatto, A. T. 115
Hawkes, J. 14
Hawthorne, N. 58, 69
Hay, R. 94
Haydon, B. R. 19
Hayes, A. 58
Hazan, M. 75
Hazlitt, W. 100
Head, J. 121
Heaney, S. 129
Hebblethwaite, P. 143
Hecht, A. 129
Hegel, G. W. F. 124
Heidegger, M. 124
Heilbroner, R. L. 47
Heilman R. E. 43
Heine, H. 129
Heinlein, R. A. 67
Heisenberg, W. 103
Helleman, L. 23
Heller, J. 58
Hellyer, A. 94
Hemingway. E. 58, 69
Hemming, J. 92
Hennessy, A. 92
Henry, O. 69
Herbert, F. 67
Herbert, G. 129
Herodotus 83
Herrick, R. 129
Hersey, J. 58
Hervey 23
Hessayon, D. G. 94
Hesse, H. 58

Hethman, R. H. 43
Hey, J. S. 103
Heyden, A. A. M. 83
Heyden, P. 38
Heydenreich, L. 16
Heyerdahl, T. 151
Hibbert, C. 85, 88
Hick, J. 143
Hicks, J. 47
Higham, D. 108
Higham, J. 80
Highet, G. 100
Highsmith, P. 52
Hiley, M. 49
Hilgard, E. R. 137
Hill, C. 88
Hillaby, J. 151
Hillier, H. 95
Hindley, G. 112
Hinton, W. 134
Hirsch, F. 47
Hitchcock, H.-R. 16
Hite, S. 145
Hoban, R. 33
Hobbes, T. 124
Hoffman, E. T. W. 69
Hoffnung, G. 112
Hofstadter, D. 103
Hofstadter, R. 81
Hogarth, W. 19
Hogben, L. 103
Hoggart, R. 108
Holden, E. 118
Hole, E. 90
Hollowood, B. 96
Holmes, R. 27
Holroyd, M. 27
Homer 129
Honour, H. 19
Hooke, S. H. 115
Hope, A. 58
Hopkins, A. 112
Hopkins, G. M. 129
Horace 100, 129
Hornung, E. W. 52
Hoskins, W. G. 78
Household, G. 52
Howarth, D. 27
Howe, I. 81
Hoyle, F. 104
Huart, C. 83
Hubbard, C. E. 118
Hudson, D. 27
Hudson, W. H. 23, 118
Hufstedler, S. M. 49
Hughes, T. 33, 129
Huizinga, J. 27, 90
Hume, D. 124
Hume, I. 14
Humphreys, C. 144
Hunter, N. 33
Husserl, E. 124
Hutchings, A. 112
Hutchinson, P. 76
Huth, H. 119
Huxley, A. 58
Huxley, F. 115
Huxley, T. H. 119
Hyde, H. M. 27

Ibsen, H. 43
Imms, A. D. 119
Ingham, K. 85
Inglis, B. 85
Innes, J. 95
Innes, M. 52
Ionesco, E. 43
Ions, V. 115
Irving, C. 85
Irving, D. 104
Isherwood, C. 69
Isted, C. R. 109
Ivins, W. M. 19

Jackson, M. 76
Jacobs, A. 112
Jacobs, J. 78
Jacobsen, D. 59
Jacoby, R. 148
James, E. P. 78
James, H. 27, 38, 59, 69, 100
James, M. R. 69
James, P. D. 52
James, W. 124, 144
Janeway, E. 49
Jansson, T. 33
Jarrell, R. 59, 100, 129
Jaspers, K. 124
Jay, P. 129
Jeans, J. 104
Jefferies, R. 119
Jeffs, A. 95
Jeffs, J. 76
Jekyll, G. 95
Jencks, C. 16
Jenkins, S. 121
Jennings, E. 129
Jerome, J. K. 96

John of the Cross 130
Johnson, H. 76, 95
Johnson, P. 83
Johnson, P. H. 43
Johnson, S. 27, 100, 139, 151
Jones, A. H. M. 83
Jones, D. 130
Jones, Daniel 139
Jones, E. 27
Jones, G. 91
Jones, H. M. 81
Jones, J. 59
Jones, M. 81
Jones, O. 19
Jonson, B. 43
Jordan, T. 78
Jordan, W. D. 81
Josephus 83
Josephy, A. M. 81
Joyce, J. 38, 59, 69
Judd, D. 85
Jung, C. 137
Juvenal 130

Kael, P. 72
Kafka, F. 38, 59, 69
Kamin, L. J. 137
Kammen, M. 81
Kaner, P. 104
Kant, I. 124
Kaplan, H. S. 109
Kapleau, P. 144
Karp, D. 59
Kasner, E. 104
Kasperson, R. K. 78
Katz, F. 92
Kaufman, W. 104
Kazin, A. 100
Keating, H. R. F. 52
Keating, R. 14
Keats, J. 100, 130
Keegan, J. 91
Keller, H. 23
Kemelman, H. 53
Keneally, T. 59
Kerenyi, C. 115
Kerouac, J. 59
Keynes, J. M. 47
Kidron, M. 47
Kierkegaard, S. 38, 125
Kilvert, F. T. 38
King, C. 108
King, L. C. 78
Kinglake, A. W. 151
Kingsley, C. 33
Kingsley, M. 151
Kinross 85
Kinsey, A. C. 145
Kipling, R. 33, 69, 130
Kirk, G. S. 115, 125
Kirkpatrick, J. 112
Kitzinger, S. 11
Klee, P. 19
Knapp, J. M. 112
Knight, A. 72
Knight, G. W. 101
Knopf, A. A. 108
Kobbe, G. 112
Koestler, A. 59, 104, 119, 121
Kolko, G. 81
Kollontai, A. 50
Konigsburg, E. L. 33
Kosinski, J. 59
Kouwenhoven, J. 16
Kovel, J. 109
Kraditor, A. S. 81
Kroeber, A. L. 11
Kron, J. 95
Kropotkin, P. 23
Krutch, J. W. 27, 119
Kuhn, T. 104
Kuper, A. 11
Kuznets, S. 48

Lachouque, H. 28
Lack, D. 119
Laclos, C. de 145
Ladurie, E. le Roy 91
Lagerkvist, P. 59
Laing, R. D. 109
Laithwaite, E. R. 104
Lancaster, O. 16
Lang, A. 33
Langley, N. 97
Lappe, F. M. 76
Laqueur, W. 134
Lardner, R. 69, 97
Larkin, M. 91
Larkin, P. 130
Larkin, S. 104
Larry, 97
Lasch, C. 81
Laslett, P. 88
Latham, A. 72
Lathen, E. 53
Laver, J. 19
Lawrence, A. 16

Author index

Lawrence, D. H. 38, 60, 69, 91, 101, 130, 151
Lawrence, T. E. 151
Leach, E. 11
Leacock, S. 97
Leavis, F. R. 101
Le Carre, J. 53
Le Corbusier 16
Lee, E. 112
Lee, L. 23
Lefebure, M. 28
Le Guin, U. 32, 33, 67
Lehmann, J. 83
Lehrer, S. 109
Leibniz, G. W. von 125
Lem, S. 67
Lempriere, J. 83
Lenin, I. I. 134
Leonard, L. W. 76
Leone, M. 14
Leopardi, G. 130
LeShan, L. 121
Lessing, D. 60
Lethbridge, T. C. 121
Levine, P. 130
Levi-Strauss, C. 11, 116
Lewis, C. S. 33, 67
Lewis, I. M. 11
Lewis, J. E. 104
Lewis, L. 116
Lewis, M. 152
Lewis, N. 83
Lewis, O. 148
Lewis, P. 91
Lewis, S. 60
Lewis, W. 60
Ley, C. D. 152
Leyda, J. 72
Libby, W. F. 14
Lichine, A. 76
Lichtheim. G. 91
Liehm, A. J. 72
Lienhardt, G. 11
Lietzmann, W. 104
Lincoln, A. 39
Lindbergh, C. 152
Lindsay, J. 28, 104
Lindsay, N. 33
Lindsay, P. H. 137
Lines, K. 33
Lipset, S. M, 148
Lisitzky, G. 12
Lively, P. 33
Livy, 83
Lloyd, P. 12
Lobel, A. 33
Locke, J. 125, 134
Lockhart, J. G. 85
Lodge, D. 60
Lofting, H. 33
Logan, N. 112
London, J. 69, 152
Longford, E. 28, 88
Loos, A. 97
Lorca, F. G. 44
Lorenz, K. 119
Love, B. 72
Lovell, B. 104
Lowell, R. 130
Lowry, M. 60, 69
Ludowyk, E. F. C. 86
Luria, A. 137
Lynch, J. 93
Lynd, R. S. 148

McAleavy, H. 86
Macartney, C. A. 91
Macauley, D. 34
Macaulay, T. B. 88, 101
McBain, E. 53
McCabe, J. 72
McCarthy, M. 60
McCoy, W. W. 86
McCrindle, J. F. 44
McCullers, C. 60
MacDonald, G. 34
MacDonald, R. 53
McEwan, P. J. M. 86
McGlashan, A. 105
Machiavelli, N. 134
Machlup, F. 48
MacKendrick, P. 14
Mackenzie, C. 60
Mackenzie, W. J. M. 134
Maclean, F. 152
McLean, R. 108
MacLeish, A. 130
McLeish, J. 137
McLuhan, M. 108
Macmillan, H. 23
McNaught, K. 81
MacNeice, L. 130
McNeill, W. H. 110
McPhee, J. 72
McWhirter, R. 139
Madariaga, S. de 28
Magnus, P. 88
Magnusson, M. 152

Mailer, N. 28, 60
Malamud, B. 60
Malcolm X 24
Malinowski, B. 12
Malory, T. 116
Malraux, A. 60
Mandler, G. 137
Mann, T. 60, 69
Manners, G. 78
Mannheim, K. 134
Mansfield, K. 39, 69
Marcel, G. 125
Marchand, L. 28
Marcus Aurelius 144
Marcuse, H. 148
Marlowe, C. 44, 130
Marquez, G. G. 61
Marshall, A. 48
Marshall, J. M. 34
Martensson, A. 95
Marvell, A. 130
Marx, K. 48, 134, 148
Masefield, J. 34, 44
Massie, R. K. 91
Mast, G. 72
Masters, E. L. 130
Masters, J. 28
Masters, W. H. 145
Mathew, G. 88
Mathews, M. M. 139
Matthiessen, P. 152
Mattingly, G. 88
Matza, D. 148
Maugham, 24, 44, 53, 61, 69
Maupassant, G. de 70
Mauriac, F. 61
Maurois, A. 91
Maxwell, G. 119
Mayne, W. 34
Mead, G. H. 148
Mead, M. 12, 24, 148
Medawar, P. B. 119
Mellen, J. 72
Mellers, W. 112
Mellersh, H. E. L. 83
Melville, H. 61
Mencken, H. L. 81
Mendelssohn, K. 105
Merleau-Ponty, M. 125
Merrill, J. C. 108
Meyer, G. 152
Meyer, J. A. 93
Meyers, M. 81
Michels, R. 134
Michener, J. A. 152
Middlebrook, M. 91
Milford, N. 28
Mitford, N. 28
Mill, J. S. 48, 50, 125, 134
Miller, A. 44
Miller, G. A. 137
Miller, H. 145
Miller, J. 110
Miller, M. 24
Miller, P. 81
Miller, W. M. 67
Millet, K. 50
Milligan, S. 34, 97
Mills, C. W. 148
Milne, A. A. 34
Milne, T. 72
Milton, J. 130
Mishan, E. J. 48
Mitchell, J. 50
Mitchell, M. 61
Mitchison, N. 116
Mitton J. and S. 105
Moliere, J. P. D. de 44
Monaco, J. F. 72
Mondrian, P. 20
Montagne, P. 76
Montagu, I. 72
Montagu, M. W. 39
Montesquieu, Baron de 134
Montgomery, L. M. 34
Moorcock, M. 67
Moore, B. 134
Moore, G. 130
Moore, G. E. 125
Moore, George 70
Moore, P. 105
Moore, R. 105
Moorehead, A. 119, 152
Moorhouse, G. 152
Moravia, A. 61
More, T. 88
Morgan, E. 78
Morgan, E. S. 81
Morgenstern, S. 112
Morison, S. 20
Morison, S. E. 28, 82, 152
Morris, D. R. 86
Morris, J. 24, 152
Morton, H. V. 152
Morton, J. B. 97
Moss, H. L. B. 91
Moszkowski, A. 105

Mountfort, S. 119
Muggeridge, M. 24
Muir, J. 152
Mulvaney, D. J. 14
Mumford, L. 16, 20
Mundy, J. H. 91
Munro, A. 50
Munrow, D. 112
Murasaki-Shikibu 70
Murdoch, I. 61
Murphy, B. 76
Murphy, D. 153
Murphy, G. 137
Murphy, P. 105
Murray, P. 16, 20
Musil, R. 61
Myers, F. W. H. 121
Myers, L. H. 61
Myrdal, G. 48

Nabokov, V. 24, 28, 61
Naipaul, V. S. 153
Narayan, R. K. 116
Neale, J. E. 88
Neatby, L. H. 153
Nefzawi 145
Negev, A. 14
Nehru, J. 86
Nelson, W. H. 91
Neruda, P. 131
Nesbit, E. 34
Newby, E. 153
Newman, E. 112
Newman, J. H. 144
Newman, O. 16
Newton, S. M. 20
Nicholas, R. 112
Nichols, R. 112
Nicolson, H. 28, 39
Nicholson, I. 105
Nicholson, M. 78
Niebuhr, R. 134
Nietzsche, F. 125
Nin, A. 146
Niven, D. 72
Nochlin, L. 20
Nolan, F. 112
Norberg-Schulz, C. 16
Norris, J. 50
Norris, K. 48
North, C. C. 148
Norton, A. 34
Norton, A. P. 105
Norton, M. 34
Nowell-Smith, S. 108
Nye, R. 61

Oakeshott, M. 134
Oates, D. 14
Oatley, K. 137
O'Brien, F. 97
O'Casey, S. 44
O'Flaherty, W. D. 116
O'Hara, J. 61, 70
Oman, J. 144
O'Neill, E. 44
Onions, C. T. 140
Opie, I. 140
Origo, I. 91
Ortega y Gasset, J. 125
Orwell, G. 61, 89, 101, 135
Osborne, C. 113
Osborne, H. 20
Osborne, J. 44
O'Sullivan, F. 153
Ovid, 116, 146
Owen, R. 135
Owen, W. 131

Packard, V. 108
Page, R. 95
Pahl, R. E. 78
Painter, G. 28
Palgrave, F. T. 131
Palladio, A. 17
Pannell, J. P. M. 105
Panovsky, E. 20
Papanek, V. 20
Pares, B. 91
Parish, P. 110
Parkman, F. 29, 82
Parrish, R. 72
Parry, J. H. 93
Partington, J. R. 105
Partridge, B. 146
Partridge, E. 140
Pascal, B. 144
Pascoe, L. C. 140
Passmore, J. 125
Paterson, J. H. 78
Patmore, J. A. 78
Patterson, J. H. 153
Pauling, L. 105
Pausanias 153
Peacock. T. L. 62
Pearce, P. 34
Peel, J. 146
Penning-Rowsell, E. 76

158

Pepys, S. 39
Perelman, S. J. 97
Perkins, V. F. 73
Pernoud, G. 91
Perrault, C. 34
Peterson, M. 82
Peterson, R. T. 119
Peterson, T. 108
Petronius 97
Pevsner, N. 17, 20
Peyton, K. M. 34
Phillips, C. E. L. 95
Phillips, D. 95
Phillips, M. M. 144
Phillips, W. 86
Phillipson, D. W. 14
Pickard, R. 73
Pickering, G. W. 29
Piggott, S. 14
Pinero, A. W. 44
Pinter, H. 44
Pirandello, L. 44, 70
Pissaro, C. 20
Piven, F. F. 135
Plato 125, 135
Pliny 39
Plutarch 29
Plumb, J. H. 89
Pocock, D. F. 12
Poe, E. A. 53, 70
Pohl, F. 67
Poincare, H. 105
Polo, M. 153
Pomeroy, S. B. 50
Pope, A. 101, 131
Pope John XXIII 39
Popper, K. 126
Porter, C. 50
Potok, C. 62
Potter, B. 34
Potter, S. 97
Potts, M. 110
Pough, F. H. 105
Pound, E. 101, 131
Poupon, P. 76
Powell, A. 62
Powell, D. 153
Power, E. 89
Powys, J. C. 62
Preble, G. H. 86
Prescott, W. H. 93
Price, A. 53
Priestley, J. B. 89
Prince, W. F. 121
Procopius, 83
Procter, P. 140
Proust, M. 62
Prøysen, A. 34
Psellus, M. 91
Pudovkin, V. I. 73
Pushkin, A. 131
Pye, M. 73
Pyke, M. 105

Queneau, R. 97
Quine, W. van O. 126

Raban, J. 149
Rabelais, F. 62
Racine, J. 45
Radice, B. 83
Radin, P. 12
Raffel, B. 116
Raglan 116
Raistrick, A. 14
Ramelson, M. 50
Ramsaye, T. 73
Ransome, A. 35
Rank, O. 116
Ransford, O. 86
Rao, K. R. 122
Raphael, F. 62
Rapoport, A. 17
Rattigan, T. 45
Rauchhaupt, U. von 113
Raven, S. 62
Rawls, J. 135
Ray, E. 76
Read, C. 89
Read, H. 20
Reage, P. 146
Rechy, J. 146
Redfield, W. 45
Rees, A. 116
Reeves, M. P. 149
Reich, W. 146
Reid, R. 105
Reisz, K. 73
Reitlinger, G. 20
Renan, E. 29
Renoir, J. 29
Reyner, J. H. 122
Reynolds, J. 20
Rhine, J. B. 122
Rhode, E. 73
Rhodes, F. H. T. 119
Rhys, J. 62
Richards, J. 17

Richardson, S. 62
Richter, J. P. 20
Ricks, C. 29
Ridley, B. K. 105
Riesman, D. 149
Rilke, R. M. 39, 131
Robbe-Grillet, A. 62
Roberts, J. M. 93
Roberts, R. 149
Roberts, V. M. 45
Robertson, A. 113
Robinson, E. A. 131
Robinson, J. 95
Robinson, Joan, 48
Robson, D. A. 105
Roden, C. 76
Roethke, T. 131
Roget, 140
Roll, W. G. 122
Rolt, L. T. C. 29
Rombauer, I. S. 76
Romer, A. S. 119
Ronay, E. 153
Rosen, C. 113
Rosen, R. 50
Rosen, S. 106
Rosenberg, H. 20
Rosenberg, I. 131
Rossi, A. 50
Rossotti, H. 106
Rostem, L. 97
Rostovtzeff, M. 83
Rostow, W. W. 48
Roth, H. 62
Roth, P. 63
Rotha, P. 73
Rothenstein, J. 21
Rourke, C. 149
Rousseau, J.-J. 24, 135
Rowbotham, S. 50
Rowse, A. L. 89
Roy, J. 153
Rude, G. 89
Runciman, S. 91
Runyon, D. 70, 97
Ruskin, J. 17, 101
Russell, B. 126
Russell, D. 50
Rutter, M. 137
Ryder, A. J. 91
Ryle, G. 126

Sacco, N. 39
Sacks, O. 110
Sade, Marquis de 146
Sadie, S. 113
Sadler, A. H. L. 86
Saggs, H. W. F. 84
St Exupery, A. de 35
Saint Simon, L. de R. 24
Saki 70
Sakoian, F. 122
Salinger, J. D. 63
Salisbury, E. J. 95
Sallust 84
Samuelson, P. A. 48
Sandars, N. K. 14, 116
Sandburg, C. 29
Sandler, I. 21
Sapir, E. 12
Saroyan, W. 70
Sarris, A. 73
Sartori, G. 135
Sartre, J.-P. 29, 45, 63, 126
Sauer, C. O. 78
Savory, T. H. 119
Sayers, D. L. 45, 53
Scarisbrick, J. J. 89
Scarry, R. 35
Schaeffer, H. 21
Schapera, I. 12
Scharf, A. 21
Schattschneider, E. E. 135
Scheffer, V. B. 119
Scheuer, S. H. 73
Schlesinger, A. M. 82
Schrodinger, E. 106
Schopenhauer, A. 126
Schulberg, B. 63
Schultz, J. W. 153
Schulz, C. 97
Schumacher, E. F. 48
Schumpeter, J. 135
Schutz, A. 149
Scott, G. 17
Scott, P. 63
Searle, J. 97
Sears, P. B. 119
Seferis, G. 131
Sellar, W. C. 97
Selye, H. 110
Selzer, M. 84
Sendak, M. 35
Seneca 39
Septon, M. 73
Serge, V. 63
Severin, T. 86
Sextus 126

Seymour, J. 95
Shaffer, P. 45
Shakespeare, W. 45, 131
Shand, P. M. 76
Shank, T. J. 45
Sharmat, M. 35
Shavelson, M. 73
Shaw, G. B. 45
Shelley, M. 63
Shelley, P. B. 101, 131
Sheridan, R. B. 45
Sherwood, M. 106
Shostakovich, D. 24
Sickert, W. R. 21
Siggwick, D. 122
Sillitoe, A. 63
Silva, K. M. da 86
Silverstein, C. 146
Simenon, G. 24, 53
Simmel, G. 149
Simmons, I. G. 78
Simon, A. L. 76
Simon, G. 113
Simpson, G. G. 120
Simpson, R. 113
Sims, G. 53
Sinclair, A. 82
Sinclair, U. 63
Singer, C. 110
Singer, I. B. 63, 70
Sisson, C. 131
Sitwell, E. 131
Sitwell, O. 24
Sitwell, S. 122
Skinner, B. F. 137
Sklar, R. 73
Slater, P. 116
Slocum, J. 153
Slonimsky, N. 113
Slotkin, R. 82
Smart, N. 144
Smith, Adam (1776) 48
Smith, Adam (1975) 122
Smith, Anthony, 110
Smith, E. B. 17
Smith, H. N. 82
Smith, J. M. 120
Smith, J. T. 21
Smith, T. 97
Smith, W. G. 141
Smollett, T. 63
Snow, C. P. 63
Snow, E. 86
Snyder, G. 131
Solzhenitsyn, A. I. 91
Sontag, S. 110
Soper, A. 17
Sophocles 45
Southern, R. W. 92
Southern, T. 146
Soyer, A. 76
Soyinka, W. 45
Spark, M. 63
Speer, A. 24
Spender, S. 131
Spenser, E. 132
Sperling, A. 106
Spinar, Z. V. 120
Spinoza, B. 126
Stableford, B. M. 106
Stamp, D. 78
Stanislavski, C. 46
Stanley, R. 86
Stapledon, Ó. 67
Stark, F. 153
Starkie, E. 29
Stead, C. 64
Steadman, R. 98
Stedman, J. 21
Steegmuller, F. 29, 39
Steiger, B. 122
Stein, G. 70
Steinbeck, J. 39, 64, 153
Steinberg, S. H. 98
Steiner, G. 101
Stendhal 64, 101
Stenton, F. M. 89
Stern, J. P. 135
Sterne, L. 64, 154
Stevens, W. 132
Stevenson, I. 122
Stevenson, R. L. 35, 70
Stewart, G. R. 141
Stigler, G. 48
Stobart, T. 76
Stodard, S. 110
Stoppard, T. 46
Storey, D. 64
Stout, R. 53
Strachey, L. 29
Stravinsky, I. 113
Street, B. V. 12
Strong, R. 89
Strunk, W. 141
Struve, N. 144
Styron, W. 64

Author index

Suetonius 84
Summers, M. 122
Summerson, J. 17
Sumner, W. G. 149
Sutcliff, R. 35
Sutherland, A. 12
Sutherland, S. 110
Suttles, G. D. 149
Suyin, H. 86
Svevo, I. 64
Swift, J. 64
Swinburne, A. 132
Syme, R. 84
Symons, J. 53
Synge, J. M. 46
Sypher, W. 21
Szasz, T. 110

Tacitus, 84
Tannahill, R. 76, 146
Tansley, A. G. 120
Targ, R. 122
Tart, C. 122
Taubman, H. 46
Tawney, R. H. 89
Taylor, A. J. P. 29, 89
Taylor, D. 106
Taylor, R. L. 73
Taylor, S. R. 106
Teilhard de Chardin 39, 144
Tennyson, A. 132
Terkel, S. 149
Tey, J. 53
Thackeray, W. M. 64
Theroux, P. 154
Thesiger, W. 154
Thomas, D. 39, 132
Thomas, E. 132
Thomas, Edith 50
Thomas, H. 93
Thomas, K. 89
Thomas, L. 110
Thomas, P. 116
Thomas, W. L. 78
Thompson, D. 92
Thompson, D'Arcy W. 106
Thompson, E. B. 86
Thompson, E. P. 30, 89
Thompson, P. 89
Thouless, R. H. 122
Thrasher, F. M. 12
Thucydides 84
Thurber, J. 98
Tiger, L. S. 12
Tilley, M. P. 141
Tillich, P. 144
Tinbergen, N. 120
Tinniswood, P. 98
Tocqueville, A. de 135
Tolkien, J. R. R. 35
Tolstoy, L. 64, 101
Tomalin, C. 30
Tomkins, P. 120
Tomlinson, H. M. 154
Tovey, D. F. 113
Toynbee, A. J. 93
Travers, B. 46
Treece, H. 35, 64
Trelawny, E. J. 30
Trevelyan, G. M. 89
Trevor-Roper, H. 30
Trevor-Roper, P. 110
Trilling, L. 65, 101
Trotsky, L. 135
Troyat, H. 30
Trudeau, G. 98
Tuchman, B. 92
Tunnard, C. 78
Turgenev, I. S. 70

Turnbull, C. M. 154
Turner, F. J. 82
Turner, V. W. 12
Tuttle, A. 40
Twain, M. 70, 65, 98
    82, 154
Tyler, E. B. 12
Tyler, R. 92
Tyrell, G. N. M. 122

Ucko, P. J. 14
Uden, G. 35
Updike, J. 65

Van Der Meer, F. 141
Van Der Post, L. 154
Van Doren, C. 30
Van Doren, M. 46
Van Gogh, V. 40
Van Vogt, A. E. 67
Varese, L. 113
Vasari, G. 21
Vatikiotis, P. J. 86
Vatsyayana 146
Vaughan, A. 122
Veblen, T. 149
Venturi, R. 17
Verne, J. 67
Veronelli, L. 76
Veut, I. 110
Victory, P.-E. 154
Vidler, A. R. 144
Villon, F. 132
Vitruvius 17
Virgil 132
Voltaire 65
Vonnegut, K. 67
Vyvyan, J. 122

Wachtel, N. 93
Waddams, A. L. 106
Wagner, C. 40
Wagner, R. 113
Wahloo, P. 53
Walker, A. 73
Walker, E. P. 120
Walker, S. 137
Wall, J. F. 30
Wallechinksy, D. 141
Wallerstein, I. 149
Walpole, H. 40
Walton, I. 120
Ward, B. 78
Ward, K. 144
Ward, R. R. 120
Warner, A. H. 76
Warner, M. 144
Warr, P. 137
Warren, N. 40
Warren, R. P. 65
Wat, W. M. 144
Waterton, C. 120
Watts, D. 78
Watson, J. D. 106
Watson, L. 122
Watson, R. I. 137
Watson-Taylor, S. 132
Waugh, E. 65
Webb, J. 122
Weber, M. 149
Webster, J. 46
Weidman, J. 65
Weil, S. 144
Welty, E. 65
Wendel, F. 144
West, N. 65
Westmore, F. 73
Weston, J. 116

Westergaard, J. 48
Westlake, D. 98
Wharton, E. 65
Whitall, A. 113
White, E. B. 35, 40, 98
White, E. W. 113
White, G. 120
White, P. 65
White, T. H. 35
White, Theodore H. 135
Whitehead, A. N. 106
Whitman, W. 132
Whyte, W. F. 149
Wilbur, R. 132
Wilde, O. 40, 46, 65
Wilder, A. 113
Wilder, L. I. 35
Wilder, T. 46
Wilk, M. 108
Willey, G. 14
Williams, R. 46, 108
Williams, T. 46
Williamson, H. 35
Wills, P. 149
Willmott, P. 149
Willson, D. H. 89
Wilmer, V. 113
Wilmot, C. 92
Wilson, A. 70
Wilson, C. 122
Wilson, C. A. 76
Wilson, D. 14
Wilson, E. 40, 82, 101, 135
Wilson, Erica, 95
Wilson, M. 86
Wilson, S. 154
Wing, J. K. 110
Winks, R. W. 154
Wittgenstein, L. 126
Wodehouse, P. G. 98
Wolf, W. 73
Wolfe, T. 65
Wolff, C. 146
Wollstonecraft, M. 50
Womack, J. 93
Woodeforde, J. 40
Woodham-Smith, C. 30, 89
Woodward, B. 135
Woodward, C. V. 82, 135
Woolf, V. 30, 40, 50, 66
Woolman, J. 24
Wordsworth, D. 40
Wordsworth, W. 132
Wright, F. L. 17
Wright, L. 106
Wright, M. 95
Wright, R. 66
Wycherley, W. 46
Wyndham, J. 67

Xenophon 84

Yeats, W. B. 46, 132
Young, J. Z. 120
Yourcenar, M. 66
Yule, H. 141

Zaehner, R. C. 144
Ziebold, N. 73
Ziman, J. 106
Zimbardo, P. G. 137
Zindel, P. 35
Zola, E. 66
Zoshchenko, M. 70
Zweig, S. 30

Printed in Great Britain by
Fakenham Press Limited